THUNDERBOLTS

VIOLENT REJECTION

THUNDERBOLTS: VIOLENT REJECTION. Contains material originally published in magazine form as THUNDERBOLTS #152-157. First printing 2011. ISBN# 978-0-7851-5221-7. Published by MARVEL WORLDWIDE, INC., a subsidiary of MARVEL ENTERTAINMENT, LLC. OFFICE OF PUBLICATION: 135 West 50th Street, New York, NY 10020. Copyright © 2011 Marvel Characters, Inc. All rights reserved. $15.99 per copy in the U.S. and $17.50 in Canada (GST #R127032852); Canadian Agreement #40668537. All characters featured in this issue and the distinctive names and likenesses thereof, and all related indicia are trademarks of Marvel Characters, Inc. No similarity between any of the names, characters, persons, and/or institutions in this magazine with those of any living or dead person or institution is intended, and any such similarity which may exist is purely coincidental. **Printed in the U.S.A.** ALAN FINE, ... N BUCKLEY, Publisher & President - Print, Animation & Digital Divisions; JOE QUESADA, Chief Creative Officer; JIM ... t; TOM BREVOORT, SVP of Publishing; C.B. CEBULSKI, SVP of Creator & Content Development; DAVID GABRIEL, ... ons; JIM O'KEEFE, VP of Operations & Logistics; DAN CARR, Executive Director of Publishing Technology; JUSTIN ... ger; ALEX MORALES, Publishing Operations Manager; STAN LEE, Chairman Emeritus. For information regarding ... s and Marketing, at jdokes@marvel.com. For Marvel subscription inquiries, please call 800-217-9158. **Manufa...**

10 9 8 7 6 5 4 3 2 1

38067160505325

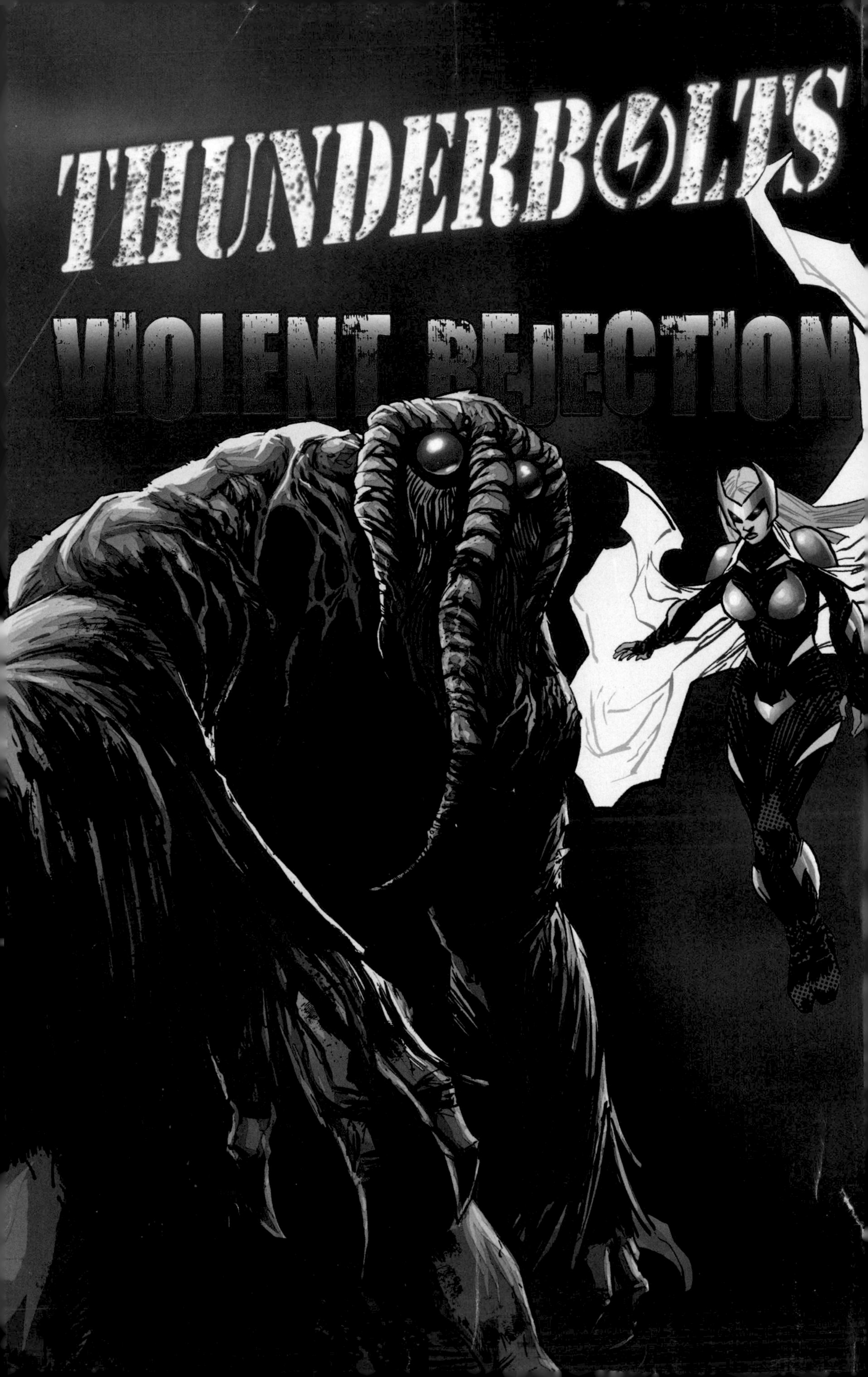
THUNDERBOLTS
VIOLENT REJECTION

WRITER
JEFF PARKER

PENCILERS
KEV WALKER (ISSUES #152-153 & 155-157)
& **DECLAN SHALVEY** (ISSUES #154 & 157)

INKERS
KEV WALKER (ISSUES #152 & 155-157),
JASON GORDER (ISSUES #153 & 155-157)
& **DECLAN SHALVEY** (ISSUES #154 & 157)

COLOR ARTIST
FRANK MARTIN
WITH FABIO D'AURIA (ISSUES #156-157)
& BRAD SIMPSON (ISSUE #157)

LETTERER
COMICRAFT'S ALBERT DESCHESNE

COVER ARTISTS
GREG LAND WITH FRANK D'ARMATA
& DAN BROWN (ISSUES #152-153),
ARTHUR ADAMS WITH FRANK D'ARMATA (ISSUE #154),
STEPHANIE HANS (ISSUE #155)
AND **JEAN-SÉBASTIEN ROSSBACH** (ISSUES #156-157)

ASSISTANT EDITOR
RACHEL PINNELAS

EDITORS
TOM BRENNAN & BILL ROSEMANN

Collection Editor
CORY LEVINE
Editorial Assistants
JAMES EMMETT & JOE HOCHSTEIN
Assistant Editors
MATT MASDEU, ALEX STARBUCK
& NELSON RIBEIRO
Editors, Special Projects
JENNIFER GRÜNWALD & MARK D. BEAZLEY
Senior Editor, Special Projects
JEFF YOUNGQUIST
Senior Vice President of Sales
DAVID GABRIEL
SVP of Brand Planning & Communications:
MICHAEL PASCIULLO
Book Design
JEFF POWELL

Editor in Chief
AXEL ALONSO
Chief Creative Officer
JOE QUESADA
Publisher
DAN BUCKLEY
Executive Producer
ALAN FINE

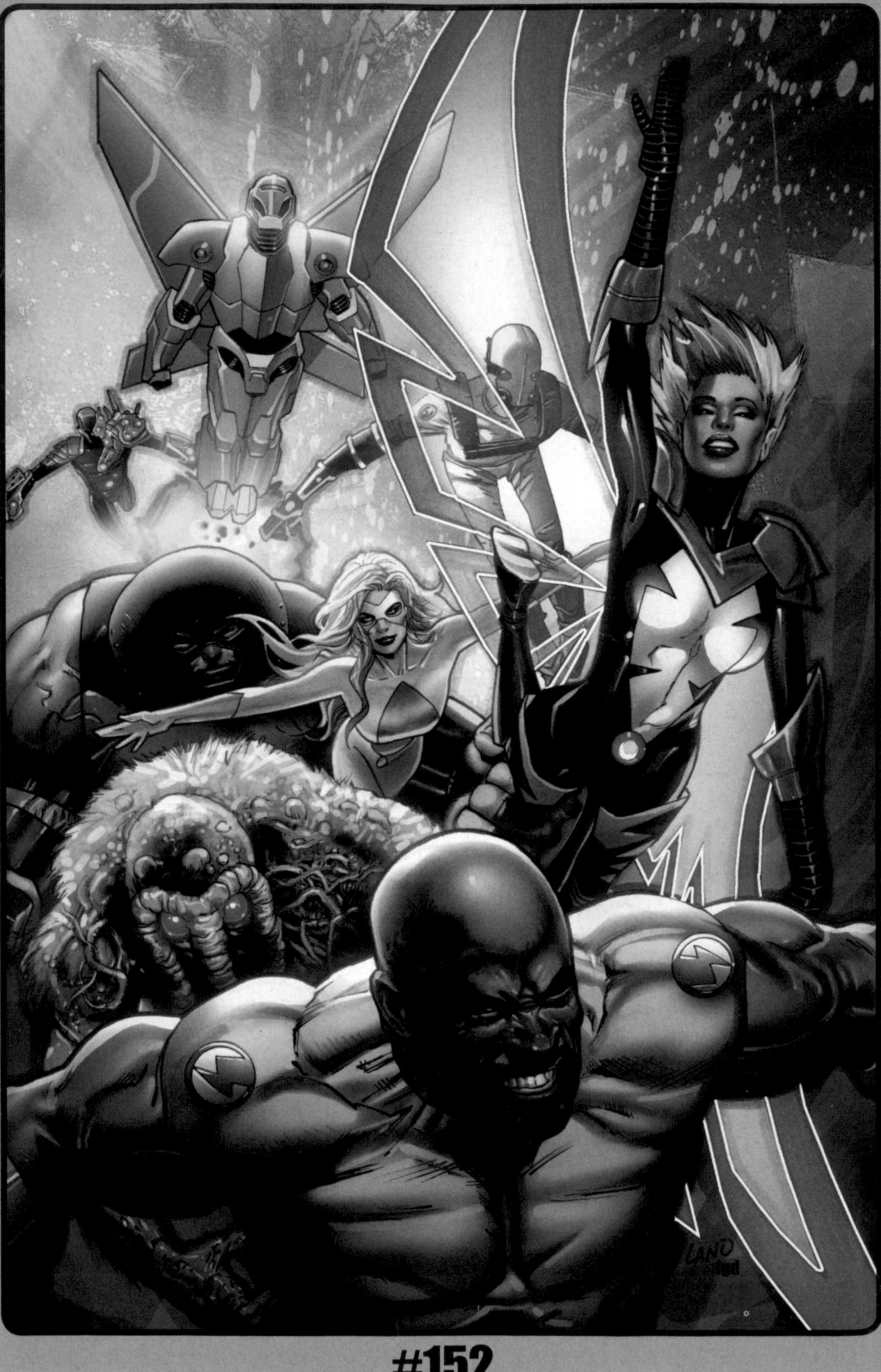

#152

Their base is a supermax facility known as The Raft. Their transport is a swamp monster. Their mission leader is the bulletproof Avenger known as Luke Cage. A handpicked team of inmates have the chance to go outside prison walls as long as they use their powers to deal with the worst the world has to offer -- they are the

THUNDERBOLTS

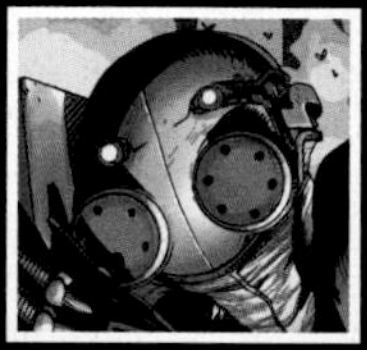

GHOST
Intangible Hacker

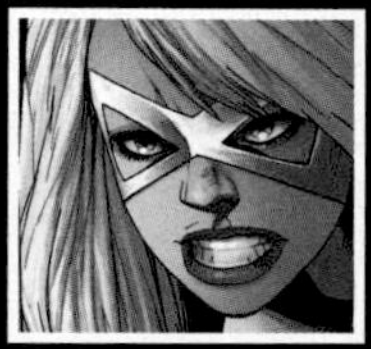

MOONSTONE
Energy Manipulator

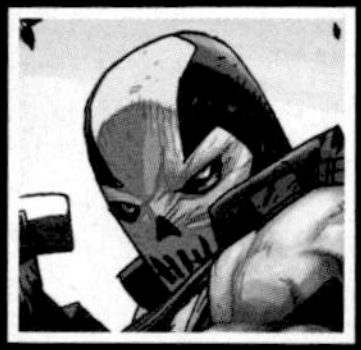

CROSSBONES
Sharpshooter

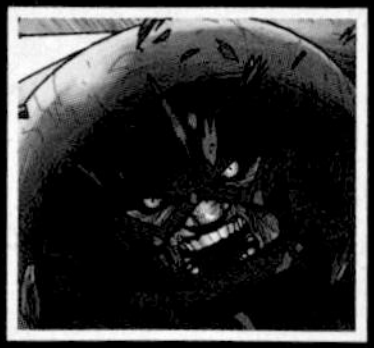

JUGGERNAUT
Unstoppable Force

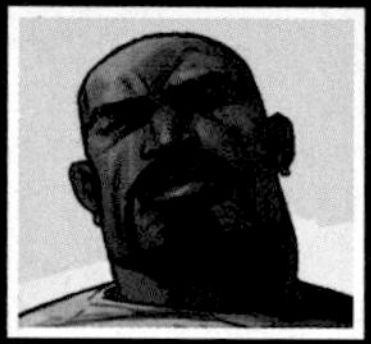

LUKE CAGE
Power Man

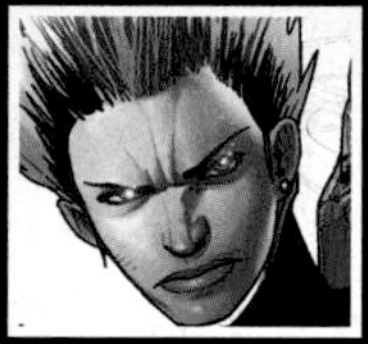

SONGBIRD
Sonic Boomer

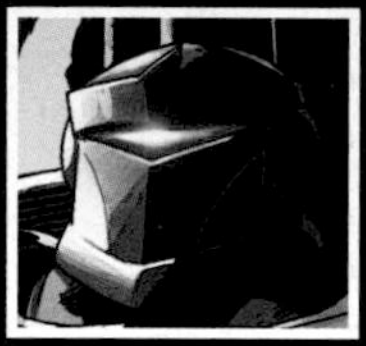

MACH V
Human Fighter Jet

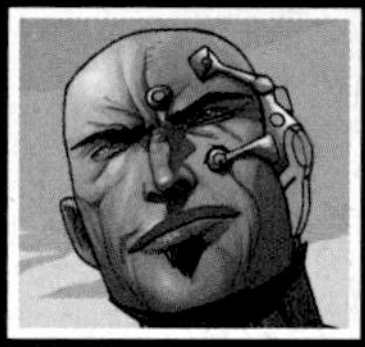

FIXER
Technological Whiz

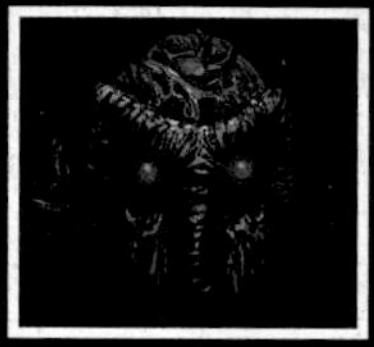

MAN-THING
Mysterious Transporter

When Norman Osborn became the Director of the Thunderbolts he restructured the team in his own dark image. He used the Thunderbolts, along with his other vast resources, to lay siege to the magical kingdom of Asgard. After failing to achieve his victory, he was sent to prison, and leadership of the Thunderbolt's transferred to Luke Cage.

Crossbones was kicked off the Thunderbolts because of exposure to Terrigen Cyrstals which mutated his cell structure, giving him unnatural power that he used to kill an innocent police officer. Because of this catastrophe the rest of the team was grounded in Thunderbolts tower.

Tensions between all members continue to mount. In an attempt to find friendship amongst her fellow teammates, Moonstone seeks out Ghost, and appealing to what is left of his humanity; he reveals to her what very few people know: his origin.

And in act of desperation, Luke Cage has hired a new team member for Thunderbolts....the all powerful Hyperion.

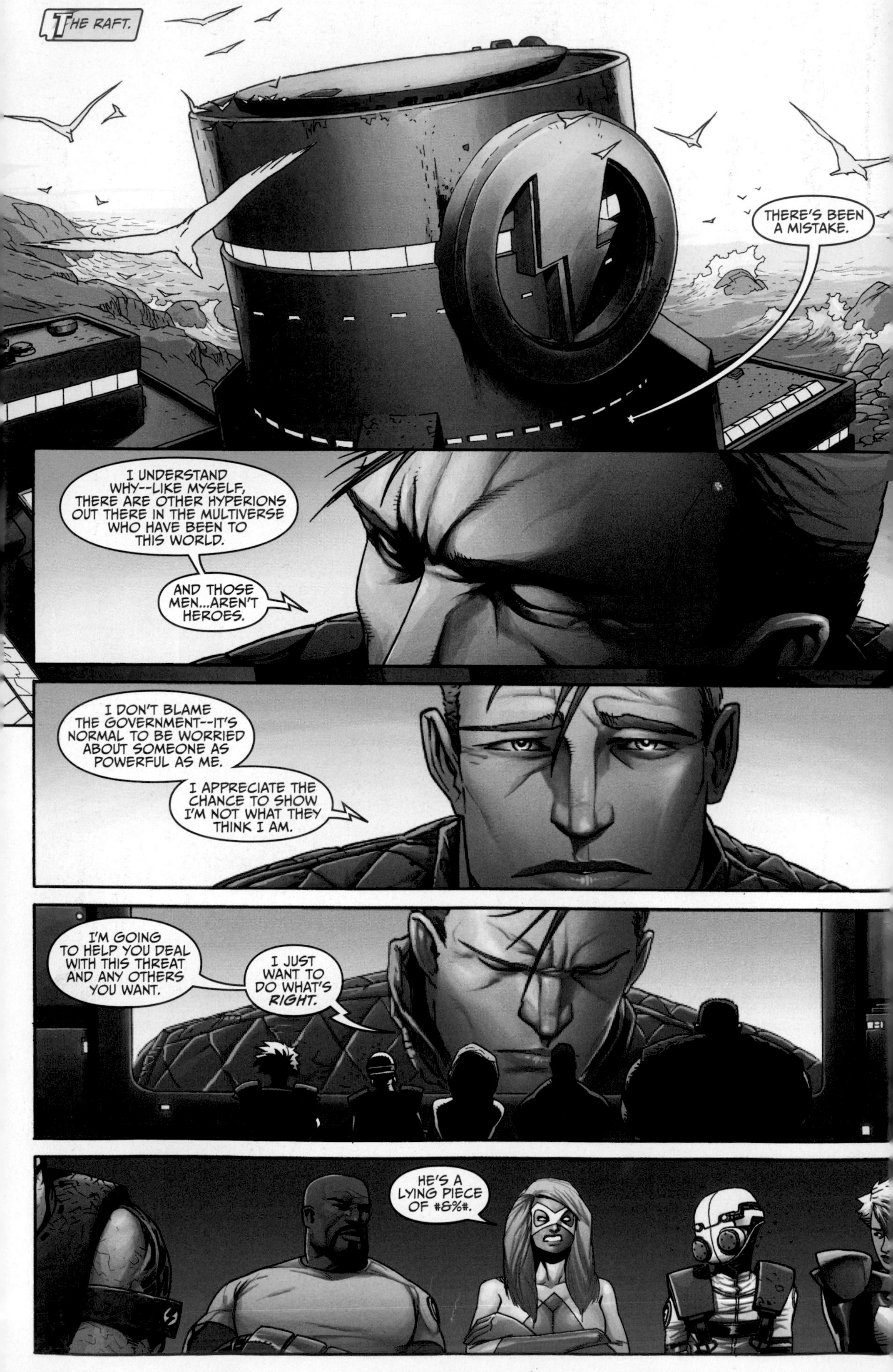
THE RAFT.
THERE'S BEEN A MISTAKE.
I UNDERSTAND WHY--LIKE MYSELF, THERE ARE OTHER HYPERIONS OUT THERE IN THE MULTIVERSE WHO HAVE BEEN TO THIS WORLD.
AND THOSE MEN...AREN'T HEROES.
I DON'T BLAME THE GOVERNMENT--IT'S NORMAL TO BE WORRIED ABOUT SOMEONE AS POWERFUL AS ME.
I APPRECIATE THE CHANCE TO SHOW I'M NOT WHAT THEY THINK I AM.
I'M GOING TO HELP YOU DEAL WITH THIS THREAT AND ANY OTHERS YOU WANT.
I JUST WANT TO DO WHAT'S *RIGHT.*
HE'S A LYING PIECE OF #&%#.

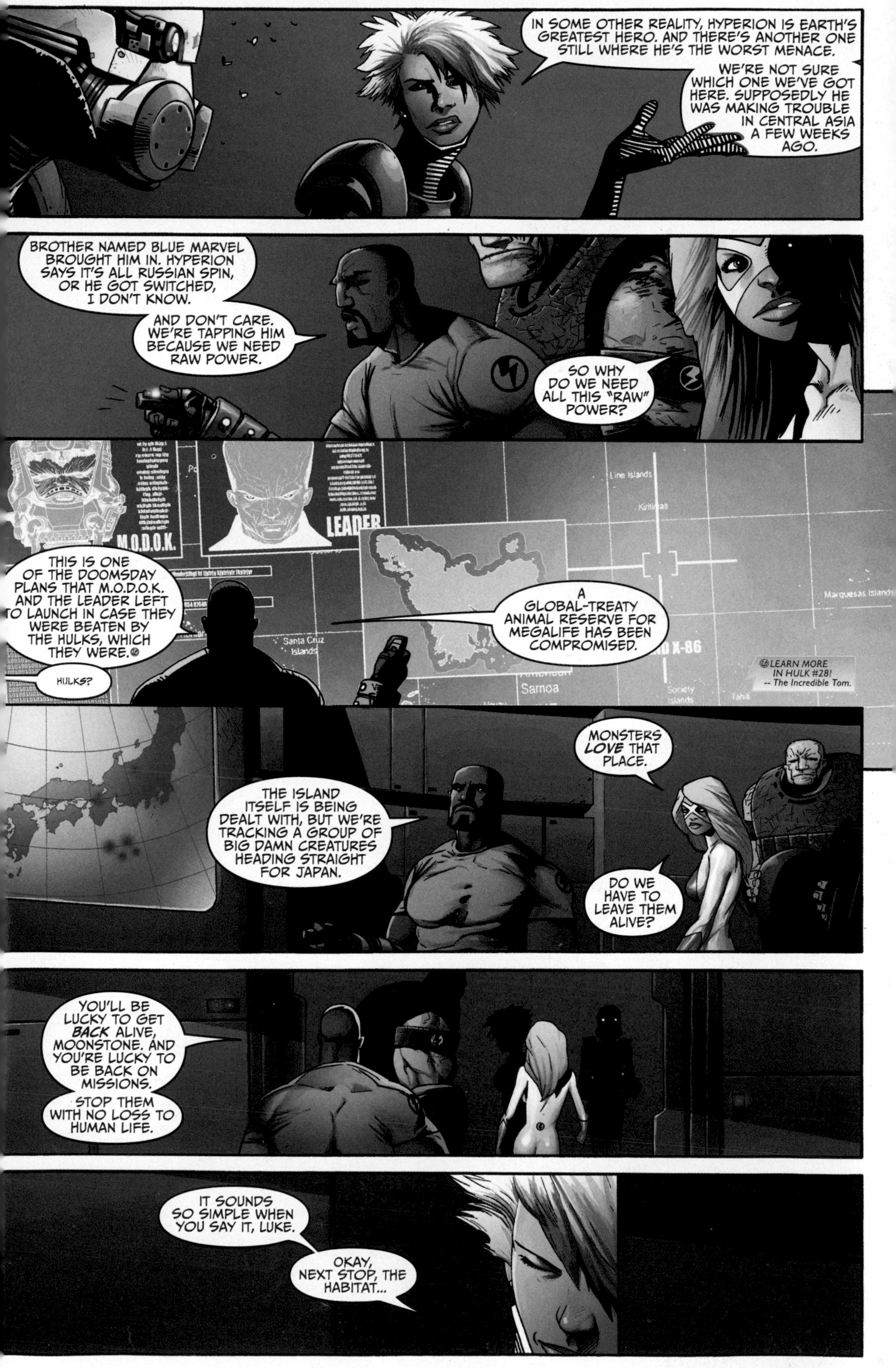
IN SOME OTHER REALITY, HYPERION IS EARTH'S GREATEST HERO. AND THERE'S ANOTHER ONE STILL WHERE HE'S THE WORST MENACE.
WE'RE NOT SURE WHICH ONE WE'VE GOT HERE. SUPPOSEDLY HE WAS MAKING TROUBLE IN CENTRAL ASIA A FEW WEEKS AGO.
BROTHER NAMED BLUE MARVEL BROUGHT HIM IN. HYPERION SAYS IT'S ALL RUSSIAN SPIN, OR HE GOT SWITCHED, I DON'T KNOW.
AND DON'T CARE. WE'RE TAPPING HIM BECAUSE WE NEED RAW POWER.
SO WHY DO WE NEED ALL THIS "RAW" POWER?
M.O.D.O.K.
LEADER
Line Islands
Marquesas Islands
Santa Cruz Islands
Samoa
Society Islands
THIS IS ONE OF THE DOOMSDAY PLANS THAT M.O.D.O.K. AND THE LEADER LEFT TO LAUNCH IN CASE THEY WERE BEATEN BY THE HULKS, WHICH THEY WERE.
HULKS?
A GLOBAL-TREATY ANIMAL RESERVE FOR MEGALIFE HAS BEEN COMPROMISED.
LEARN MORE IN HULK #28! -- The Incredible Tom.
MONSTERS LOVE THAT PLACE.
THE ISLAND ITSELF IS BEING DEALT WITH, BUT WE'RE TRACKING A GROUP OF BIG DAMN CREATURES HEADING STRAIGHT FOR JAPAN.
DO WE HAVE TO LEAVE THEM ALIVE?
YOU'LL BE LUCKY TO GET BACK ALIVE, MOONSTONE. AND YOU'RE LUCKY TO BE BACK ON MISSIONS.
STOP THEM WITH NO LOSS TO HUMAN LIFE.
IT SOUNDS SO SIMPLE WHEN YOU SAY IT, LUKE.
OKAY, NEXT STOP, THE HABITAT...

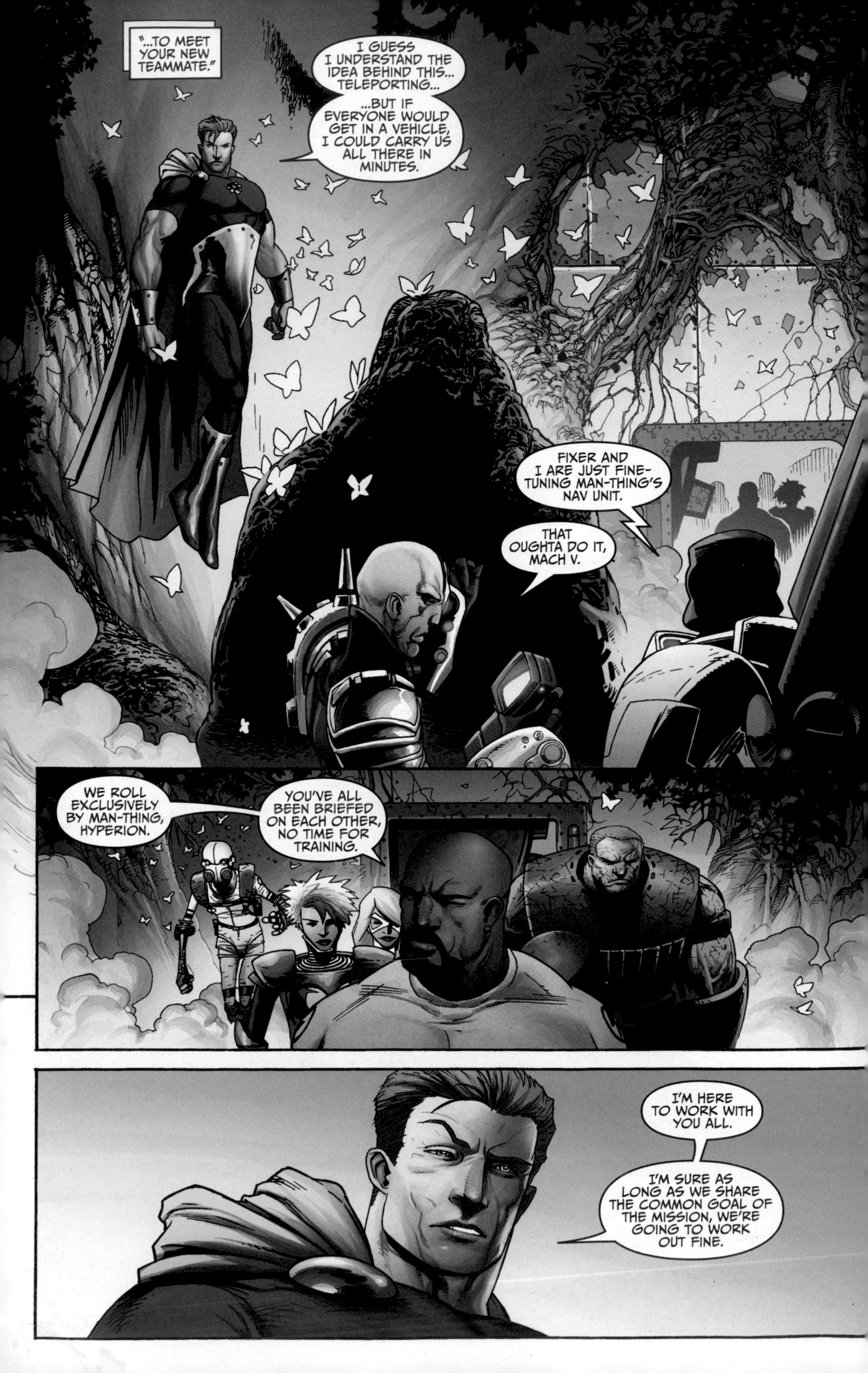
"...TO MEET YOUR NEW TEAMMATE."
I GUESS I UNDERSTAND THE IDEA BEHIND THIS... TELEPORTING...
...BUT IF EVERYONE WOULD GET IN A VEHICLE, I COULD CARRY US ALL THERE IN MINUTES.
FIXER AND I ARE JUST FINE-TUNING MAN-THING'S NAV UNIT.
THAT OUGHTA DO IT, MACH V.
WE ROLL EXCLUSIVELY BY MAN-THING, HYPERION.
YOU'VE ALL BEEN BRIEFED ON EACH OTHER, NO TIME FOR TRAINING.
I'M HERE TO WORK WITH YOU ALL.
I'M SURE AS LONG AS WE SHARE THE COMMON GOAL OF THE MISSION, WE'RE GOING TO WORK OUT FINE.

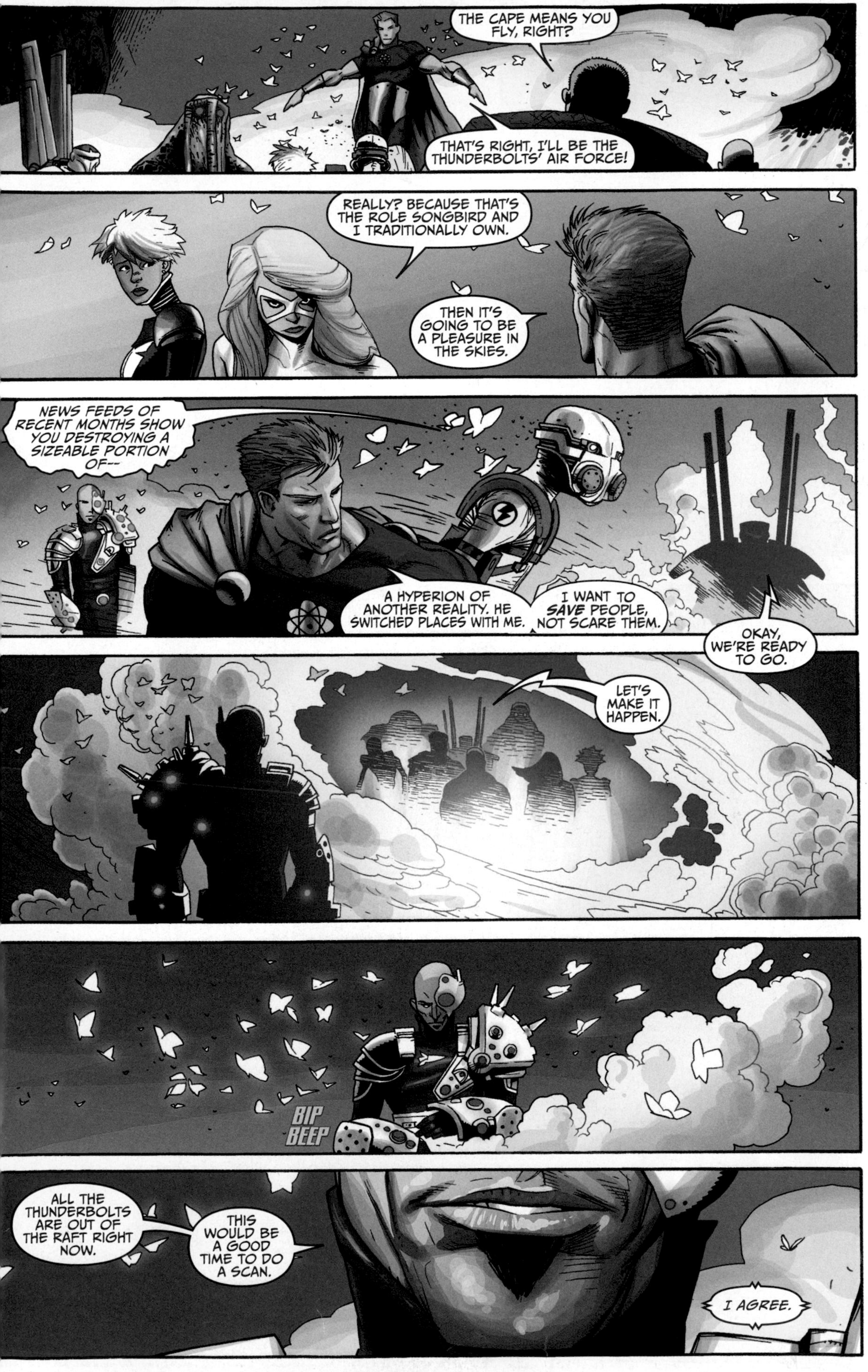
THE CAPE MEANS YOU FLY, RIGHT?
THAT'S RIGHT, I'LL BE THE THUNDERBOLTS' AIR FORCE!
REALLY? BECAUSE THAT'S THE ROLE SONGBIRD AND I TRADITIONALLY OWN.
THEN IT'S GOING TO BE A PLEASURE IN THE SKIES.
NEWS FEEDS OF RECENT MONTHS SHOW YOU DESTROYING A SIZEABLE PORTION OF--
A HYPERION OF ANOTHER REALITY. HE SWITCHED PLACES WITH ME.
I WANT TO SAVE PEOPLE, NOT SCARE THEM.
OKAY, WE'RE READY TO GO.
LET'S MAKE IT HAPPEN.
BIP BEEP
ALL THE THUNDERBOLTS ARE OUT OF THE RAFT RIGHT NOW.
THIS WOULD BE A GOOD TIME TO DO A SCAN.
I AGREE.

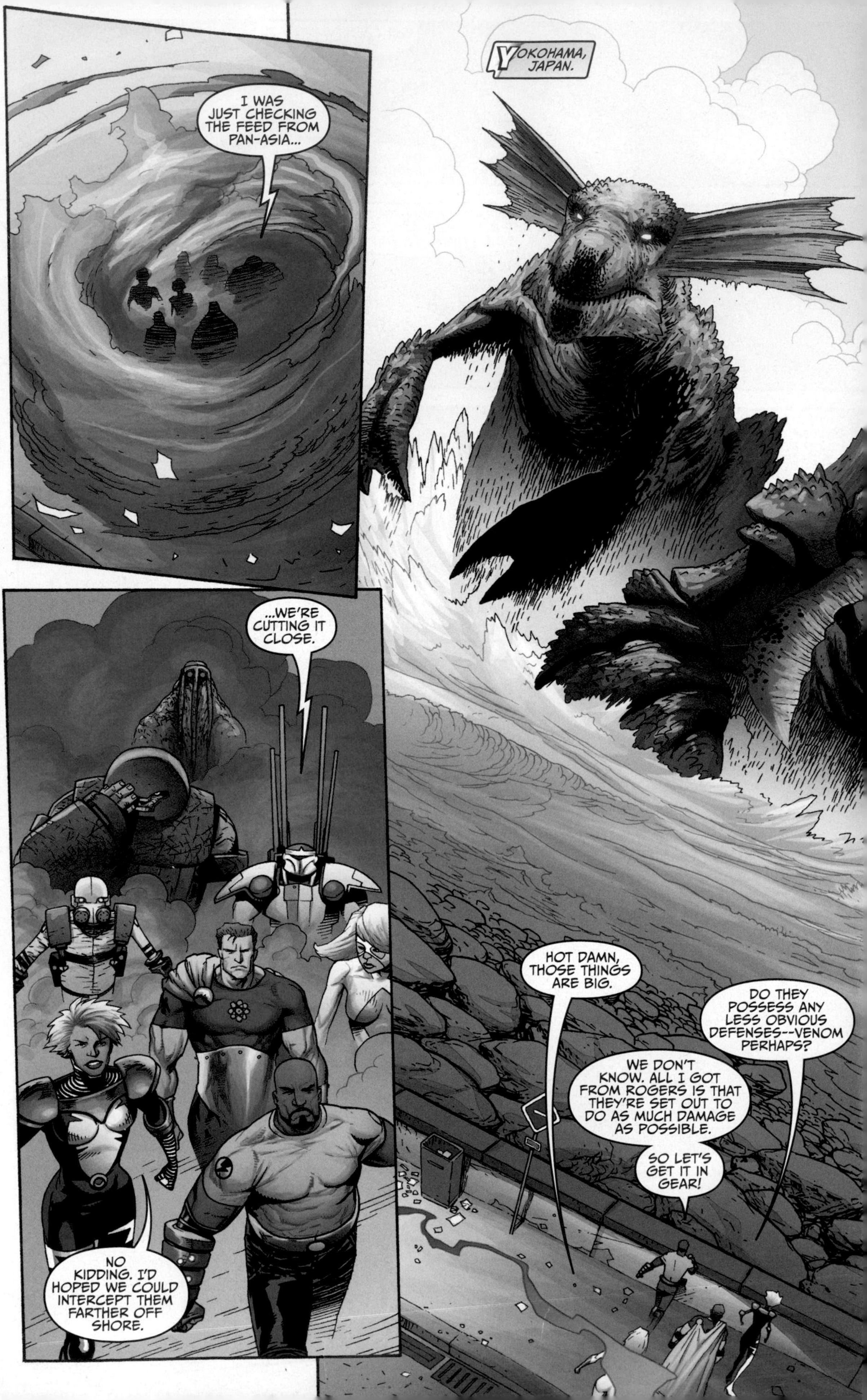
I WAS JUST CHECKING THE FEED FROM PAN-ASIA...
...WE'RE CUTTING IT CLOSE.
NO KIDDING. I'D HOPED WE COULD INTERCEPT THEM FARTHER OFF SHORE.
YOKOHAMA, JAPAN.
HOT DAMN, THOSE THINGS ARE BIG.
DO THEY POSSESS ANY LESS OBVIOUS DEFENSES--VENOM PERHAPS?
WE DON'T KNOW. ALL I GOT FROM ROGERS IS THAT THEY'RE SET OUT TO DO AS MUCH DAMAGE AS POSSIBLE.
SO LET'S GET IT IN GEAR!

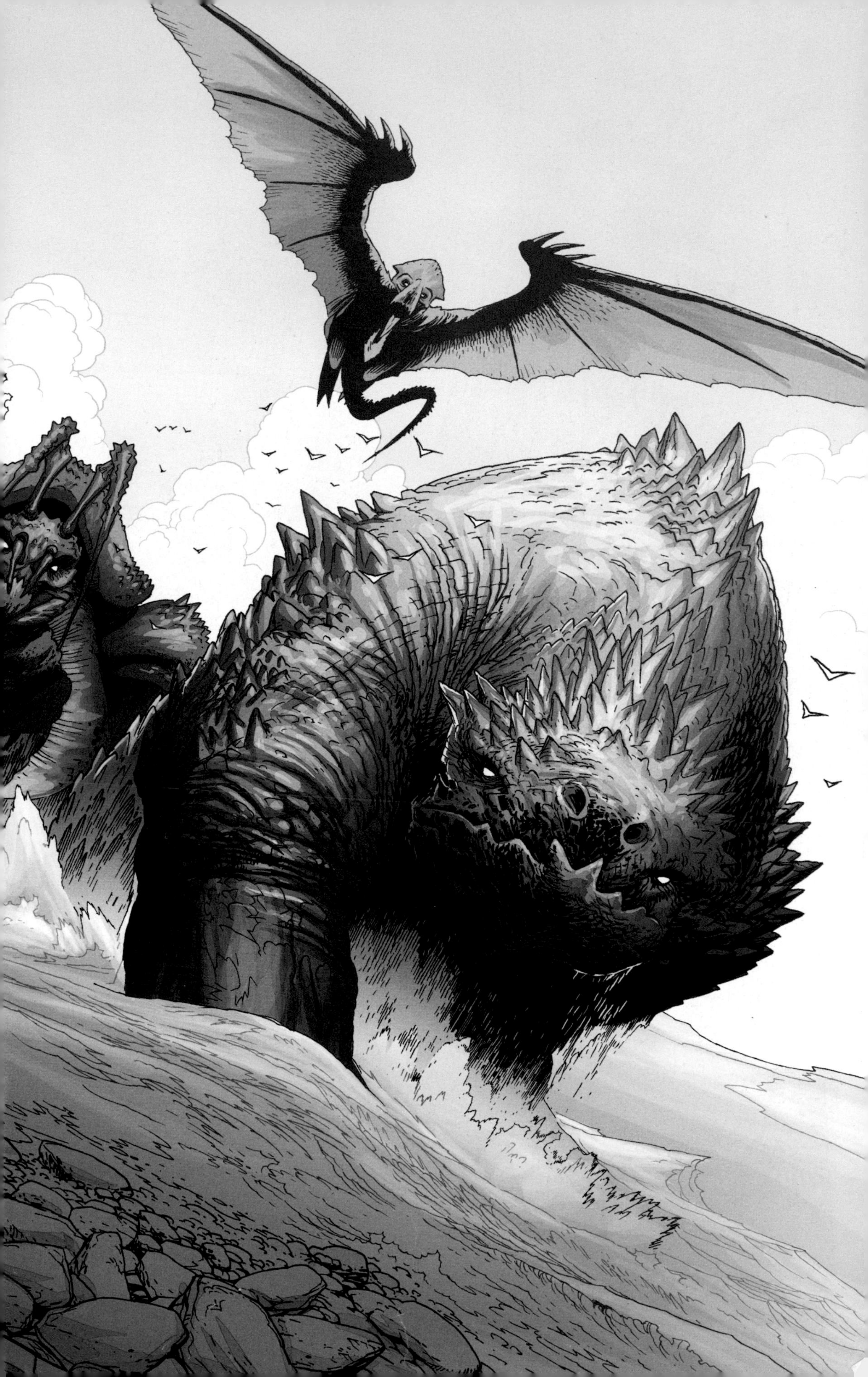

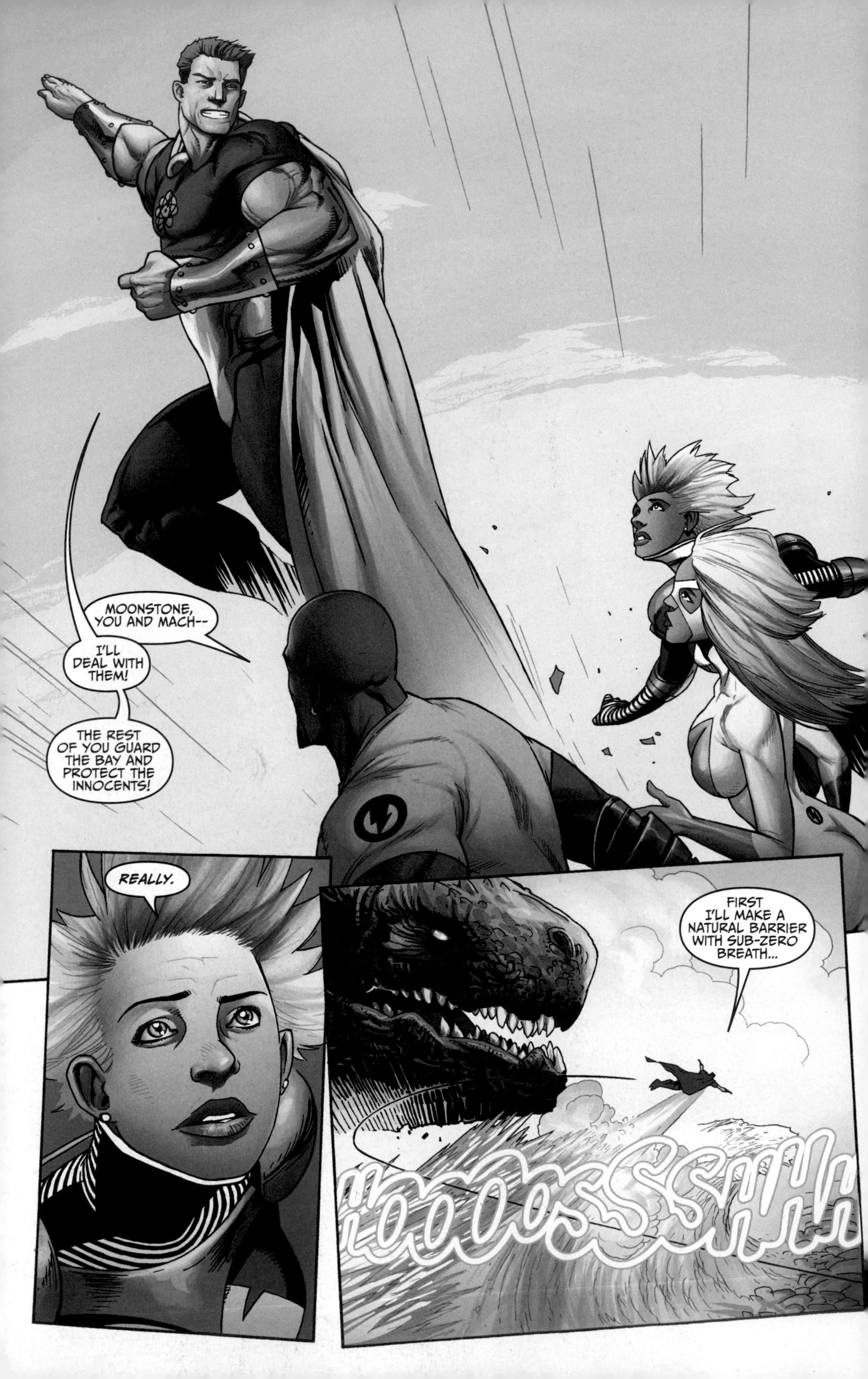
MOONSTONE, YOU AND MACH--
I'LL DEAL WITH THEM!
THE REST OF YOU GUARD THE BAY AND PROTECT THE INNOCENTS!
REALLY.
FIRST I'LL MAKE A NATURAL BARRIER WITH SUB-ZERO BREATH...

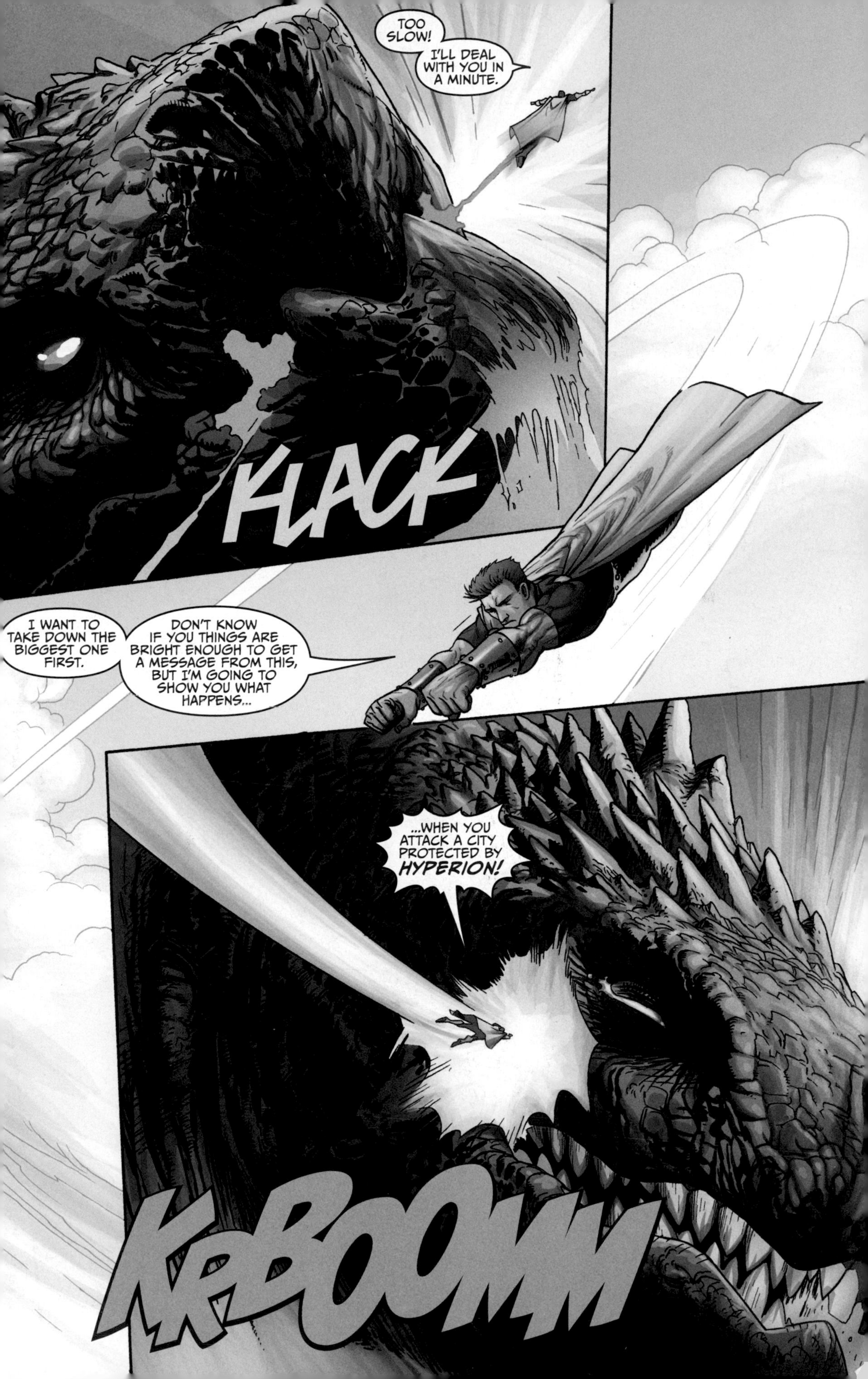
TOO SLOW!
I'LL DEAL WITH YOU IN A MINUTE.
KLACK
I WANT TO TAKE DOWN THE BIGGEST ONE FIRST.
DON'T KNOW IF YOU THINGS ARE BRIGHT ENOUGH TO GET A MESSAGE FROM THIS, BUT I'M GOING TO SHOW YOU WHAT HAPPENS...
...WHEN YOU ATTACK A CITY PROTECTED BY HYPERION!
KRBOOMM

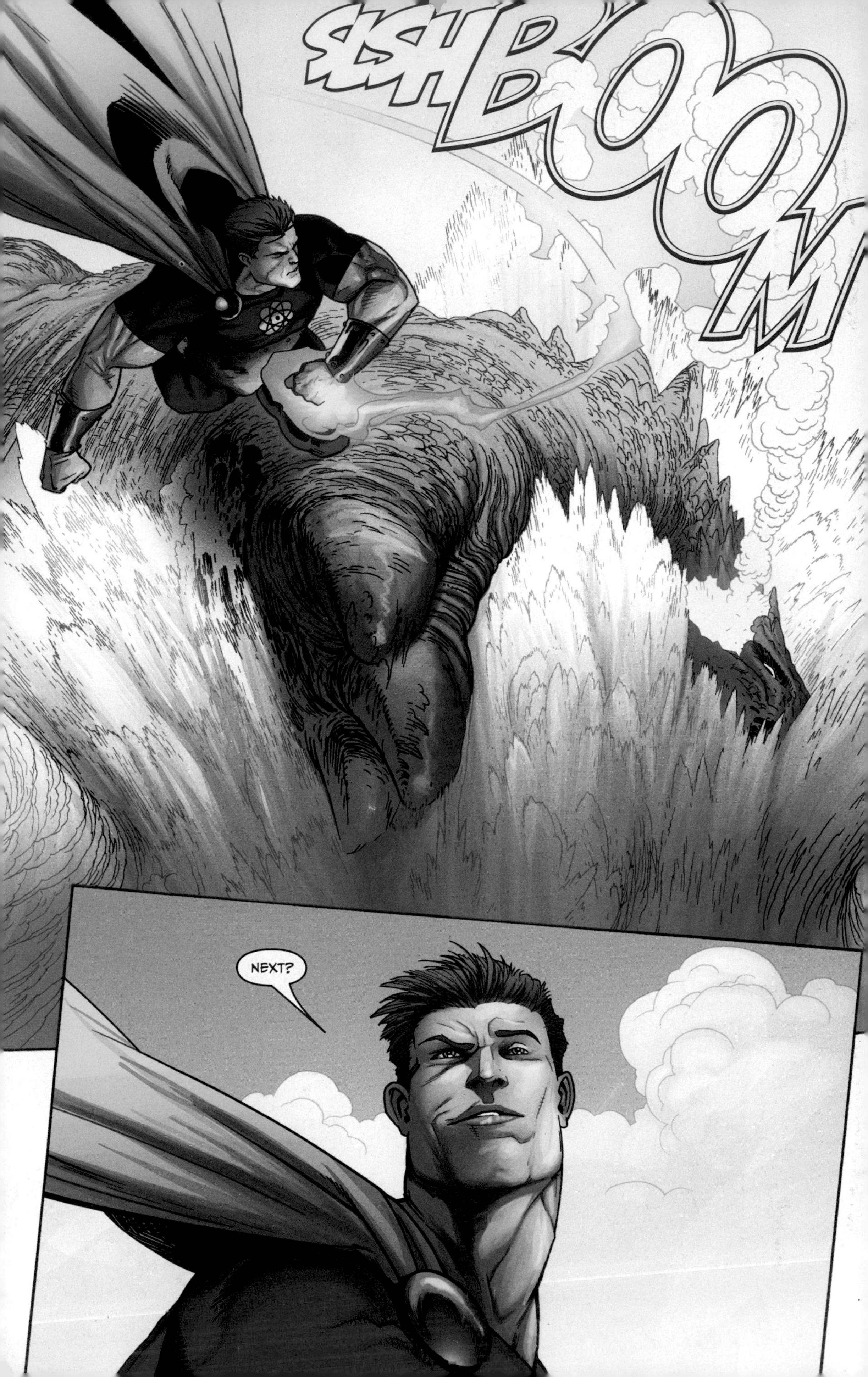
SSHBOOM
NEXT?

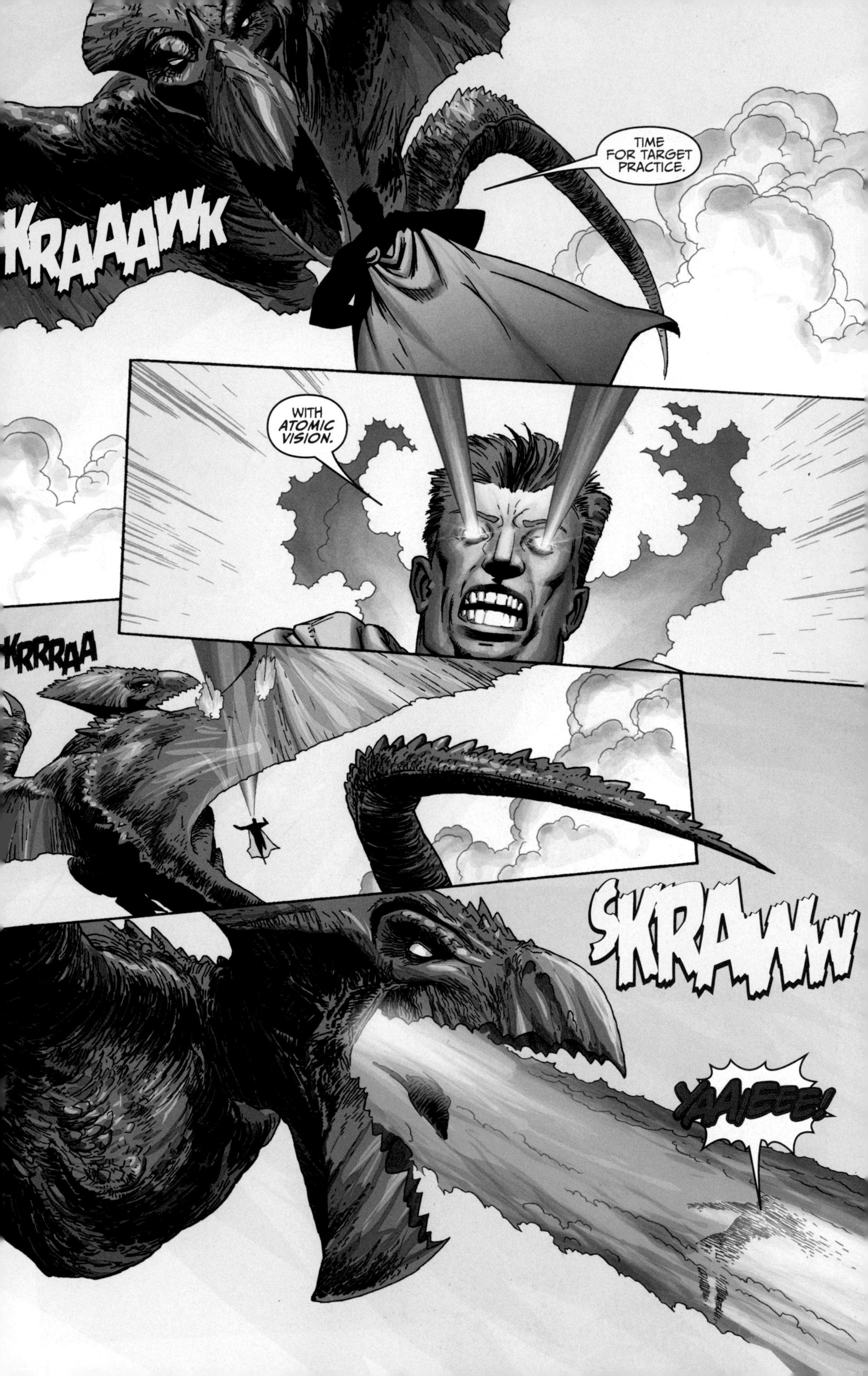

KRAAAWK
TIME FOR TARGET PRACTICE.
WITH *ATOMIC VISION.*
KRRRAA
SKRAWW
YAAIEEE!

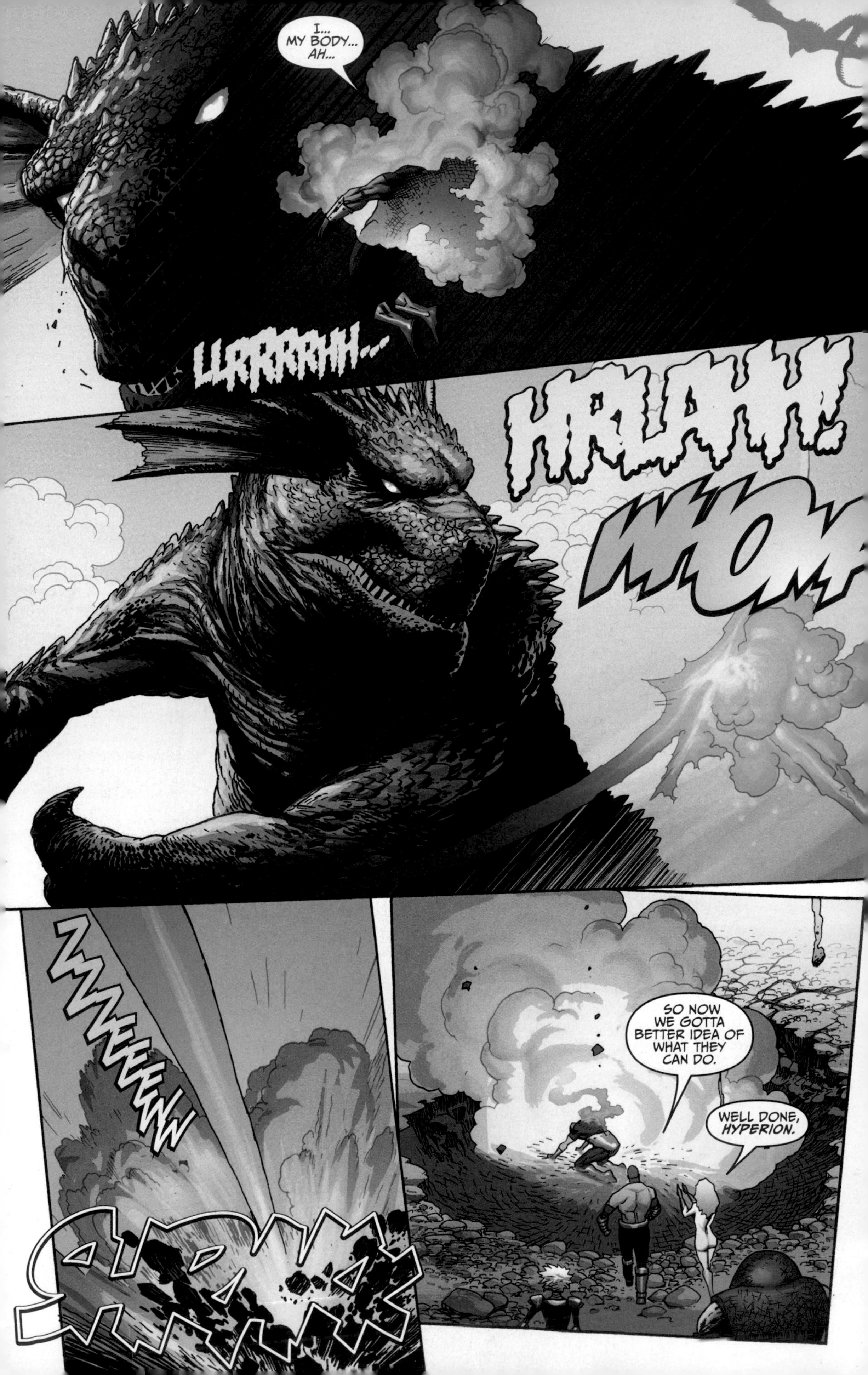
I... MY BODY... AH...
LLRRRRHH--
HRLAHH!
WHOM
ZZZEEEEWW
SO NOW WE GOTTA BETTER IDEA OF WHAT THEY CAN DO.
WELL DONE, *HYPERION.*

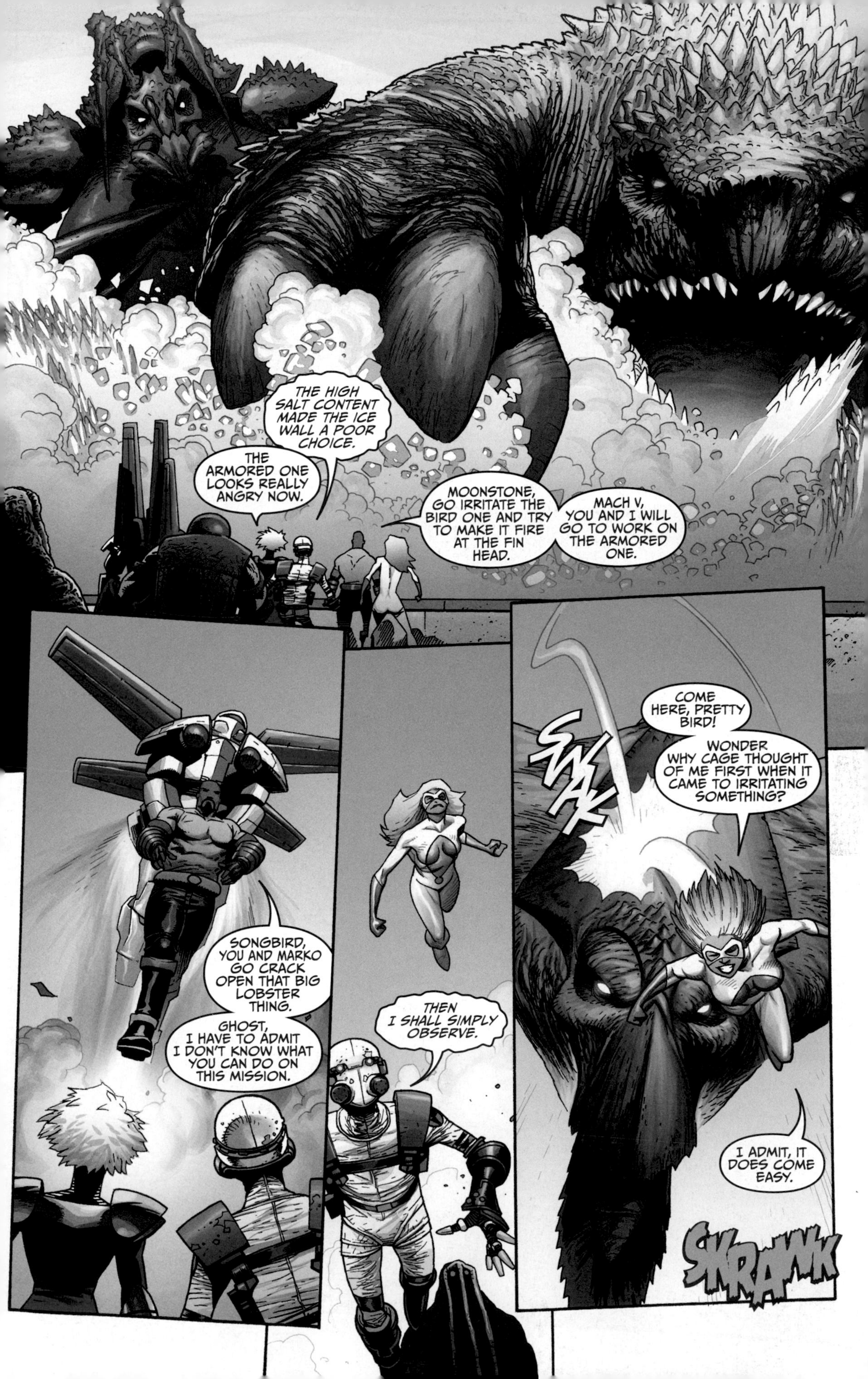
THE HIGH SALT CONTENT MADE THE ICE WALL A POOR CHOICE.
THE ARMORED ONE LOOKS REALLY ANGRY NOW.
MOONSTONE, GO IRRITATE THE BIRD ONE AND TRY TO MAKE IT FIRE AT THE FIN HEAD.
MACH V, YOU AND I WILL GO TO WORK ON THE ARMORED ONE.
SONGBIRD, YOU AND MARKO GO CRACK OPEN THAT BIG LOBSTER THING.
GHOST, I HAVE TO ADMIT I DON'T KNOW WHAT YOU CAN DO ON THIS MISSION.
THEN I SHALL SIMPLY OBSERVE.
SWAK
COME HERE, PRETTY BIRD!
WONDER WHY CAGE THOUGHT OF ME FIRST WHEN IT CAME TO IRRITATING SOMETHING?
I ADMIT, IT DOES COME EASY.
SKRAWK

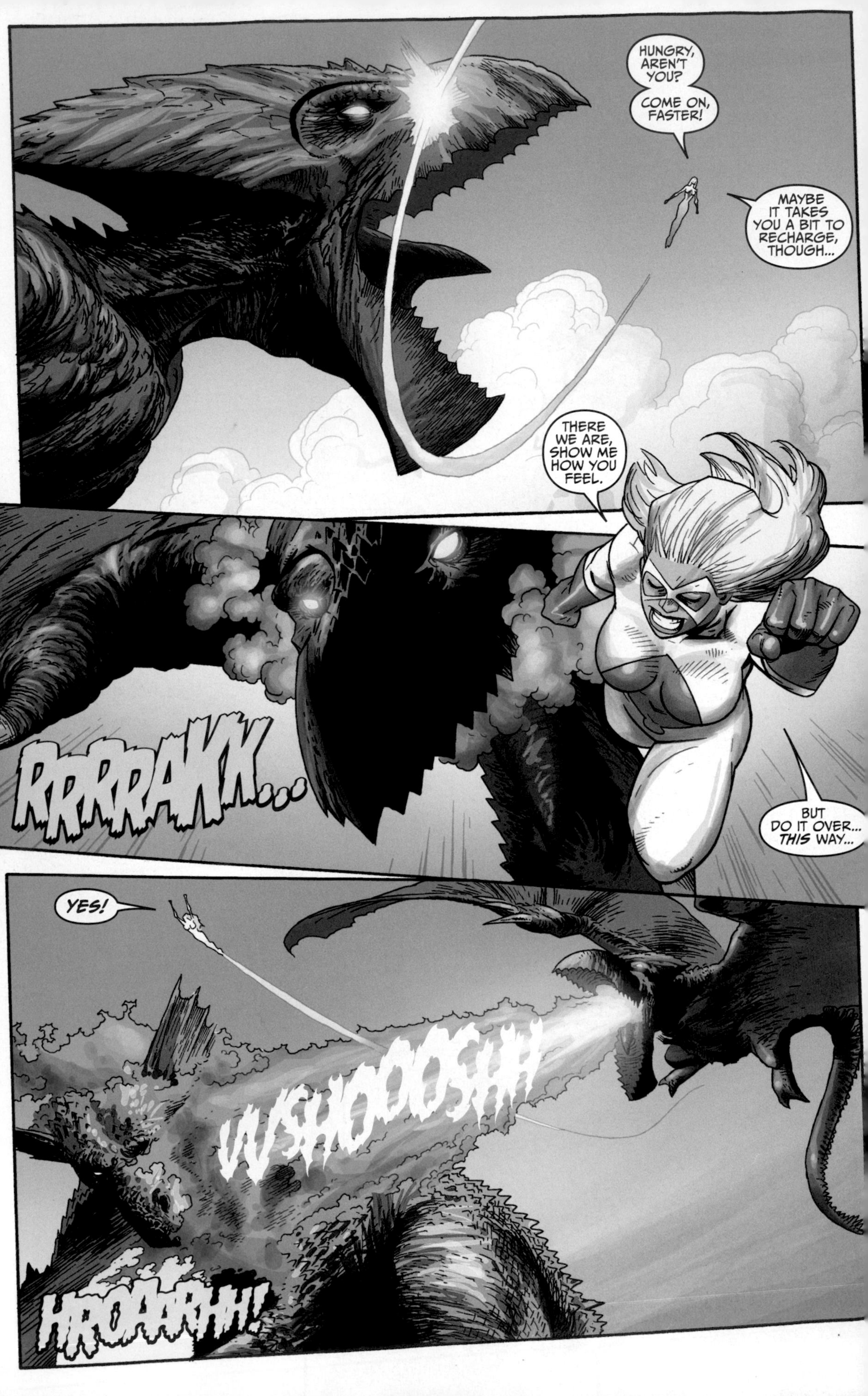
HUNGRY, AREN'T YOU?
COME ON, FASTER!
MAYBE IT TAKES YOU A BIT TO RECHARGE, THOUGH...
THERE WE ARE, SHOW ME HOW YOU FEEL.
RRRRAKK...
BUT DO IT OVER... *THIS* WAY...
YES!
VVSHOOOSH
HROARRHH!

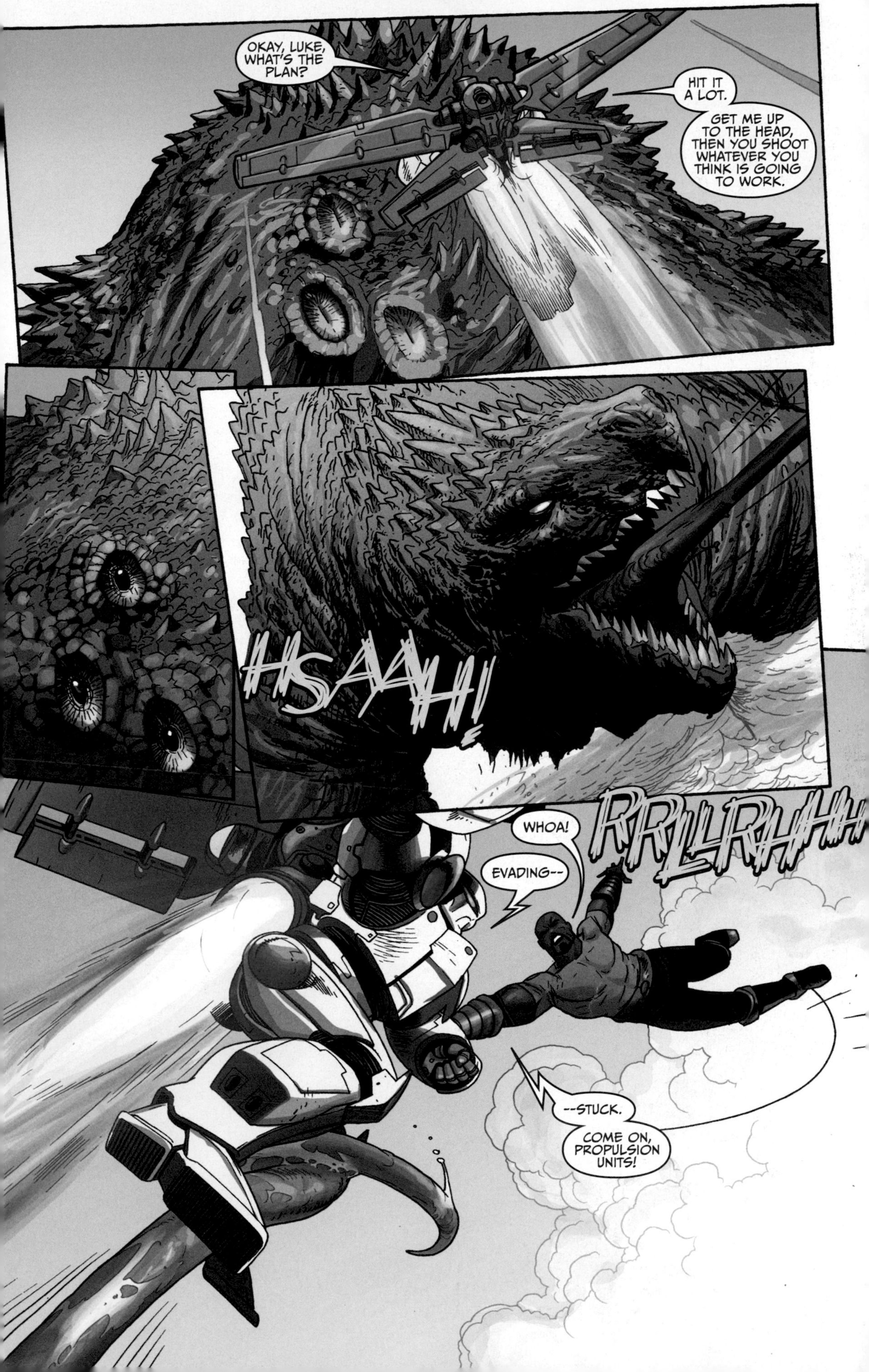
OKAY, LUKE, WHAT'S THE PLAN?
HIT IT A LOT.
GET ME UP TO THE HEAD, THEN YOU SHOOT WHATEVER YOU THINK IS GOING TO WORK.
HSAAH!
RRLLRHHH
WHOA!
EVADING--
--STUCK.
COME ON, PROPULSION UNITS!

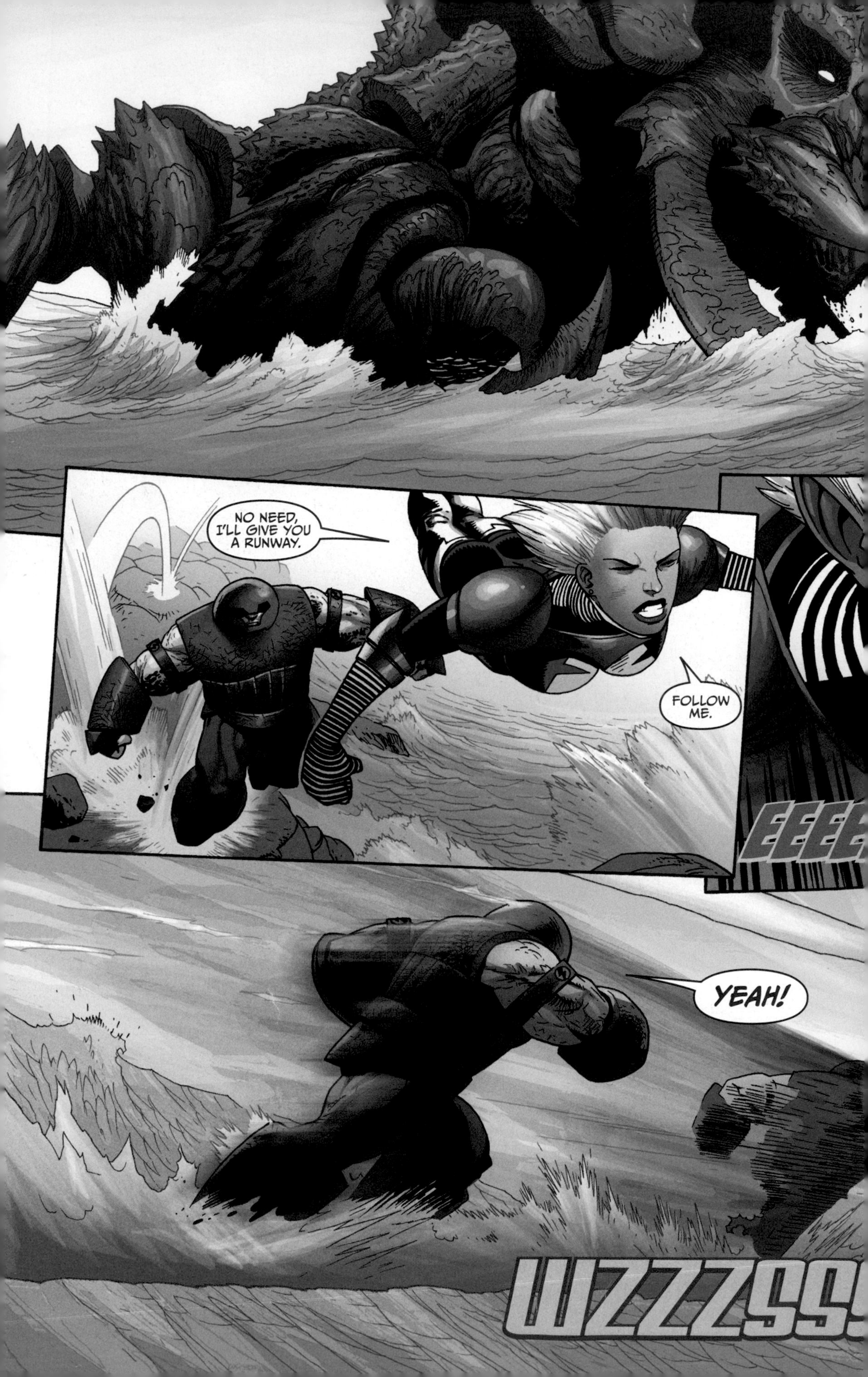

NO NEED, I'LL GIVE YOU A RUNWAY.
FOLLOW ME.
EEEE
YEAH!
WZZZSSS

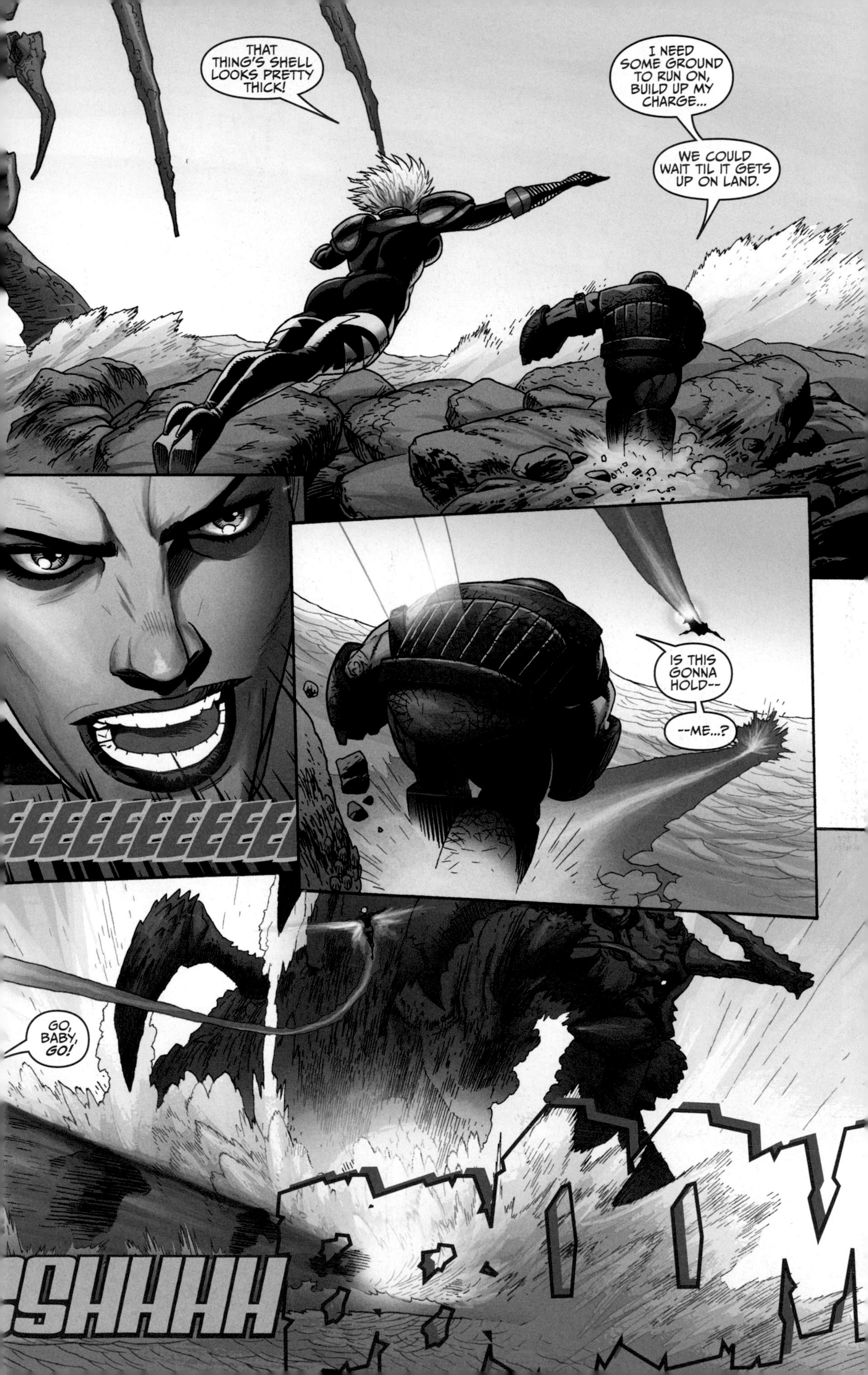
THAT THING'S SHELL LOOKS PRETTY THICK!
I NEED SOME GROUND TO RUN ON, BUILD UP MY CHARGE...
WE COULD WAIT TIL IT GETS UP ON LAND.
EEEEEEEEEEEE
IS THIS GONNA HOLD--
--ME...?
GO, BABY, GO!
SHHHH

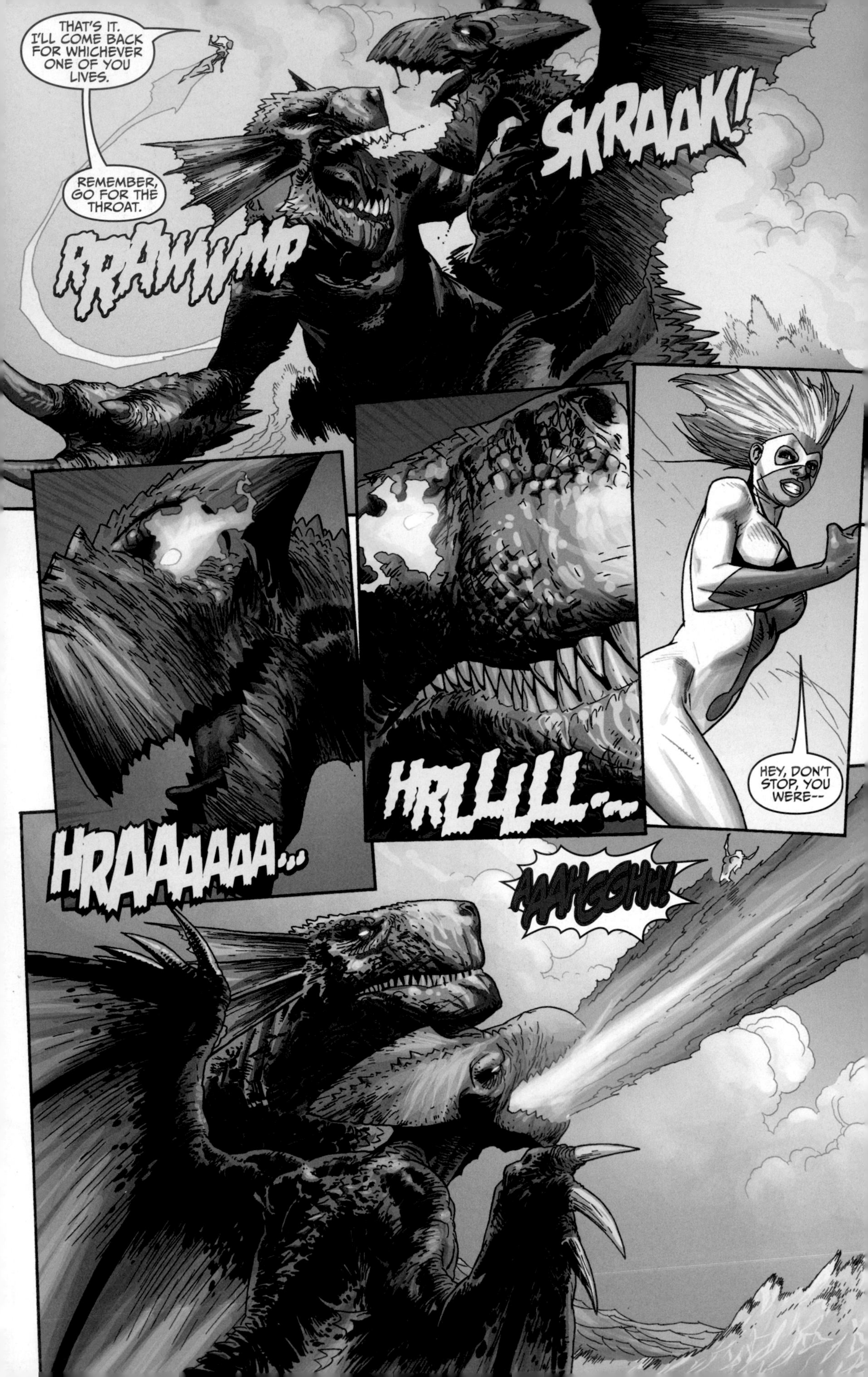
THAT'S IT. I'LL COME BACK FOR WHICHEVER ONE OF YOU LIVES.
REMEMBER, GO FOR THE THROAT.
SKRAAK!
RRAWWMP
HRAAAAAA...
HRLLLL--
HEY, DON'T STOP, YOU WERE--
AAAHGGHH!

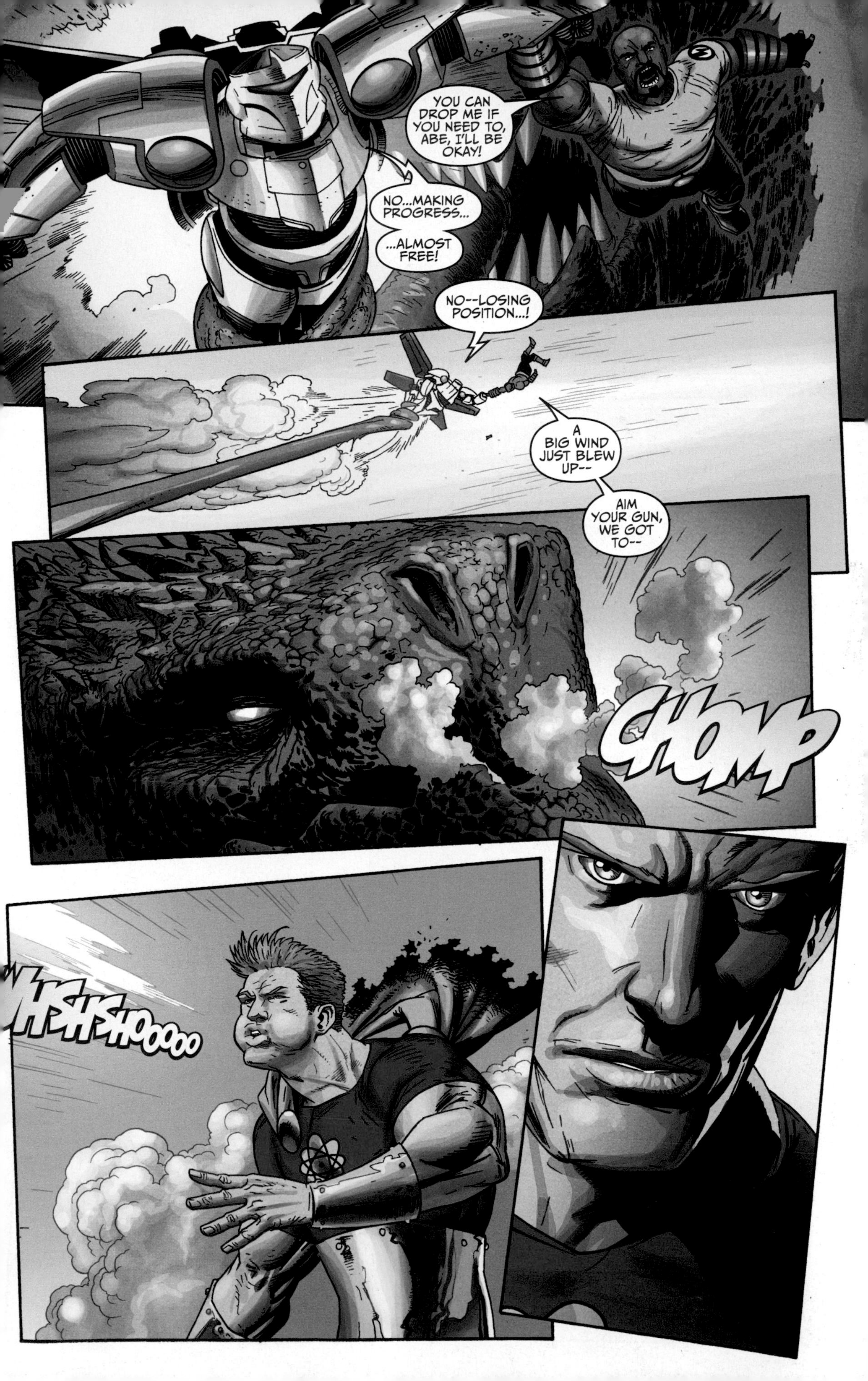

YOU CAN DROP ME IF YOU NEED TO, ABE, I'LL BE OKAY!
NO...MAKING PROGRESS...
...ALMOST FREE!
NO--LOSING POSITION...!
A BIG WIND JUST BLEW UP--
AIM YOUR GUN, WE GOT TO--
CHOMP
HSHSHOOOOO

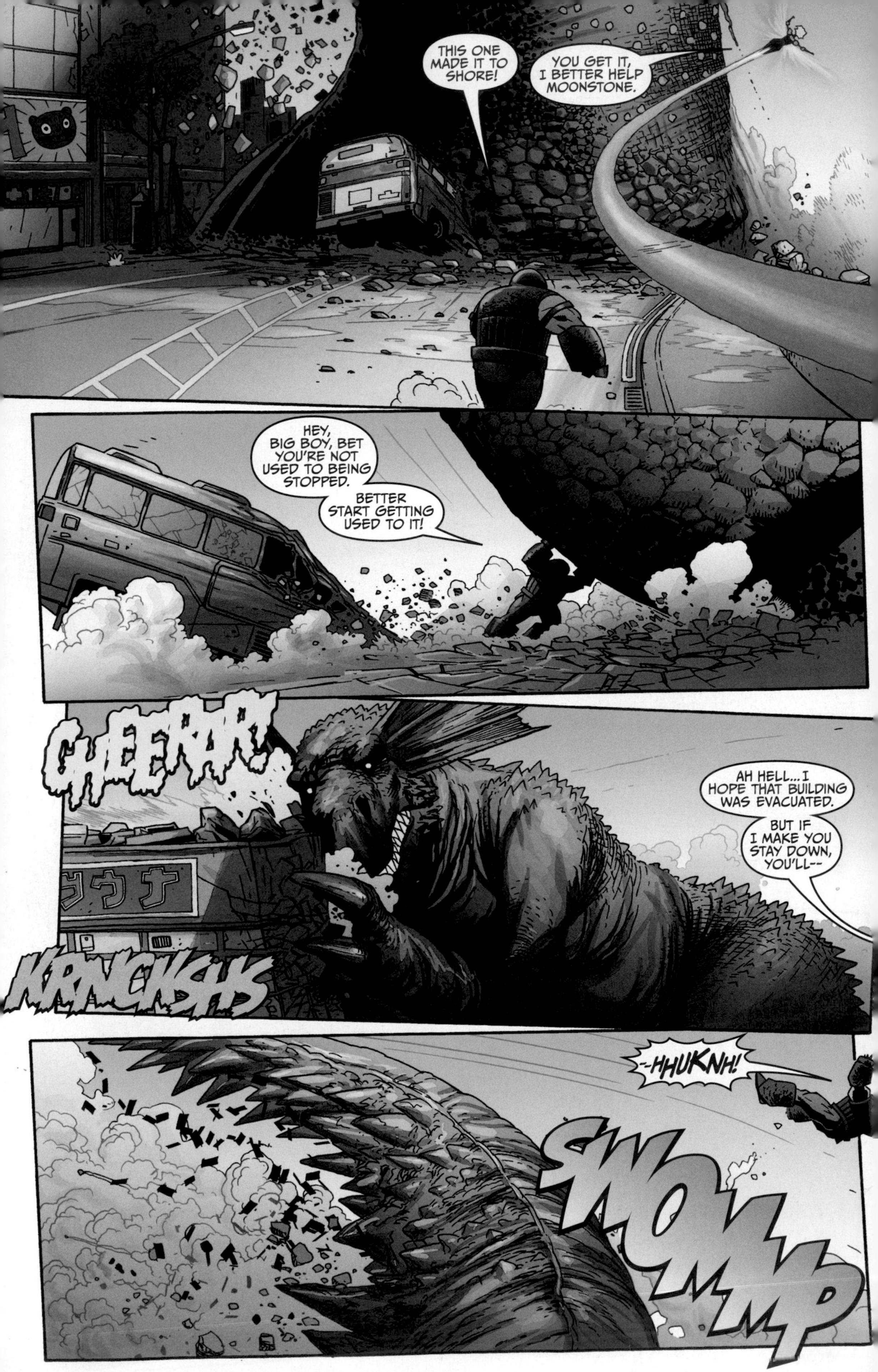
THIS ONE MADE IT TO SHORE!
YOU GET IT, I BETTER HELP MOONSTONE.
HEY, BIG BOY, BET YOU'RE NOT USED TO BEING STOPPED.
BETTER START GETTING USED TO IT!
GHEERAR!
AH HELL... I HOPE THAT BUILDING WAS EVACUATED.
BUT IF I MAKE YOU STAY DOWN, YOU'LL--
KRNCKSHS
--HHUKNH!
SWOMP

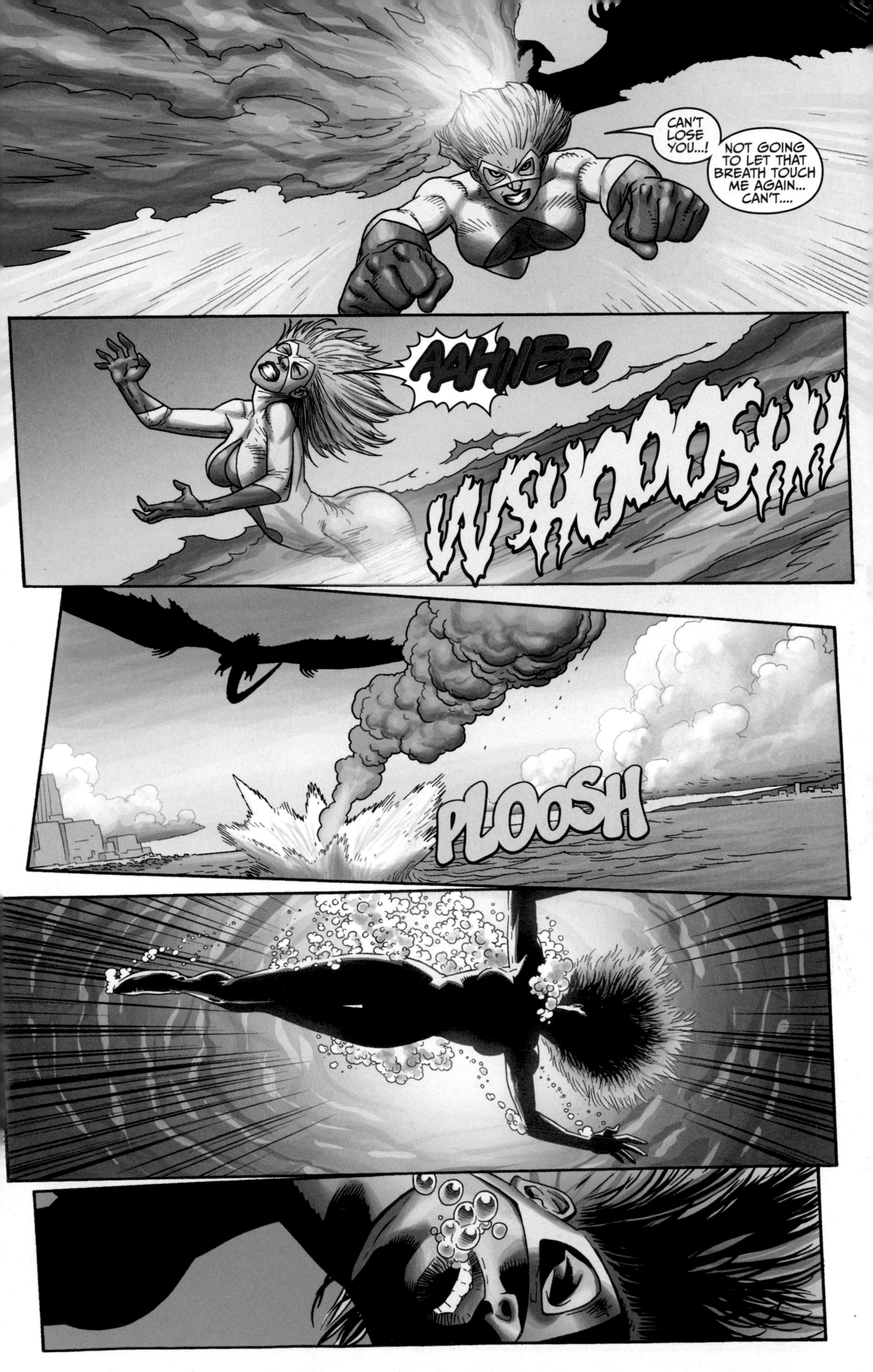
CAN'T LOSE YOU...!
NOT GOING TO LET THAT BREATH TOUCH ME AGAIN... CAN'T....
AAHIIEE!
WHOOOSH
PLOOSH

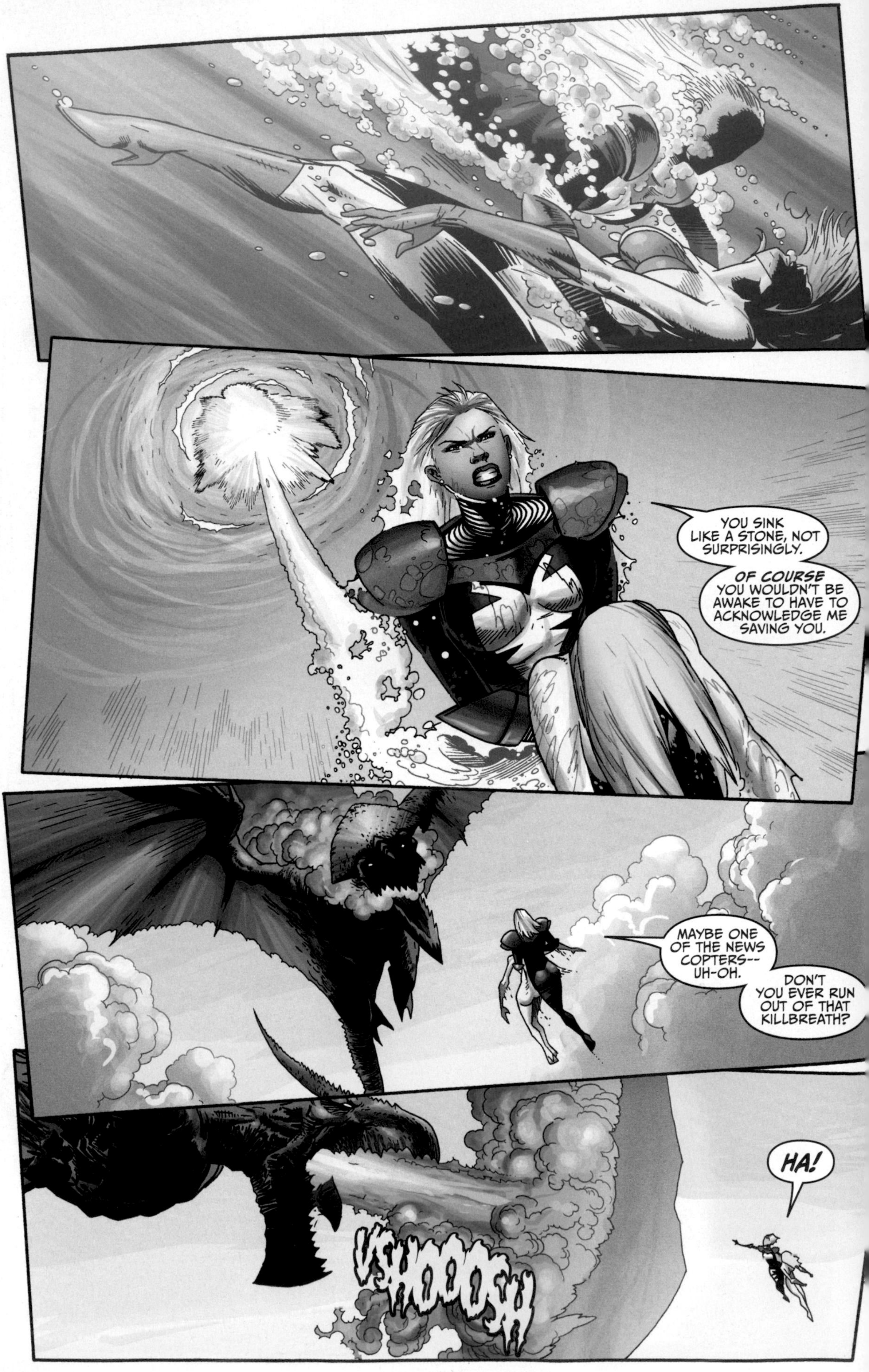
YOU SINK LIKE A STONE, NOT SURPRISINGLY.
OF COURSE YOU WOULDN'T BE AWAKE TO HAVE TO ACKNOWLEDGE ME SAVING YOU.
MAYBE ONE OF THE NEWS COPTERS-- UH-OH.
DON'T YOU EVER RUN OUT OF THAT KILLBREATH?
HA!
VSHOOOSH

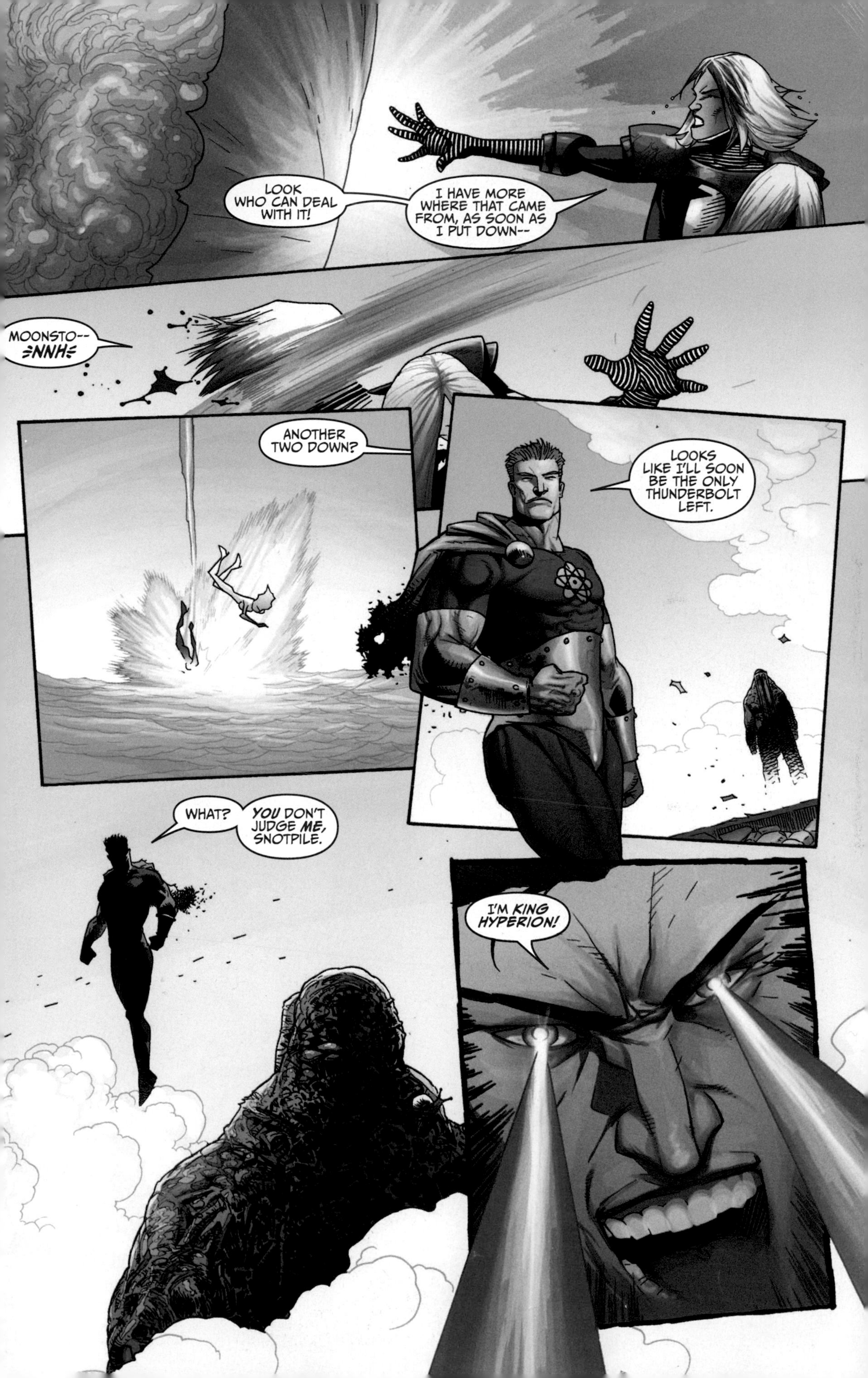
LOOK WHO CAN DEAL WITH IT!
I HAVE MORE WHERE THAT CAME FROM, AS SOON AS I PUT DOWN--
MOONSTO-- NNH
ANOTHER TWO DOWN?
LOOKS LIKE I'LL SOON BE THE ONLY THUNDERBOLT LEFT.
WHAT?
YOU DON'T JUDGE ME, SNOTPILE.
I'M KING HYPERION!

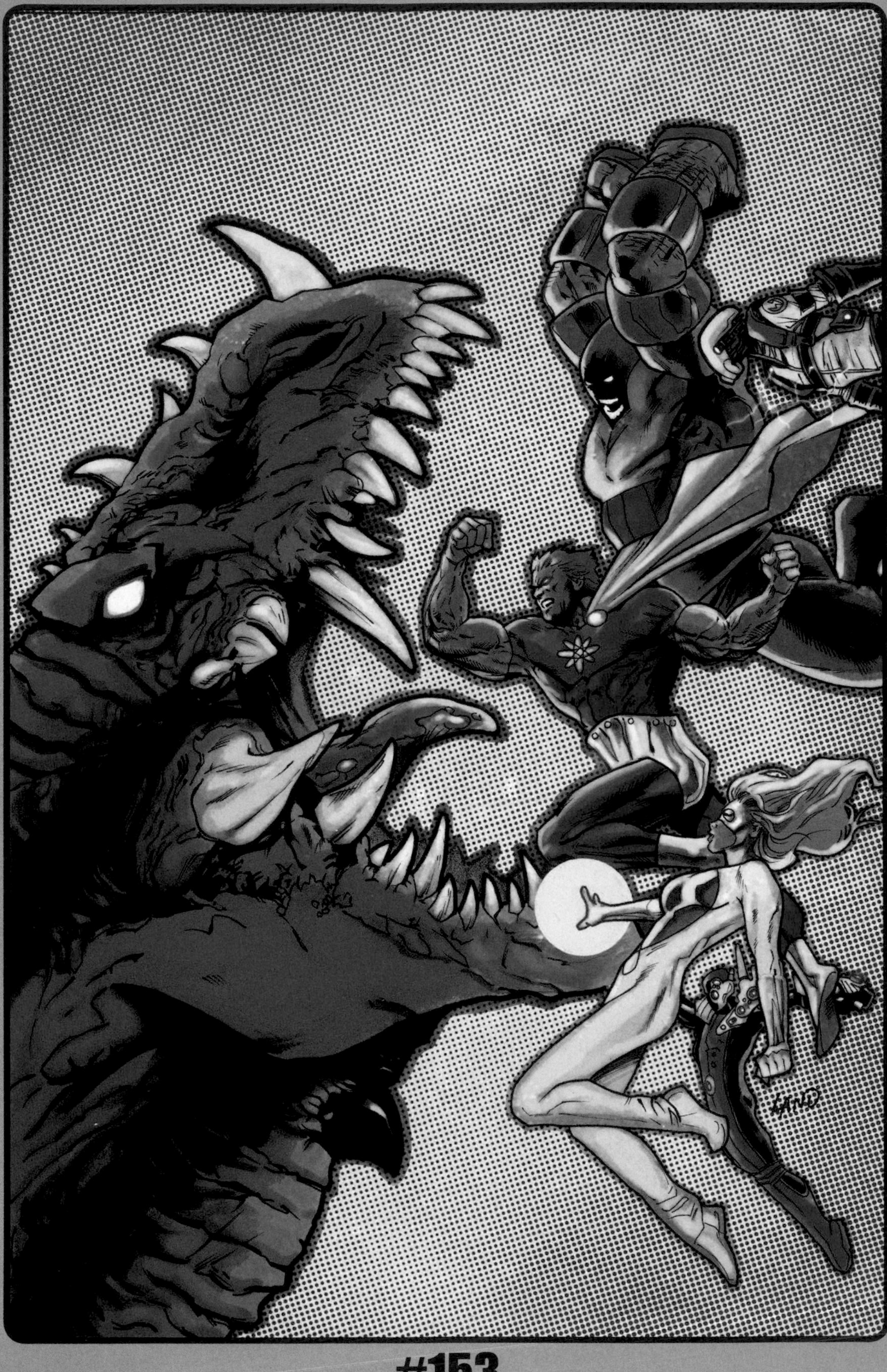
LAND

#153

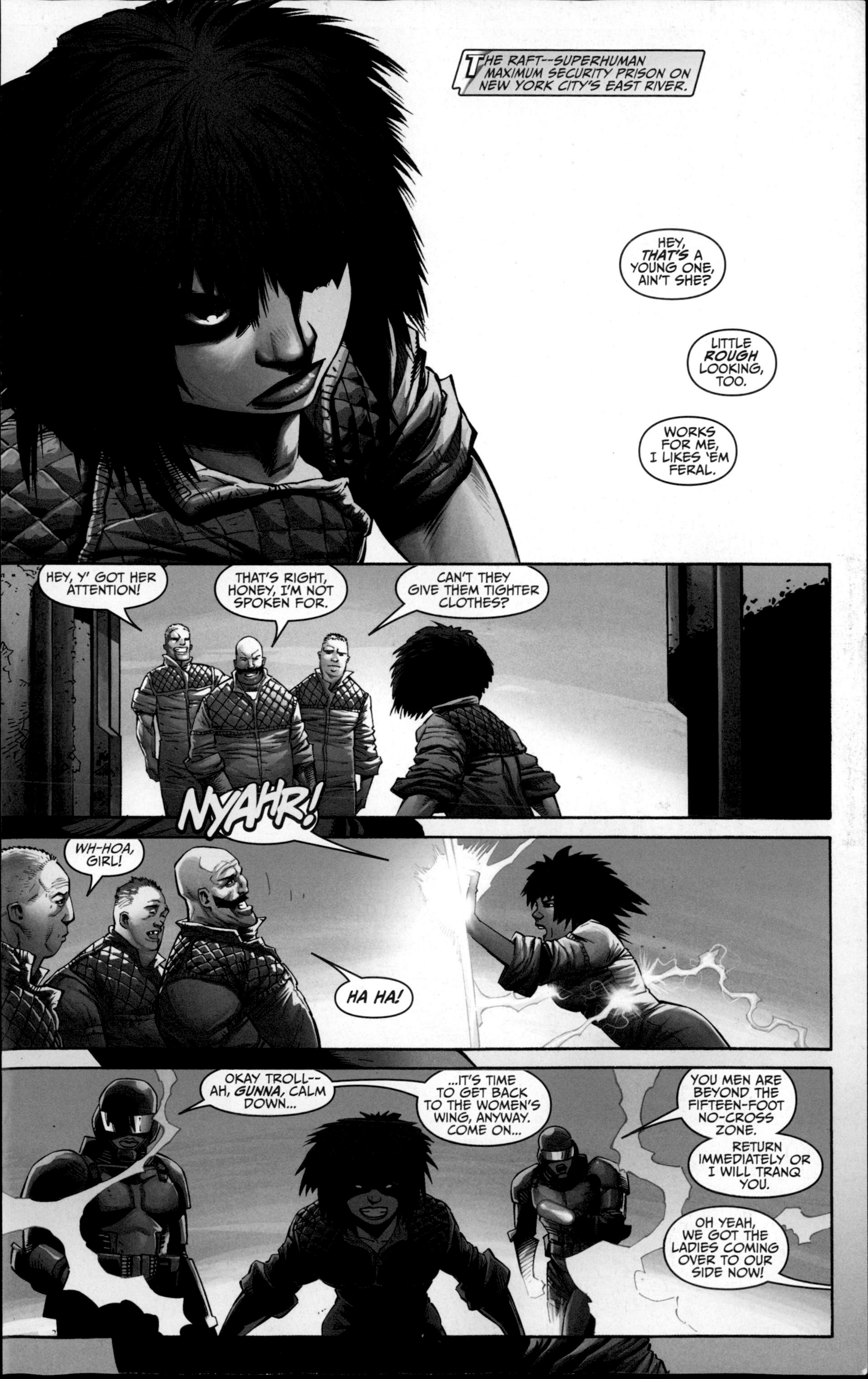
THE RAFT--SUPERHUMAN MAXIMUM SECURITY PRISON ON NEW YORK CITY'S EAST RIVER.
HEY, THAT'S A YOUNG ONE, AIN'T SHE?
LITTLE ROUGH LOOKING, TOO.
WORKS FOR ME, I LIKES 'EM FERAL.
HEY, Y' GOT HER ATTENTION!
THAT'S RIGHT, HONEY, I'M NOT SPOKEN FOR.
CAN'T THEY GIVE THEM TIGHTER CLOTHES?
NYAHR!
WH-HOA, GIRL!
HA HA!
OKAY TROLL-- AH, GUNNA, CALM DOWN...
...IT'S TIME TO GET BACK TO THE WOMEN'S WING, ANYWAY. COME ON...
YOU MEN ARE BEYOND THE FIFTEEN-FOOT NO-CROSS ZONE.
RETURN IMMEDIATELY OR I WILL TRANQ YOU.
OH YEAH, WE GOT THE LADIES COMING OVER TO OUR SIDE NOW!

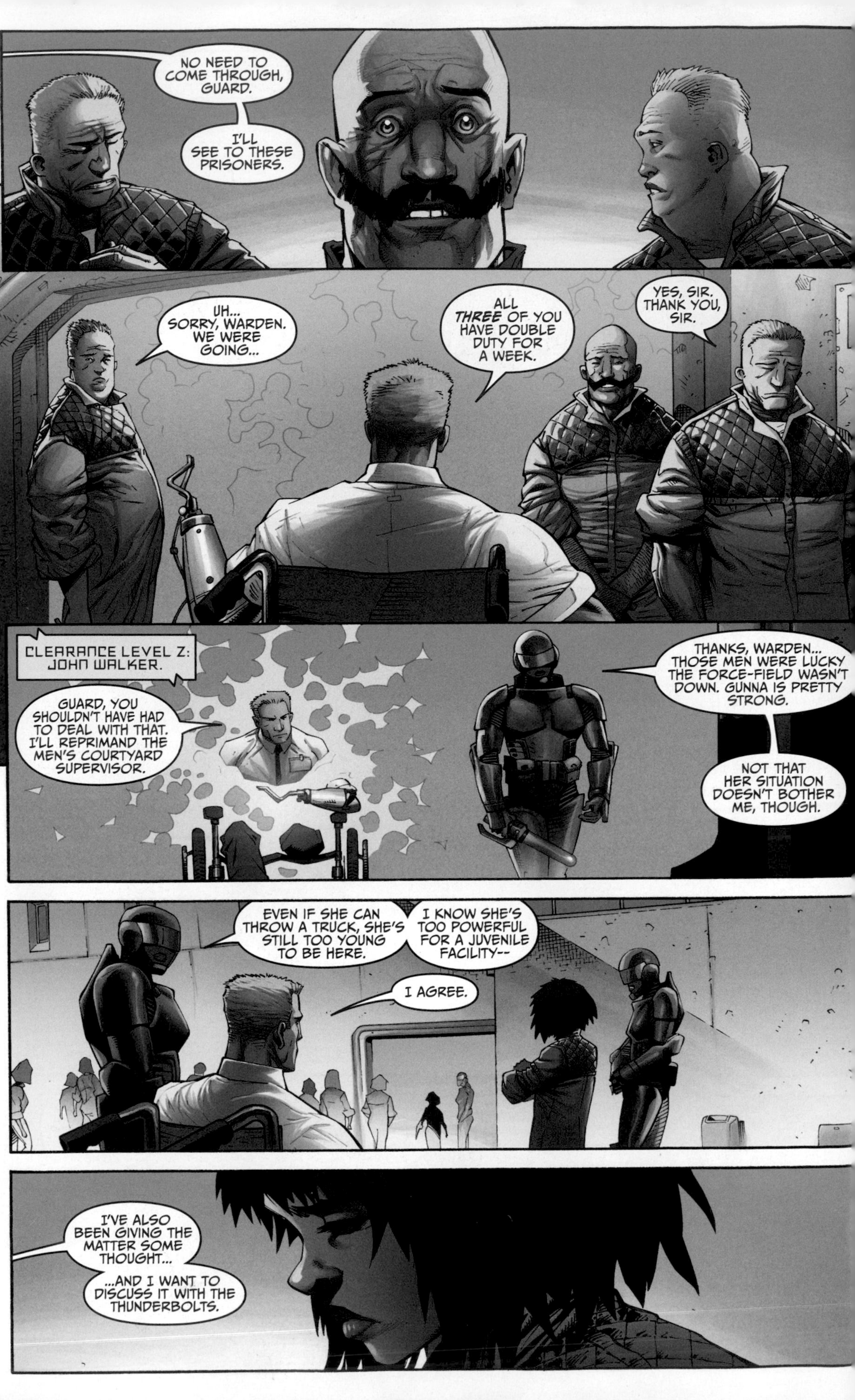
NO NEED TO COME THROUGH, GUARD.
I'LL SEE TO THESE PRISONERS.
UH... SORRY, WARDEN. WE WERE GOING...
ALL THREE OF YOU HAVE DOUBLE DUTY FOR A WEEK.
YES, SIR. THANK YOU, SIR.
CLEARANCE LEVEL Z: JOHN WALKER.
GUARD, YOU SHOULDN'T HAVE HAD TO DEAL WITH THAT. I'LL REPRIMAND THE MEN'S COURTYARD SUPERVISOR.
THANKS, WARDEN... THOSE MEN WERE LUCKY THE FORCE-FIELD WASN'T DOWN. GUNNA IS PRETTY STRONG.
NOT THAT HER SITUATION DOESN'T BOTHER ME, THOUGH.
EVEN IF SHE CAN THROW A TRUCK, SHE'S STILL TOO YOUNG TO BE HERE.
I KNOW SHE'S TOO POWERFUL FOR A JUVENILE FACILITY--
I AGREE.
I'VE ALSO BEEN GIVING THE MATTER SOME THOUGHT...
...AND I WANT TO DISCUSS IT WITH THE THUNDERBOLTS.

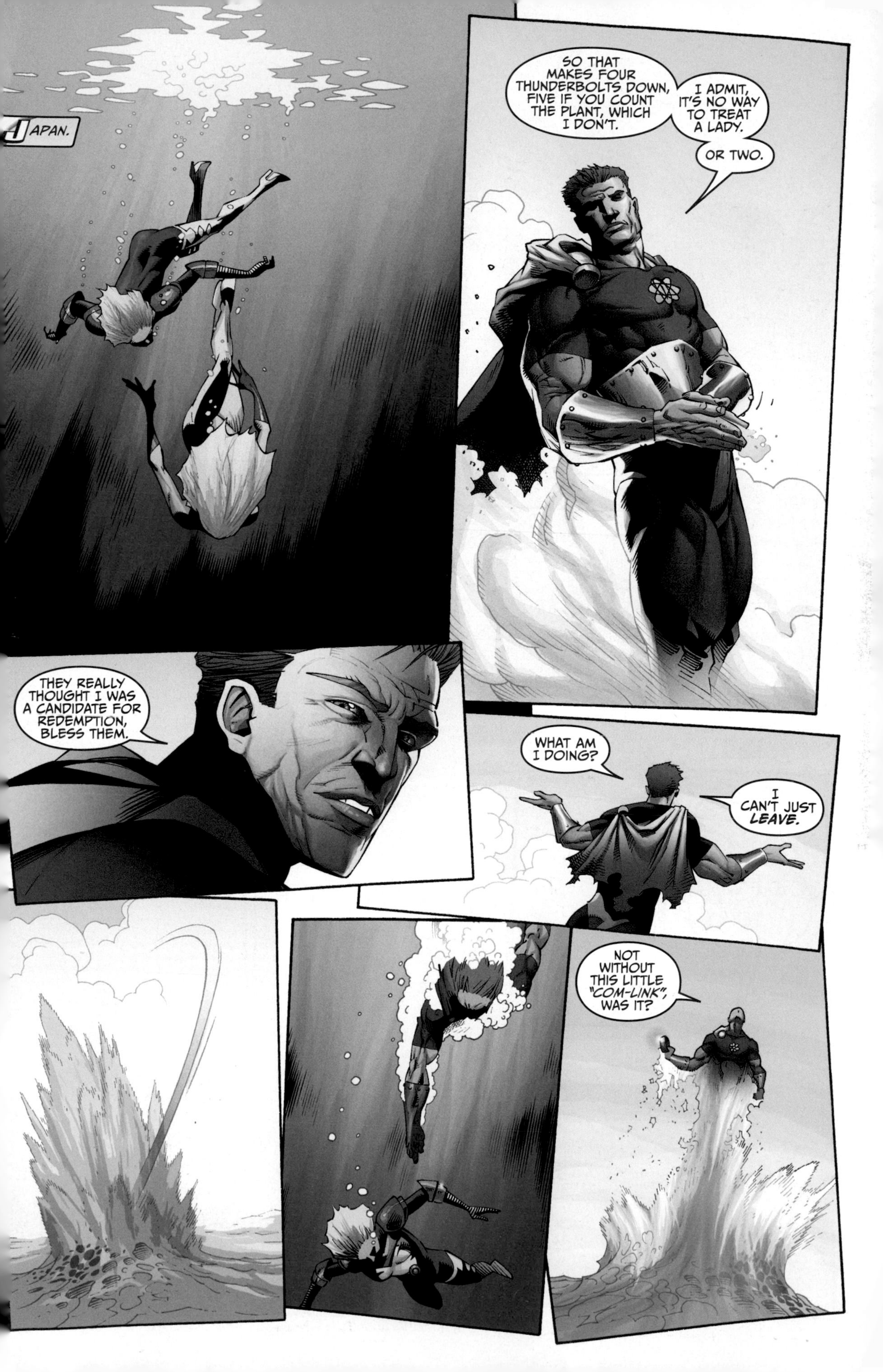
JAPAN.
SO THAT MAKES FOUR THUNDERBOLTS DOWN, FIVE IF YOU COUNT THE PLANT, WHICH I DON'T.
I ADMIT, IT'S NO WAY TO TREAT A LADY.
OR TWO.
THEY REALLY THOUGHT I WAS A CANDIDATE FOR REDEMPTION, BLESS THEM.
WHAT AM I DOING?
I CAN'T JUST LEAVE.
NOT WITHOUT THIS LITTLE "COM-LINK", WAS IT?

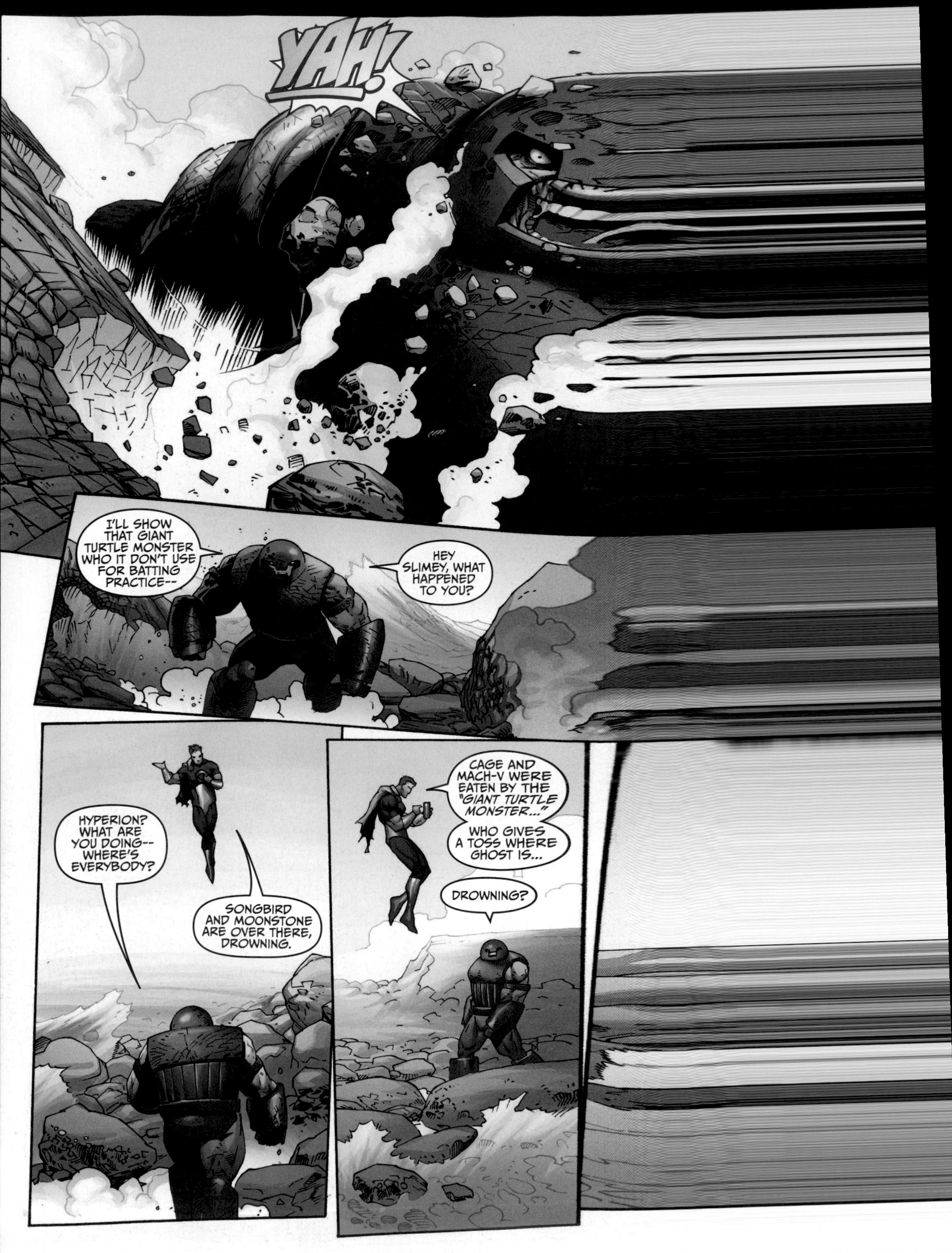
YAH!
I'LL SHOW THAT GIANT TURTLE MONSTER WHO IT DON'T USE FOR BATTING PRACTICE--
HEY SLIMEY, WHAT HAPPENED TO YOU?
HYPERION? WHAT ARE YOU DOING-- WHERE'S EVERYBODY?
SONGBIRD AND MOONSTONE ARE OVER THERE, DROWNING.
CAGE AND MACH-V WERE EATEN BY THE "GIANT TURTLE MONSTER..."
WHO GIVES A TOSS WHERE GHOST IS...
DROWNING?

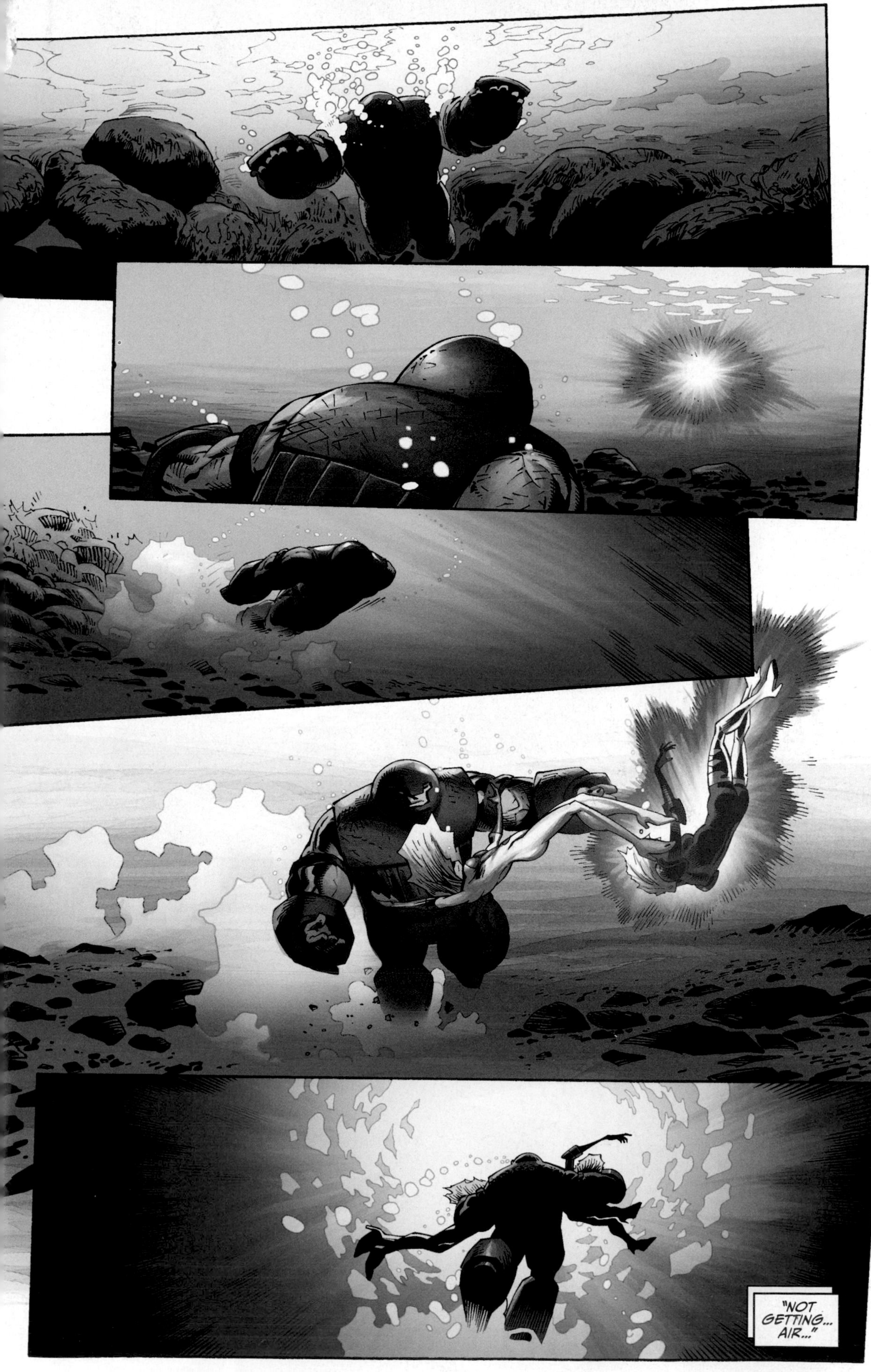
"NOT GETTING... AIR..."

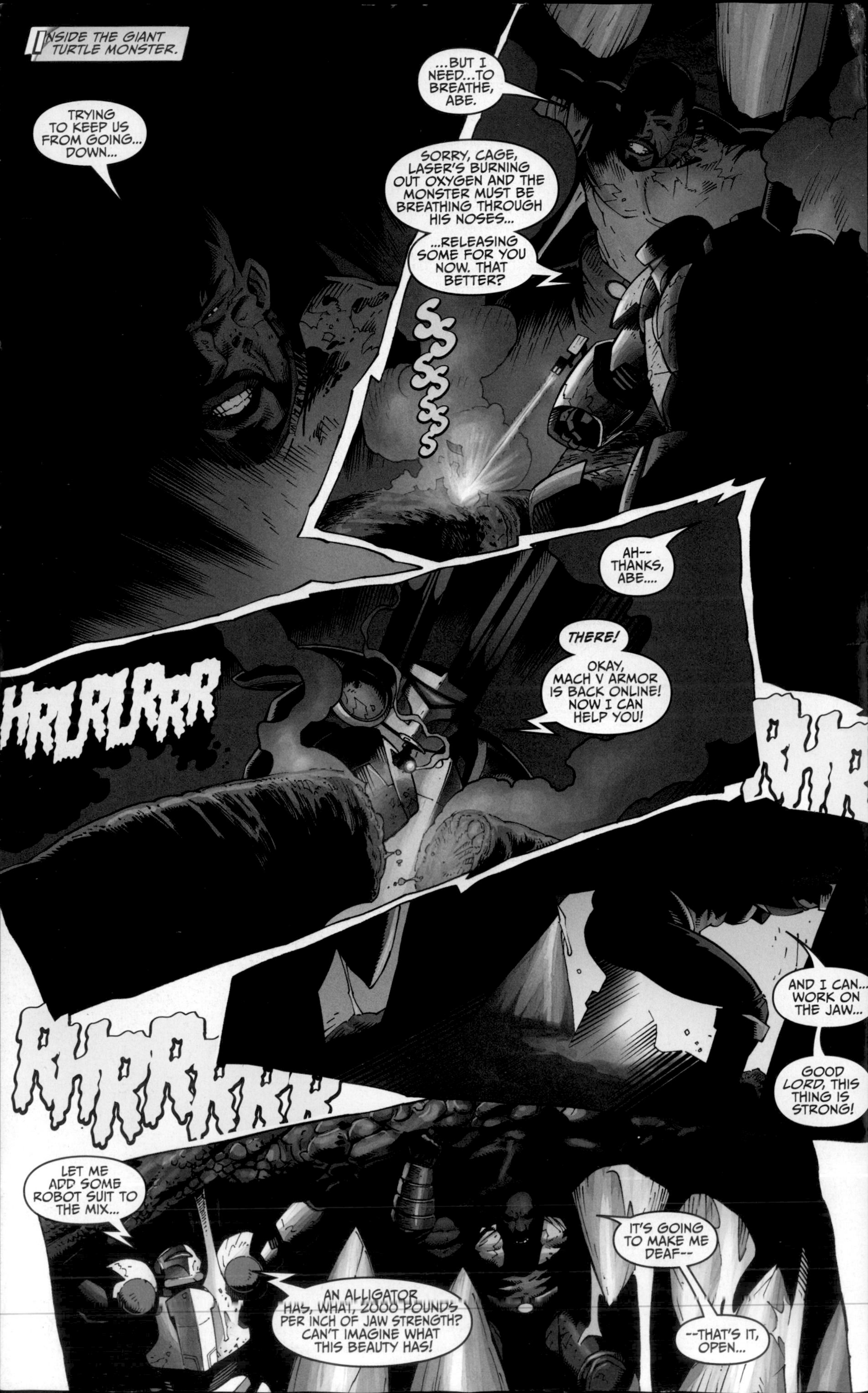
INSIDE THE GIANT TURTLE MONSTER.
TRYING TO KEEP US FROM GOING... DOWN...
...BUT I NEED...TO BREATHE, ABE.
SORRY, CAGE, LASER'S BURNING OUT OXYGEN AND THE MONSTER MUST BE BREATHING THROUGH HIS NOSES...
...RELEASING SOME FOR YOU NOW. THAT BETTER?
SSSSSS
AH-- THANKS, ABE....
THERE!
OKAY, MACH V ARMOR IS BACK ONLINE! NOW I CAN HELP YOU!
HRURRR
RHRR
RHRRRRRR
AND I CAN... WORK ON THE JAW...
GOOD LORD, THIS THING IS STRONG!
LET ME ADD SOME ROBOT SUIT TO THE MIX...
AN ALLIGATOR HAS, WHAT, 2000 POUNDS PER INCH OF JAW STRENGTH? CAN'T IMAGINE WHAT THIS BEAUTY HAS!
IT'S GOING TO MAKE ME DEAF--
--THAT'S IT, OPEN...

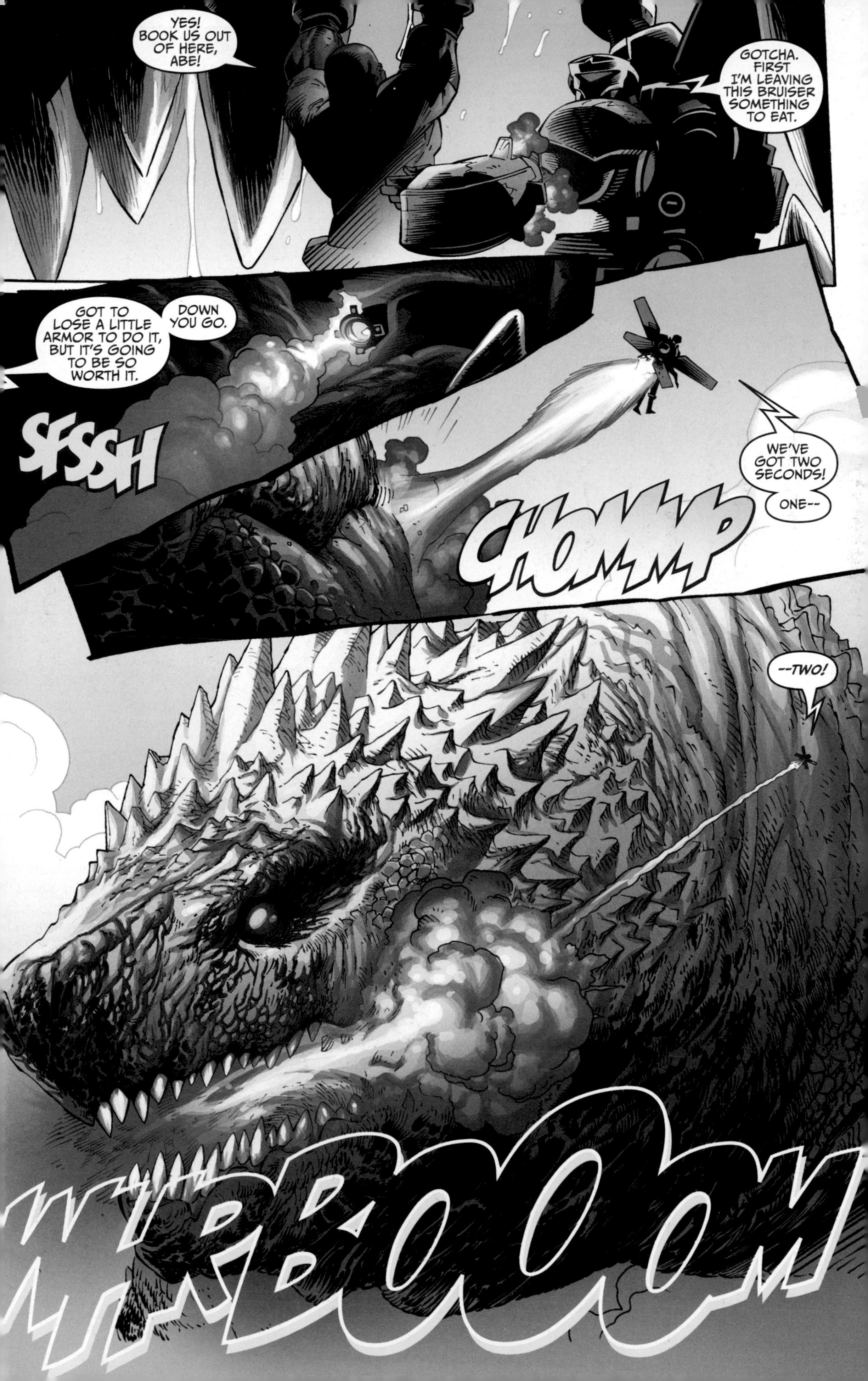
YES! BOOK US OUT OF HERE, ABE!
GOTCHA. FIRST I'M LEAVING THIS BRUISER SOMETHING TO EAT.
GOT TO LOSE A LITTLE ARMOR TO DO IT, BUT IT'S GOING TO BE SO WORTH IT.
DOWN YOU GO.
SFSSH
WE'VE GOT TWO SECONDS!
ONE--
CHOMP
--TWO!
WHBOOOM

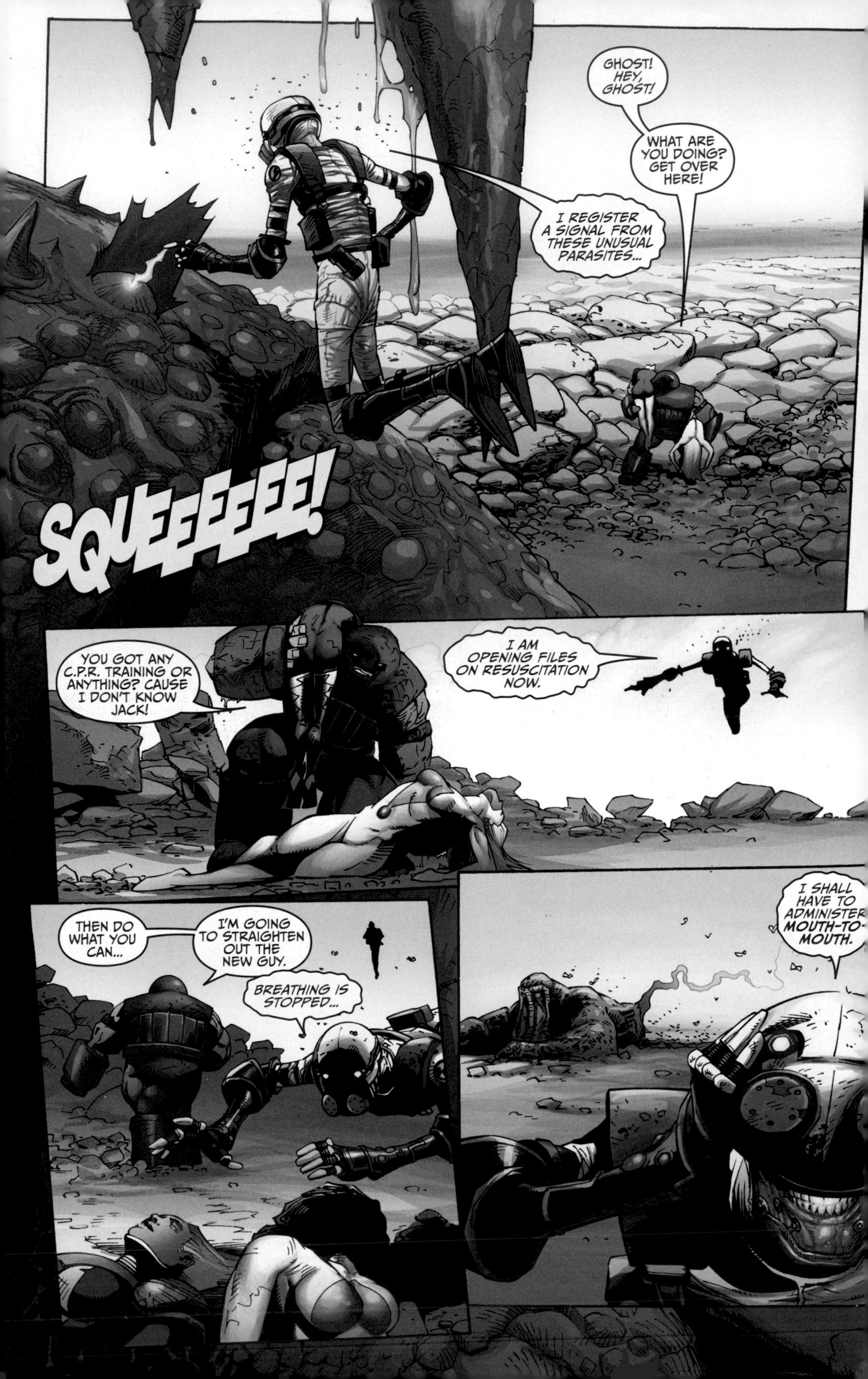
GHOST! HEY, GHOST!
WHAT ARE YOU DOING? GET OVER HERE!
I REGISTER A SIGNAL FROM THESE UNUSUAL PARASITES...
SQUEEEEEE!
YOU GOT ANY C.P.R. TRAINING OR ANYTHING? CAUSE I DON'T KNOW JACK!
I AM OPENING FILES ON RESUSCITATION NOW.
THEN DO WHAT YOU CAN...
I'M GOING TO STRAIGHTEN OUT THE NEW GUY.
BREATHING IS STOPPED...
I SHALL HAVE TO ADMINISTER MOUTH-TO-MOUTH.

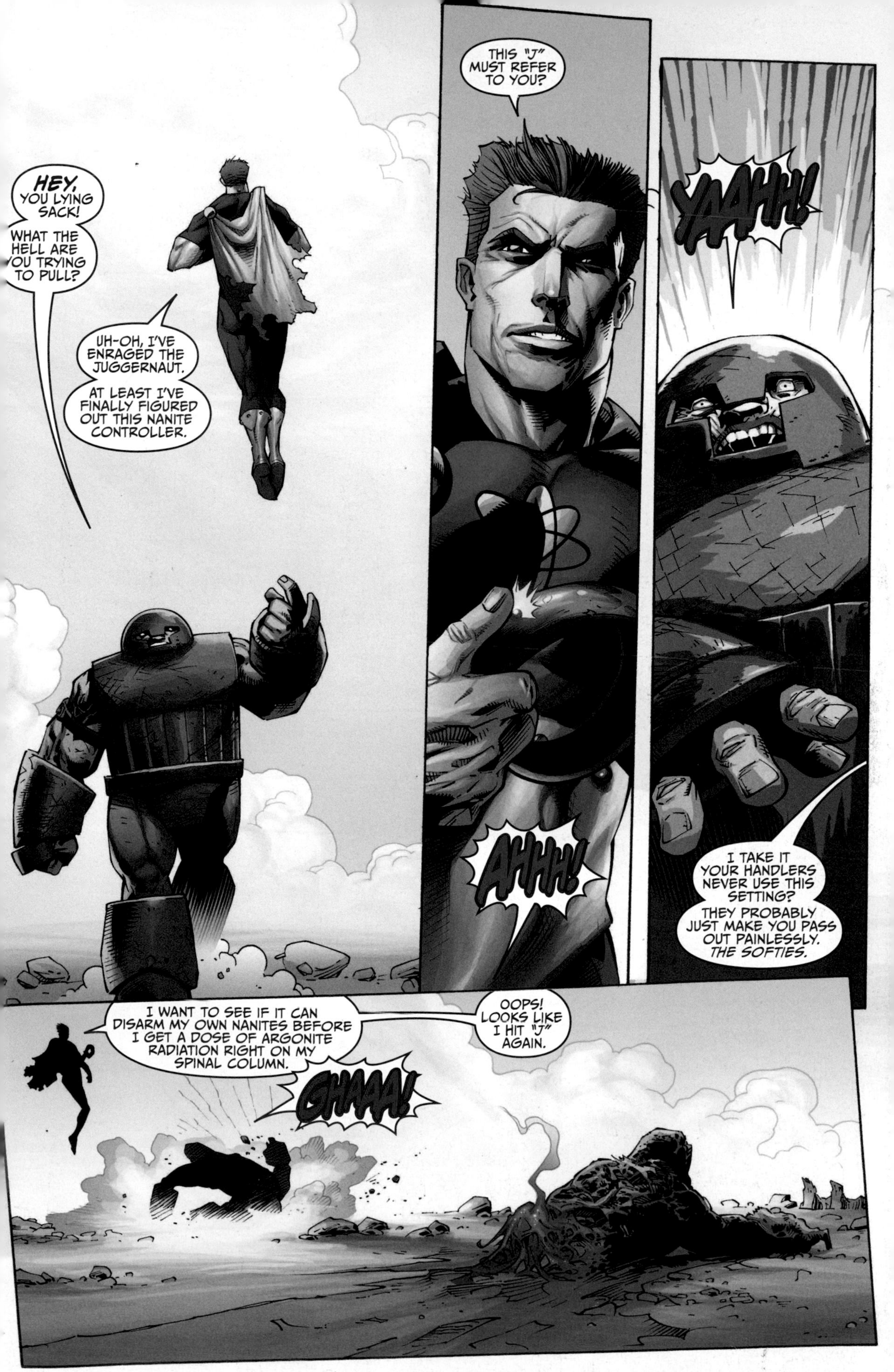
HEY, YOU LYING SACK!
WHAT THE HELL ARE YOU TRYING TO PULL?
UH-OH, I'VE ENRAGED THE JUGGERNAUT.
AT LEAST I'VE FINALLY FIGURED OUT THIS NANITE CONTROLLER.
THIS "J" MUST REFER TO YOU?
AHHH!
YAAHH!
I TAKE IT YOUR HANDLERS NEVER USE THIS SETTING?
THEY PROBABLY JUST MAKE YOU PASS OUT PAINLESSLY. THE SOFTIES.
I WANT TO SEE IF IT CAN DISARM MY OWN NANITES BEFORE I GET A DOSE OF ARGONITE RADIATION RIGHT ON MY SPINAL COLUMN.
OOPS! LOOKS LIKE I HIT "J" AGAIN.
GHAAA!

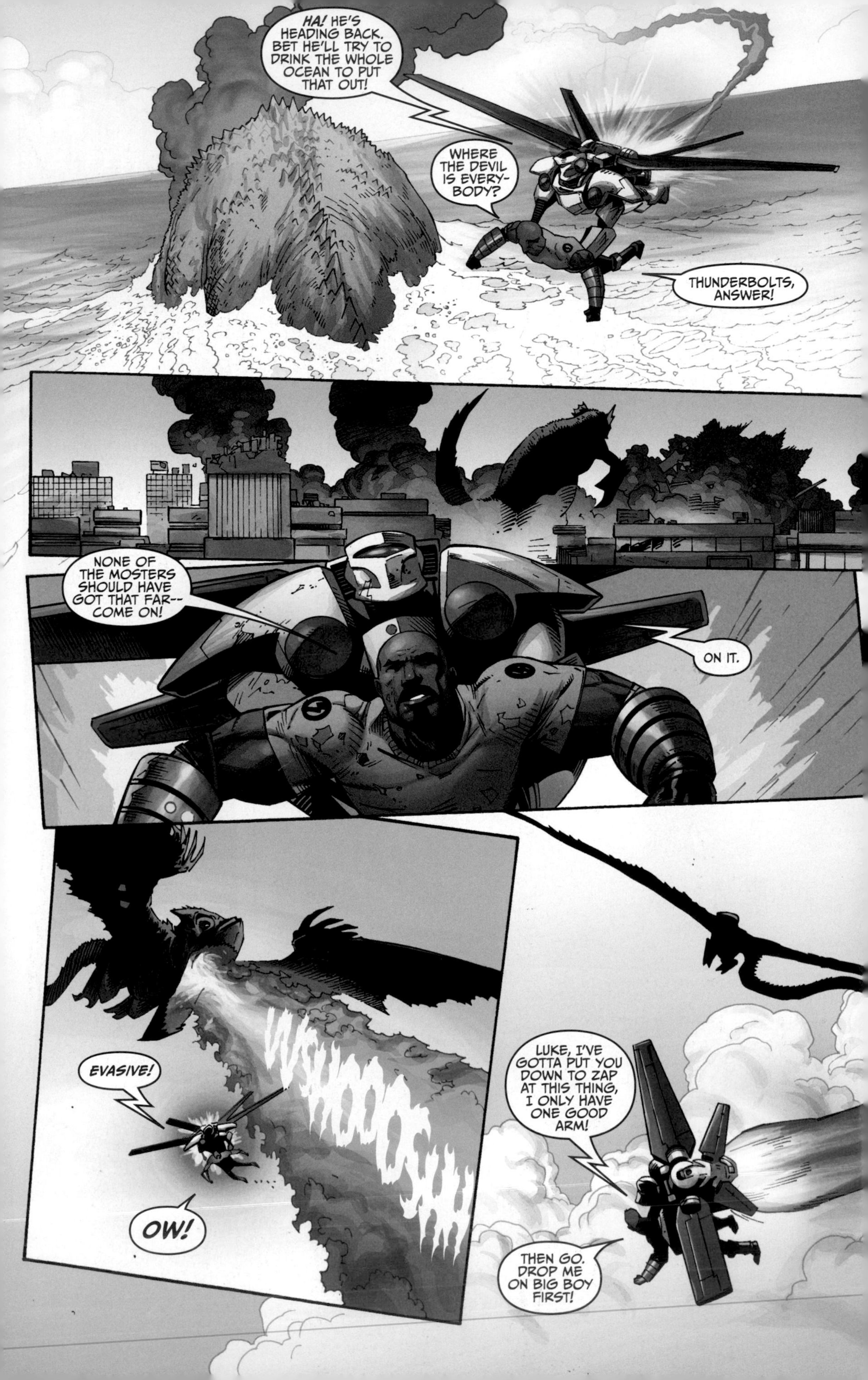

HA! HE'S HEADING BACK. BET HE'LL TRY TO DRINK THE WHOLE OCEAN TO PUT THAT OUT!
WHERE THE DEVIL IS EVERY-BODY?
THUNDERBOLTS, ANSWER!
NONE OF THE MOSTERS SHOULD HAVE GOT THAT FAR-- COME ON!
ON IT.
WHOOOSH
EVASIVE!
OW!
LUKE, I'VE GOTTA PUT YOU DOWN TO ZAP AT THIS THING, I ONLY HAVE ONE GOOD ARM!
THEN GO. DROP ME ON BIG BOY FIRST!

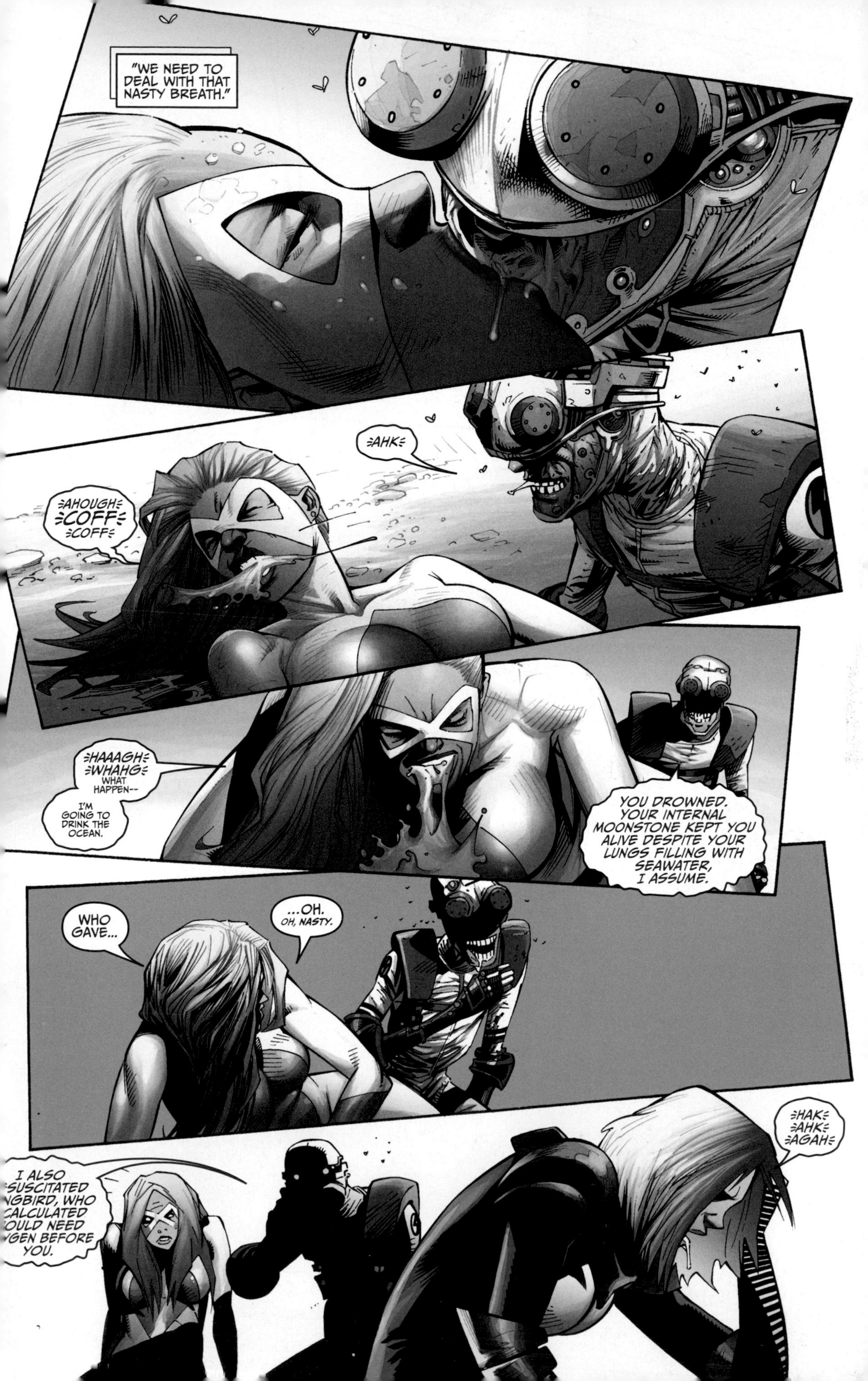
"WE NEED TO DEAL WITH THAT NASTY BREATH."
AHK
AHOUGH COFF COFF
HAAAGH WHAHG WHAT HAPPEN--
I'M GOING TO DRINK THE OCEAN.
YOU DROWNED. YOUR INTERNAL MOONSTONE KEPT YOU ALIVE DESPITE YOUR LUNGS FILLING WITH SEAWATER, I ASSUME.
WHO GAVE...
...OH. OH, NASTY.
HAK AHK AGAH
I ALSO ESUSCITATED NGBIRD, WHO CALCULATED OULD NEED YGEN BEFORE YOU.

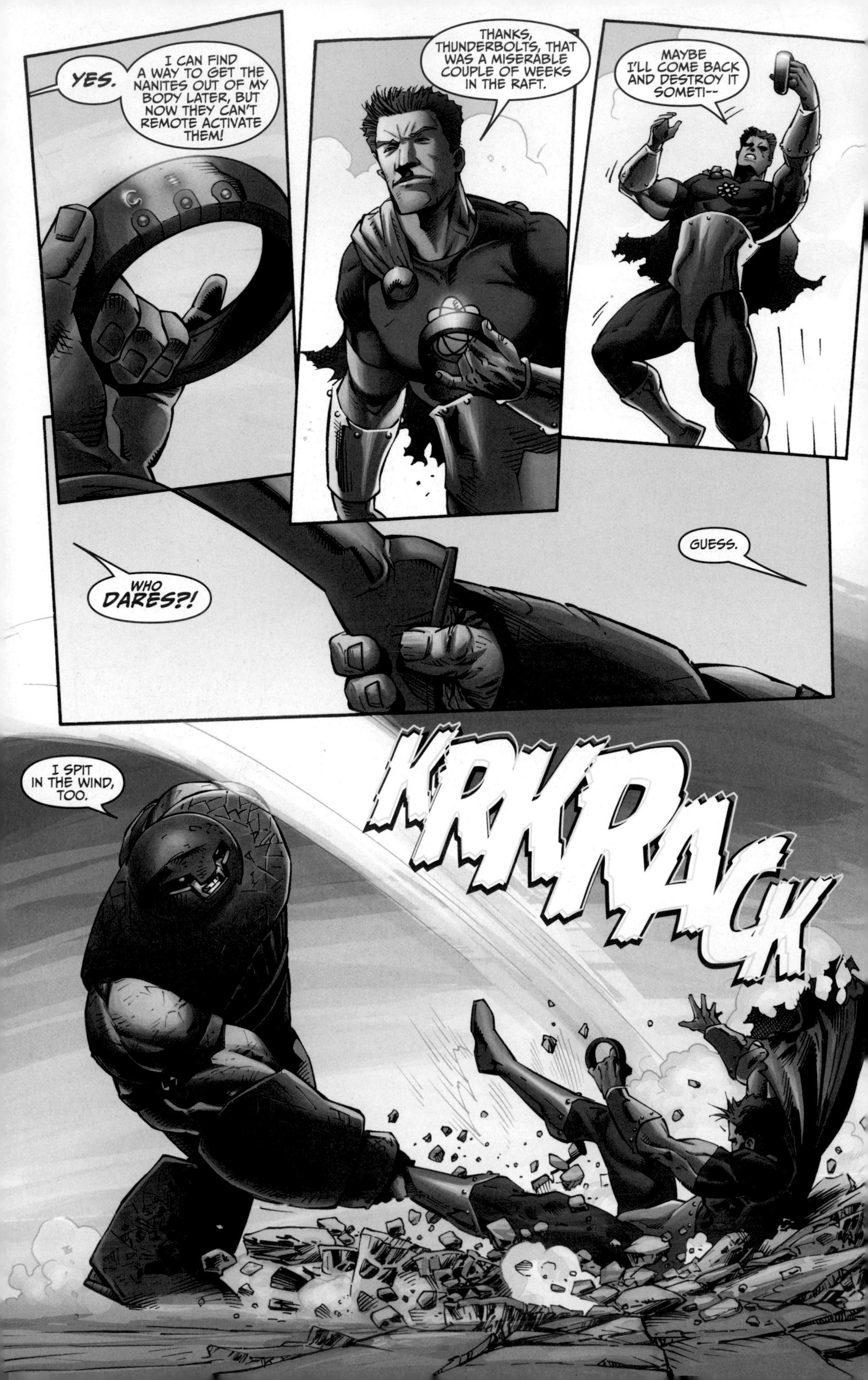
YES.
I CAN FIND A WAY TO GET THE NANITES OUT OF MY BODY LATER, BUT NOW THEY CAN'T REMOTE ACTIVATE THEM!
THANKS, THUNDERBOLTS, THAT WAS A MISERABLE COUPLE OF WEEKS IN THE RAFT.
MAYBE I'LL COME BACK AND DESTROY IT SOMETI--
WHO DARES?!
GUESS.
I SPIT IN THE WIND, TOO.
KRKRACK

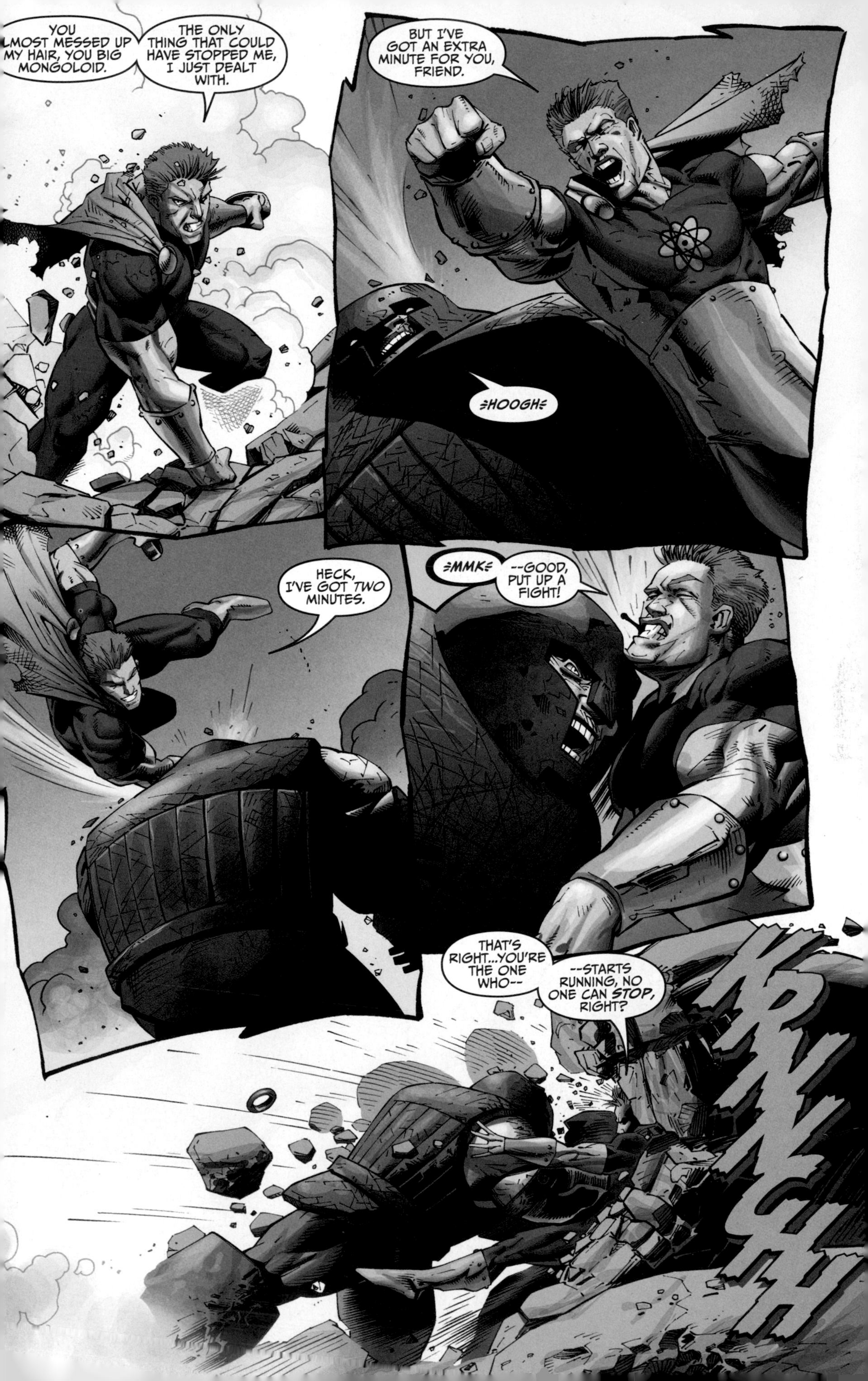

YOU ALMOST MESSED UP MY HAIR, YOU BIG MONGOLOID.
THE ONLY THING THAT COULD HAVE STOPPED ME, I JUST DEALT WITH.
BUT I'VE GOT AN EXTRA MINUTE FOR YOU, FRIEND.
HOOGH
HECK, I'VE GOT TWO MINUTES.
MMK
--GOOD, PUT UP A FIGHT!
THAT'S RIGHT...YOU'RE THE ONE WHO--
--STARTS RUNNING, NO ONE CAN STOP, RIGHT?
KRUNCH

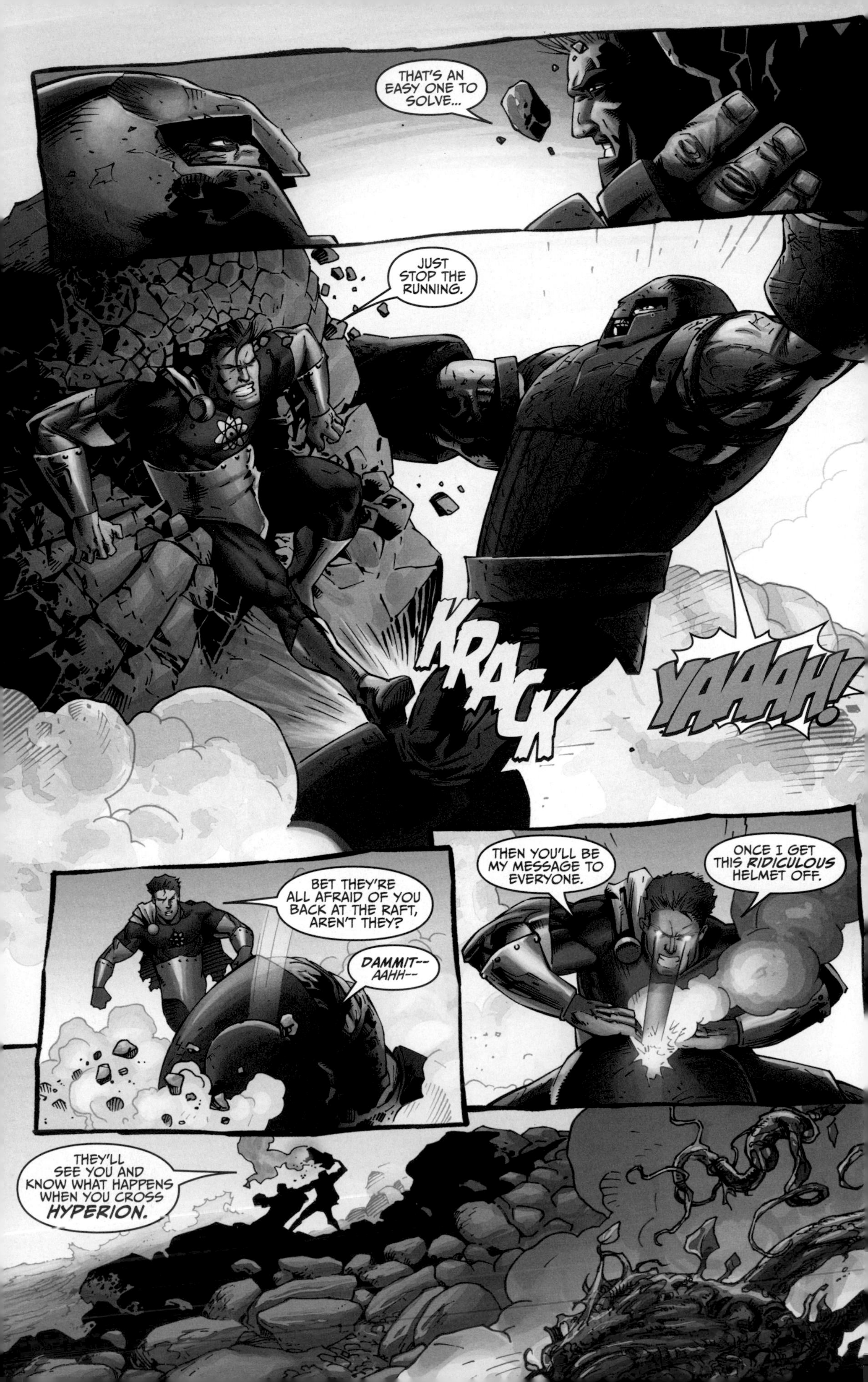
THAT'S AN EASY ONE TO SOLVE...
JUST STOP THE RUNNING.
KRACK
YAAAH!
BET THEY'RE ALL AFRAID OF YOU BACK AT THE RAFT, AREN'T THEY?
DAMMIT-- AAHH--
THEN YOU'LL BE MY MESSAGE TO EVERYONE.
ONCE I GET THIS *RIDICULOUS* HELMET OFF.
THEY'LL SEE YOU AND KNOW WHAT HAPPENS WHEN YOU CROSS **HYPERION.**

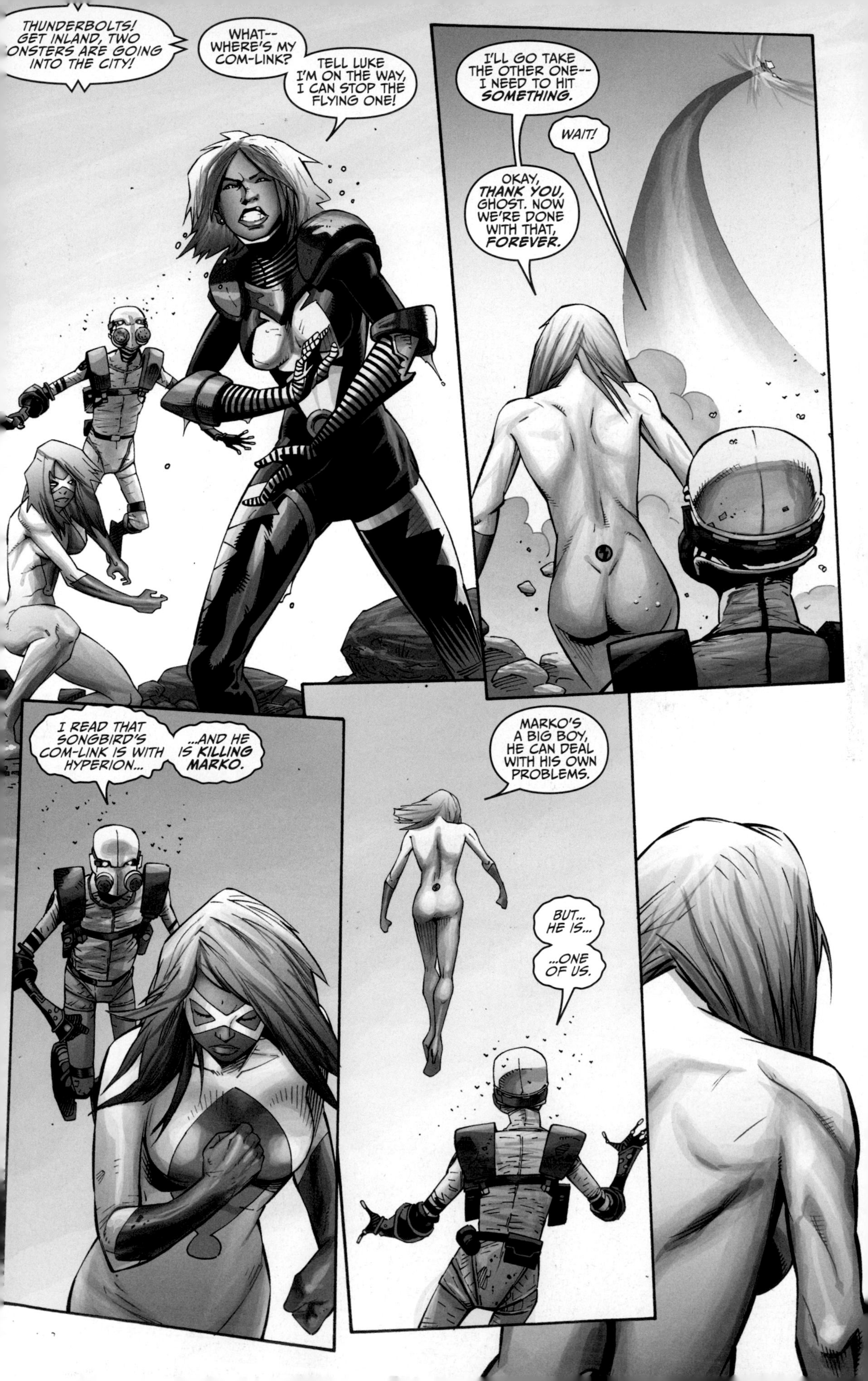
THUNDERBOLTS! GET INLAND, TWO ONSTERS ARE GOING INTO THE CITY!
WHAT-- WHERE'S MY COM-LINK?
TELL LUKE I'M ON THE WAY, I CAN STOP THE FLYING ONE!
I'LL GO TAKE THE OTHER ONE-- I NEED TO HIT SOMETHING.
WAIT!
OKAY, THANK YOU, GHOST. NOW WE'RE DONE WITH THAT, FOREVER.
I READ THAT SONGBIRD'S COM-LINK IS WITH HYPERION...
...AND HE IS KILLING MARKO.
MARKO'S A BIG BOY, HE CAN DEAL WITH HIS OWN PROBLEMS.
BUT... HE IS...
...ONE OF US.

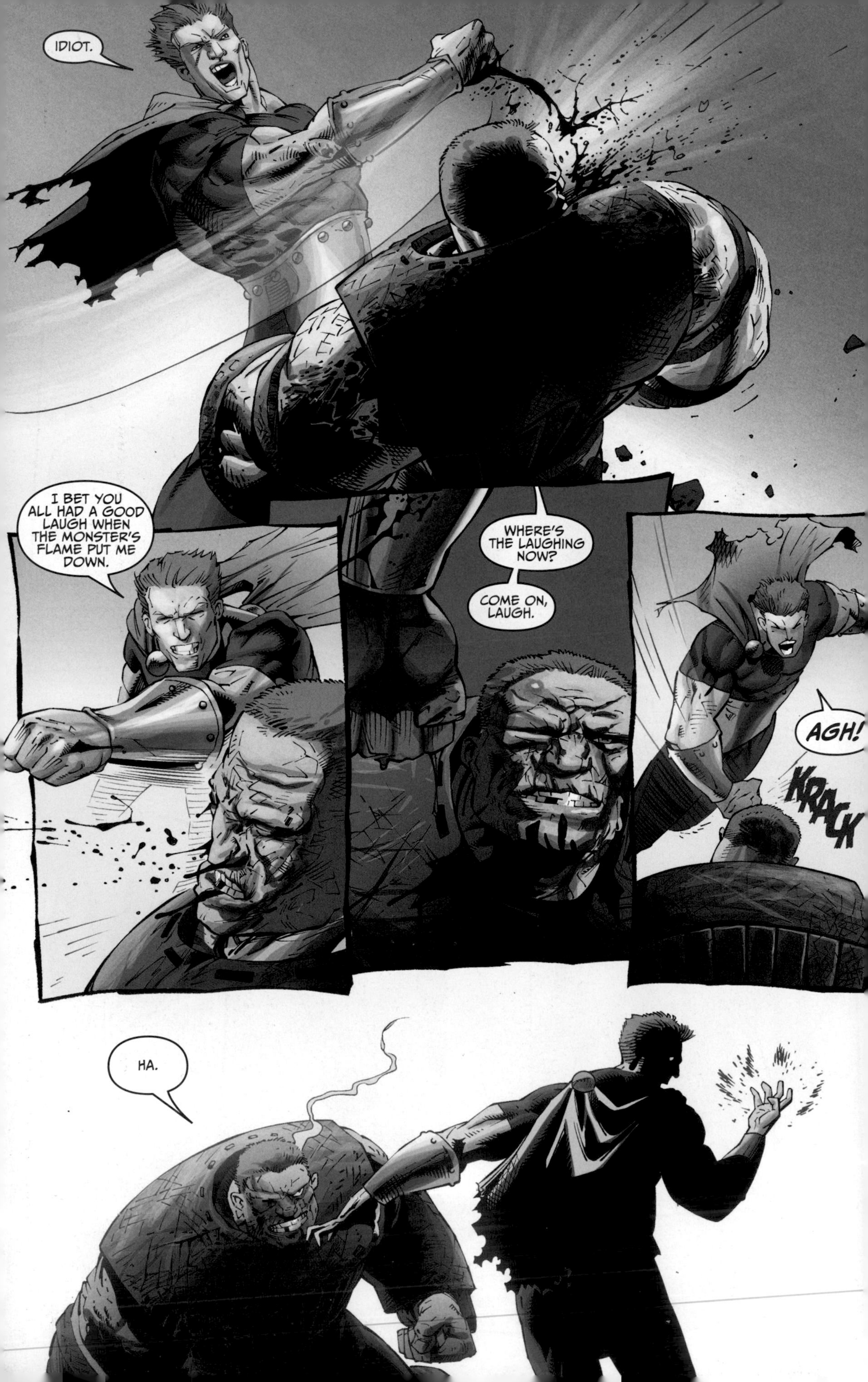
IDIOT.
I BET YOU ALL HAD A GOOD LAUGH WHEN THE MONSTER'S FLAME PUT ME DOWN.
WHERE'S THE LAUGHING NOW?
COME ON, LAUGH.
AGH!
KRACK
HA.

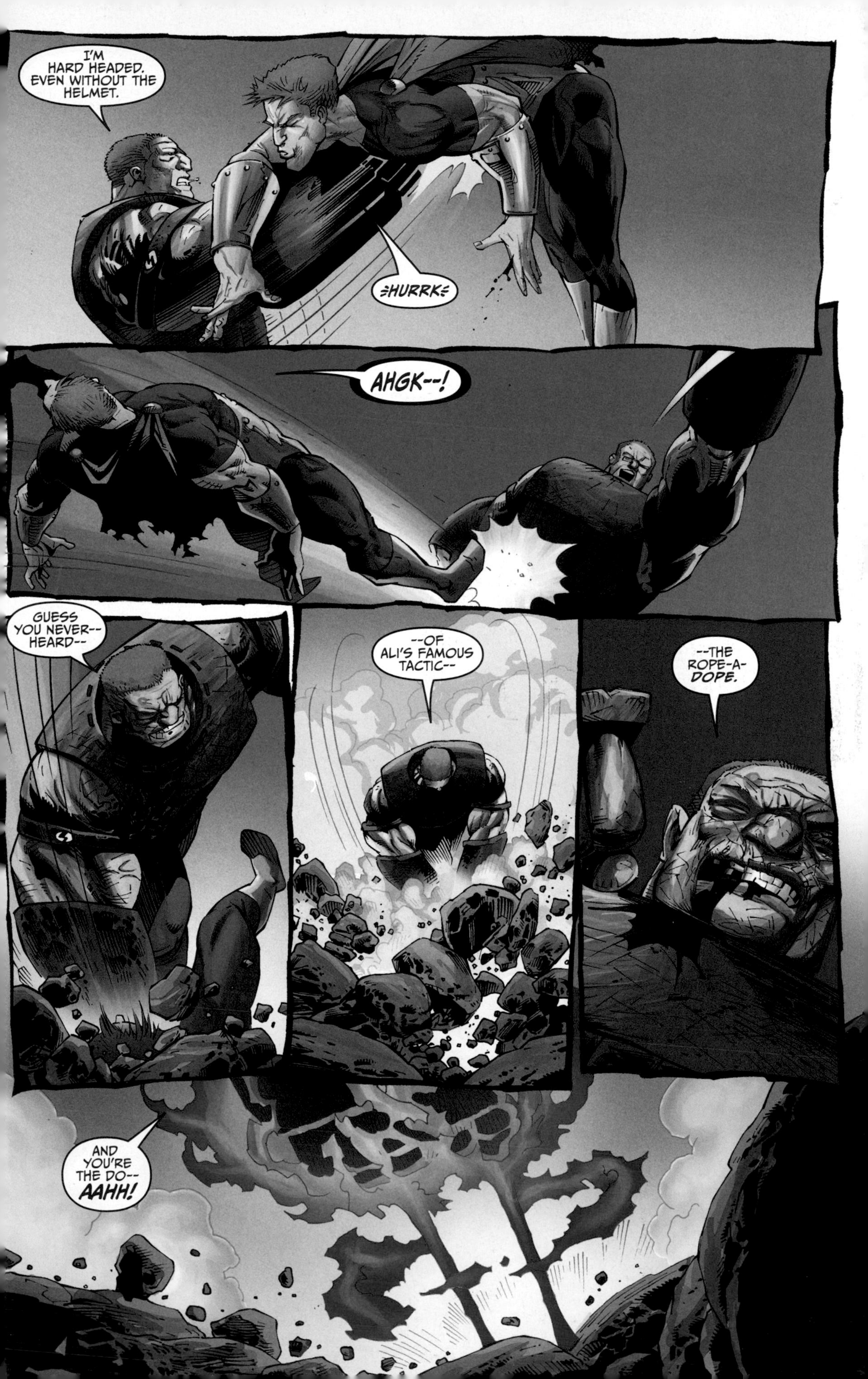

I'M HARD HEADED. EVEN WITHOUT THE HELMET.
HURRK
AHGK--!
GUESS YOU NEVER--HEARD--
--OF ALI'S FAMOUS TACTIC--
--THE ROPE-A-DOPE.
AND YOU'RE THE DO--AAHH!

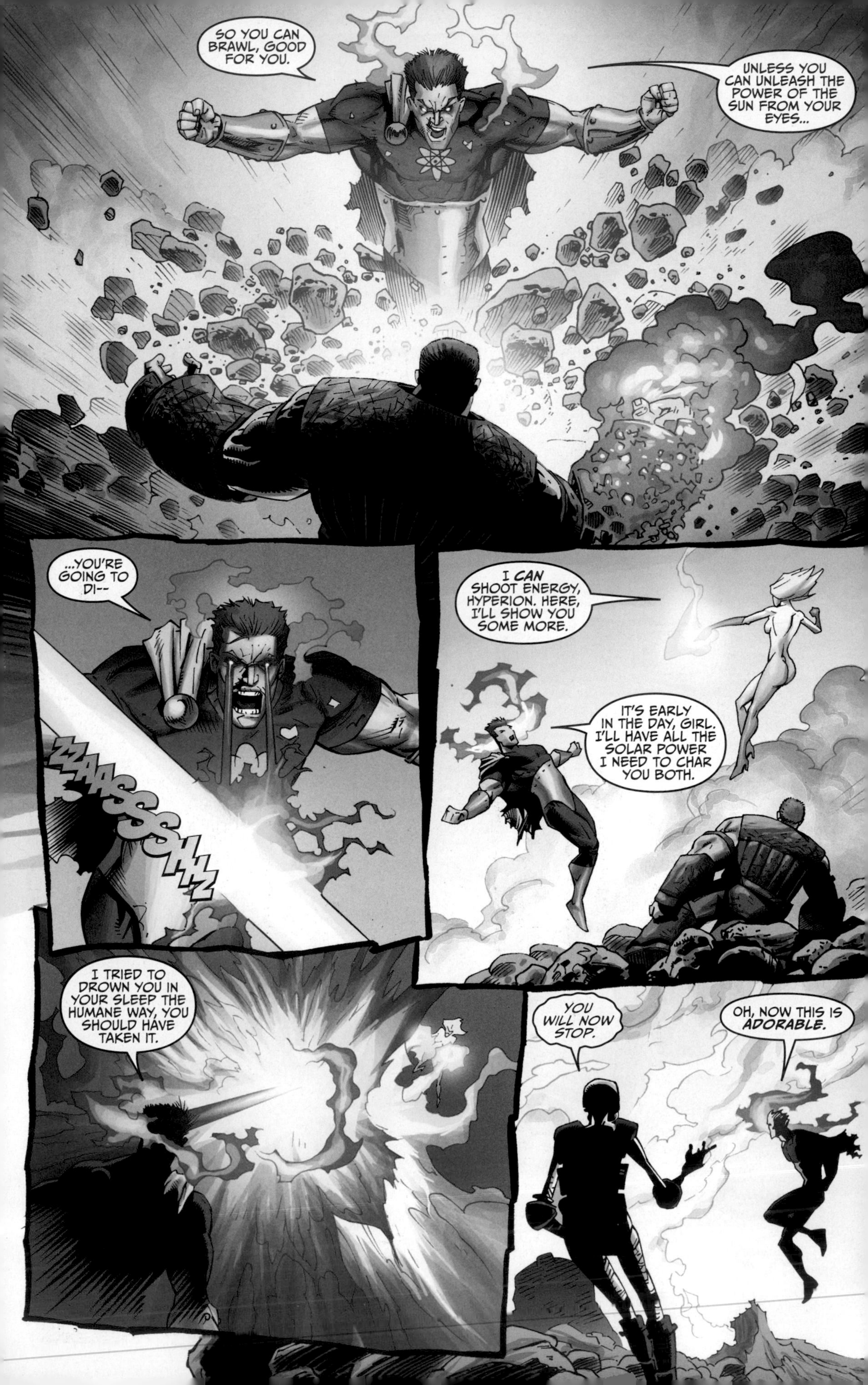
SO YOU CAN BRAWL, GOOD FOR YOU.
UNLESS YOU CAN UNLEASH THE POWER OF THE SUN FROM YOUR EYES...
...YOU'RE GOING TO DI--
ZZAASSSSHHZZ
I *CAN* SHOOT ENERGY, HYPERION. HERE, I'LL SHOW YOU SOME MORE.
IT'S EARLY IN THE DAY, GIRL. I'LL HAVE ALL THE SOLAR POWER I NEED TO CHAR YOU BOTH.
I TRIED TO DROWN YOU IN YOUR SLEEP THE HUMANE WAY, YOU SHOULD HAVE TAKEN IT.
YOU WILL NOW STOP.
OH, NOW THIS IS *ADORABLE.*

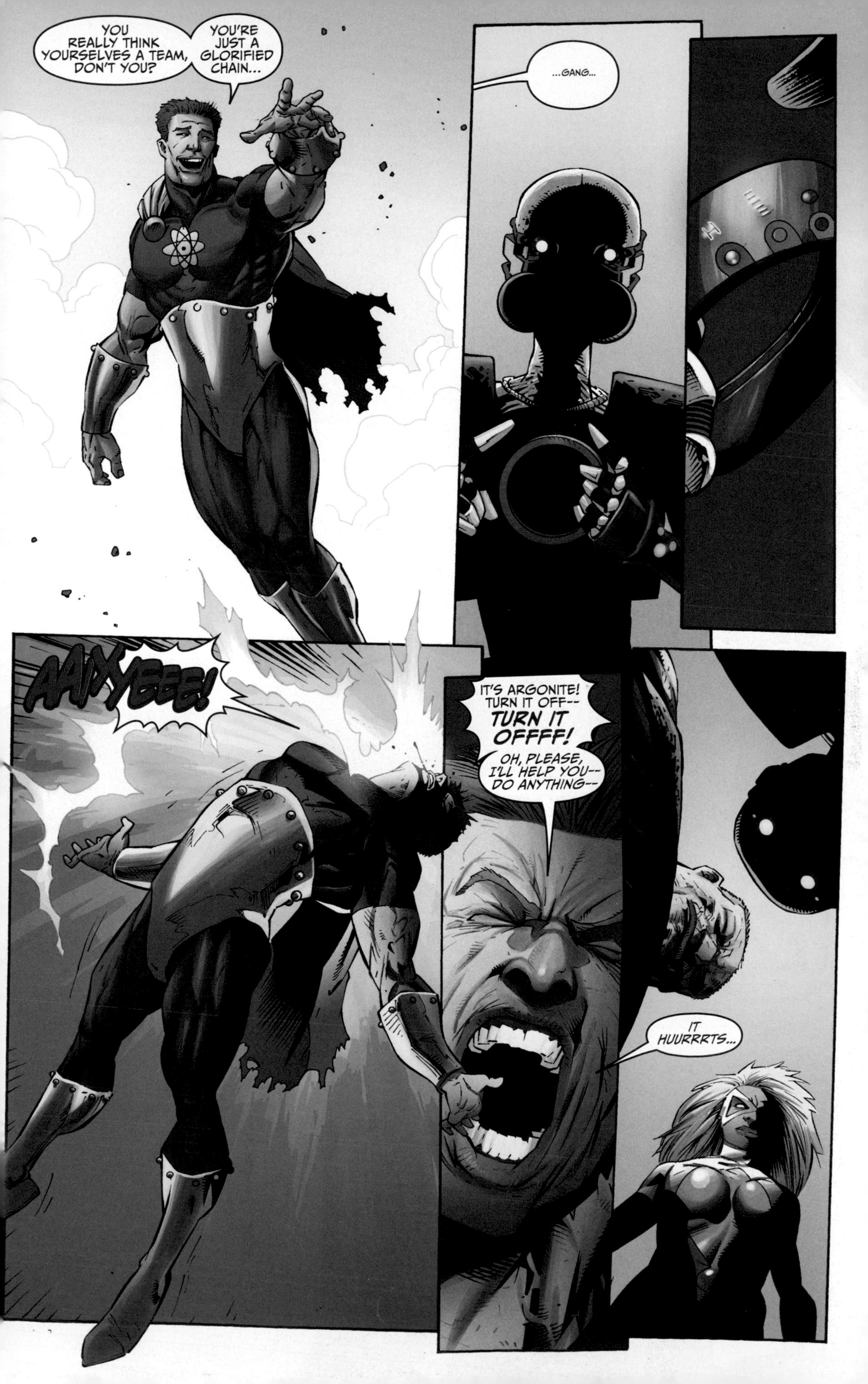
YOU REALLY THINK YOURSELVES A TEAM, DON'T YOU?
YOU'RE JUST A GLORIFIED CHAIN...
...GANG...
AAIXYEEE!
IT'S ARGONITE! TURN IT OFF-- TURN IT OFFFF!
OH, PLEASE, I'LL HELP YOU-- DO ANYTHING--
IT HUURRRTS...

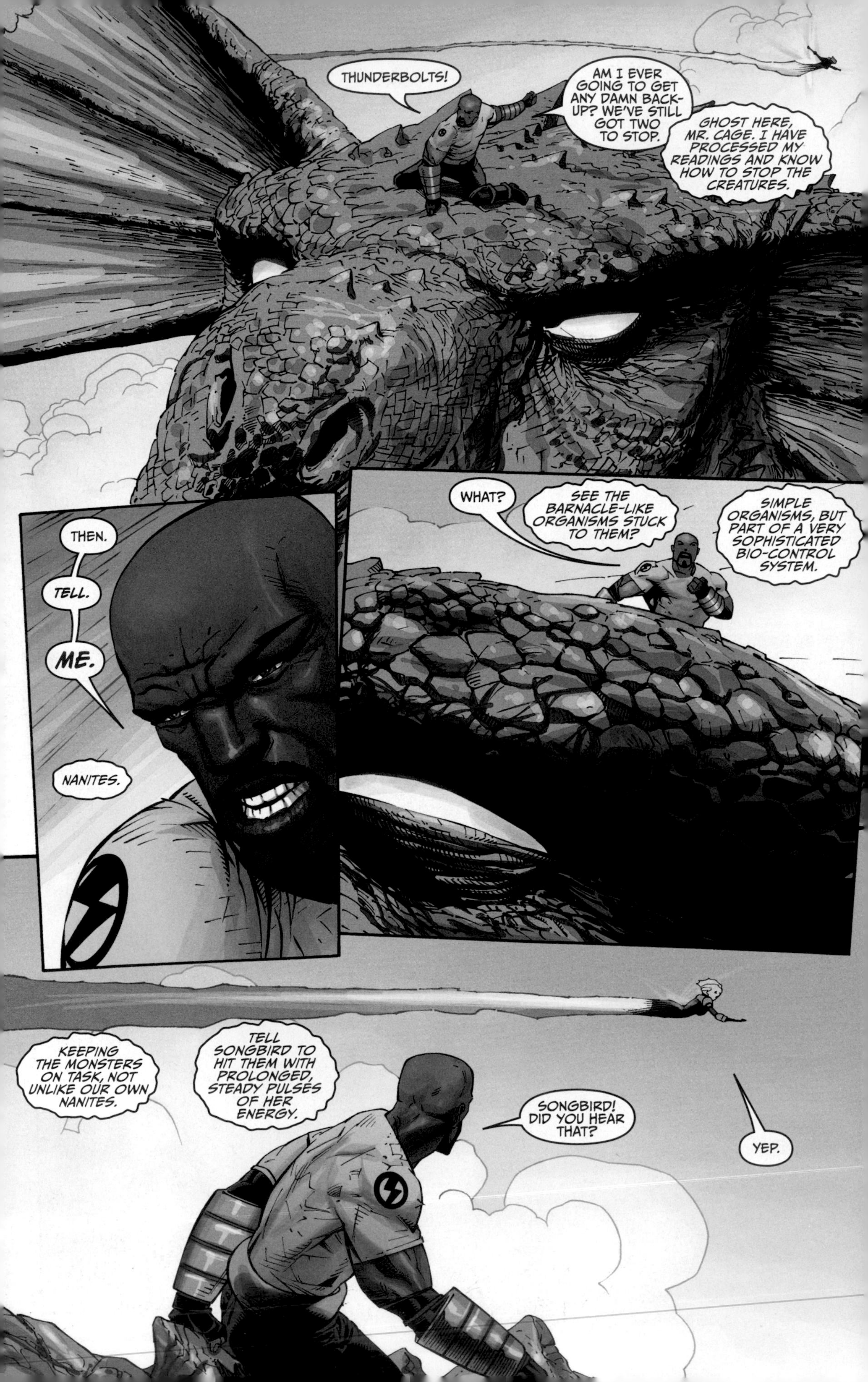
THUNDERBOLTS!
AM I EVER GOING TO GET ANY DAMN BACK-UP? WE'VE STILL GOT TWO TO STOP.
GHOST HERE, MR. CAGE. I HAVE PROCESSED MY READINGS AND KNOW HOW TO STOP THE CREATURES.
THEN.
TELL.
ME.
NANITES.
WHAT?
SEE THE BARNACLE-LIKE ORGANISMS STUCK TO THEM?
SIMPLE ORGANISMS, BUT PART OF A VERY SOPHISTICATED BIO-CONTROL SYSTEM.
KEEPING THE MONSTERS ON TASK, NOT UNLIKE OUR OWN NANITES.
TELL SONGBIRD TO HIT THEM WITH PROLONGED, STEADY PULSES OF HER ENERGY.
SONGBIRD! DID YOU HEAR THAT?
YEP.

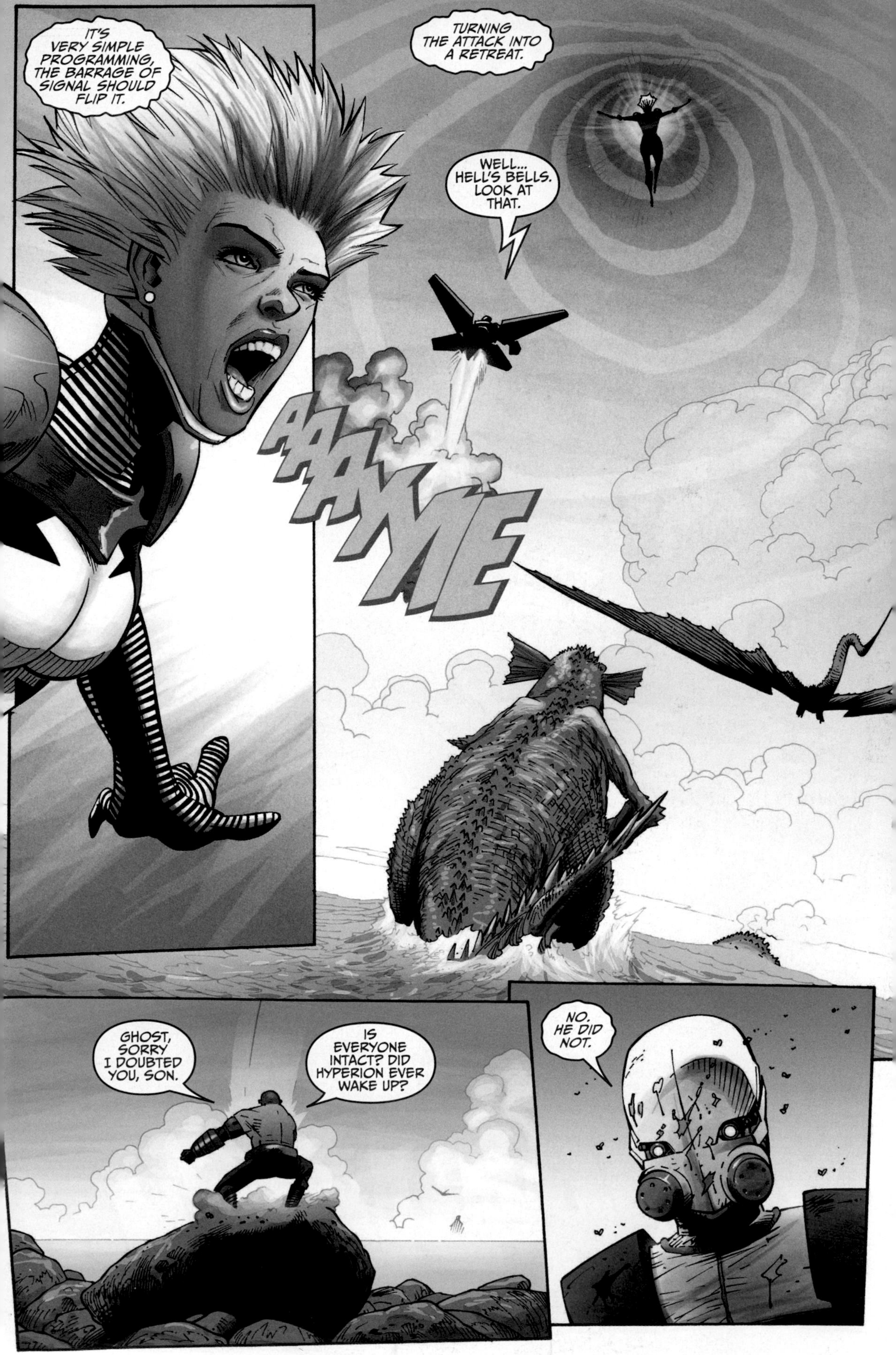
IT'S VERY SIMPLE PROGRAMMING, THE BARRAGE OF SIGNAL SHOULD FLIP IT.
TURNING THE ATTACK INTO A RETREAT.
WELL... HELL'S BELLS. LOOK AT THAT.
AAAWYE
GHOST, SORRY I DOUBTED YOU, SON.
IS EVERYONE INTACT? DID HYPERION EVER WAKE UP?
NO. HE DID NOT.

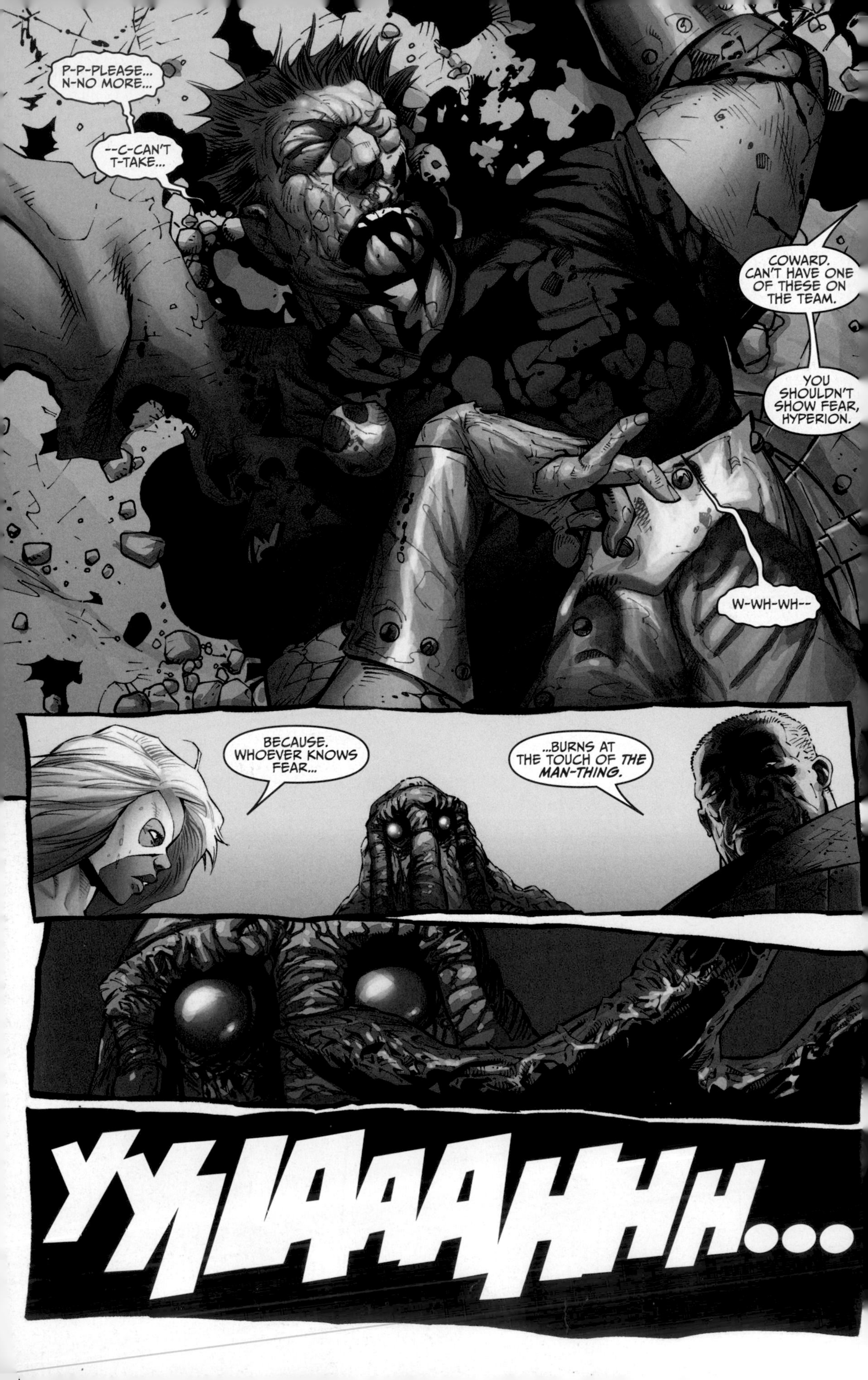
P-P-PLEASE... N-NO MORE...
--C-CAN'T T-TAKE...
COWARD. CAN'T HAVE ONE OF THESE ON THE TEAM.
YOU SHOULDN'T SHOW FEAR, HYPERION.
W-WH-WH--
BECAUSE. WHOEVER KNOWS FEAR...
...BURNS AT THE TOUCH OF *THE MAN-THING.*
YYAAAAHHH...

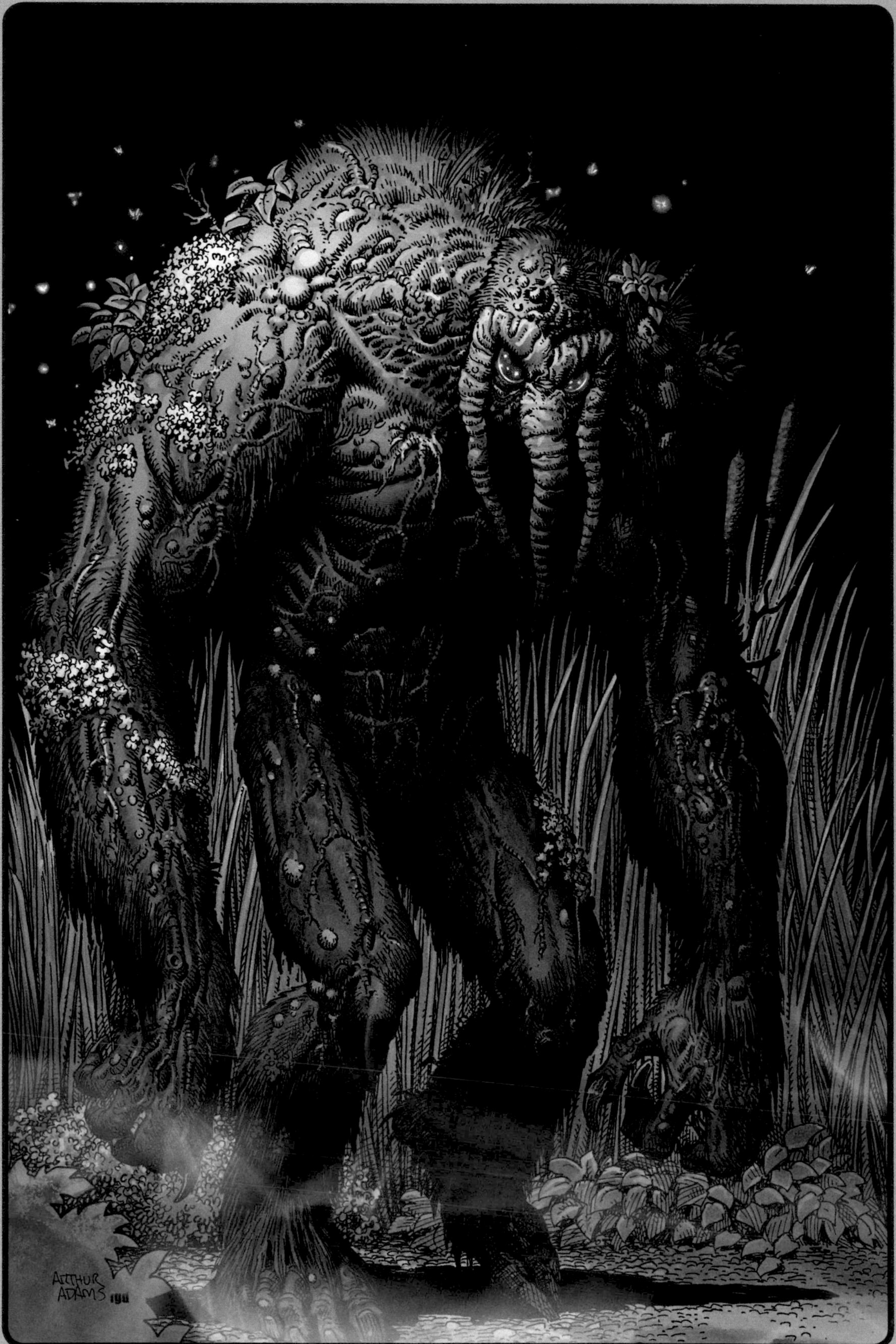
ARTHUR ADAMS

#154

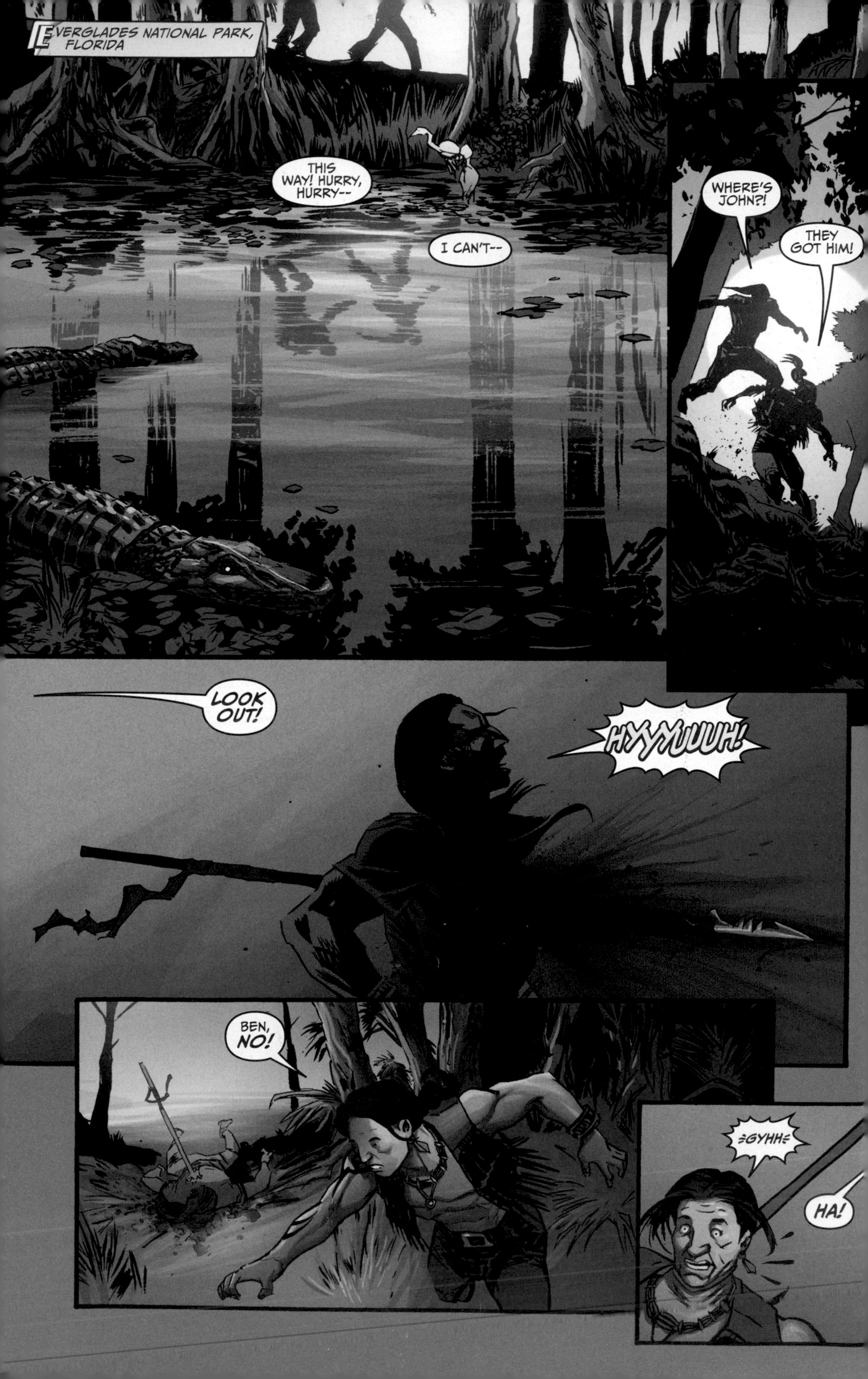
EVERGLADES NATIONAL PARK, FLORIDA
THIS WAY! HURRY, HURRY--
I CAN'T--
WHERE'S JOHN?!
THEY GOT HIM!
LOOK OUT!
HYYYUUUH!
BEN, NO!
GYHH
HA!

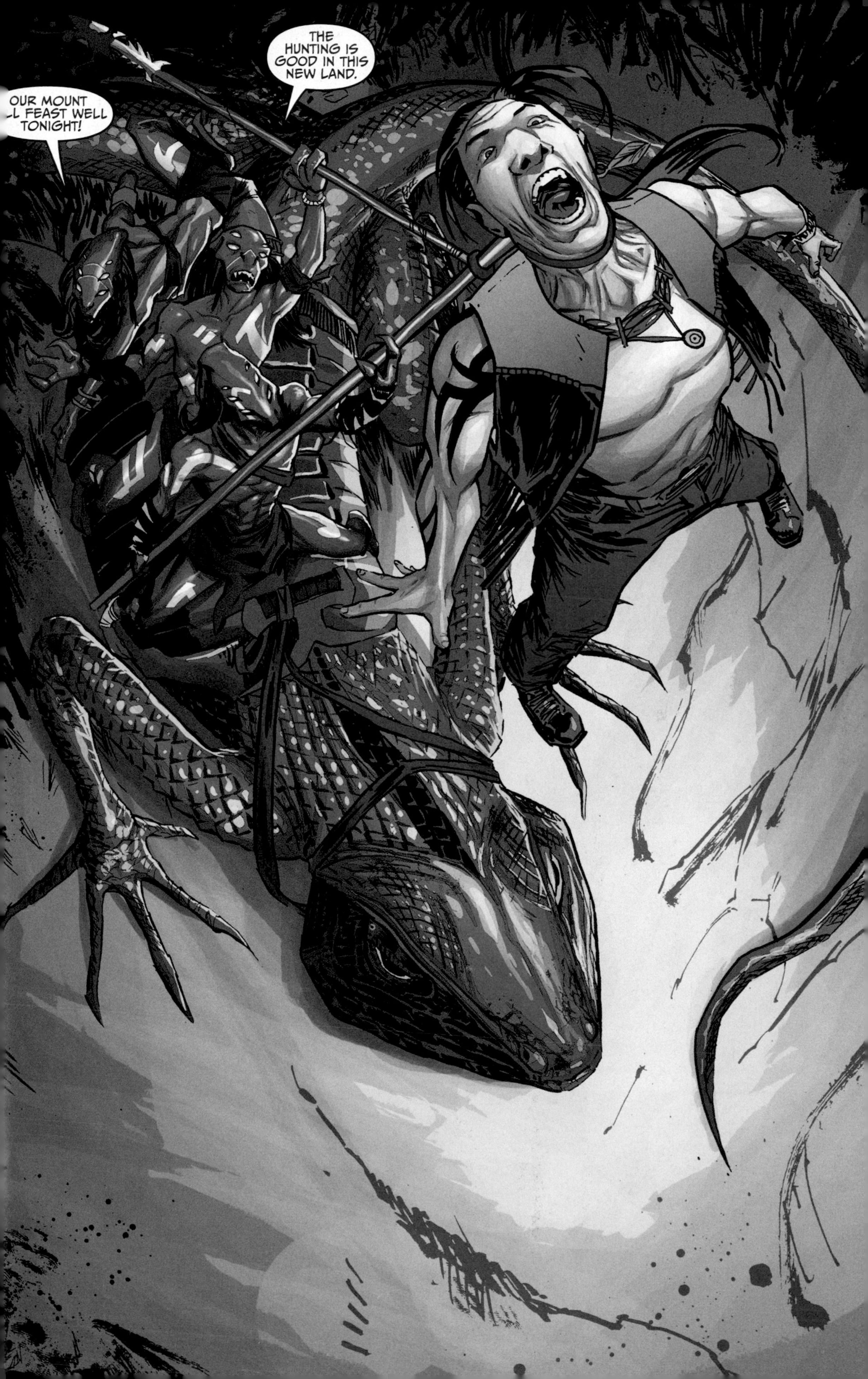
OUR MOUNT L FEAST WELL TONIGHT!
THE HUNTING IS GOOD IN THIS NEW LAND.

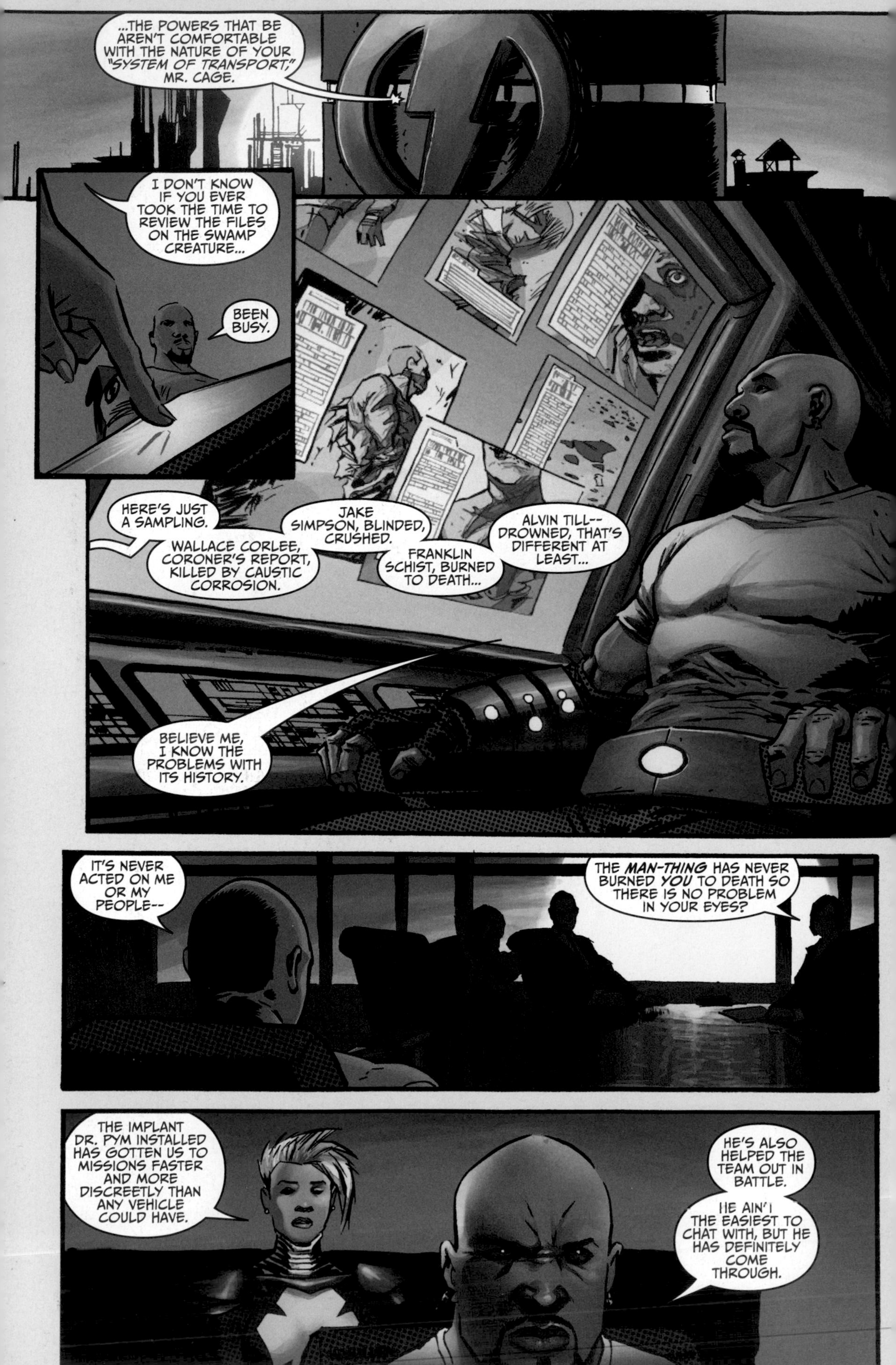

...THE POWERS THAT BE AREN'T COMFORTABLE WITH THE NATURE OF YOUR "SYSTEM OF TRANSPORT," MR. CAGE.
I DON'T KNOW IF YOU EVER TOOK THE TIME TO REVIEW THE FILES ON THE SWAMP CREATURE...
BEEN BUSY.
HERE'S JUST A SAMPLING.
WALLACE CORLEE, CORONER'S REPORT, KILLED BY CAUSTIC CORROSION.
JAKE SIMPSON, BLINDED, CRUSHED.
FRANKLIN SCHIST, BURNED TO DEATH...
ALVIN TILL--DROWNED, THAT'S DIFFERENT AT LEAST...
BELIEVE ME, I KNOW THE PROBLEMS WITH ITS HISTORY.
IT'S NEVER ACTED ON ME OR MY PEOPLE--
THE MAN-THING HAS NEVER BURNED YOU TO DEATH SO THERE IS NO PROBLEM IN YOUR EYES?
THE IMPLANT DR. PYM INSTALLED HAS GOTTEN US TO MISSIONS FASTER AND MORE DISCREETLY THAN ANY VEHICLE COULD HAVE.
HE'S ALSO HELPED THE TEAM OUT IN BATTLE.
HE AIN'T THE EASIEST TO CHAT WITH, BUT HE HAS DEFINITELY COME THROUGH.

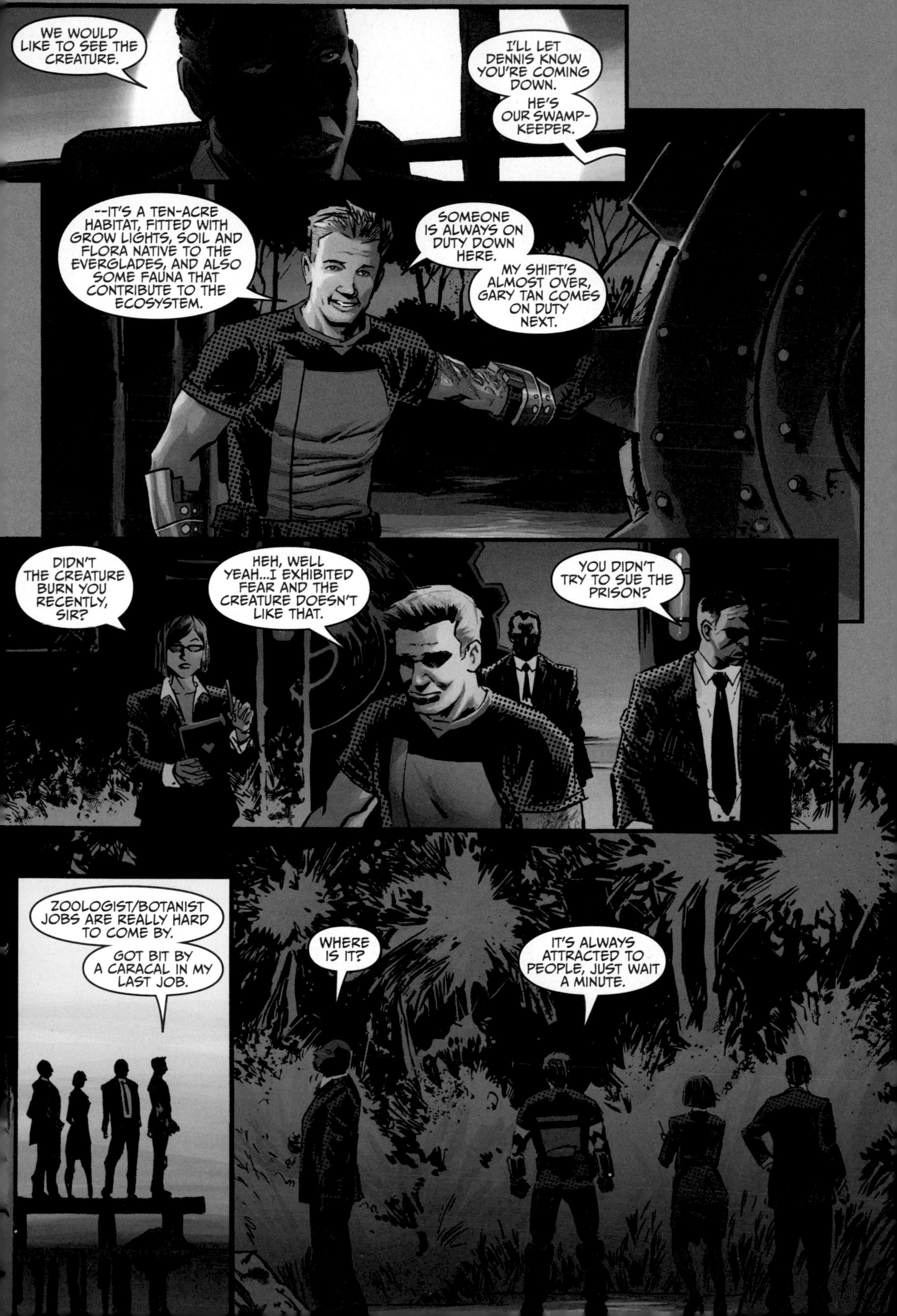
WE WOULD LIKE TO SEE THE CREATURE.
I'LL LET DENNIS KNOW YOU'RE COMING DOWN.
HE'S OUR SWAMP-KEEPER.
--IT'S A TEN-ACRE HABITAT, FITTED WITH GROW LIGHTS, SOIL AND FLORA NATIVE TO THE EVERGLADES, AND ALSO SOME FAUNA THAT CONTRIBUTE TO THE ECOSYSTEM.
SOMEONE IS ALWAYS ON DUTY DOWN HERE.
MY SHIFT'S ALMOST OVER, GARY TAN COMES ON DUTY NEXT.
DIDN'T THE CREATURE BURN YOU RECENTLY, SIR?
HEH, WELL YEAH...I EXHIBITED FEAR AND THE CREATURE DOESN'T LIKE THAT.
YOU DIDN'T TRY TO SUE THE PRISON?
ZOOLOGIST/BOTANIST JOBS ARE REALLY HARD TO COME BY.
GOT BIT BY A CARACAL IN MY LAST JOB.
WHERE IS IT?
IT'S ALWAYS ATTRACTED TO PEOPLE, JUST WAIT A MINUTE.

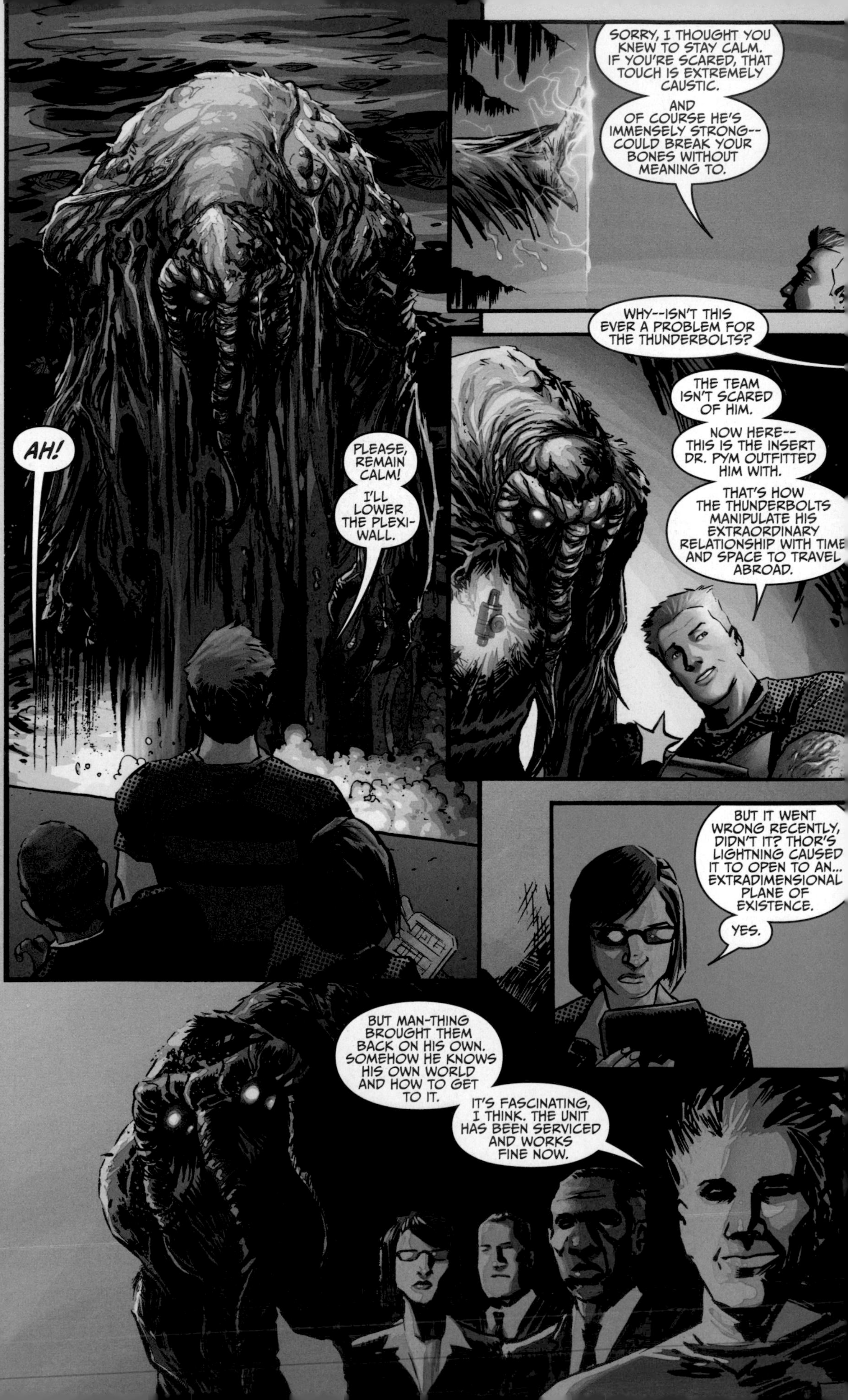
SORRY, I THOUGHT YOU KNEW TO STAY CALM. IF YOU'RE SCARED, THAT TOUCH IS EXTREMELY CAUSTIC.
AND OF COURSE HE'S IMMENSELY STRONG-- COULD BREAK YOUR BONES WITHOUT MEANING TO.
AH!
PLEASE, REMAIN CALM!
I'LL LOWER THE PLEXI-WALL.
WHY--ISN'T THIS EVER A PROBLEM FOR THE THUNDERBOLTS?
THE TEAM ISN'T SCARED OF HIM.
NOW HERE-- THIS IS THE INSERT DR. PYM OUTFITTED HIM WITH.
THAT'S HOW THE THUNDERBOLTS MANIPULATE HIS EXTRAORDINARY RELATIONSHIP WITH TIME AND SPACE TO TRAVEL ABROAD.
BUT IT WENT WRONG RECENTLY, DIDN'T IT? THOR'S LIGHTNING CAUSED IT TO OPEN TO AN... EXTRADIMENSIONAL PLANE OF EXISTENCE.
YES.
BUT MAN-THING BROUGHT THEM BACK ON HIS OWN. SOMEHOW HE KNOWS HIS OWN WORLD AND HOW TO GET TO IT.
IT'S FASCINATING, I THINK. THE UNIT HAS BEEN SERVICED AND WORKS FINE NOW.

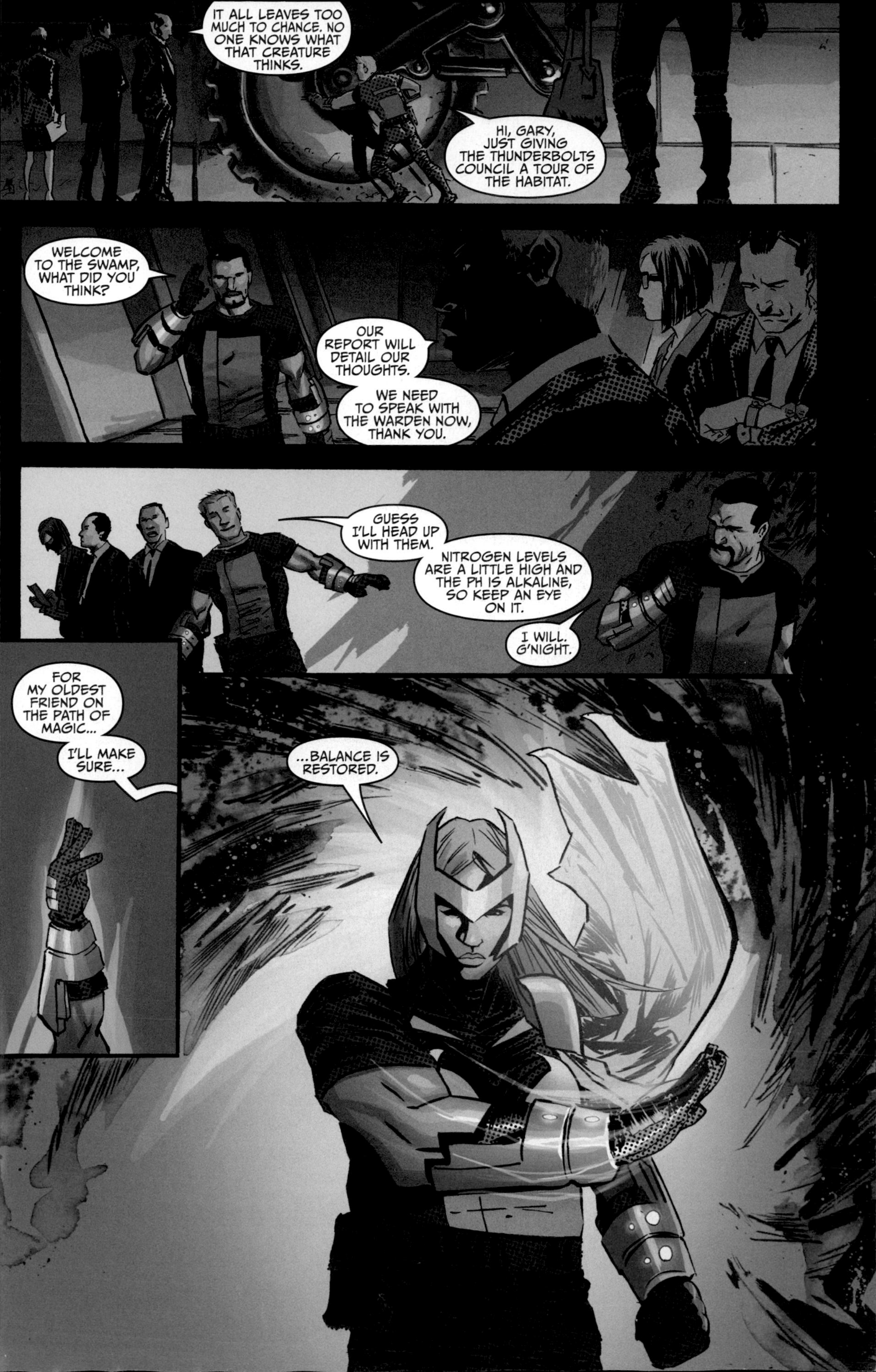
IT ALL LEAVES TOO MUCH TO CHANCE. NO ONE KNOWS WHAT THAT CREATURE THINKS.
HI, GARY, JUST GIVING THE THUNDERBOLTS COUNCIL A TOUR OF THE HABITAT.
WELCOME TO THE SWAMP, WHAT DID YOU THINK?
OUR REPORT WILL DETAIL OUR THOUGHTS.
WE NEED TO SPEAK WITH THE WARDEN NOW, THANK YOU.
GUESS I'LL HEAD UP WITH THEM.
NITROGEN LEVELS ARE A LITTLE HIGH AND THE PH IS ALKALINE, SO KEEP AN EYE ON IT.
I WILL. G'NIGHT.
FOR MY OLDEST FRIEND ON THE PATH OF MAGIC...
I'LL MAKE SURE...
...BALANCE IS RESTORED.

HERE, CUTTING THROUGH FIXER'S CONTROL ROOM IS THE FASTEST WAY.

HEY, 'BERT.

DENNIS? WHY ARE YOU LEAVING?

SHIFT'S OVER.

BUT GARY'S RUNNING LATE. HE CALLED IN EARLIER WITH CAR TROUBLE.

WOULDN'T MAKE THE FERRY UNTIL FOUR.

BUT...I JUST SAW HIM IN OUR STATION.

HABITAT VIDEO FEED ON SCREEN FOUR.

THE VAULT DOOR IS OPEN!

I'M NOT READING ANY HUMAN LIFE IN THAT CHAMBER.

TRACING MAN-THING BY HIS TELEPORT SYSTEM...

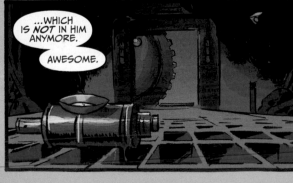

...WHICH IS *NOT* IN HIM ANYMORE.

AWESOME.

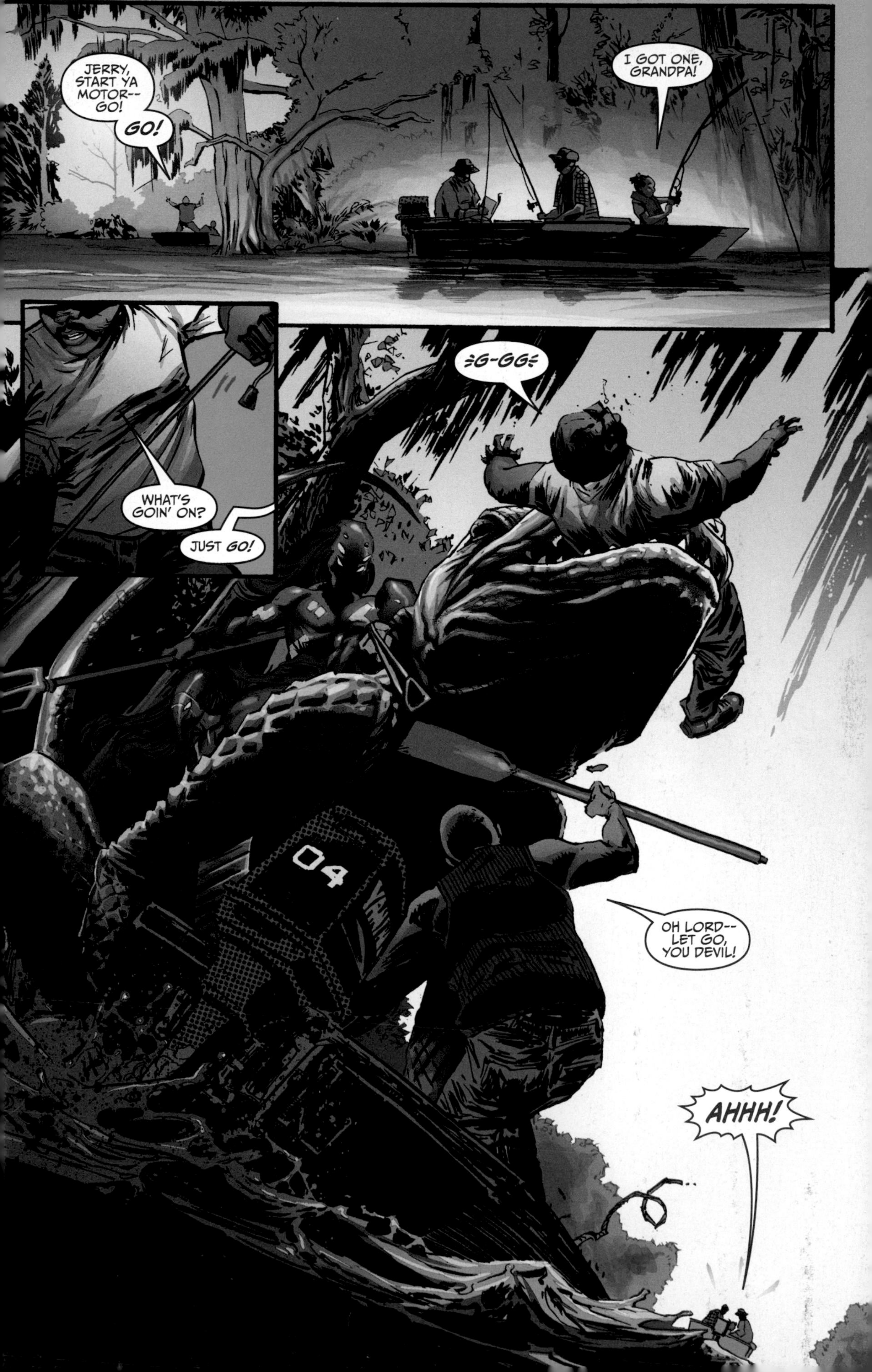

JERRY, START YA MOTOR--GO!
GO!
I GOT ONE, GRANDPA!
WHAT'S GOIN' ON?
JUST GO!
G-GG
OH LORD--LET GO, YOU DEVIL!
AHHH!

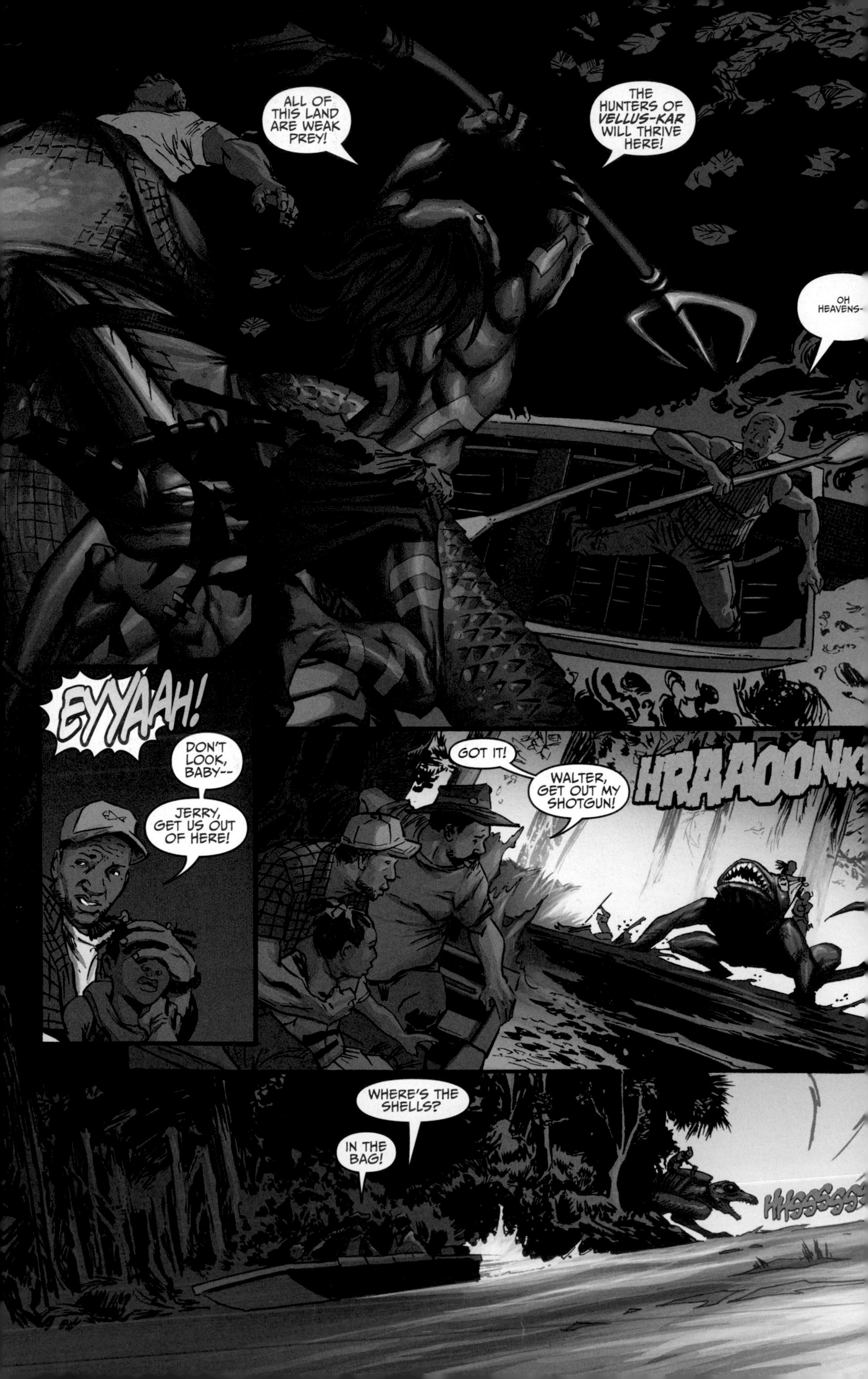
ALL OF THIS LAND ARE WEAK PREY!
THE HUNTERS OF VELLUS-KAR WILL THRIVE HERE!
OH HEAVENS-
EYYAAH!
DON'T LOOK, BABY--
JERRY, GET US OUT OF HERE!
GOT IT!
WALTER, GET OUT MY SHOTGUN!
HRAAOONK
WHERE'S THE SHELLS?
IN THE BAG!

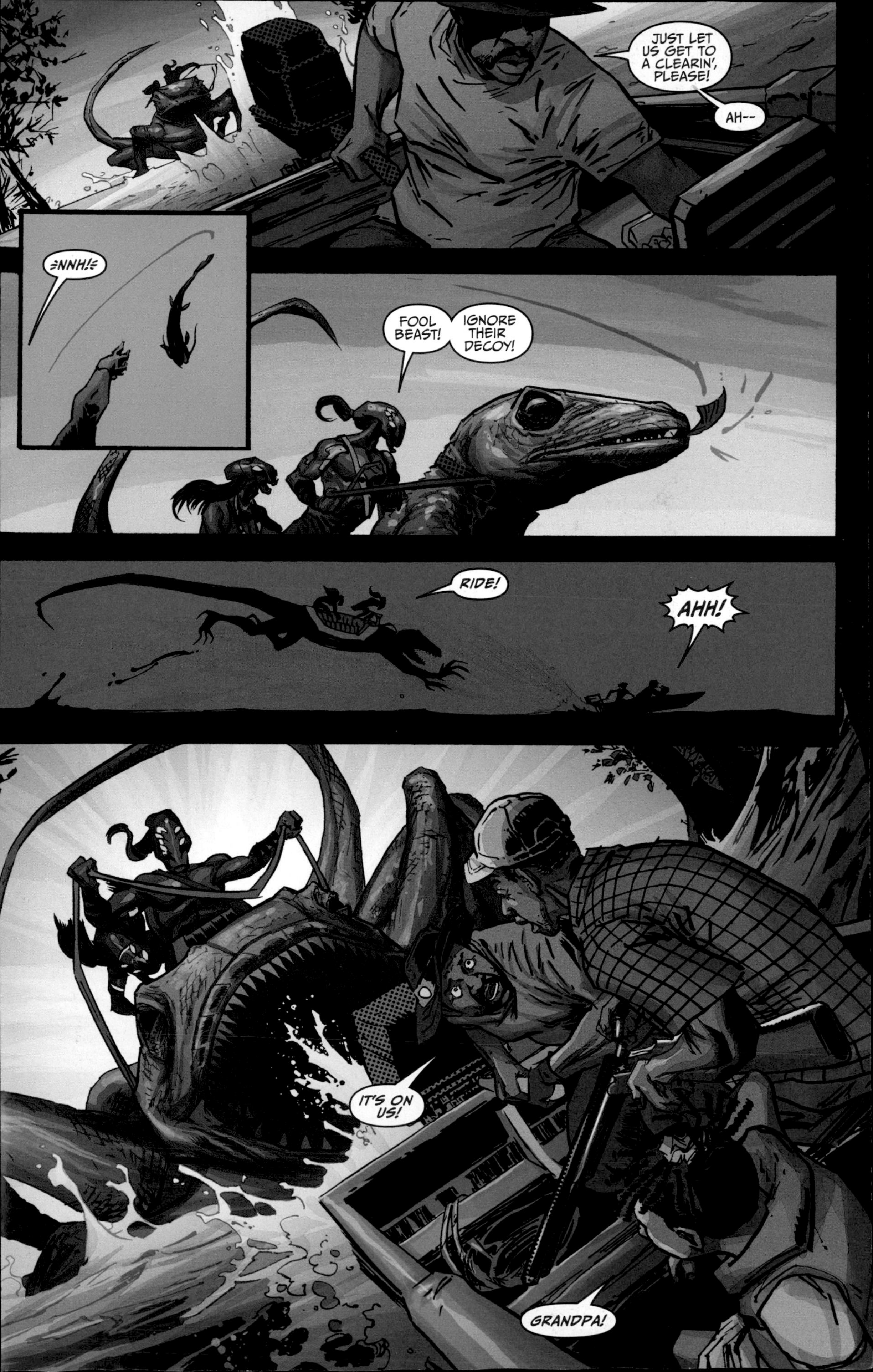
JUST LET US GET TO A CLEARIN', PLEASE!
AH--
≠NNH!≠
FOOL BEAST!
IGNORE THEIR DECOY!
RIDE!
AHH!
IT'S ON US!
GRANDPA!

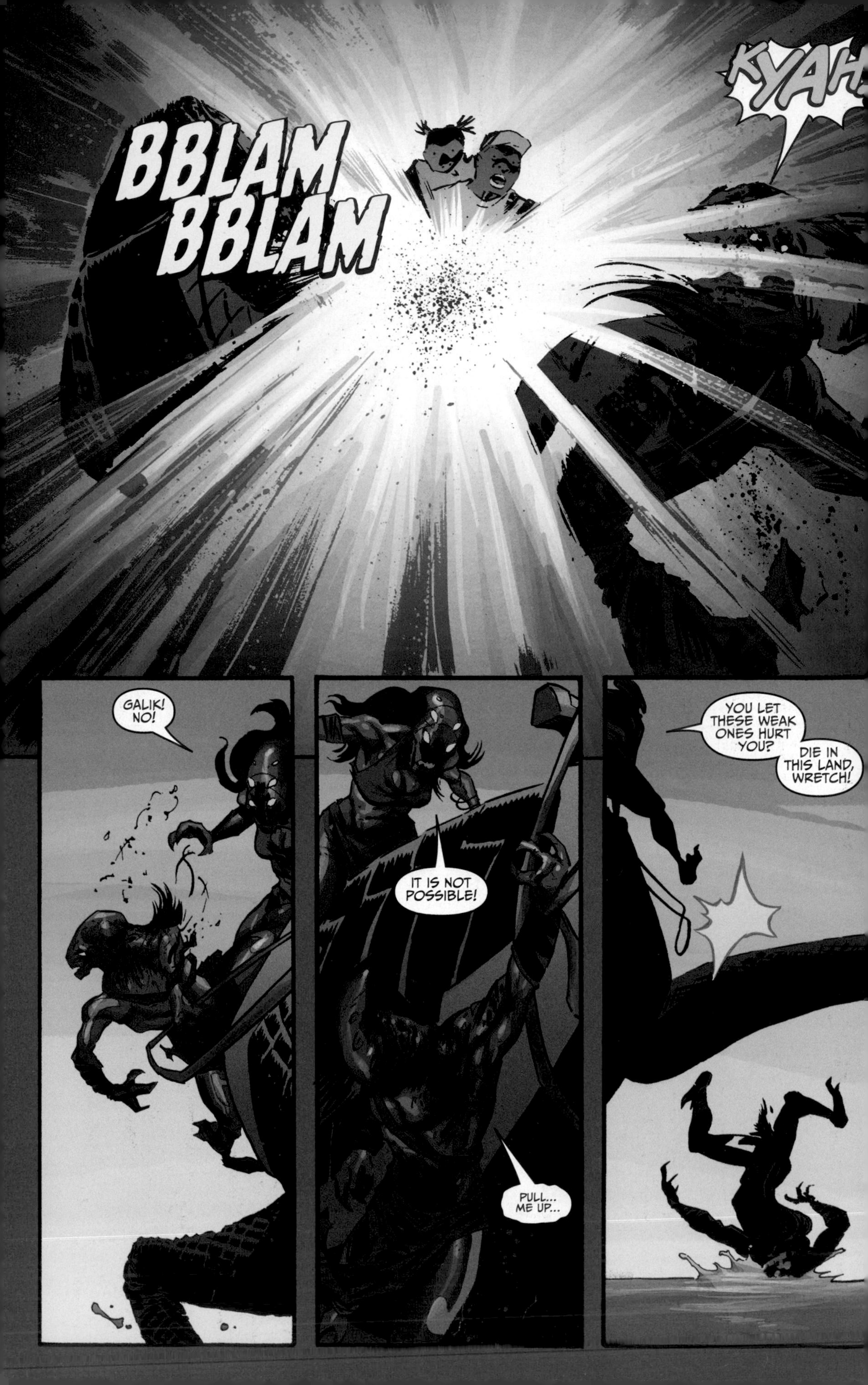
BBLAM
BBLAM
KYAH
GALIK! NO!
IT IS NOT POSSIBLE!
PULL... ME UP...
YOU LET THESE WEAK ONES HURT YOU?
DIE IN THIS LAND, WRETCH!

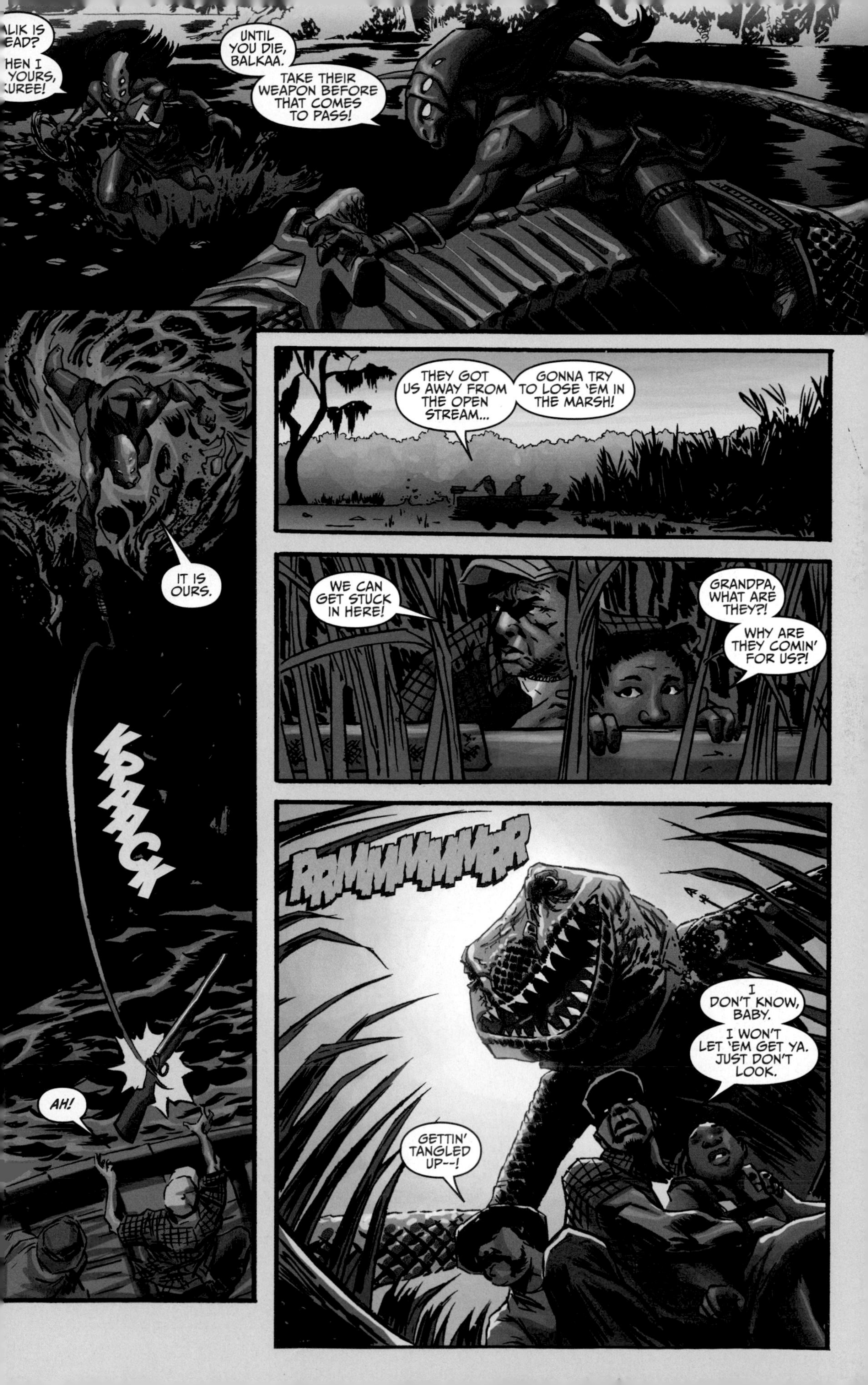

ALIK IS
EAD?
HEN I
YOURS,
KUREE!
UNTIL YOU DIE, BALKAA.
TAKE THEIR WEAPON BEFORE THAT COMES TO PASS!
IT IS OURS.
KRAAACK
AH!
THEY GOT US AWAY FROM THE OPEN STREAM...
GONNA TRY TO LOSE 'EM IN THE MARSH!
WE CAN GET STUCK IN HERE!
GRANDPA, WHAT ARE THEY?!
WHY ARE THEY COMIN' FOR US?!
RRMMMMMMR
I DON'T KNOW, BABY.
I WON'T LET 'EM GET YA. JUST DON'T LOOK.
GETTIN' TANGLED UP--!

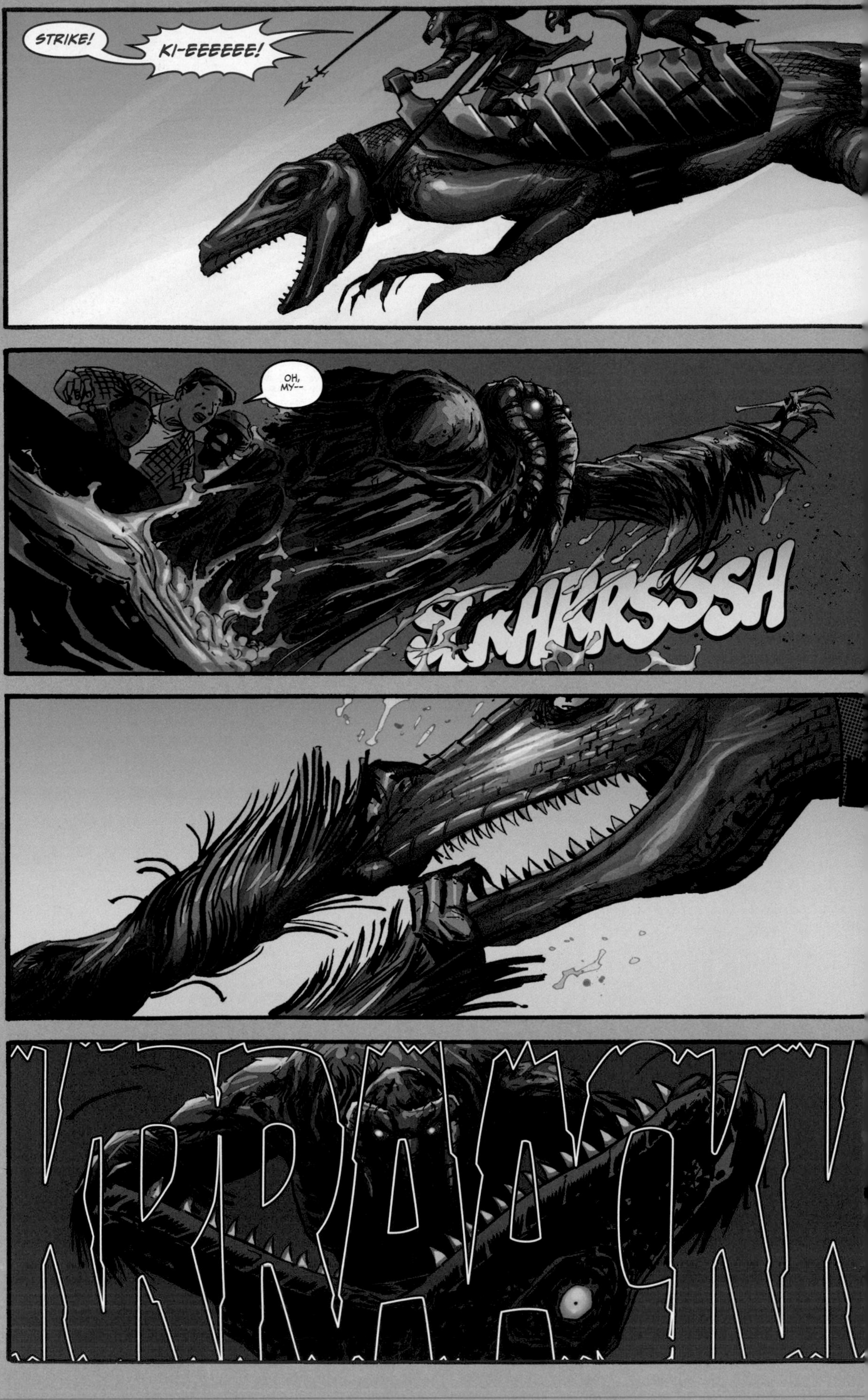
STRIKE!
KI-EEEEEE!
OH, MY--
SKHKRSSSH
KRRAAACK

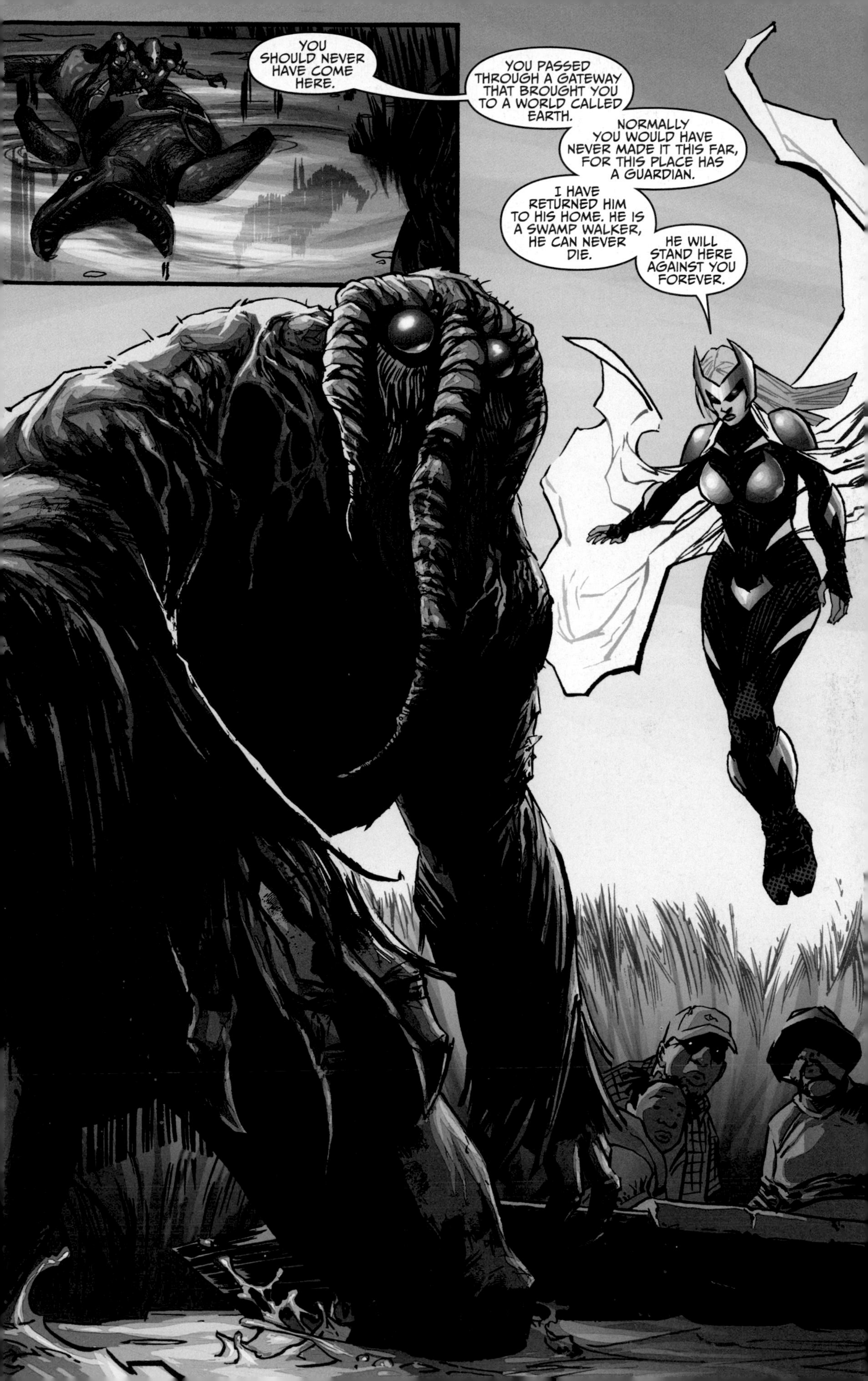
YOU SHOULD NEVER HAVE COME HERE.
YOU PASSED THROUGH A GATEWAY THAT BROUGHT YOU TO A WORLD CALLED EARTH.
NORMALLY YOU WOULD HAVE NEVER MADE IT THIS FAR, FOR THIS PLACE HAS A GUARDIAN.
I HAVE RETURNED HIM TO HIS HOME. HE IS A SWAMP WALKER, HE CAN NEVER DIE.
HE WILL STAND HERE AGAINST YOU FOREVER.

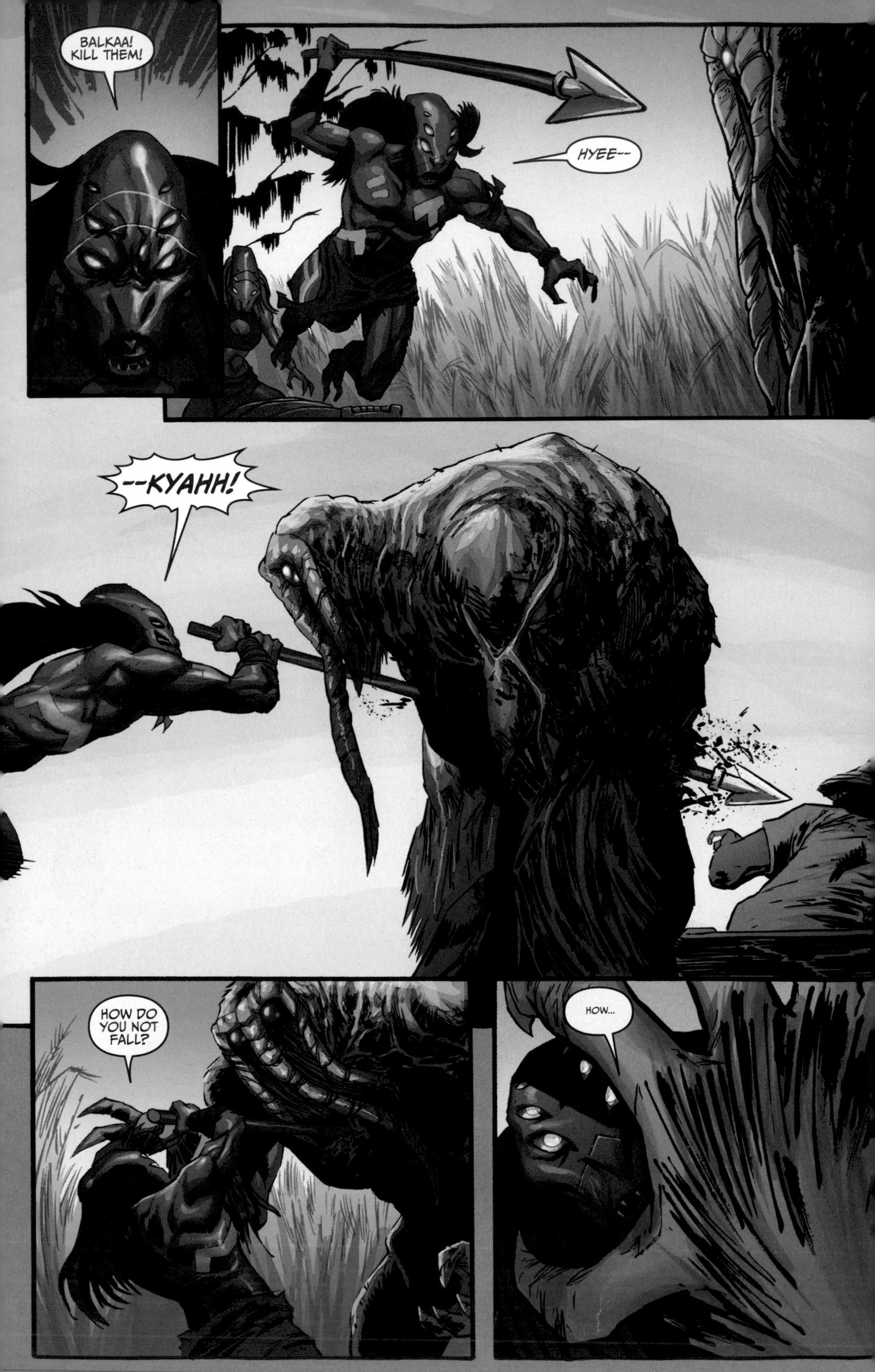
BALKAA! KILL THEM!
HYEE--
--KYAHH!
HOW DO YOU NOT FALL?
HOW...

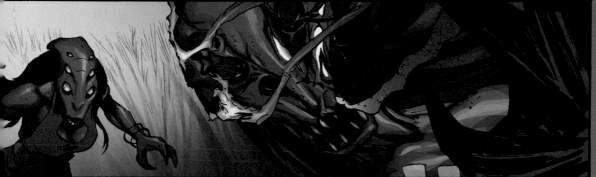

WHATEVER KNOWS FEAR...

...BURNS AT THE MAN-THING'S TOUCH.

LOOK BEHIND YOU, HUNTER.

MY HOME!

IT IS. IN SECONDS I SHALL SEAL THAT GATEWAY OFF.

STEP THROUGH NOW OR NEVER SEE IT AGAIN.

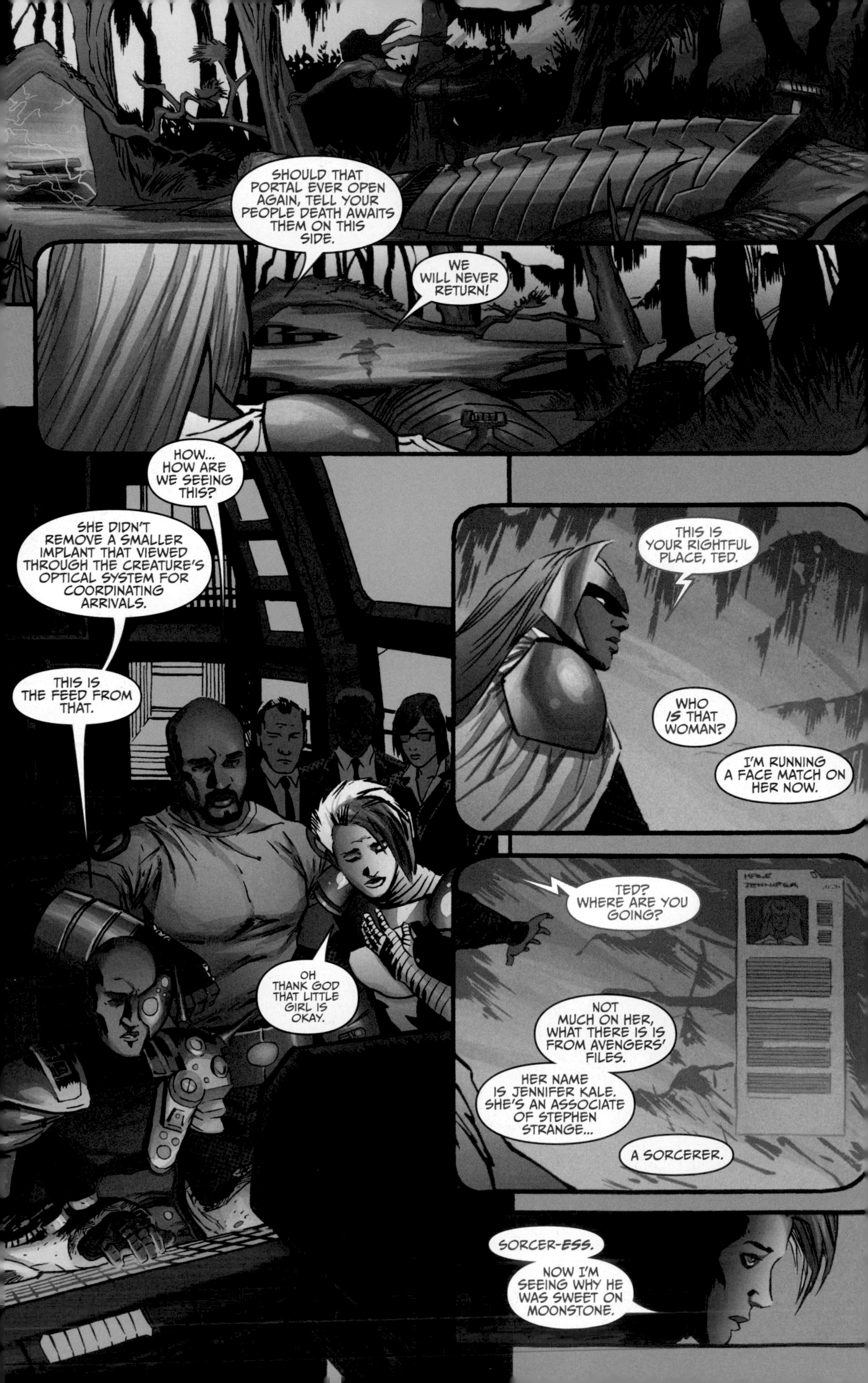
SHOULD THAT PORTAL EVER OPEN AGAIN, TELL YOUR PEOPLE DEATH AWAITS THEM ON THIS SIDE.
WE WILL NEVER RETURN!
HOW... HOW ARE WE SEEING THIS?
SHE DIDN'T REMOVE A SMALLER IMPLANT THAT VIEWED THROUGH THE CREATURE'S OPTICAL SYSTEM FOR COORDINATING ARRIVALS.
THIS IS THE FEED FROM THAT.
THIS IS YOUR RIGHTFUL PLACE, TED.
WHO *IS* THAT WOMAN?
I'M RUNNING A FACE MATCH ON HER NOW.
OH THANK GOD THAT LITTLE GIRL IS OKAY.
TED? WHERE ARE YOU GOING?
NOT MUCH ON HER, WHAT THERE IS IS FROM AVENGERS' FILES.
HER NAME IS JENNIFER KALE. SHE'S AN ASSOCIATE OF STEPHEN STRANGE...
A SORCERER.
SORCER-**ESS.**
NOW I'M SEEING WHY HE WAS SWEET ON MOONSTONE.

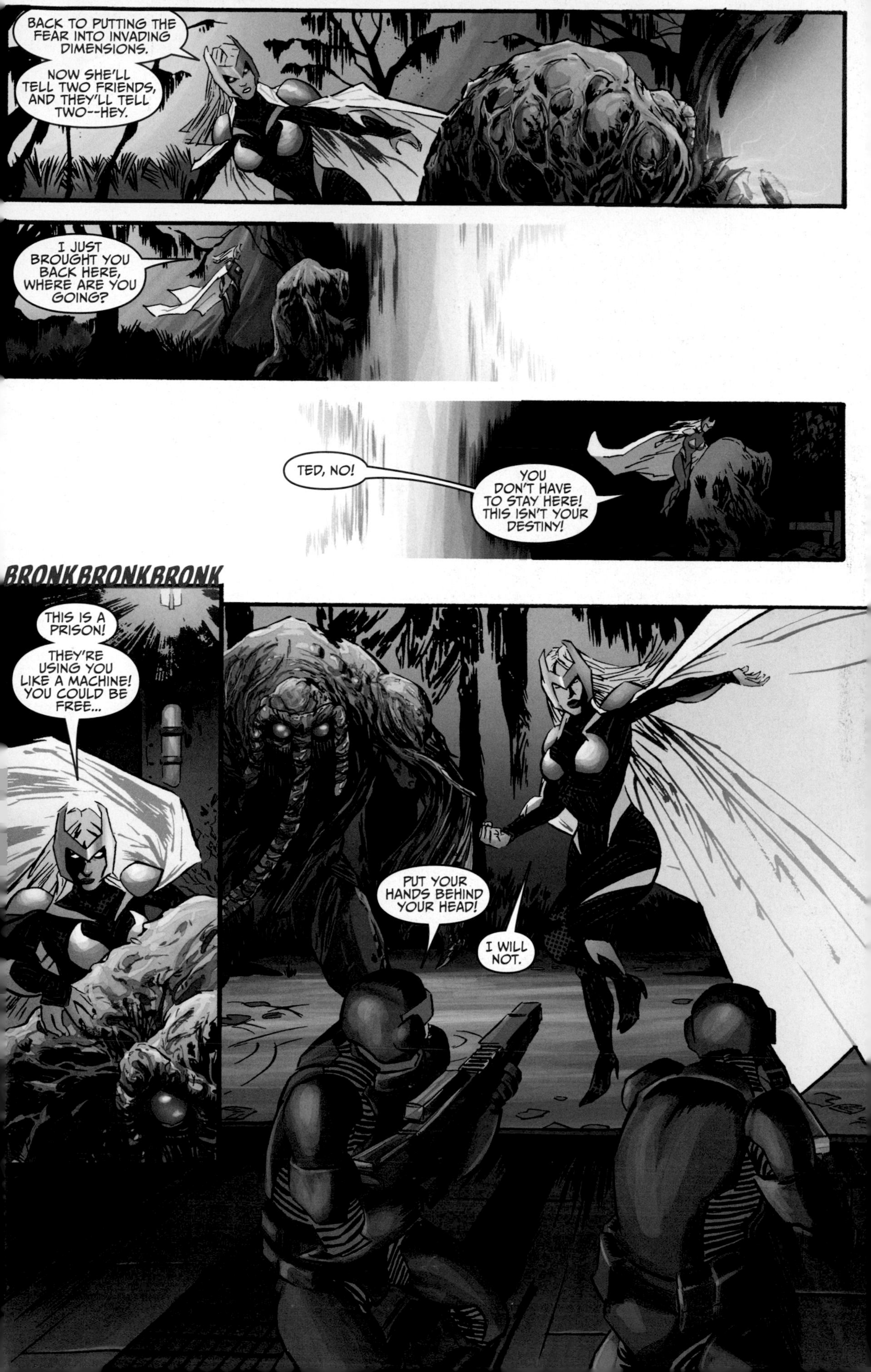
BACK TO PUTTING THE FEAR INTO INVADING DIMENSIONS.
NOW SHE'LL TELL TWO FRIENDS, AND THEY'LL TELL TWO--HEY.
I JUST BROUGHT YOU BACK HERE, WHERE ARE YOU GOING?
TED, NO!
YOU DON'T HAVE TO STAY HERE! THIS ISN'T YOUR DESTINY!
BRONKBRONKBRONK
THIS IS A PRISON!
THEY'RE USING YOU LIKE A MACHINE! YOU COULD BE FREE...
PUT YOUR HANDS BEHIND YOUR HEAD!
I WILL NOT.

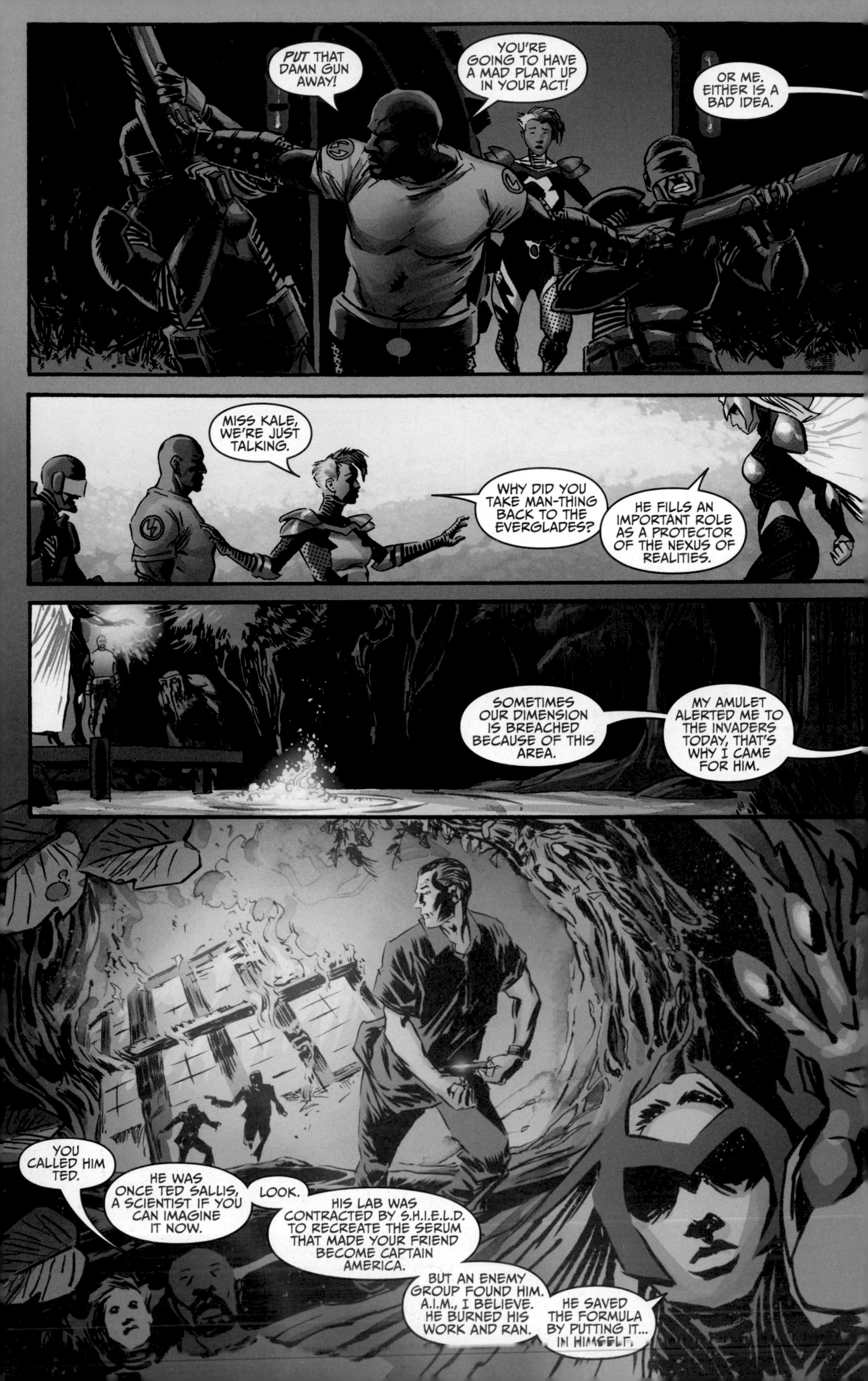
PUT THAT DAMN GUN AWAY!
YOU'RE GOING TO HAVE A MAD PLANT UP IN YOUR ACT!
OR ME. EITHER IS A BAD IDEA.
MISS KALE, WE'RE JUST TALKING.
WHY DID YOU TAKE MAN-THING BACK TO THE EVERGLADES?
HE FILLS AN IMPORTANT ROLE AS A PROTECTOR OF THE NEXUS OF REALITIES.
SOMETIMES OUR DIMENSION IS BREACHED BECAUSE OF THIS AREA.
MY AMULET ALERTED ME TO THE INVADERS TODAY, THAT'S WHY I CAME FOR HIM.
YOU CALLED HIM TED.
HE WAS ONCE TED SALLIS, A SCIENTIST IF YOU CAN IMAGINE IT NOW.
LOOK.
HIS LAB WAS CONTRACTED BY S.H.I.E.L.D. TO RECREATE THE SERUM THAT MADE YOUR FRIEND BECOME CAPTAIN AMERICA.
BUT AN ENEMY GROUP FOUND HIM. A.I.M., I BELIEVE. HE BURNED HIS WORK AND RAN.
HE SAVED THE FORMULA BY PUTTING IT... IN HIMSELF.

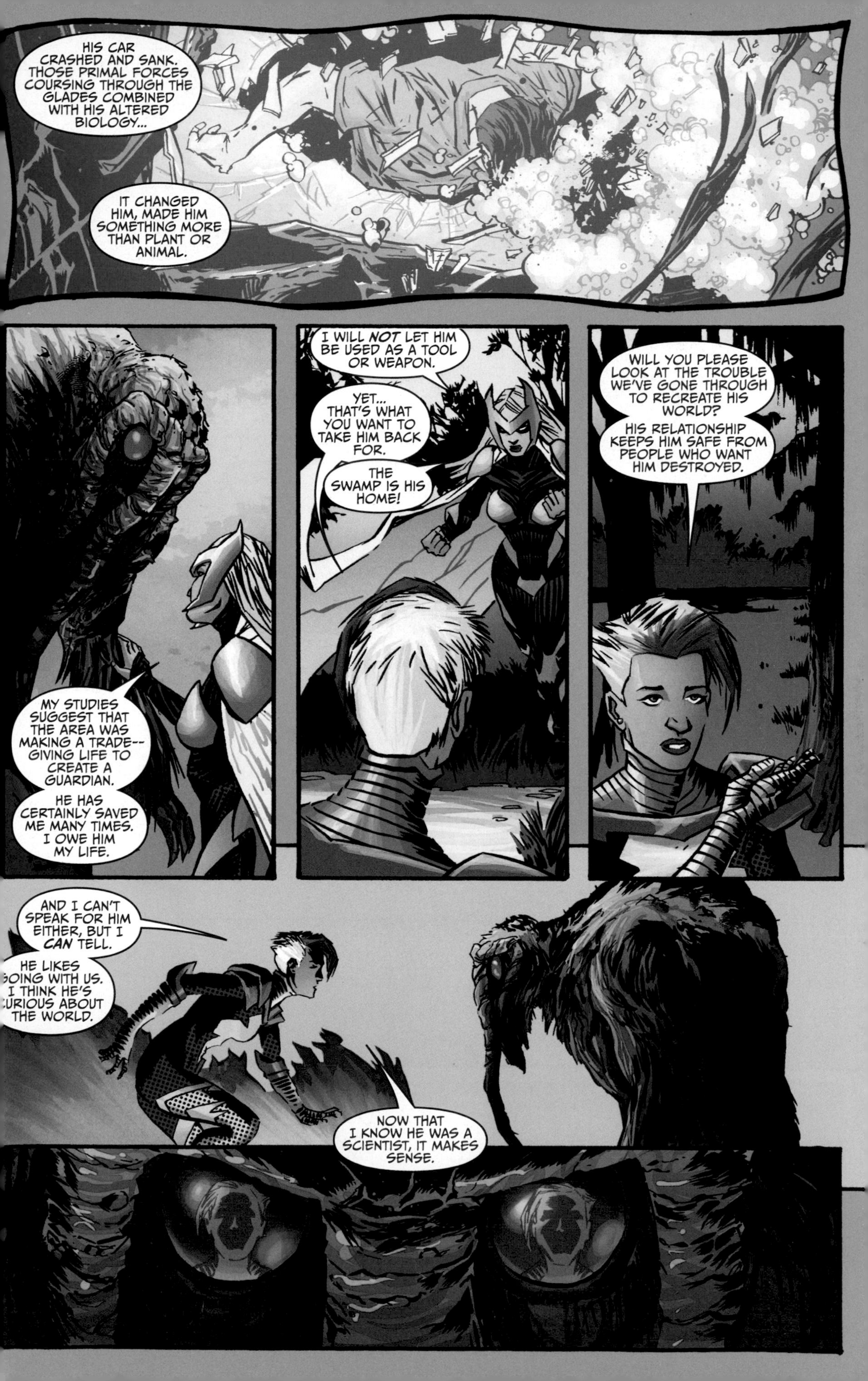
HIS CAR CRASHED AND SANK. THOSE PRIMAL FORCES COURSING THROUGH THE GLADES COMBINED WITH HIS ALTERED BIOLOGY...
IT CHANGED HIM, MADE HIM SOMETHING MORE THAN PLANT OR ANIMAL.
MY STUDIES SUGGEST THAT THE AREA WAS MAKING A TRADE-- GIVING LIFE TO CREATE A GUARDIAN.
HE HAS CERTAINLY SAVED ME MANY TIMES. I OWE HIM MY LIFE.
I WILL NOT LET HIM BE USED AS A TOOL OR WEAPON.
YET... THAT'S WHAT YOU WANT TO TAKE HIM BACK FOR.
THE SWAMP IS HIS HOME!
WILL YOU PLEASE LOOK AT THE TROUBLE WE'VE GONE THROUGH TO RECREATE HIS WORLD?
HIS RELATIONSHIP KEEPS HIM SAFE FROM PEOPLE WHO WANT HIM DESTROYED.
AND I CAN'T SPEAK FOR HIM EITHER, BUT I CAN TELL.
HE LIKES GOING WITH US. I THINK HE'S CURIOUS ABOUT THE WORLD.
NOW THAT I KNOW HE WAS A SCIENTIST, IT MAKES SENSE.

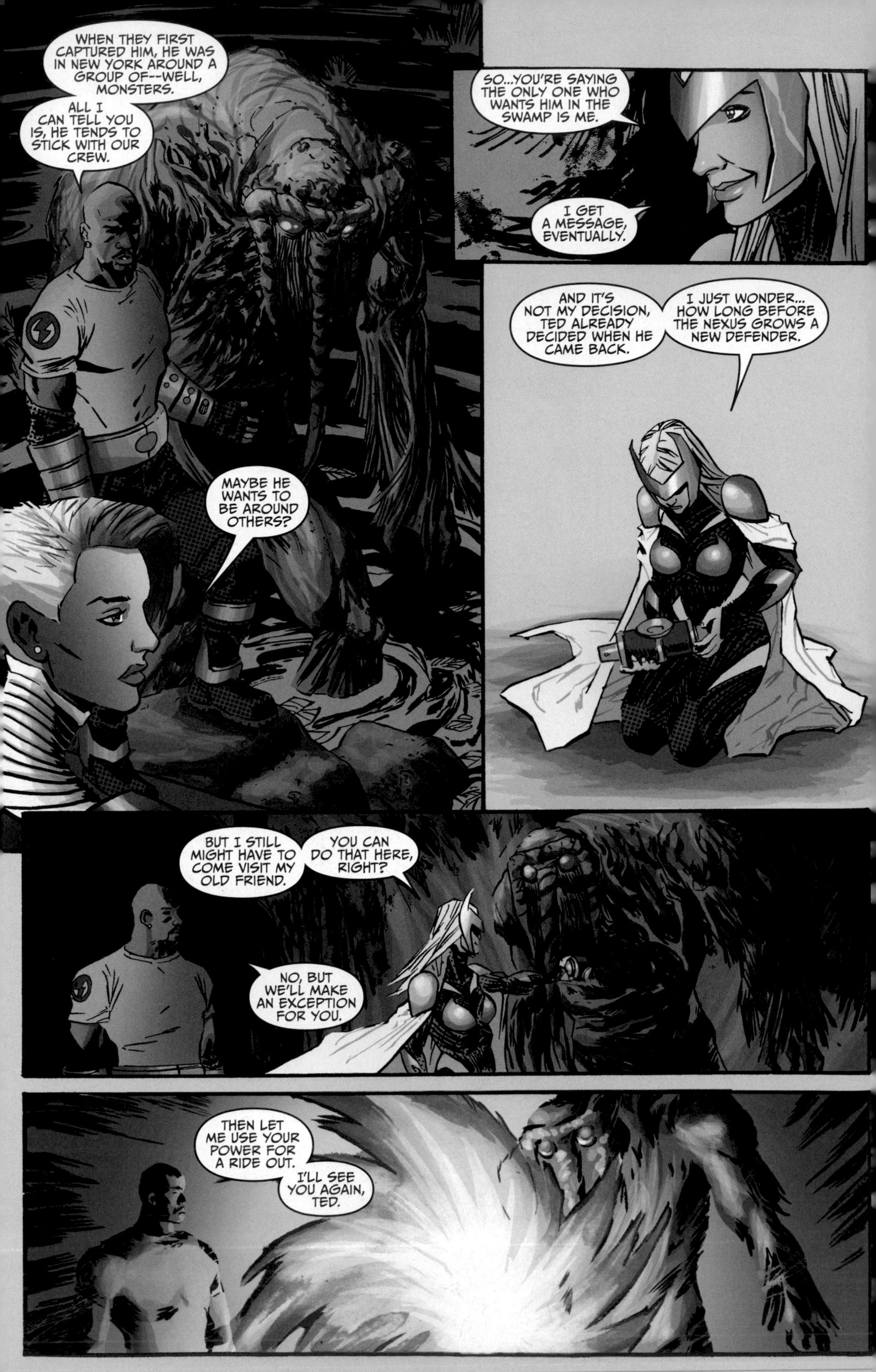
WHEN THEY FIRST CAPTURED HIM, HE WAS IN NEW YORK AROUND A GROUP OF--WELL, MONSTERS.
ALL I CAN TELL YOU IS, HE TENDS TO STICK WITH OUR CREW.
SO...YOU'RE SAYING THE ONLY ONE WHO WANTS HIM IN THE SWAMP IS ME.
I GET A MESSAGE, EVENTUALLY.
AND IT'S NOT MY DECISION, TED ALREADY DECIDED WHEN HE CAME BACK.
I JUST WONDER... HOW LONG BEFORE THE NEXUS GROWS A NEW DEFENDER.
MAYBE HE WANTS TO BE AROUND OTHERS?
BUT I STILL MIGHT HAVE TO COME VISIT MY OLD FRIEND.
YOU CAN DO THAT HERE, RIGHT?
NO, BUT WE'LL MAKE AN EXCEPTION FOR YOU.
THEN LET ME USE YOUR POWER FOR A RIDE OUT.
I'LL SEE YOU AGAIN, TED.

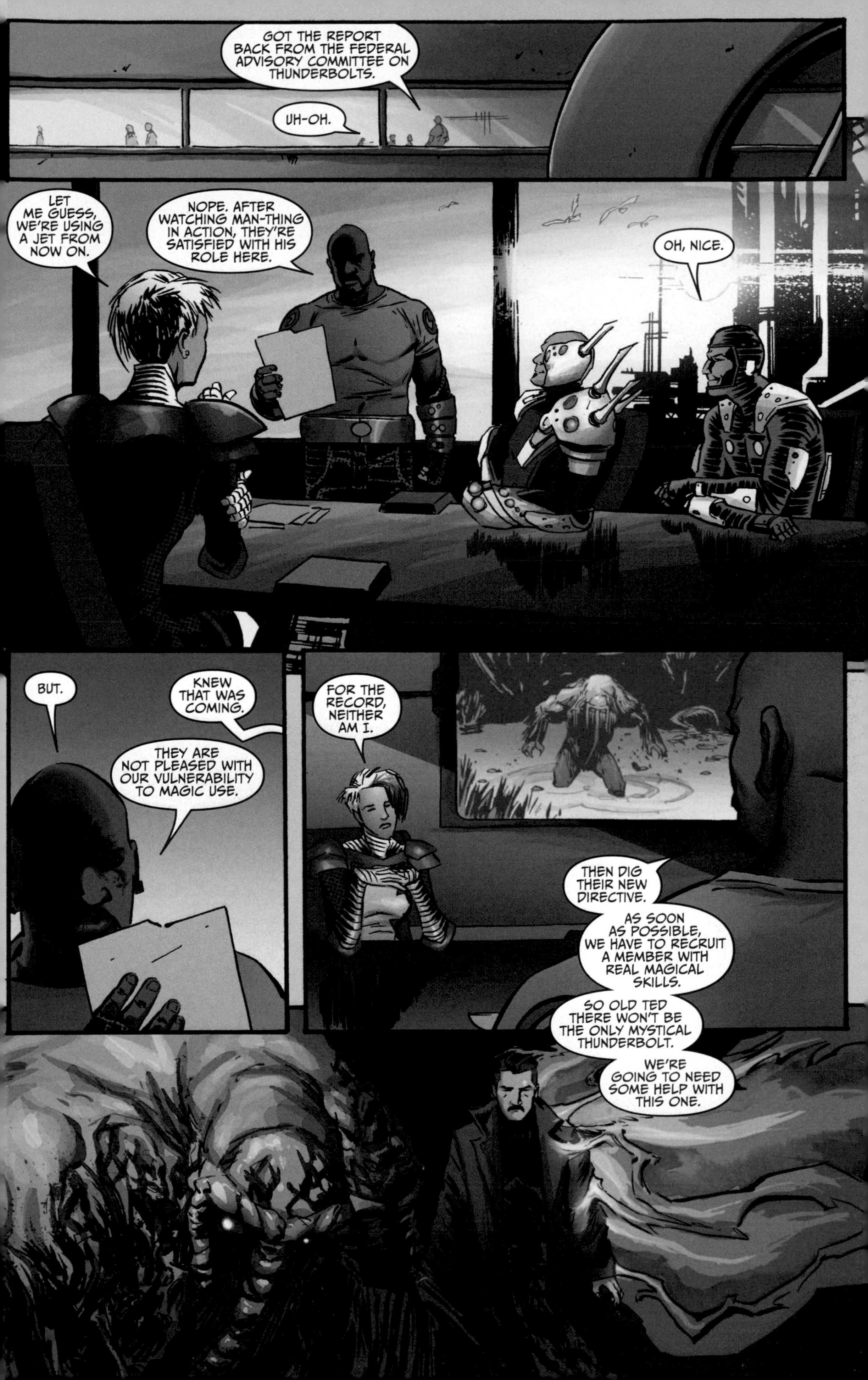
GOT THE REPORT BACK FROM THE FEDERAL ADVISORY COMMITTEE ON THUNDERBOLTS.
UH-OH.
LET ME GUESS, WE'RE USING A JET FROM NOW ON.
NOPE. AFTER WATCHING MAN-THING IN ACTION, THEY'RE SATISFIED WITH HIS ROLE HERE.
OH, NICE.
BUT.
KNEW THAT WAS COMING.
THEY ARE NOT PLEASED WITH OUR VULNERABILITY TO MAGIC USE.
FOR THE RECORD, NEITHER AM I.
THEN DIG THEIR NEW DIRECTIVE.
AS SOON AS POSSIBLE, WE HAVE TO RECRUIT A MEMBER WITH REAL MAGICAL SKILLS.
SO OLD TED THERE WON'T BE THE ONLY MYSTICAL THUNDERBOLT.
WE'RE GOING TO NEED SOME HELP WITH THIS ONE.

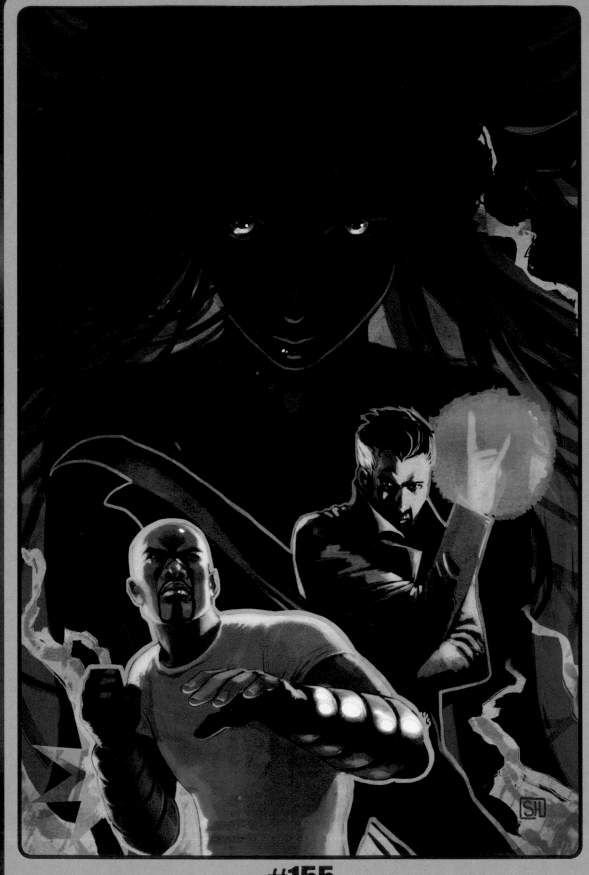

#155

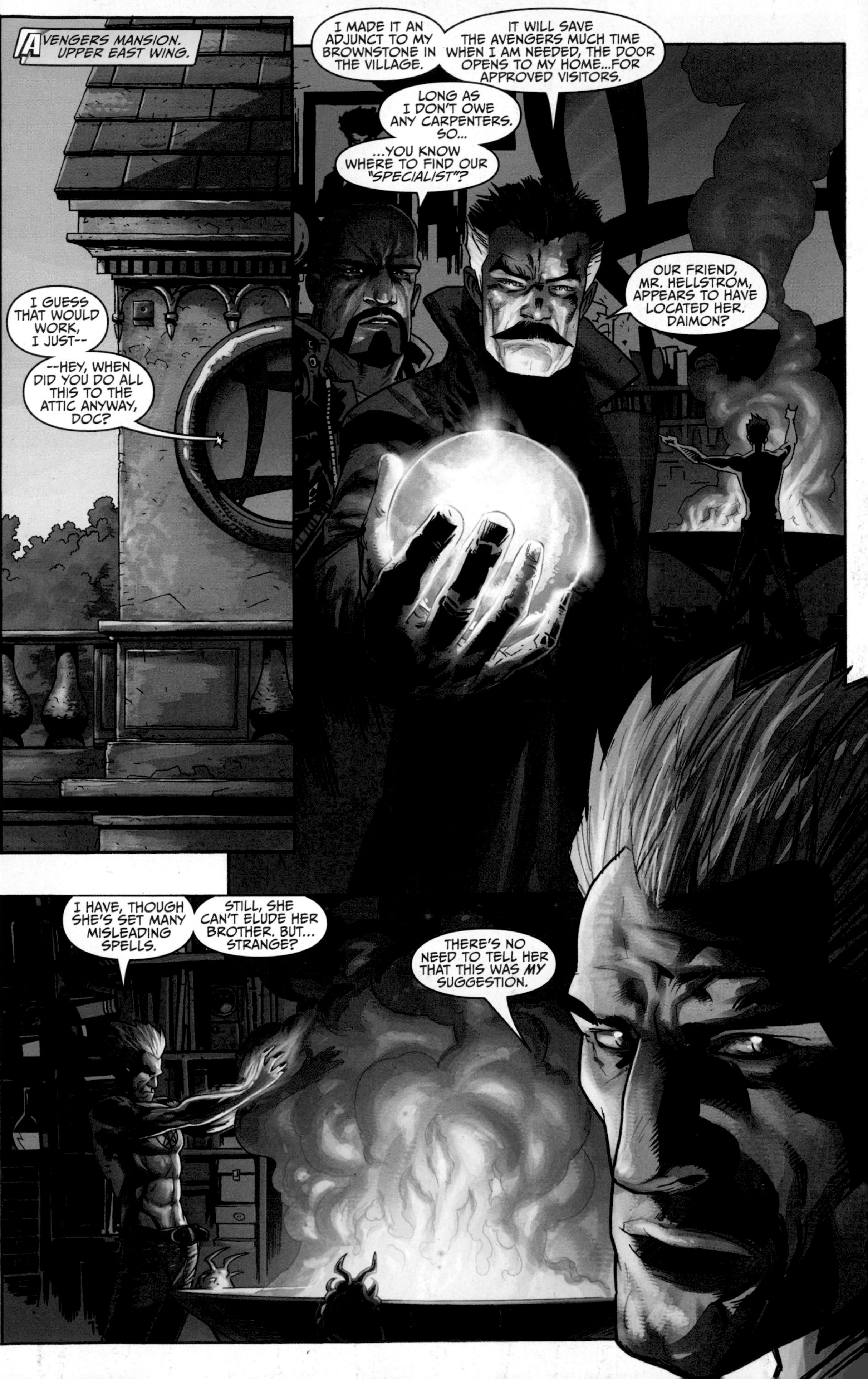
AVENGERS MANSION. UPPER EAST WING.
I MADE IT AN ADJUNCT TO MY BROWNSTONE IN THE VILLAGE.
IT WILL SAVE THE AVENGERS MUCH TIME WHEN I AM NEEDED, THE DOOR OPENS TO MY HOME...FOR APPROVED VISITORS.
I GUESS THAT WOULD WORK, I JUST--
--HEY, WHEN DID YOU DO ALL THIS TO THE ATTIC ANYWAY, DOC?
LONG AS I DON'T OWE ANY CARPENTERS. SO...
...YOU KNOW WHERE TO FIND OUR "SPECIALIST"?
OUR FRIEND, MR. HELLSTROM, APPEARS TO HAVE LOCATED HER. DAIMON?
I HAVE, THOUGH SHE'S SET MANY MISLEADING SPELLS.
STILL, SHE CAN'T ELUDE HER BROTHER. BUT... STRANGE?
THERE'S NO NEED TO TELL HER THAT THIS WAS MY SUGGESTION.

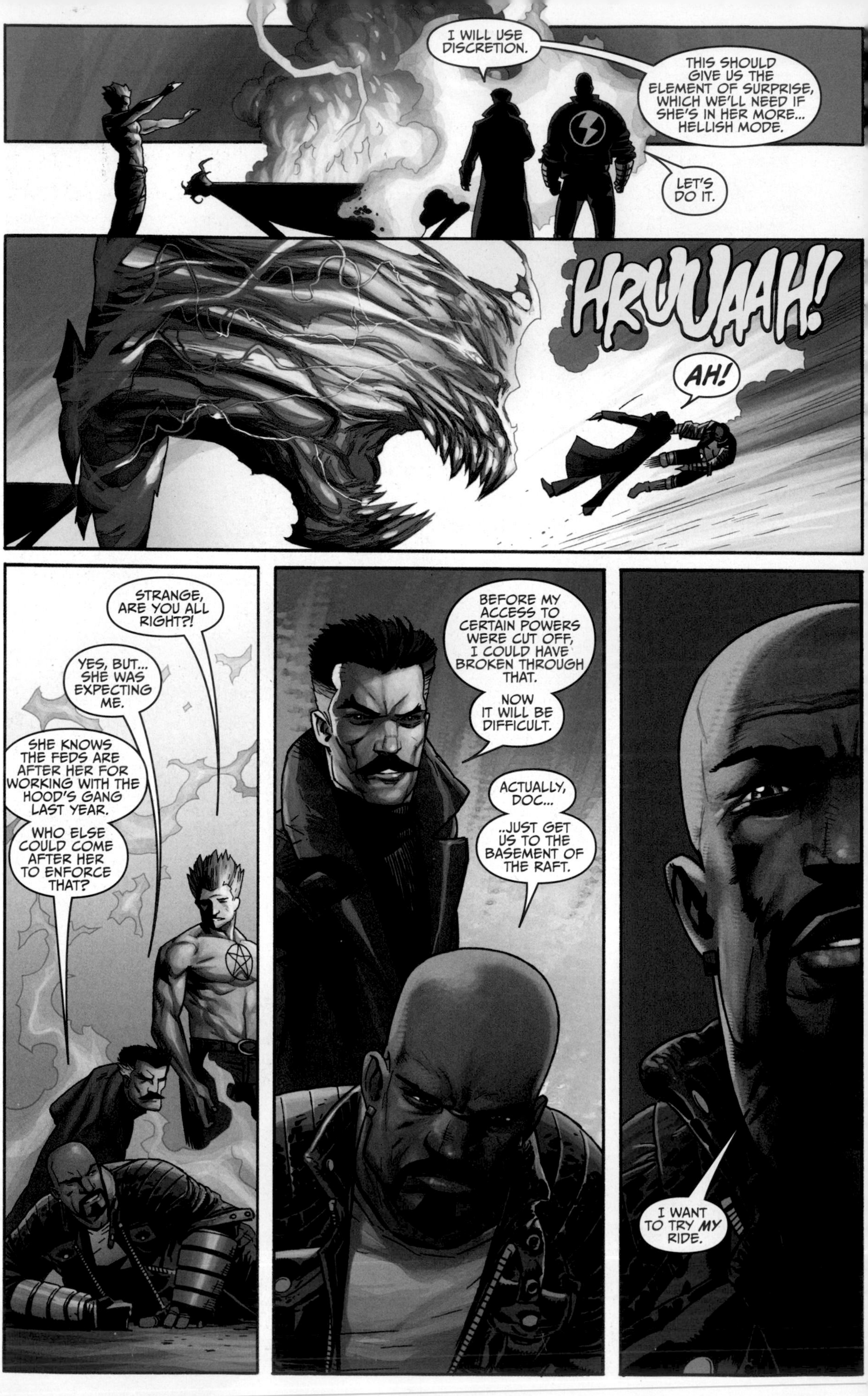
I WILL USE DISCRETION.
THIS SHOULD GIVE US THE ELEMENT OF SURPRISE, WHICH WE'LL NEED IF SHE'S IN HER MORE... HELLISH MODE.
LET'S DO IT.
HRUUAAH!
AH!
STRANGE, ARE YOU ALL RIGHT?!
YES, BUT... SHE WAS EXPECTING ME.
SHE KNOWS THE FEDS ARE AFTER HER FOR WORKING WITH THE HOOD'S GANG LAST YEAR.
WHO ELSE COULD COME AFTER HER TO ENFORCE THAT?
BEFORE MY ACCESS TO CERTAIN POWERS WERE CUT OFF, I COULD HAVE BROKEN THROUGH THAT.
NOW IT WILL BE DIFFICULT.
ACTUALLY, DOC...
..JUST GET US TO THE BASEMENT OF THE RAFT.
I WANT TO TRY *MY* RIDE.

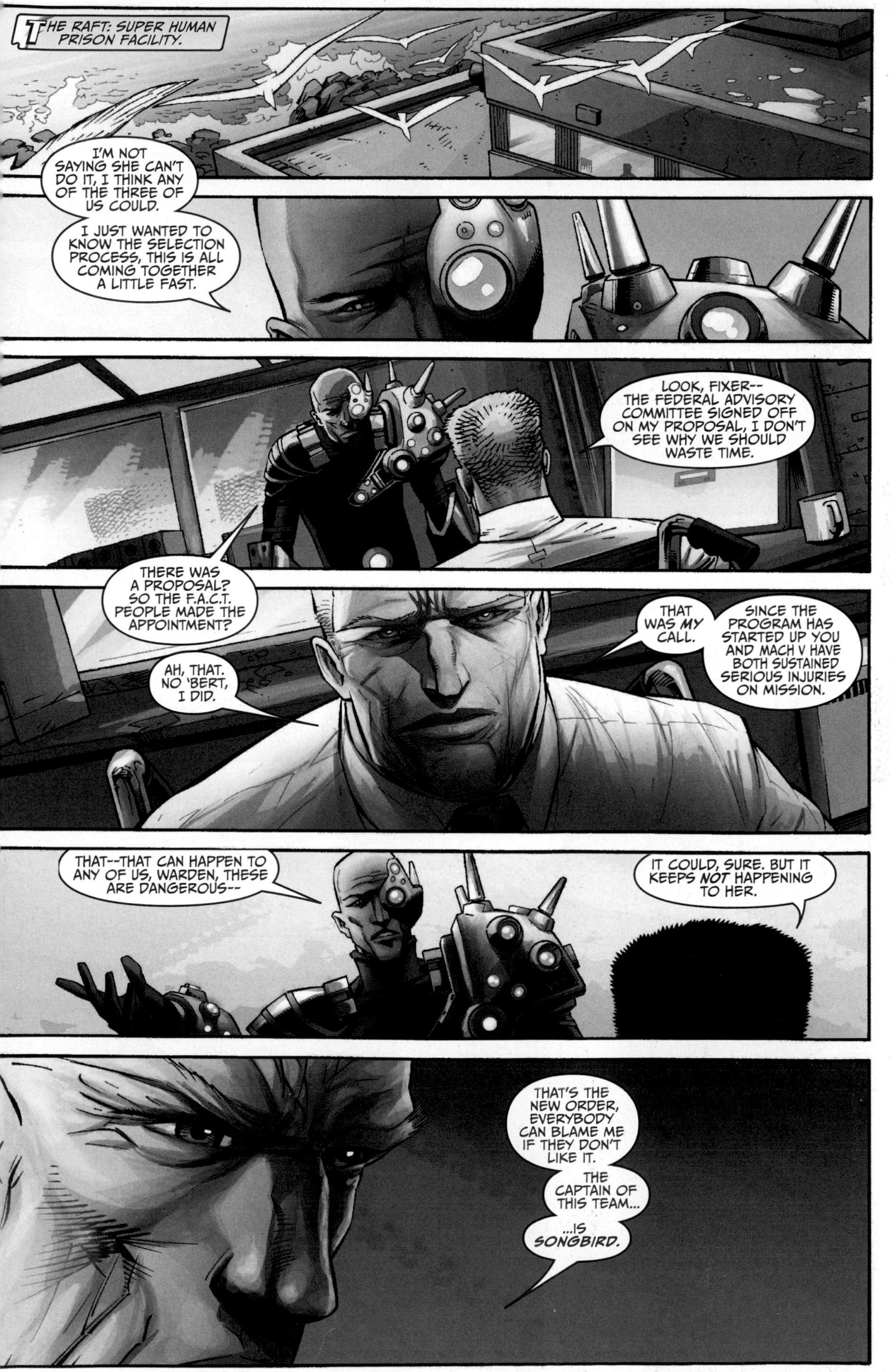
THE RAFT: SUPER HUMAN PRISON FACILITY.
I'M NOT SAYING SHE CAN'T DO IT, I THINK ANY OF THE THREE OF US COULD.
I JUST WANTED TO KNOW THE SELECTION PROCESS, THIS IS ALL COMING TOGETHER A LITTLE FAST.
LOOK, FIXER-- THE FEDERAL ADVISORY COMMITTEE SIGNED OFF ON MY PROPOSAL, I DON'T SEE WHY WE SHOULD WASTE TIME.
THERE WAS A PROPOSAL? SO THE F.A.C.T. PEOPLE MADE THE APPOINTMENT?
AH, THAT. NO 'BERT, I DID.
THAT WAS MY CALL.
SINCE THE PROGRAM HAS STARTED UP YOU AND MACH V HAVE BOTH SUSTAINED SERIOUS INJURIES ON MISSION.
THAT--THAT CAN HAPPEN TO ANY OF US, WARDEN, THESE ARE DANGEROUS--
IT COULD, SURE. BUT IT KEEPS NOT HAPPENING TO HER.
THAT'S THE NEW ORDER, EVERYBODY CAN BLAME ME IF THEY DON'T LIKE IT.
THE CAPTAIN OF THIS TEAM...
...IS SONGBIRD.

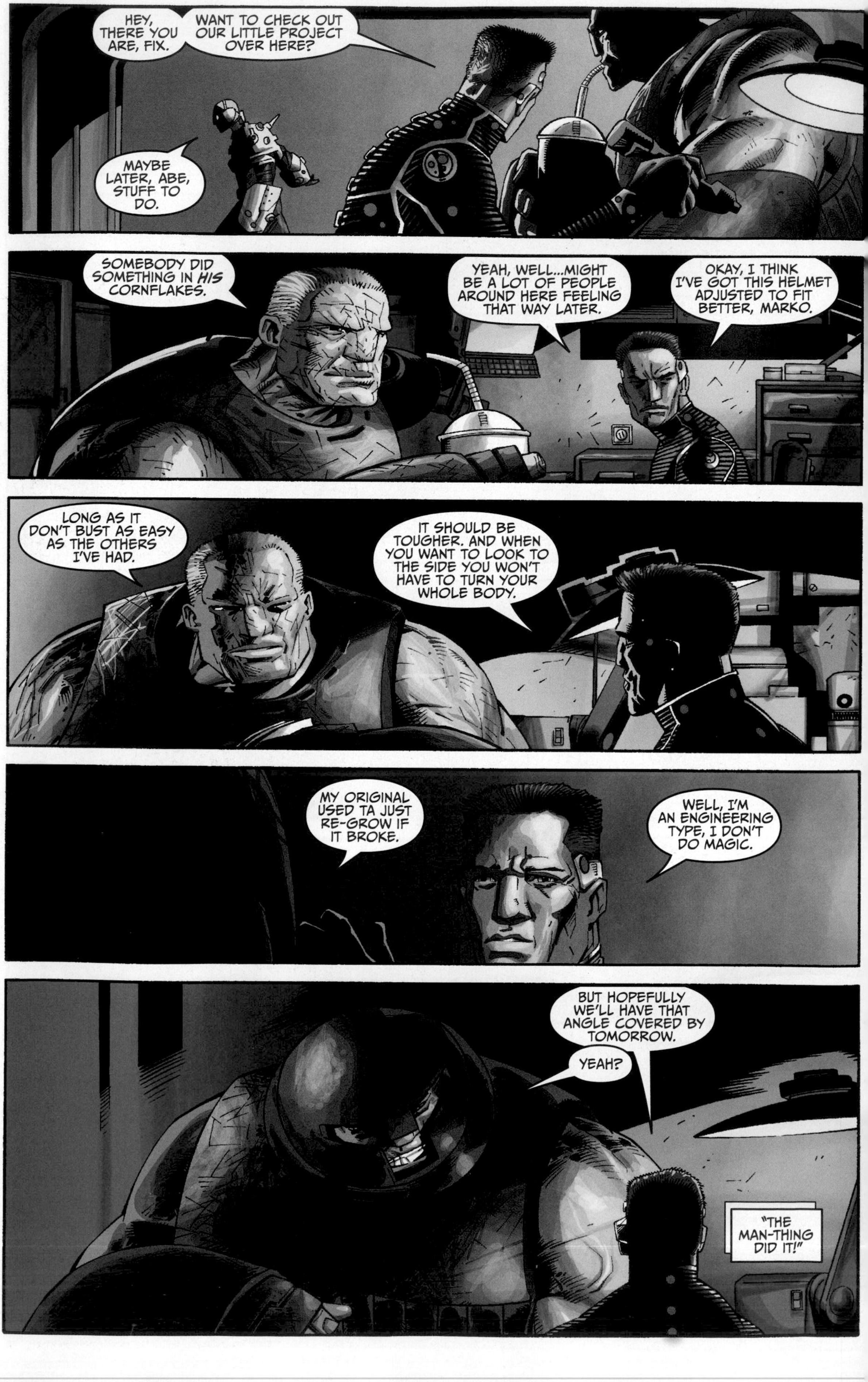
HEY, THERE YOU ARE, FIX.
WANT TO CHECK OUT OUR LITTLE PROJECT OVER HERE?
MAYBE LATER, ABE, STUFF TO DO.
SOMEBODY DID SOMETHING IN HIS CORNFLAKES.
YEAH, WELL...MIGHT BE A LOT OF PEOPLE AROUND HERE FEELING THAT WAY LATER.
OKAY, I THINK I'VE GOT THIS HELMET ADJUSTED TO FIT BETTER, MARKO.
LONG AS IT DON'T BUST AS EASY AS THE OTHERS I'VE HAD.
IT SHOULD BE TOUGHER. AND WHEN YOU WANT TO LOOK TO THE SIDE YOU WON'T HAVE TO TURN YOUR WHOLE BODY.
MY ORIGINAL USED TA JUST RE-GROW IF IT BROKE.
WELL, I'M AN ENGINEERING TYPE, I DON'T DO MAGIC.
BUT HOPEFULLY WE'LL HAVE THAT ANGLE COVERED BY TOMORROW.
YEAH?
"THE MAN-THING DID IT!"

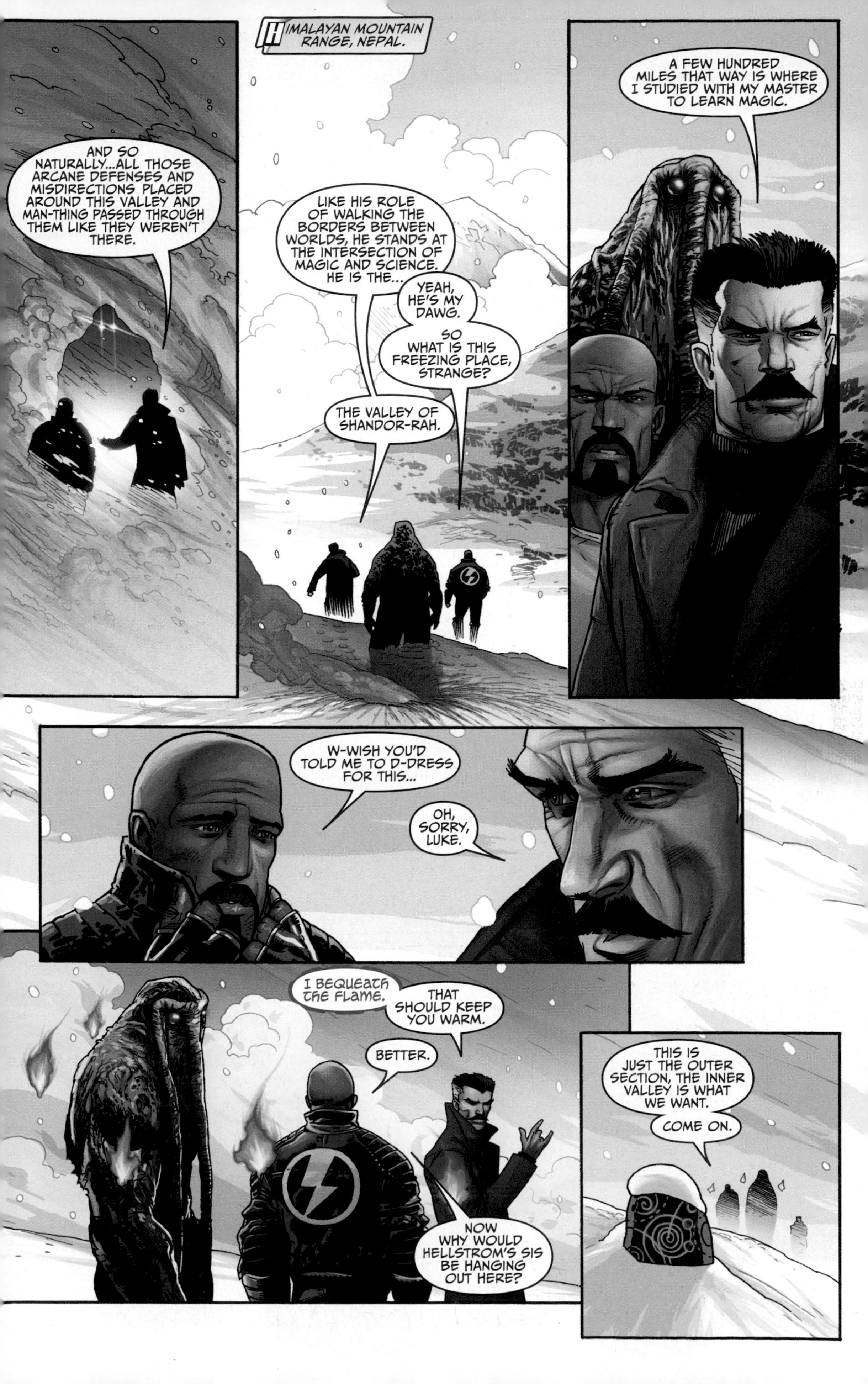
HIMALAYAN MOUNTAIN RANGE, NEPAL.
AND SO NATURALLY...ALL THOSE ARCANE DEFENSES AND MISDIRECTIONS PLACED AROUND THIS VALLEY AND MAN-THING PASSED THROUGH THEM LIKE THEY WEREN'T THERE.
LIKE HIS ROLE OF WALKING THE BORDERS BETWEEN WORLDS, HE STANDS AT THE INTERSECTION OF MAGIC AND SCIENCE. HE IS THE...
YEAH, HE'S MY DAWG.
SO WHAT IS THIS FREEZING PLACE, STRANGE?
THE VALLEY OF SHANDOR-RAH.
A FEW HUNDRED MILES THAT WAY IS WHERE I STUDIED WITH MY MASTER TO LEARN MAGIC.
W-WISH YOU'D TOLD ME TO D-DRESS FOR THIS...
OH, SORRY, LUKE.
I BEQUEATH THE FLAME.
THAT SHOULD KEEP YOU WARM.
BETTER.
NOW WHY WOULD HELLSTROM'S SIS BE HANGING OUT HERE?
THIS IS JUST THE OUTER SECTION, THE INNER VALLEY IS WHAT WE WANT.
COME ON.

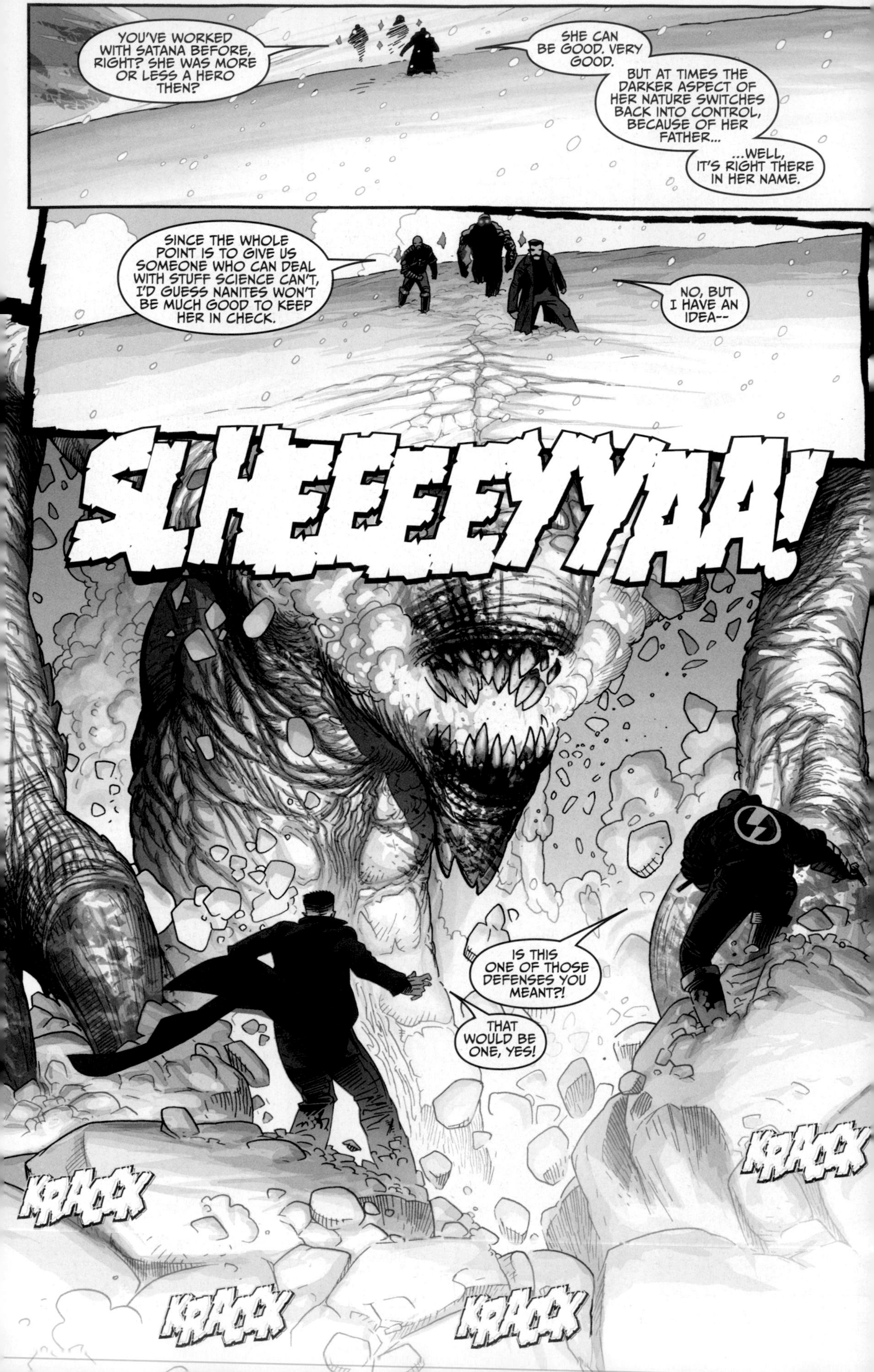
YOU'VE WORKED WITH SATANA BEFORE, RIGHT? SHE WAS MORE OR LESS A HERO THEN?
SHE CAN BE GOOD. VERY GOOD.
BUT AT TIMES THE DARKER ASPECT OF HER NATURE SWITCHES BACK INTO CONTROL, BECAUSE OF HER FATHER...
...WELL, IT'S RIGHT THERE IN HER NAME.
SINCE THE WHOLE POINT IS TO GIVE US SOMEONE WHO CAN DEAL WITH STUFF SCIENCE CAN'T, I'D GUESS NANITES WON'T BE MUCH GOOD TO KEEP HER IN CHECK.
NO, BUT I HAVE AN IDEA--
SKREEEEYYAA!
IS THIS ONE OF THOSE DEFENSES YOU MEANT?!
THAT WOULD BE ONE, YES!
KRACCK
KRACCK
KRACCK
KRACCK

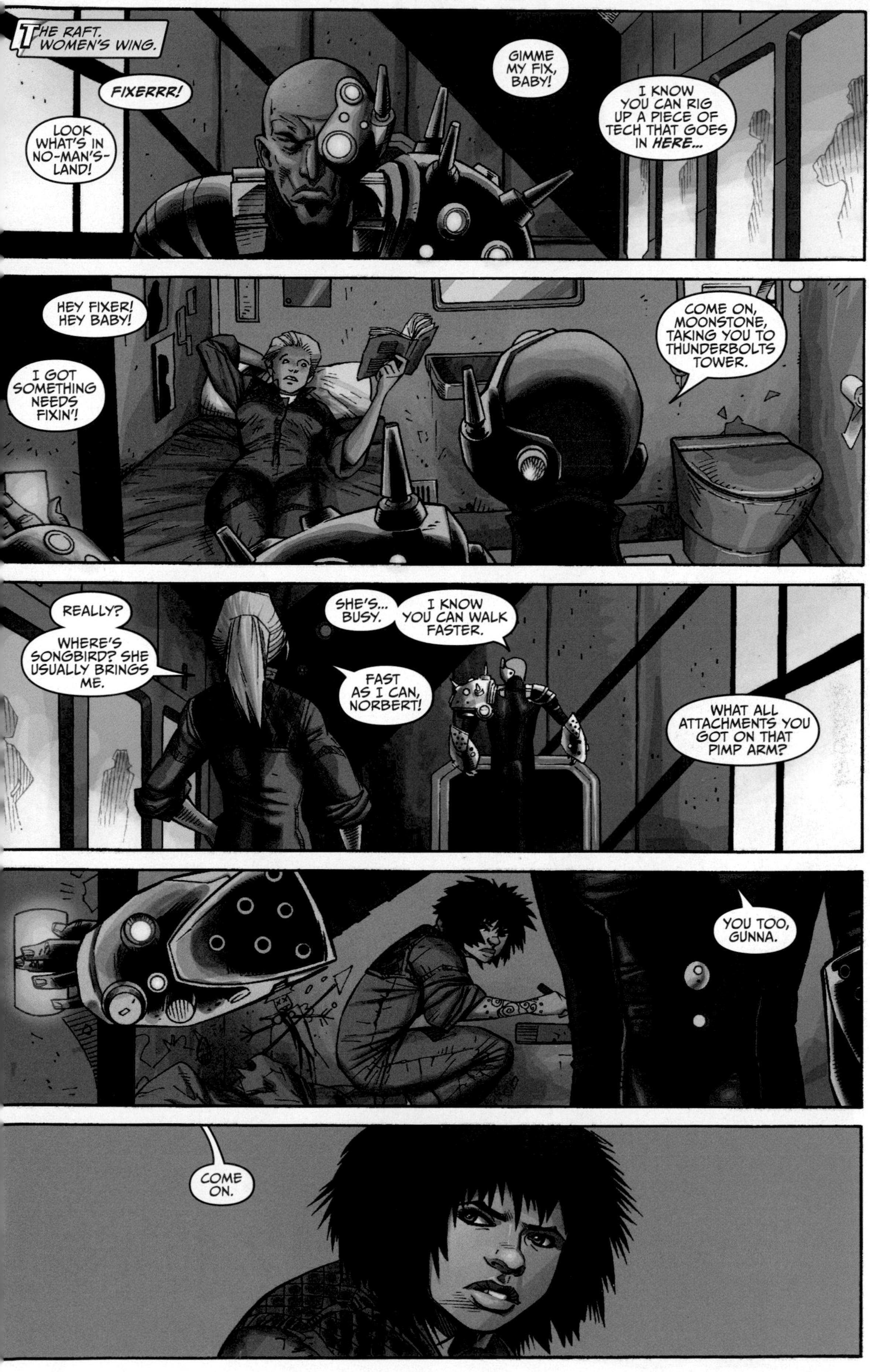
THE RAFT. WOMEN'S WING.
FIXERRR!
LOOK WHAT'S IN NO-MAN'S-LAND!
GIMME MY FIX, BABY!
I KNOW YOU CAN RIG UP A PIECE OF TECH THAT GOES IN HERE...
HEY FIXER! HEY BABY!
I GOT SOMETHING NEEDS FIXIN'!
COME ON, MOONSTONE, TAKING YOU TO THUNDERBOLTS TOWER.
REALLY?
WHERE'S SONGBIRD? SHE USUALLY BRINGS ME.
SHE'S... BUSY.
I KNOW YOU CAN WALK FASTER.
FAST AS I CAN, NORBERT!
WHAT ALL ATTACHMENTS YOU GOT ON THAT PIMP ARM?
YOU TOO, GUNNA.
COME ON.

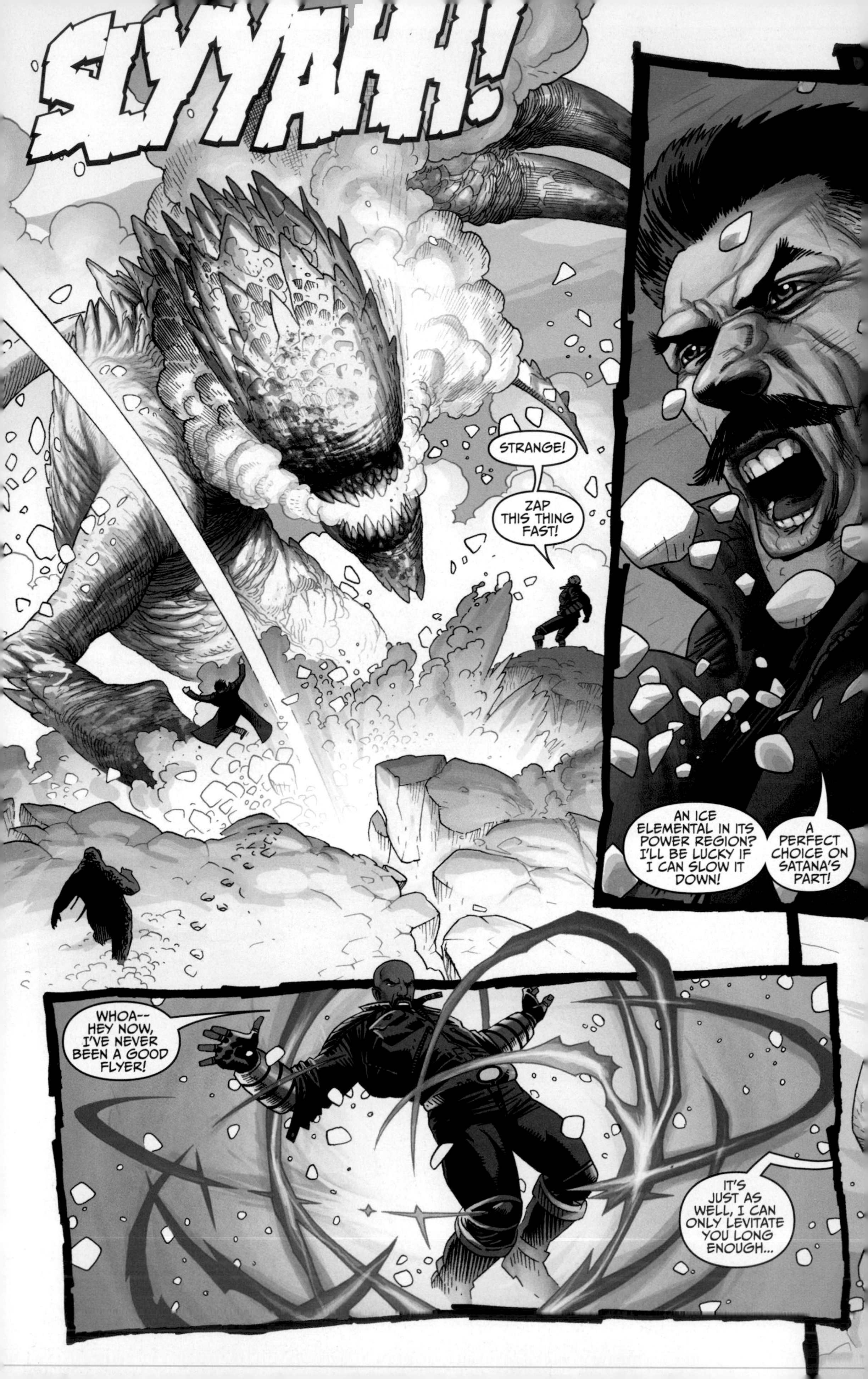
SLYAHH!
STRANGE!
ZAP THIS THING FAST!
AN ICE ELEMENTAL IN ITS POWER REGION? I'LL BE LUCKY IF I CAN SLOW IT DOWN!
A PERFECT CHOICE ON SATANA'S PART!
WHOA-- HEY NOW, I'VE NEVER BEEN A GOOD FLYER!
IT'S JUST AS WELL, I CAN ONLY LEVITATE YOU LONG ENOUGH...

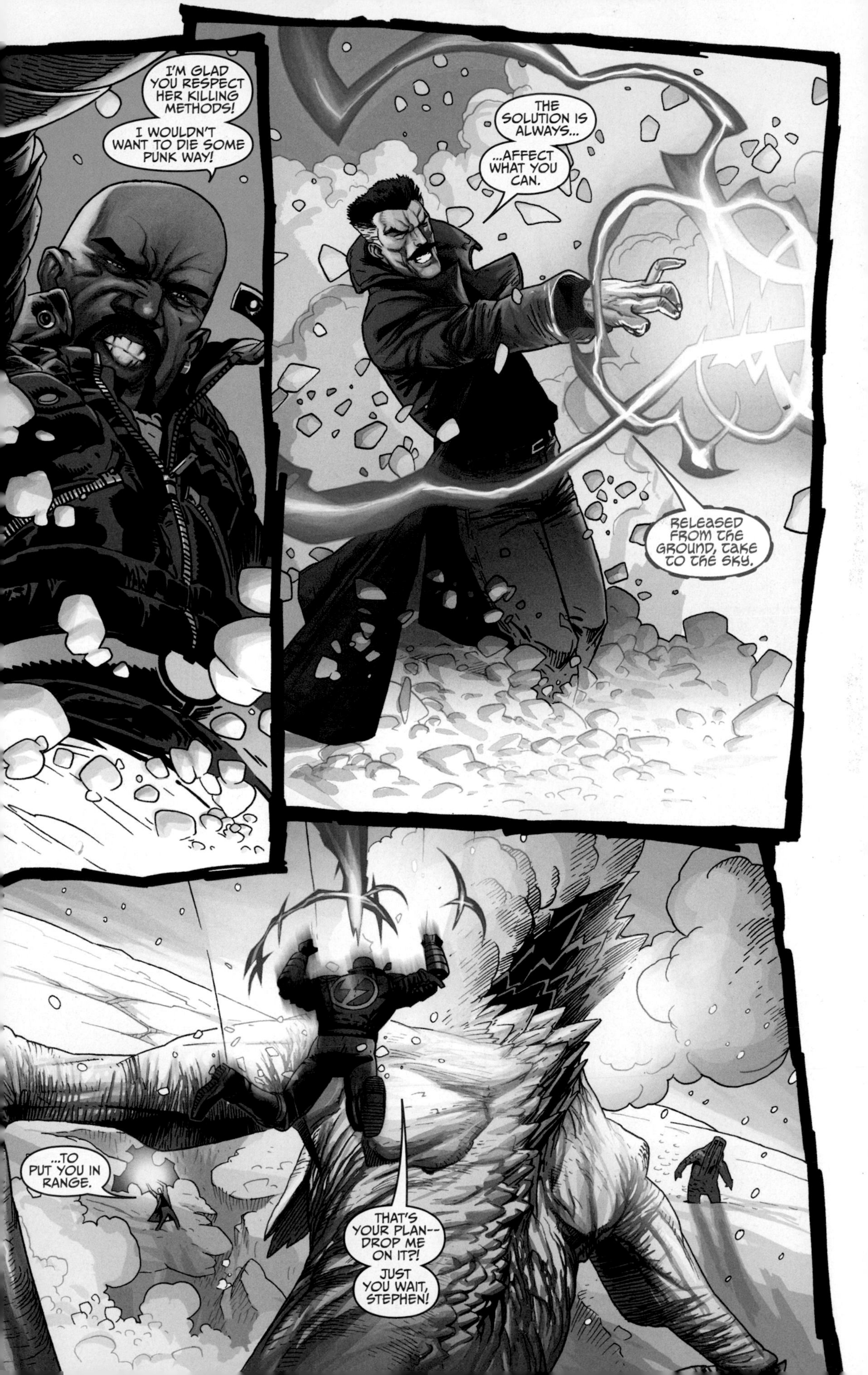
I'M GLAD YOU RESPECT HER KILLING METHODS!
I WOULDN'T WANT TO DIE SOME PUNK WAY!
THE SOLUTION IS ALWAYS...
...AFFECT WHAT YOU CAN.
RELEASED FROM THE GROUND, TAKE TO THE SKY.
...TO PUT YOU IN RANGE.
THAT'S YOUR PLAN--DROP ME ON IT?!
JUST YOU WAIT, STEPHEN!

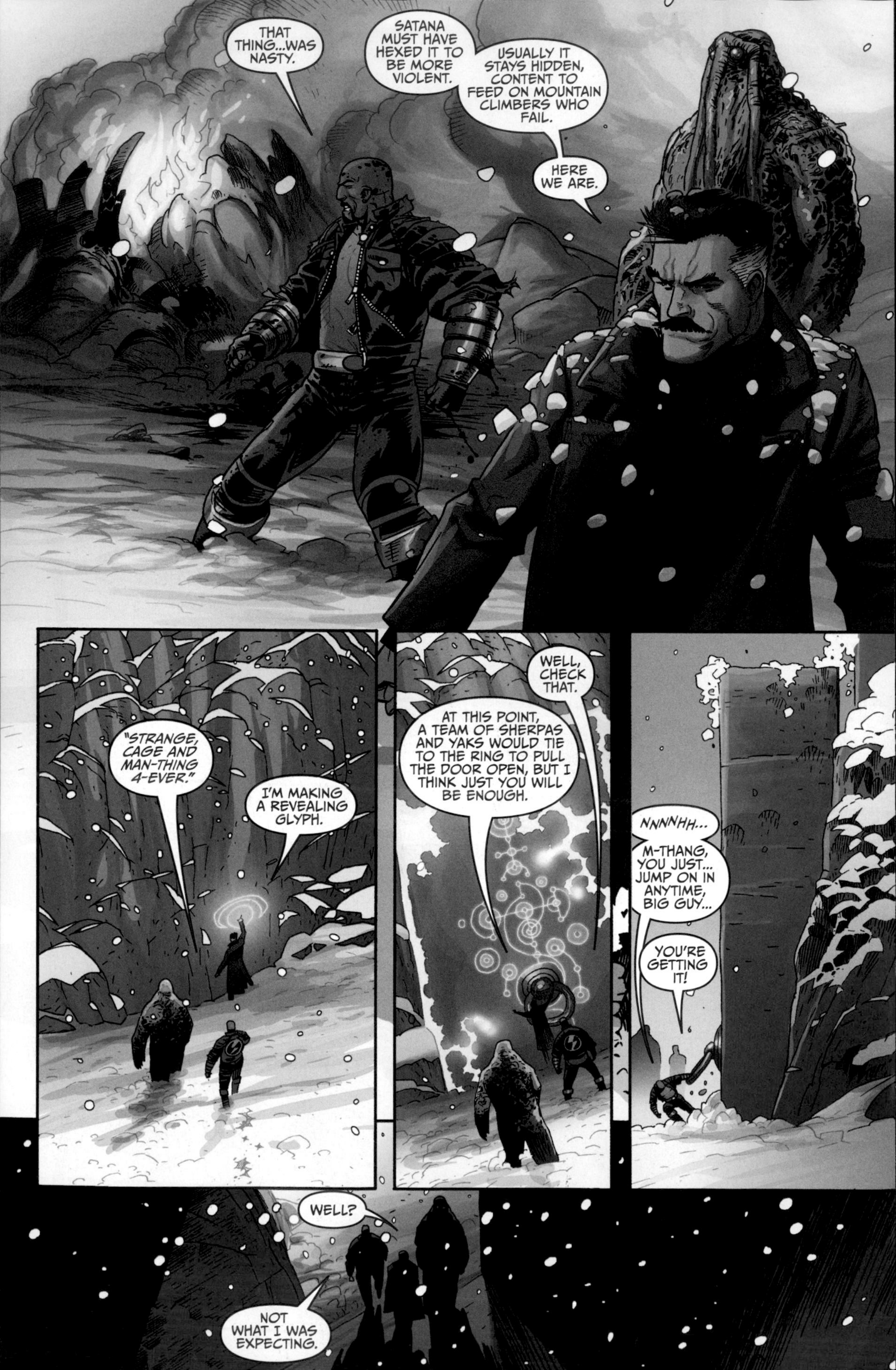
THAT THING...WAS NASTY.
SATANA MUST HAVE HEXED IT TO BE MORE VIOLENT.
USUALLY IT STAYS HIDDEN, CONTENT TO FEED ON MOUNTAIN CLIMBERS WHO FAIL.
HERE WE ARE.
"STRANGE, CAGE AND MAN-THING 4-EVER."
I'M MAKING A REVEALING GLYPH.
WELL, CHECK THAT.
AT THIS POINT, A TEAM OF SHERPAS AND YAKS WOULD TIE TO THE RING TO PULL THE DOOR OPEN, BUT I THINK JUST YOU WILL BE ENOUGH.
NNNNHH...
M-THANG, YOU JUST... JUMP ON IN ANYTIME, BIG GUY...
YOU'RE GETTING IT!
WELL?
NOT WHAT I WAS EXPECTING.

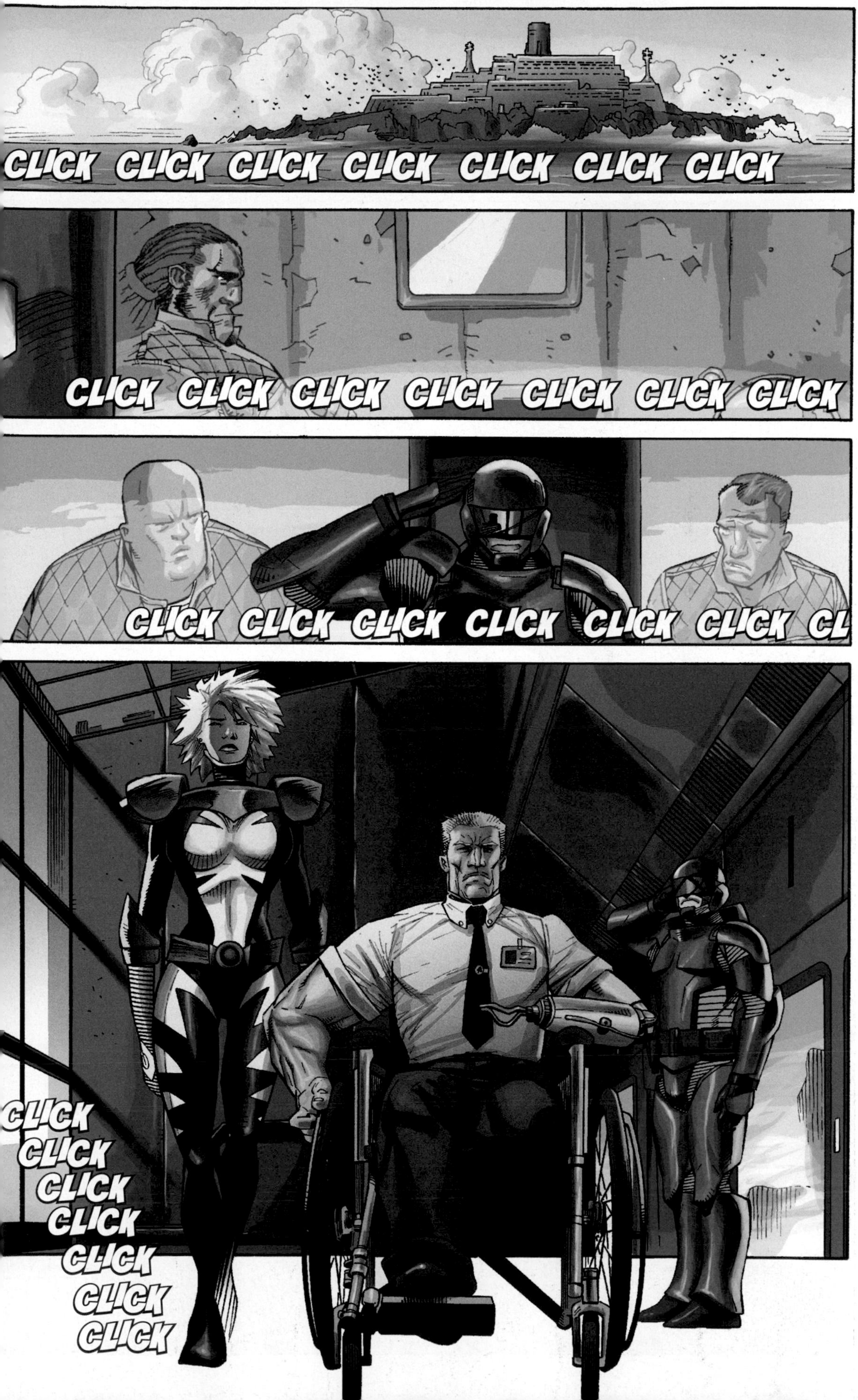
CLICK CLICK CLICK CLICK CLICK CLICK CLICK
CLICK CLICK CLICK CLICK CLICK CLICK CLICK
CLICK CLICK CLICK CLICK CLICK CLICK CL
CLICK
CLICK
CLICK
CLICK
CLICK
CLICK
CLICK

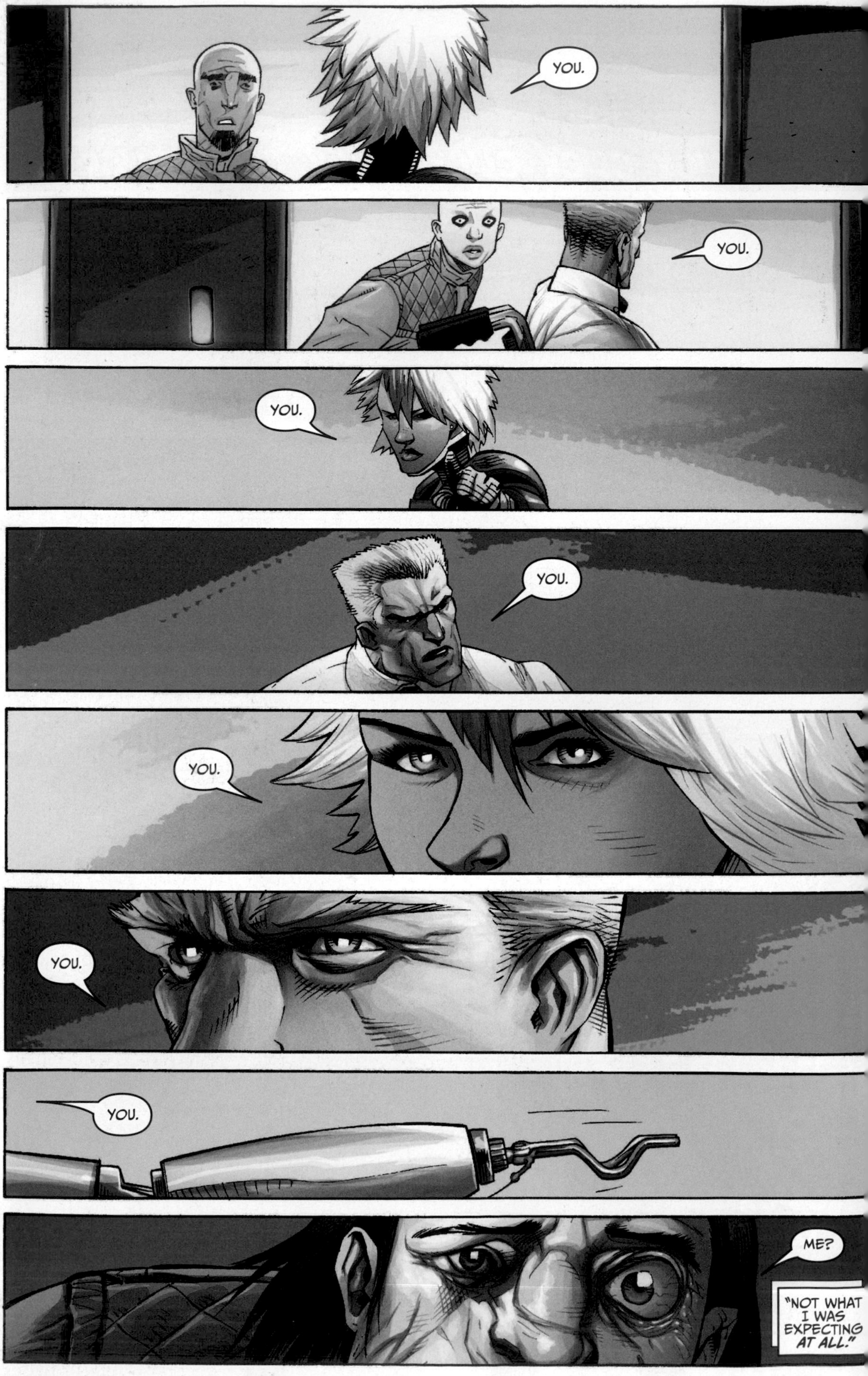
YOU.
YOU.
YOU.
YOU.
YOU.
YOU.
YOU.
ME?
"NOT WHAT I WAS EXPECTING AT ALL."

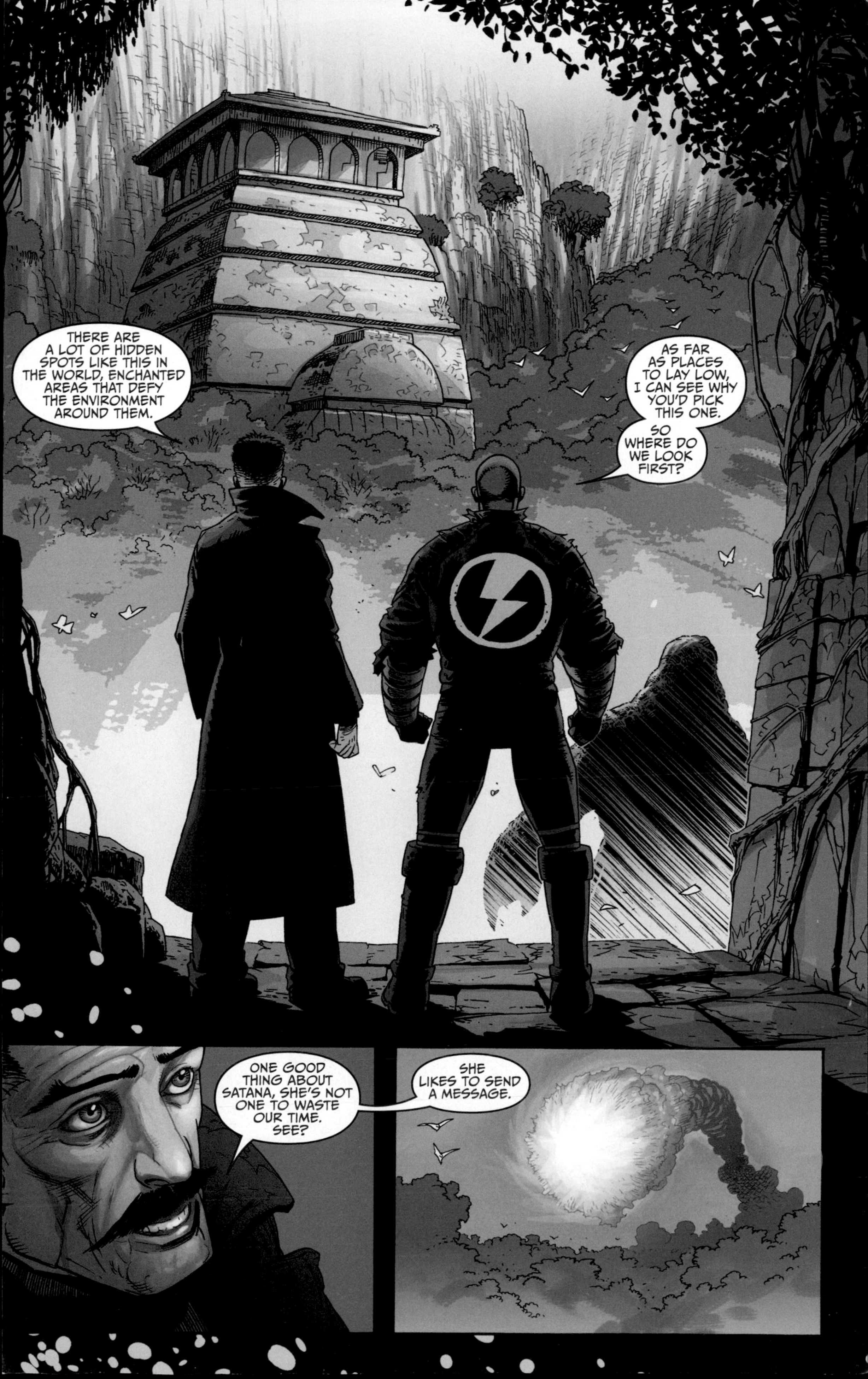
THERE ARE A LOT OF HIDDEN SPOTS LIKE THIS IN THE WORLD, ENCHANTED AREAS THAT DEFY THE ENVIRONMENT AROUND THEM.
AS FAR AS PLACES TO LAY LOW, I CAN SEE WHY YOU'D PICK THIS ONE.
SO WHERE DO WE LOOK FIRST?
ONE GOOD THING ABOUT SATANA, SHE'S NOT ONE TO WASTE OUR TIME. SEE?
SHE LIKES TO SEND A MESSAGE.

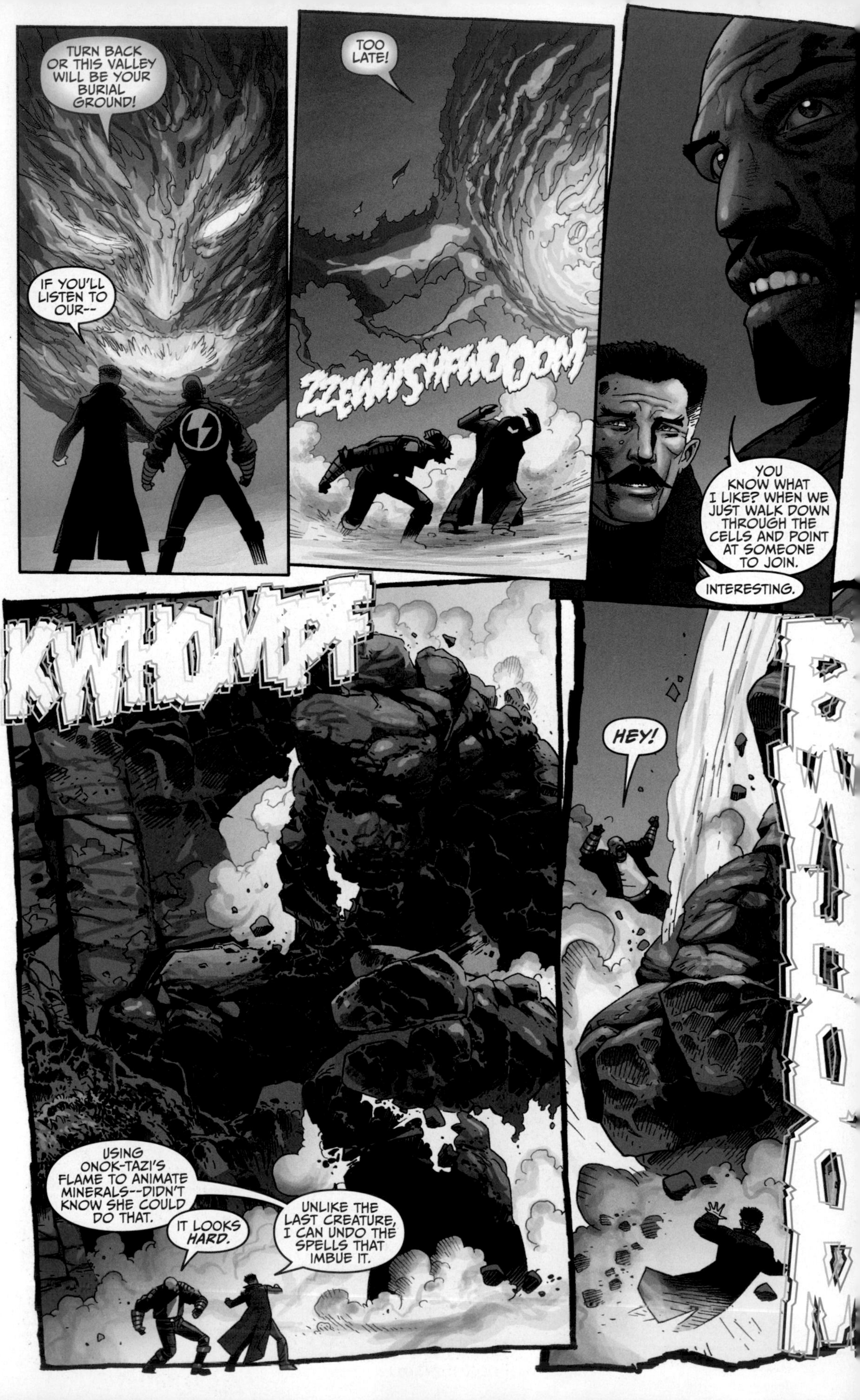
TURN BACK OR THIS VALLEY WILL BE YOUR BURIAL GROUND!
IF YOU'LL LISTEN TO OUR--
TOO LATE!
ZZEWWSHFWOOOM
YOU KNOW WHAT I LIKE? WHEN WE JUST WALK DOWN THROUGH THE CELLS AND POINT AT SOMEONE TO JOIN.
INTERESTING.
KWHOMPF
USING ONOK-TAZI'S FLAME TO ANIMATE MINERALS--DIDN'T KNOW SHE COULD DO THAT.
IT LOOKS HARD.
UNLIKE THE LAST CREATURE, I CAN UNDO THE SPELLS THAT IMBUE IT.
HEY!

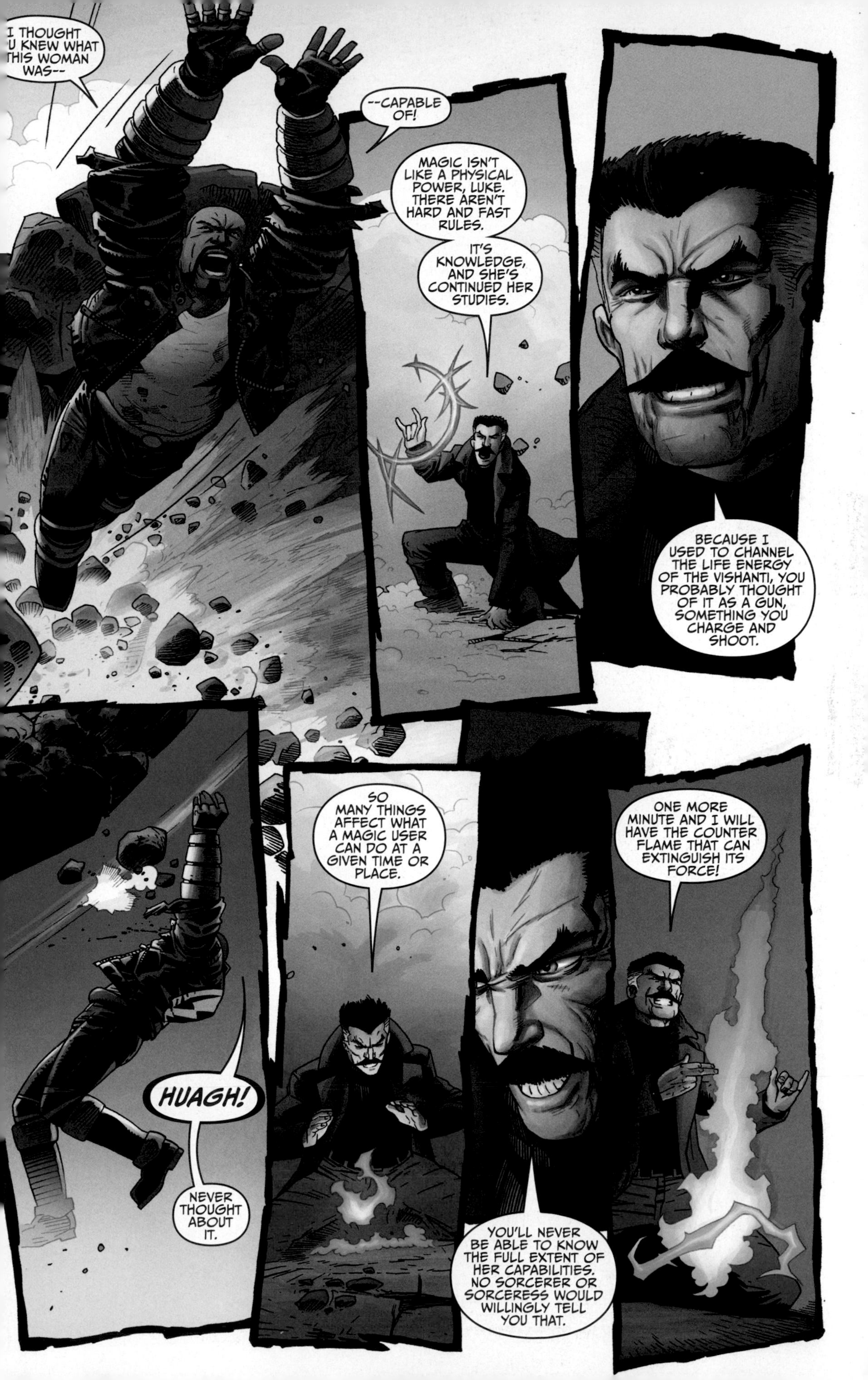
I THOUGHT U KNEW WHAT THIS WOMAN WAS--
--CAPABLE OF!
MAGIC ISN'T LIKE A PHYSICAL POWER, LUKE. THERE AREN'T HARD AND FAST RULES.
IT'S KNOWLEDGE, AND SHE'S CONTINUED HER STUDIES.
BECAUSE I USED TO CHANNEL THE LIFE ENERGY OF THE VISHANTI, YOU PROBABLY THOUGHT OF IT AS A GUN, SOMETHING YOU CHARGE AND SHOOT.
HUAGH!
NEVER THOUGHT ABOUT IT.
SO MANY THINGS AFFECT WHAT A MAGIC USER CAN DO AT A GIVEN TIME OR PLACE.
YOU'LL NEVER BE ABLE TO KNOW THE FULL EXTENT OF HER CAPABILITIES. NO SORCERER OR SORCERESS WOULD WILLINGLY TELL YOU THAT.
ONE MORE MINUTE AND I WILL HAVE THE COUNTER FLAME THAT CAN EXTINGUISH ITS FORCE!

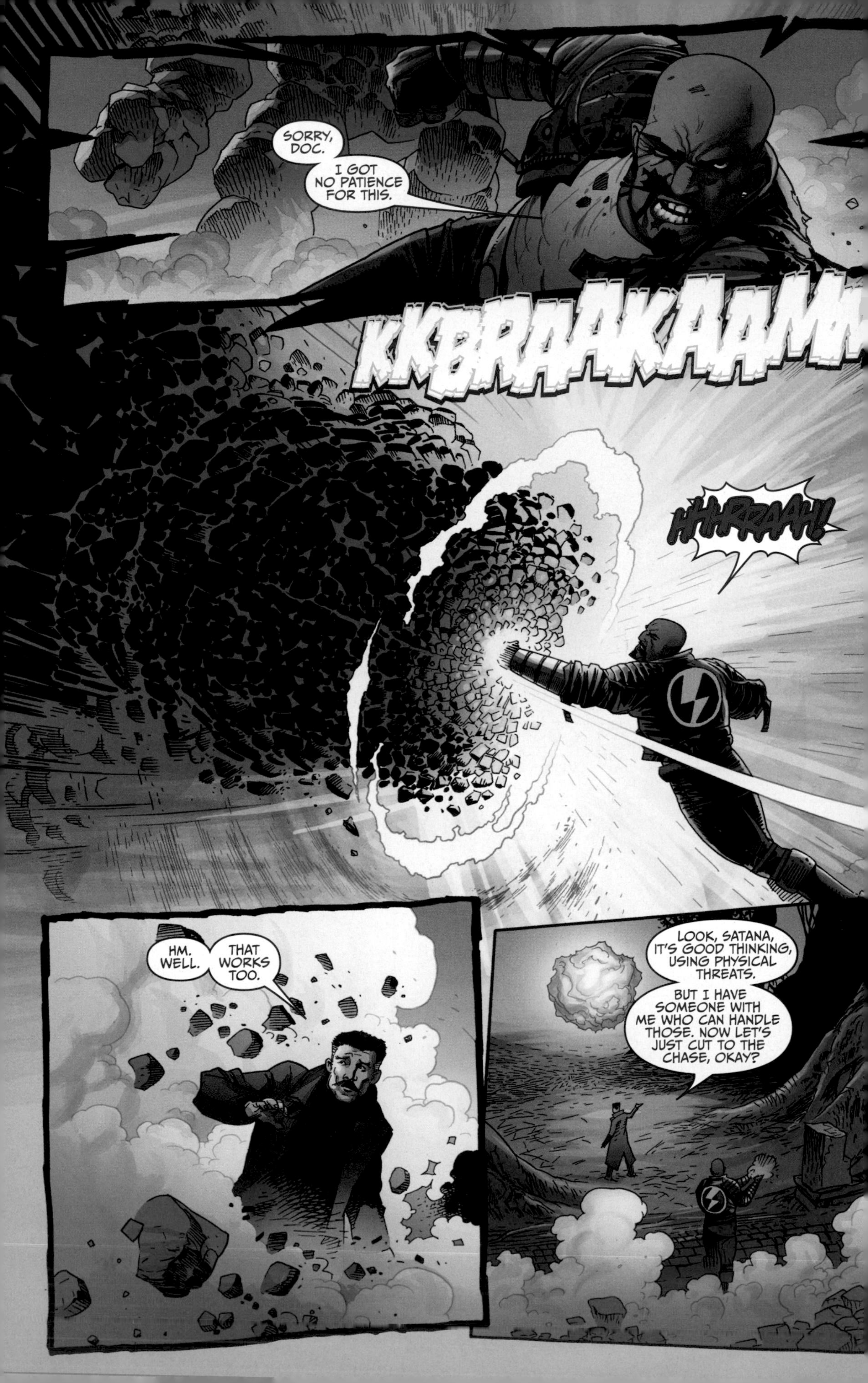
SORRY, DOC.
I GOT NO PATIENCE FOR THIS.
KKBRAAKAAMM
HHRRAAH!
HM. WELL.
THAT WORKS TOO.
LOOK, SATANA, IT'S GOOD THINKING, USING PHYSICAL THREATS.
BUT I HAVE SOMEONE WITH ME WHO CAN HANDLE THOSE. NOW LET'S JUST CUT TO THE CHASE, OKAY?

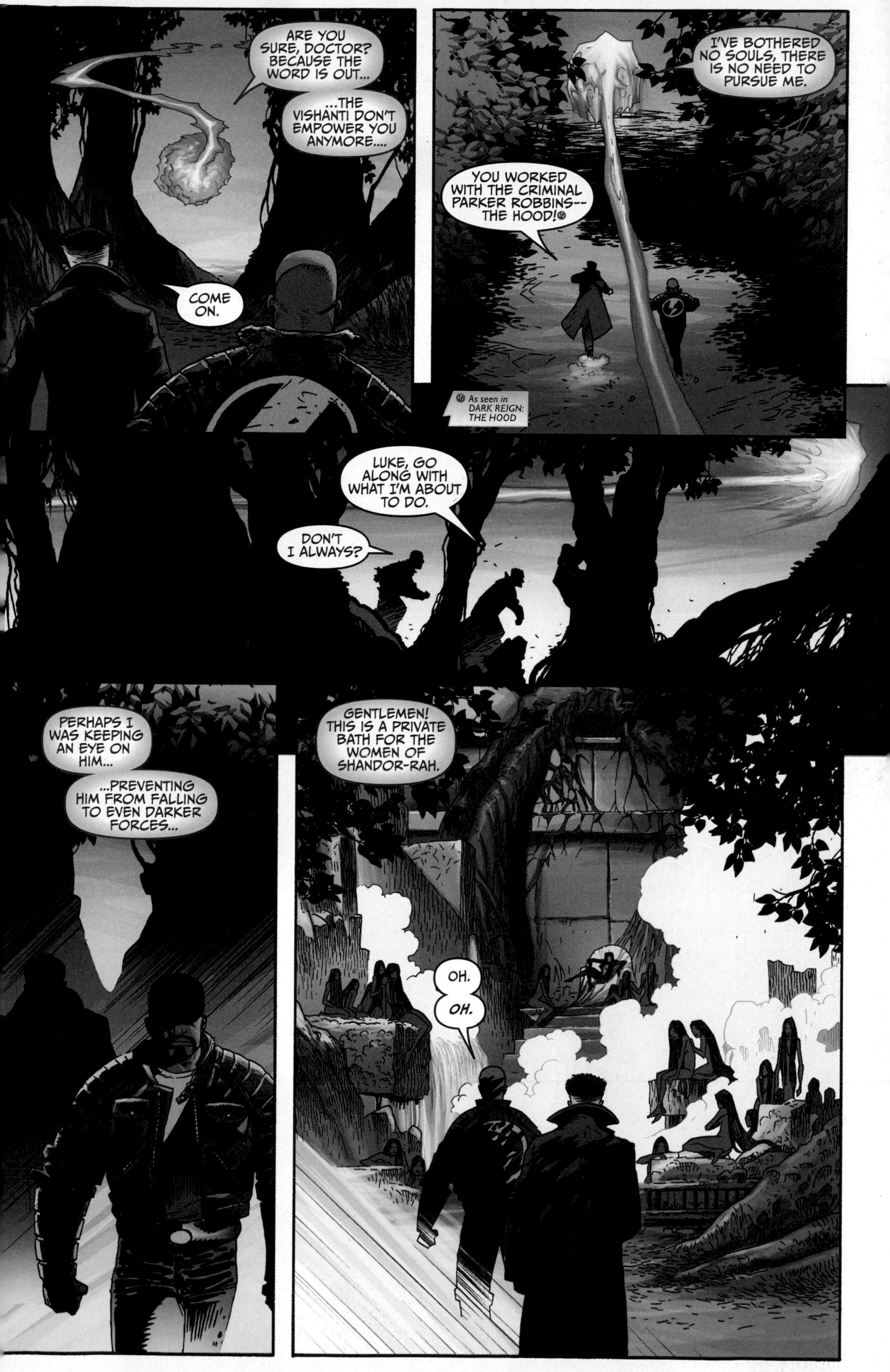
ARE YOU SURE, DOCTOR? BECAUSE THE WORD IS OUT...
...THE VISHANTI DON'T EMPOWER YOU ANYMORE....
COME ON.
I'VE BOTHERED NO SOULS, THERE IS NO NEED TO PURSUE ME.
YOU WORKED WITH THE CRIMINAL PARKER ROBBINS-- THE HOOD!
As seen in DARK REIGN: THE HOOD
LUKE, GO ALONG WITH WHAT I'M ABOUT TO DO.
DON'T I ALWAYS?
PERHAPS I WAS KEEPING AN EYE ON HIM...
...PREVENTING HIM FROM FALLING TO EVEN DARKER FORCES...
GENTLEMEN! THIS IS A PRIVATE BATH FOR THE WOMEN OF SHANDOR-RAH.
OH.
OH.

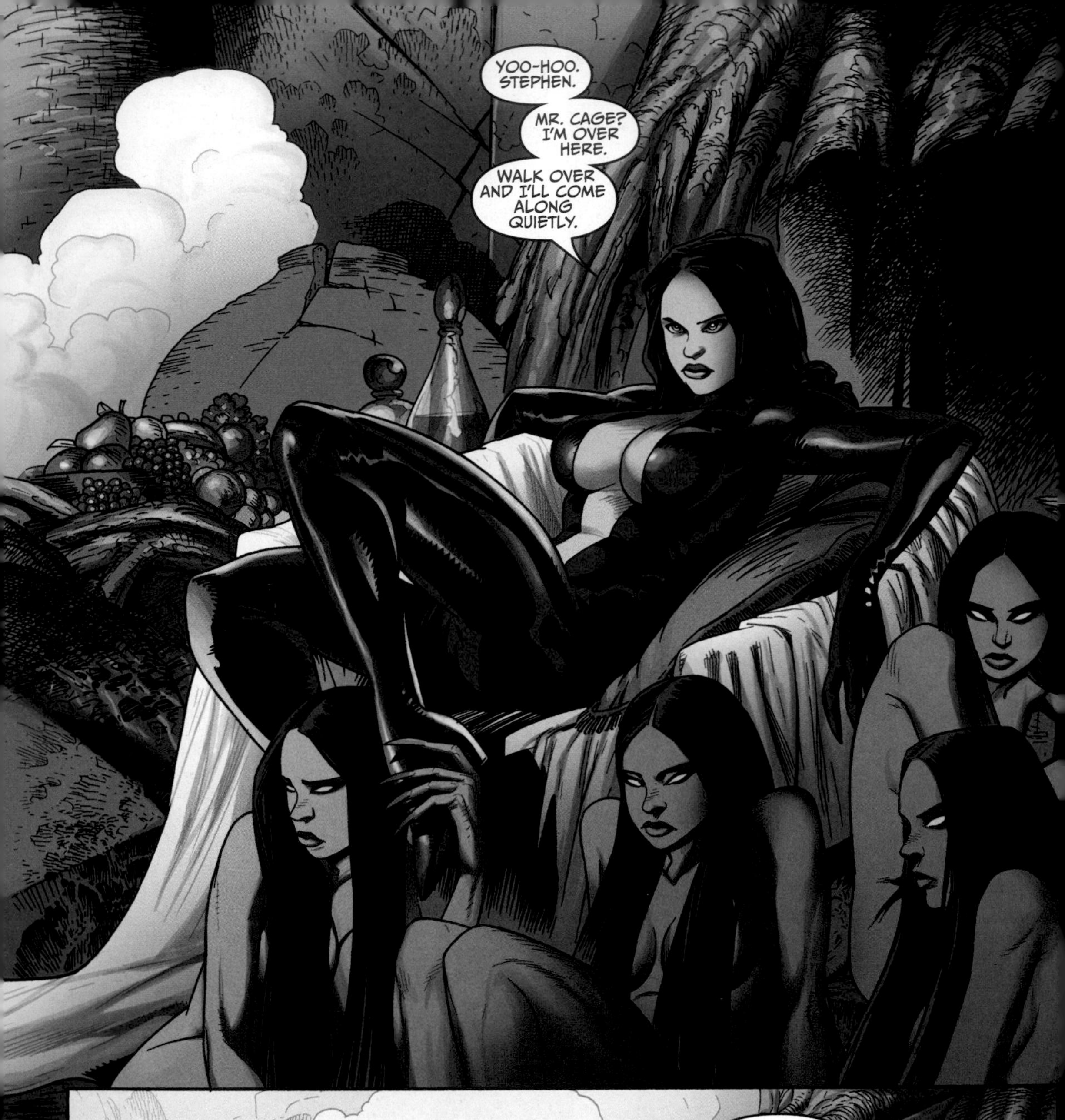
YOO-HOO. STEPHEN.
MR. CAGE? I'M OVER HERE.
WALK OVER AND I'LL COME ALONG QUIETLY.

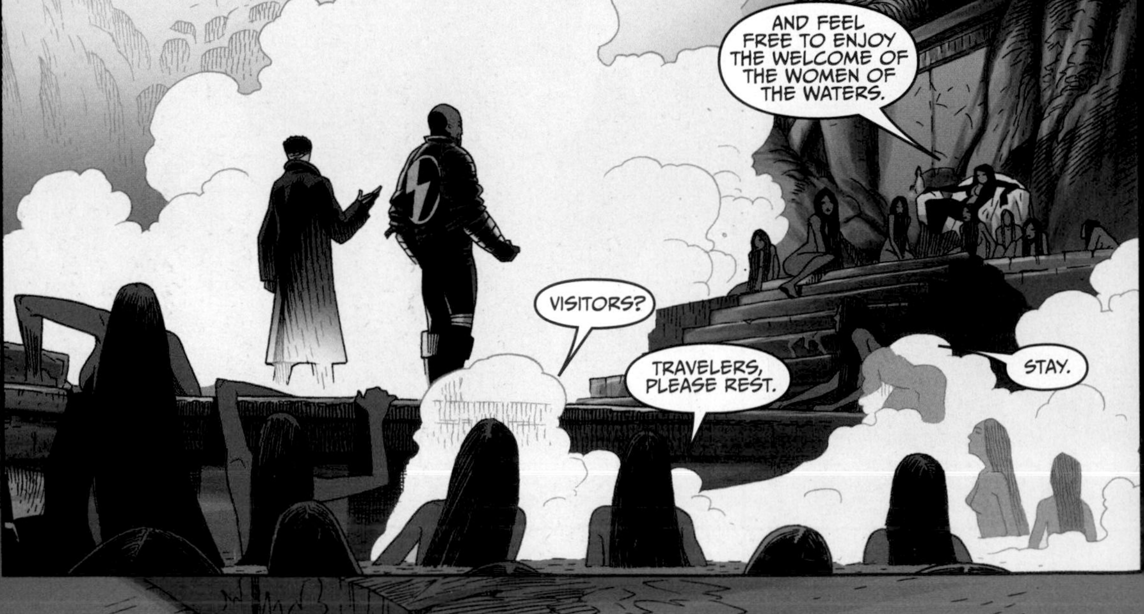
AND FEEL FREE TO ENJOY THE WELCOME OF THE WOMEN OF THE WATERS.
VISITORS?
TRAVELERS, PLEASE REST.
STAY.

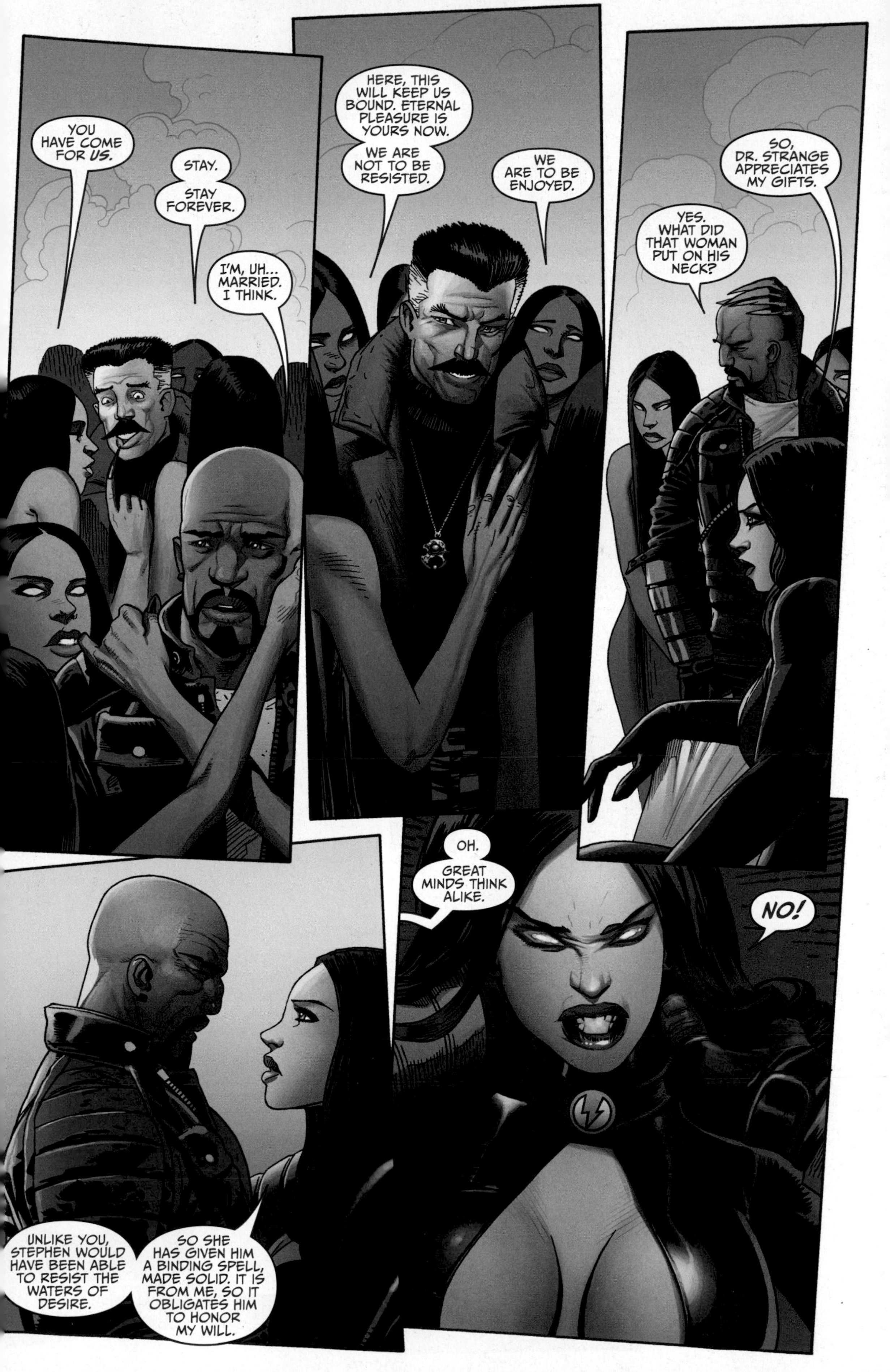
YOU HAVE COME FOR *US*.
STAY.
STAY FOREVER.
I'M, UH... MARRIED. I THINK.
HERE, THIS WILL KEEP US BOUND. ETERNAL PLEASURE IS YOURS NOW.
WE ARE NOT TO BE RESISTED.
WE ARE TO BE ENJOYED.
SO, DR. STRANGE APPRECIATES MY GIFTS.
YES. WHAT DID THAT WOMAN PUT ON HIS NECK?
UNLIKE YOU, STEPHEN WOULD HAVE BEEN ABLE TO RESIST THE WATERS OF DESIRE.
SO SHE HAS GIVEN HIM A BINDING SPELL, MADE SOLID. IT IS FROM ME, SO IT OBLIGATES HIM TO HONOR MY WILL.
OH.
GREAT MINDS THINK ALIKE.
NO!

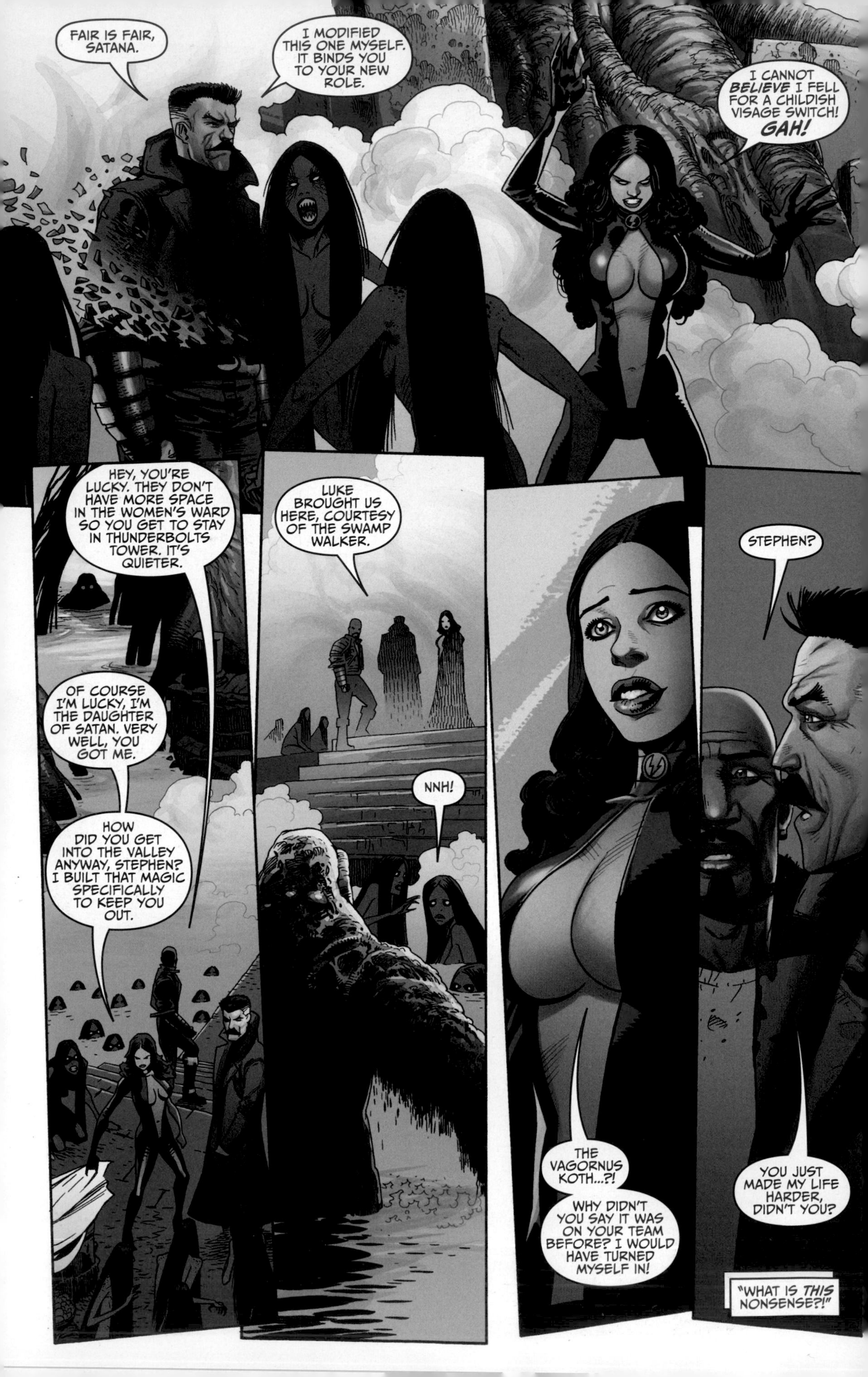
FAIR IS FAIR, SATANA.
I MODIFIED THIS ONE MYSELF. IT BINDS YOU TO YOUR NEW ROLE.
I CANNOT *BELIEVE* I FELL FOR A CHILDISH VISAGE SWITCH! *GAH!*
HEY, YOU'RE LUCKY. THEY DON'T HAVE MORE SPACE IN THE WOMEN'S WARD SO YOU GET TO STAY IN THUNDERBOLTS TOWER. IT'S QUIETER.
OF COURSE I'M LUCKY, I'M THE DAUGHTER OF SATAN. VERY WELL, YOU GOT ME.
HOW DID YOU GET INTO THE VALLEY ANYWAY, STEPHEN? I BUILT THAT MAGIC SPECIFICALLY TO KEEP YOU OUT.
LUKE BROUGHT US HERE, COURTESY OF THE SWAMP WALKER.
NNH!
THE VAGORNUS KOTH...?!
WHY DIDN'T YOU SAY IT WAS ON YOUR TEAM BEFORE? I WOULD HAVE TURNED MYSELF IN!
STEPHEN?
YOU JUST MADE MY LIFE HARDER, DIDN'T YOU?
"WHAT IS *THIS* NONSENSE?!"

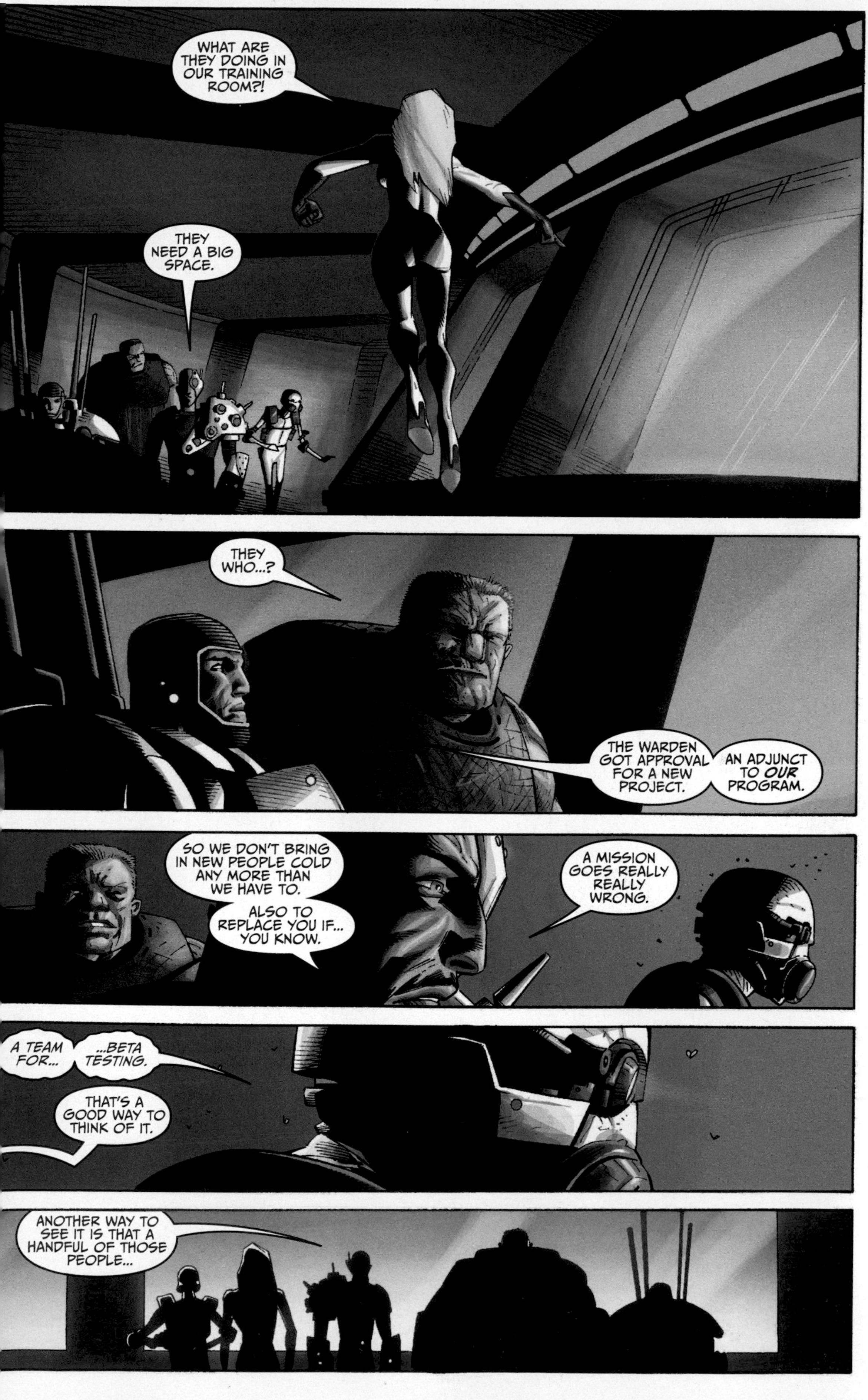
WHAT ARE THEY DOING IN OUR TRAINING ROOM?!
THEY NEED A BIG SPACE.
THEY WHO...?
THE WARDEN GOT APPROVAL FOR A NEW PROJECT.
AN ADJUNCT TO *OUR* PROGRAM.
SO WE DON'T BRING IN NEW PEOPLE COLD ANY MORE THAN WE HAVE TO.
ALSO TO REPLACE YOU IF... YOU KNOW.
A MISSION GOES REALLY REALLY WRONG.
A TEAM FOR...
...BETA TESTING.
THAT'S A GOOD WAY TO THINK OF IT.
ANOTHER WAY TO SEE IT IS THAT A HANDFUL OF THOSE PEOPLE...

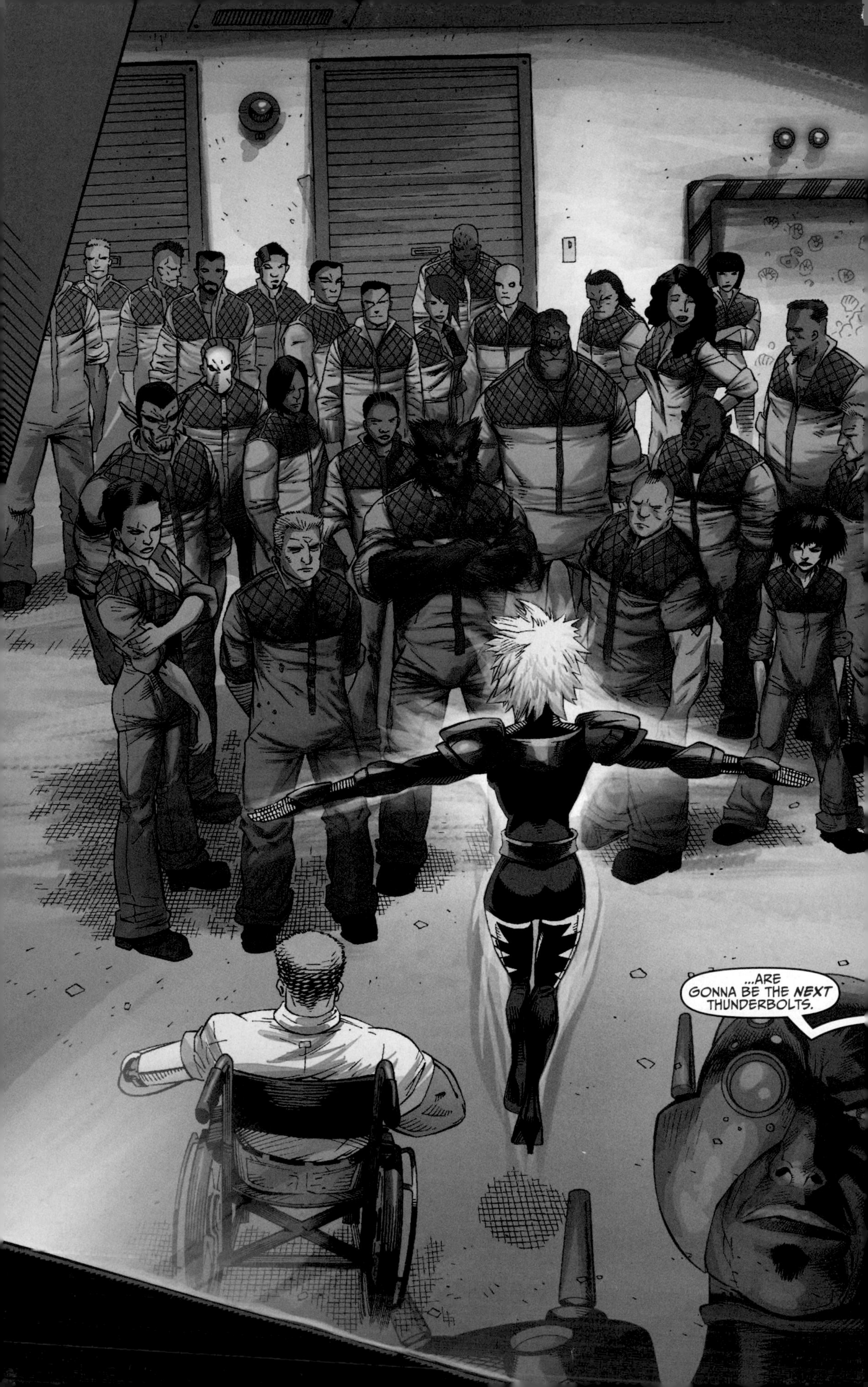
...ARE GONNA BE THE NEXT THUNDERBOLTS.

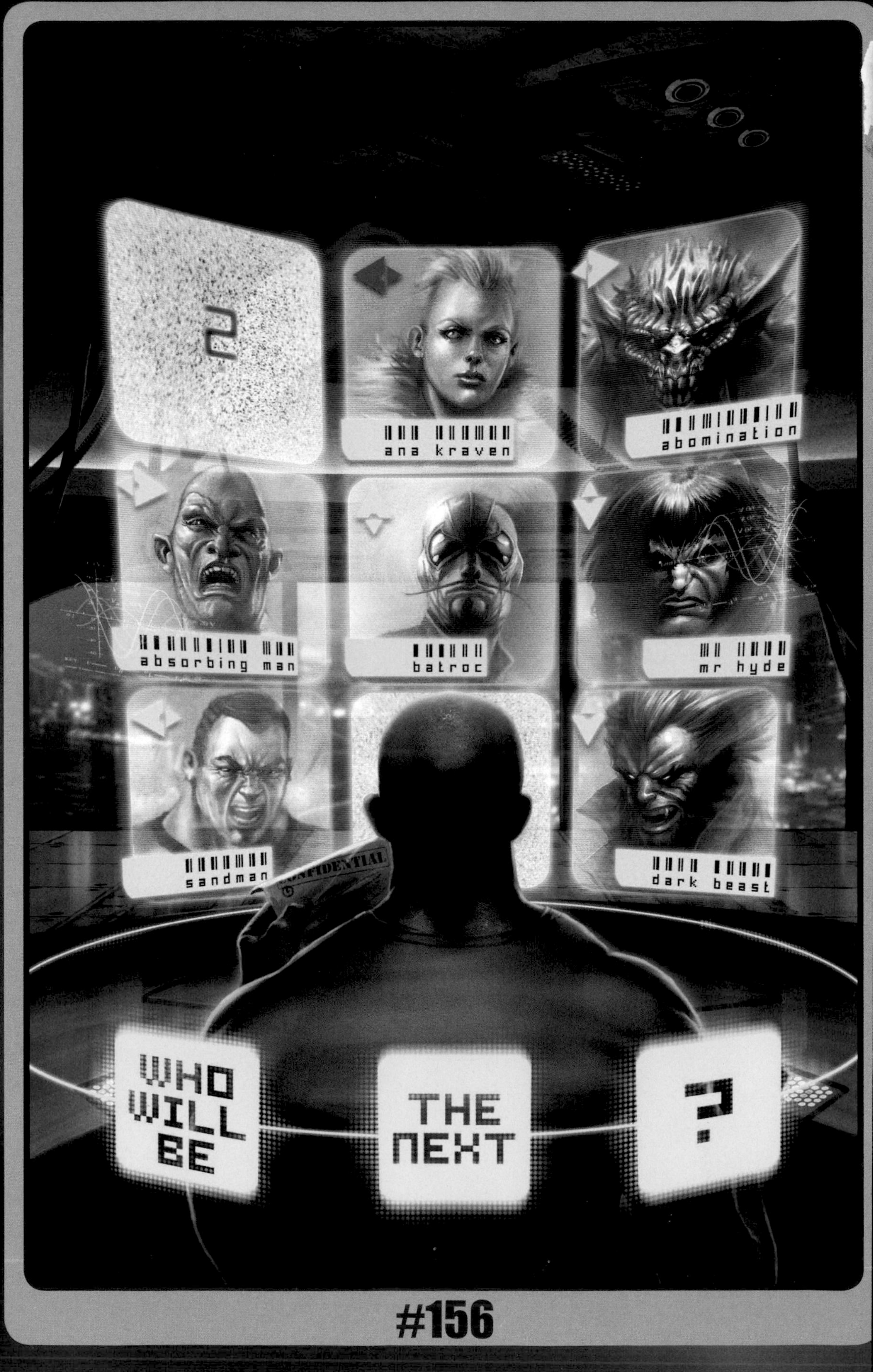
ana kraven
abomination
absorbing man
batroc
mr hyde
sandman
dark beast
CONFIDENTIAL
WHO WILL BE
THE NEXT
?

#156

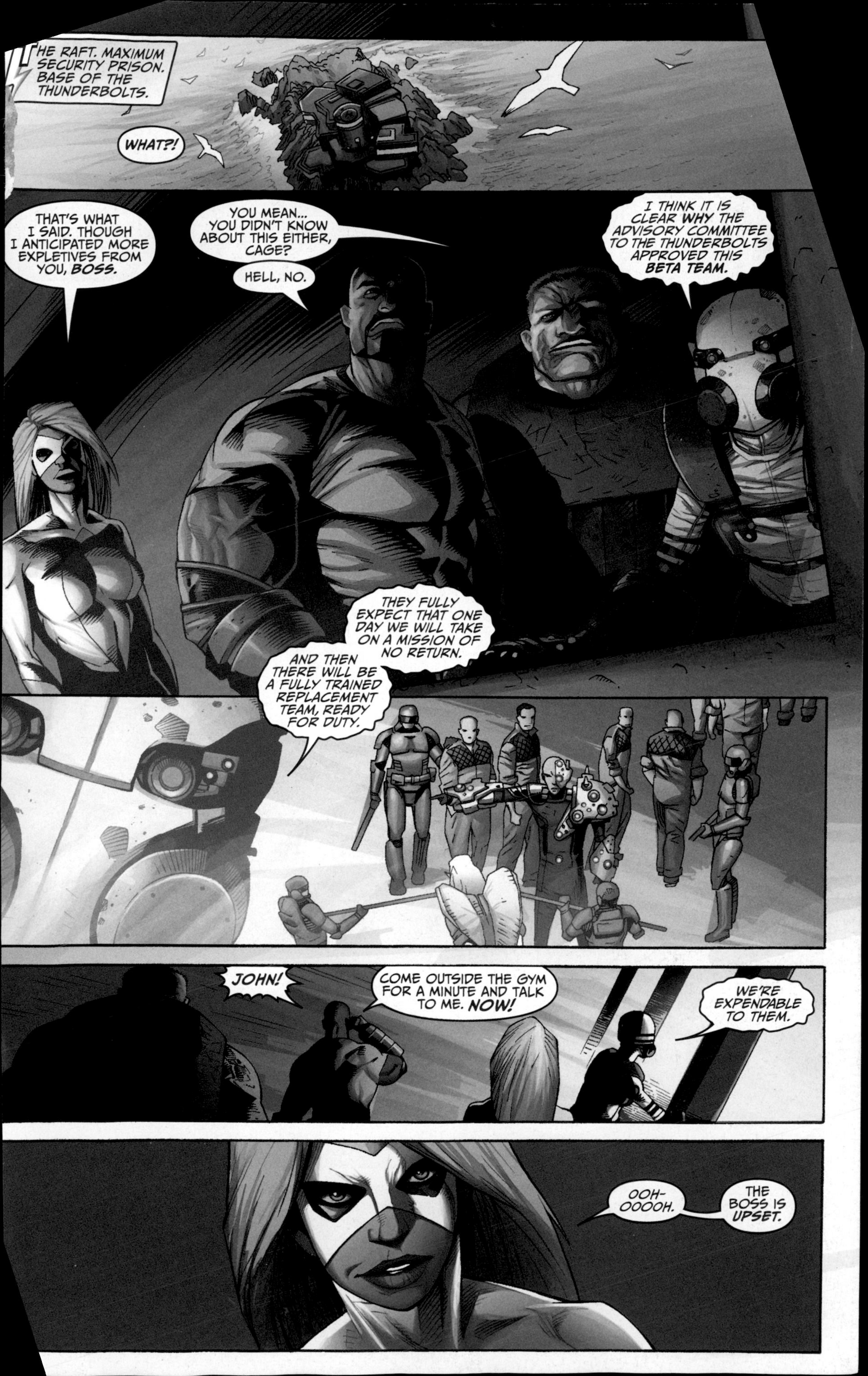
THE RAFT. MAXIMUM SECURITY PRISON. BASE OF THE THUNDERBOLTS.
WHAT?!
THAT'S WHAT I SAID. THOUGH I ANTICIPATED MORE EXPLETIVES FROM YOU, BOSS.
YOU MEAN... YOU DIDN'T KNOW ABOUT THIS EITHER, CAGE?
HELL, NO.
I THINK IT IS CLEAR WHY THE ADVISORY COMMITTEE TO THE THUNDERBOLTS APPROVED THIS BETA TEAM.
THEY FULLY EXPECT THAT ONE DAY WE WILL TAKE ON A MISSION OF NO RETURN.
AND THEN THERE WILL BE A FULLY TRAINED REPLACEMENT TEAM, READY FOR DUTY.
JOHN!
COME OUTSIDE THE GYM FOR A MINUTE AND TALK TO ME. NOW!
WE'RE EXPENDABLE TO THEM.
OOH-OOOOH.
THE BOSS IS UPSET.

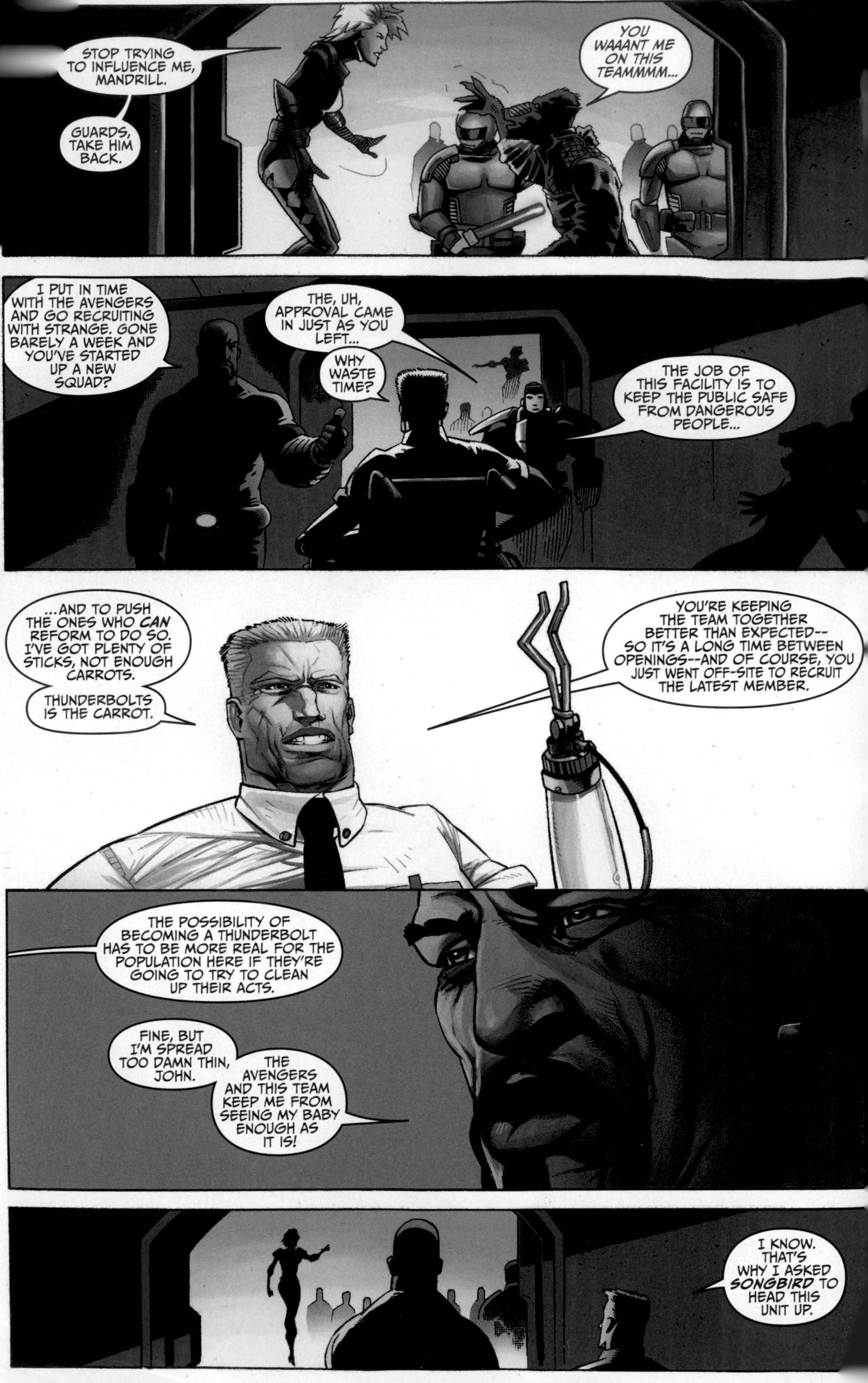
STOP TRYING TO INFLUENCE ME, MANDRILL.
GUARDS, TAKE HIM BACK.
YOU WAAANT ME ON THIS TEAMMMM...
I PUT IN TIME WITH THE AVENGERS AND GO RECRUITING WITH STRANGE. GONE BARELY A WEEK AND YOU'VE STARTED UP A NEW SQUAD?
THE, UH, APPROVAL CAME IN JUST AS YOU LEFT...
WHY WASTE TIME?
THE JOB OF THIS FACILITY IS TO KEEP THE PUBLIC SAFE FROM DANGEROUS PEOPLE...
...AND TO PUSH THE ONES WHO CAN REFORM TO DO SO. I'VE GOT PLENTY OF STICKS, NOT ENOUGH CARROTS.
THUNDERBOLTS IS THE CARROT.
YOU'RE KEEPING THE TEAM TOGETHER BETTER THAN EXPECTED-- SO IT'S A LONG TIME BETWEEN OPENINGS--AND OF COURSE, YOU JUST WENT OFF-SITE TO RECRUIT THE LATEST MEMBER.
THE POSSIBILITY OF BECOMING A THUNDERBOLT HAS TO BE MORE REAL FOR THE POPULATION HERE IF THEY'RE GOING TO TRY TO CLEAN UP THEIR ACTS.
FINE, BUT I'M SPREAD TOO DAMN THIN, JOHN.
THE AVENGERS AND THIS TEAM KEEP ME FROM SEEING MY BABY ENOUGH AS IT IS!
I KNOW. THAT'S WHY I ASKED SONGBIRD TO HEAD THIS UNIT UP.

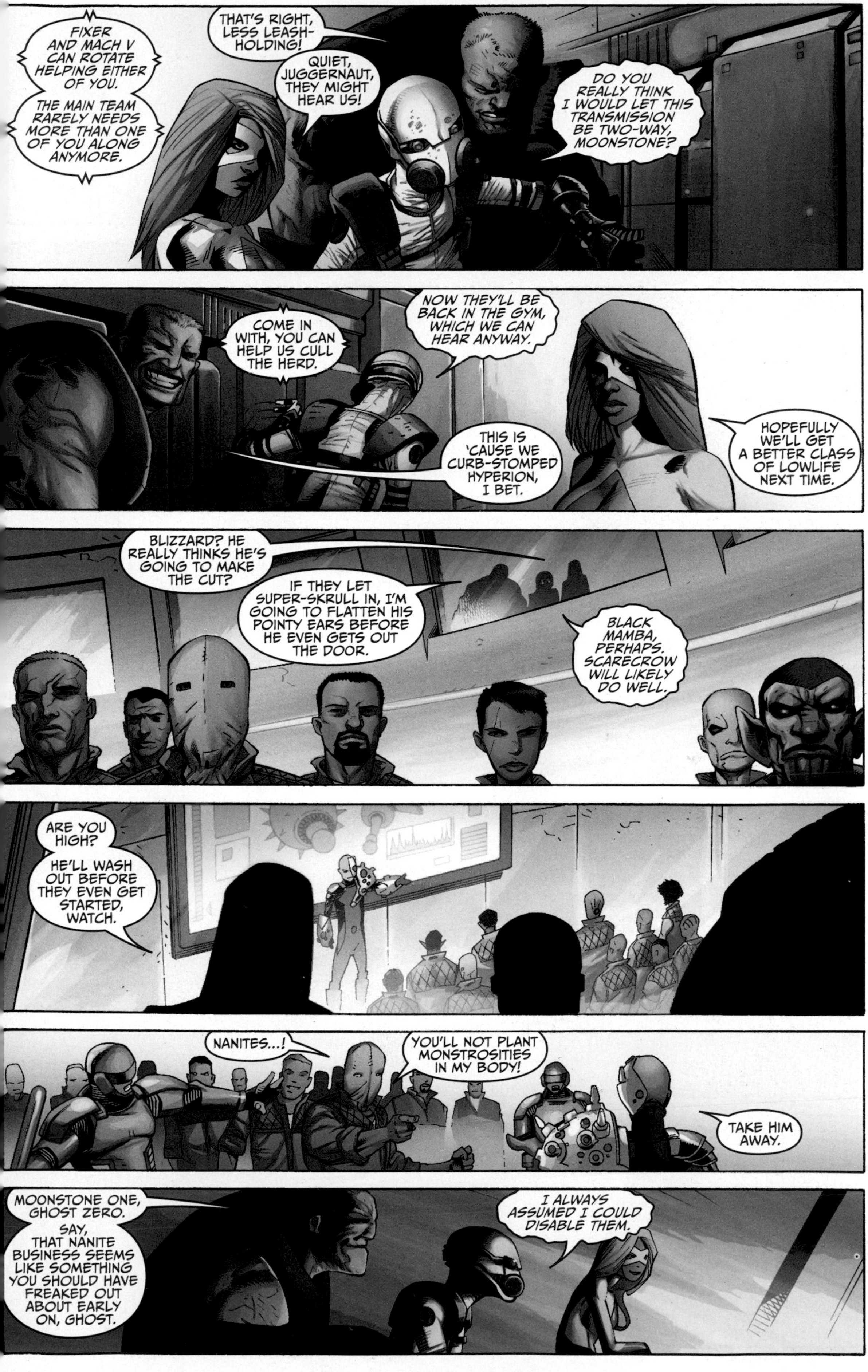
FIXER AND MACH V CAN ROTATE HELPING EITHER OF YOU.
THE MAIN TEAM RARELY NEEDS MORE THAN ONE OF YOU ALONG ANYMORE.
THAT'S RIGHT, LESS LEASH-HOLDING!
QUIET, JUGGERNAUT, THEY MIGHT HEAR US!
DO YOU REALLY THINK I WOULD LET THIS TRANSMISSION BE TWO-WAY, MOONSTONE?
COME IN WITH, YOU CAN HELP US CULL THE HERD.
NOW THEY'LL BE BACK IN THE GYM, WHICH WE CAN HEAR ANYWAY.
THIS IS 'CAUSE WE CURB-STOMPED HYPERION, I BET.
HOPEFULLY WE'LL GET A BETTER CLASS OF LOWLIFE NEXT TIME.
BLIZZARD? HE REALLY THINKS HE'S GOING TO MAKE THE CUT?
IF THEY LET SUPER-SKRULL IN, I'M GOING TO FLATTEN HIS POINTY EARS BEFORE HE EVEN GETS OUT THE DOOR.
BLACK MAMBA, PERHAPS. SCARECROW WILL LIKELY DO WELL.
ARE YOU HIGH?
HE'LL WASH OUT BEFORE THEY EVEN GET STARTED, WATCH.
NANITES...!
YOU'LL NOT PLANT MONSTROSITIES IN MY BODY!
TAKE HIM AWAY.
MOONSTONE ONE, GHOST ZERO.
SAY, THAT NANITE BUSINESS SEEMS LIKE SOMETHING YOU SHOULD HAVE FREAKED OUT ABOUT EARLY ON, GHOST.
I ALWAYS ASSUMED I COULD DISABLE THEM.

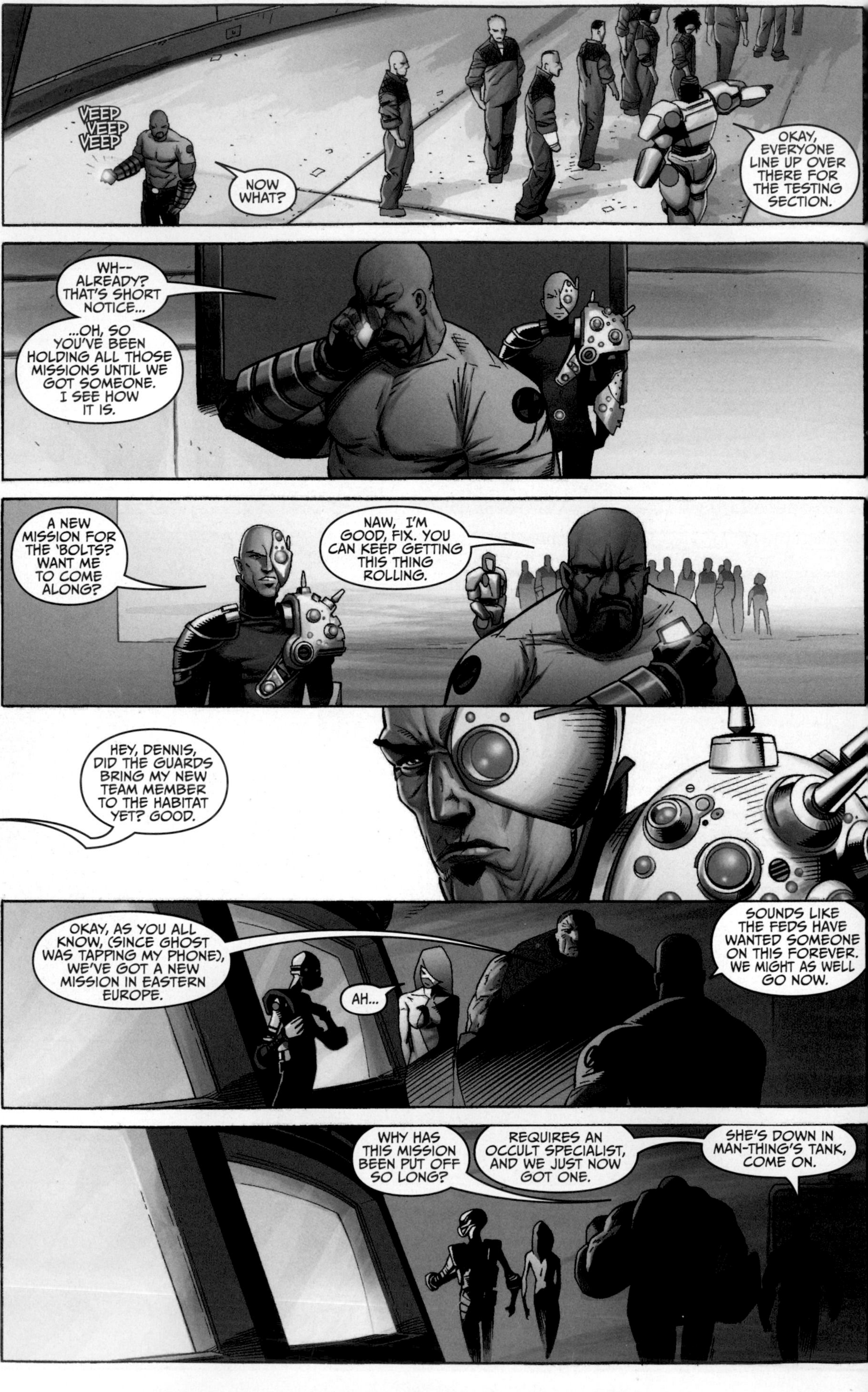
VEEP VEEP VEEP
NOW WHAT?
OKAY, EVERYONE LINE UP OVER THERE FOR THE TESTING SECTION.
WH-- ALREADY? THAT'S SHORT NOTICE...
...OH, SO YOU'VE BEEN HOLDING ALL THOSE MISSIONS UNTIL WE GOT SOMEONE. I SEE HOW IT IS.
A NEW MISSION FOR THE 'BOLTS? WANT ME TO COME ALONG?
NAW, I'M GOOD, FIX. YOU CAN KEEP GETTING THIS THING ROLLING.
HEY, DENNIS, DID THE GUARDS BRING MY NEW TEAM MEMBER TO THE HABITAT YET? GOOD.
OKAY, AS YOU ALL KNOW, (SINCE GHOST WAS TAPPING MY PHONE), WE'VE GOT A NEW MISSION IN EASTERN EUROPE.
AH...
SOUNDS LIKE THE FEDS HAVE WANTED SOMEONE ON THIS FOREVER. WE MIGHT AS WELL GO NOW.
WHY HAS THIS MISSION BEEN PUT OFF SO LONG?
REQUIRES AN OCCULT SPECIALIST, AND WE JUST NOW GOT ONE.
SHE'S DOWN IN MAN-THING'S TANK, COME ON.

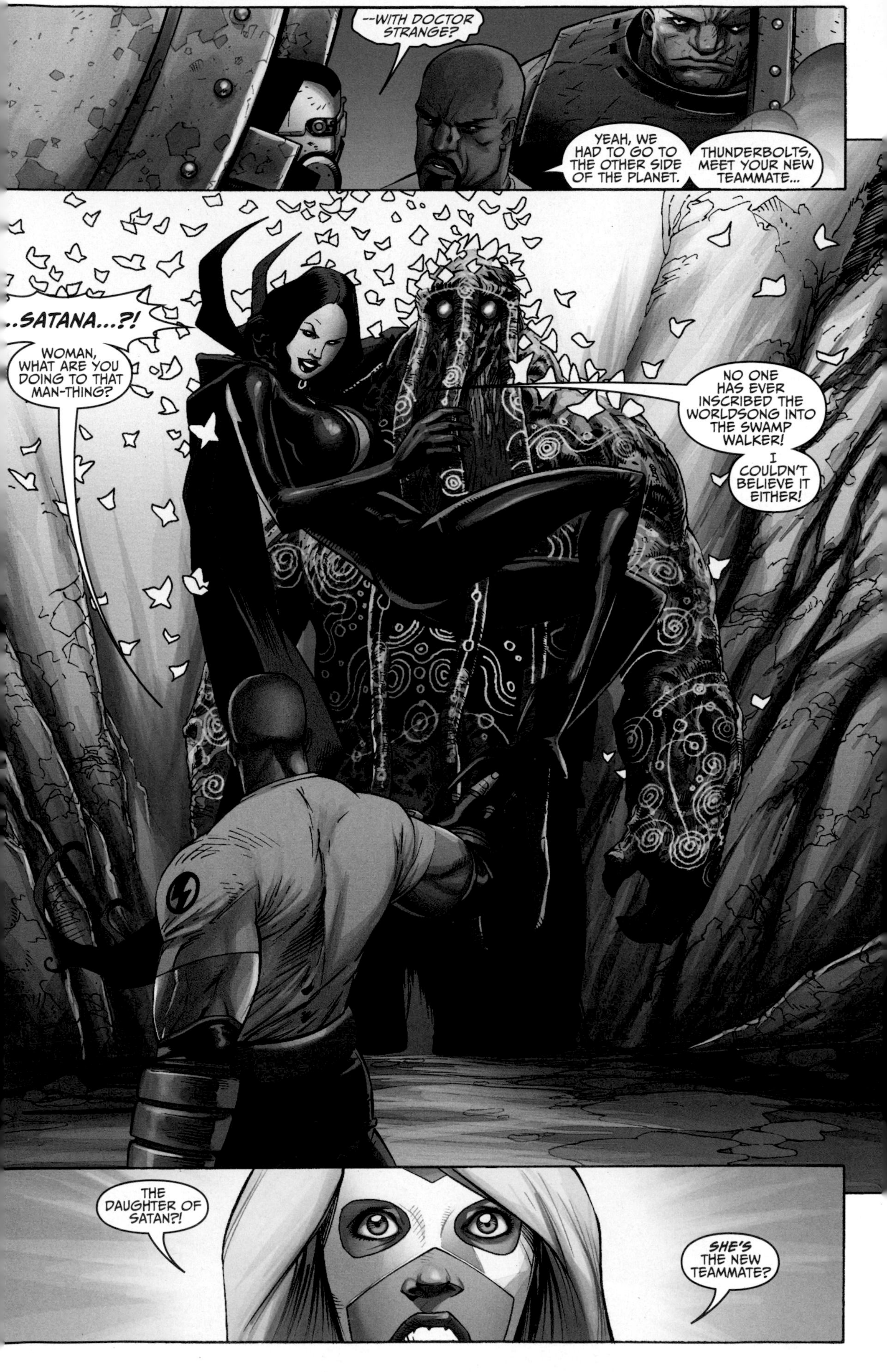
--WITH DOCTOR STRANGE?
YEAH, WE HAD TO GO TO THE OTHER SIDE OF THE PLANET.
THUNDERBOLTS, MEET YOUR NEW TEAMMATE...
..SATANA...?!
WOMAN, WHAT ARE YOU DOING TO THAT MAN-THING?
NO ONE HAS EVER INSCRIBED THE WORLDSONG INTO THE SWAMP WALKER!
I COULDN'T BELIEVE IT EITHER!
THE DAUGHTER OF SATAN?!
SHE'S THE NEW TEAMMATE?

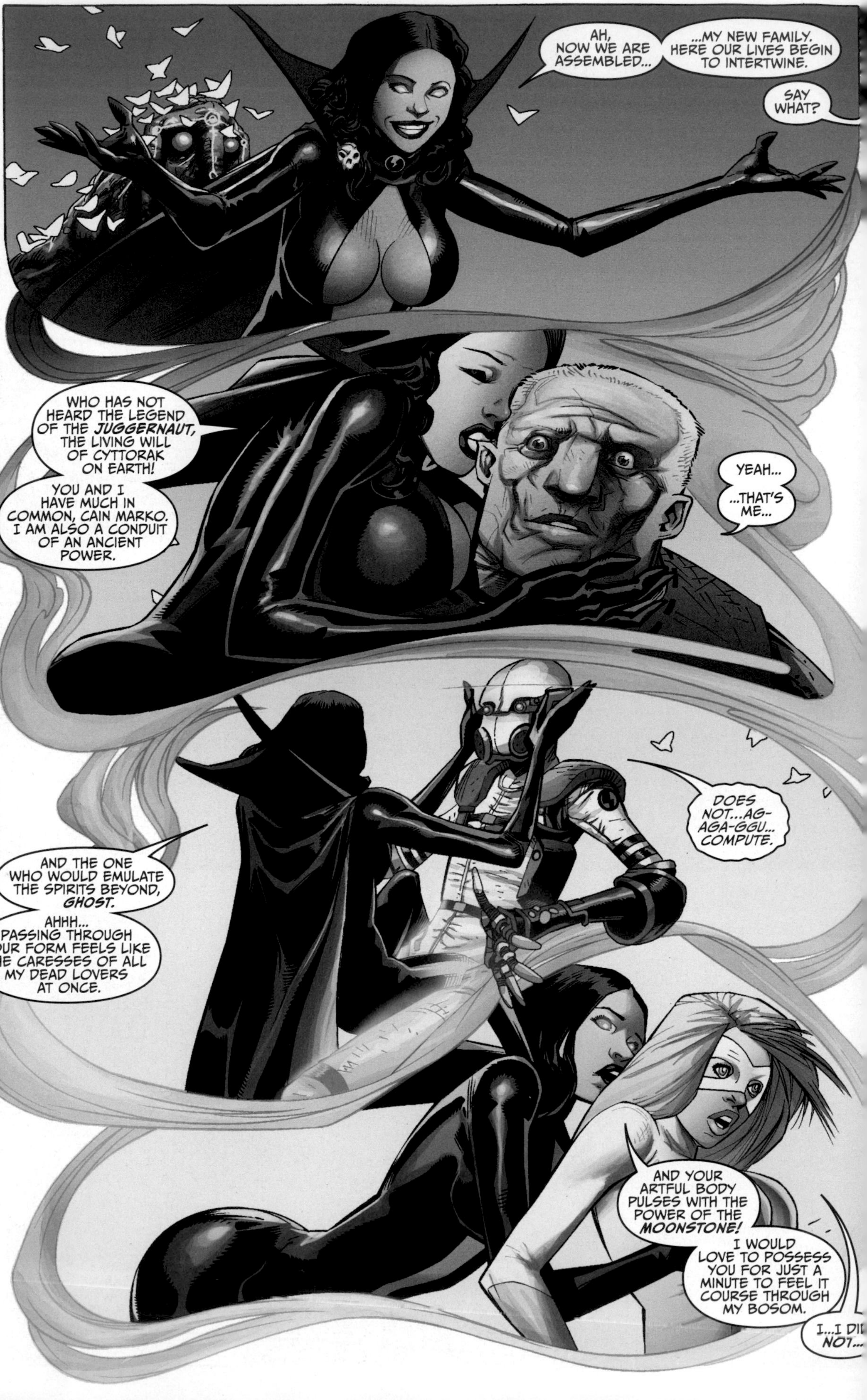
AH, NOW WE ARE ASSEMBLED...
...MY NEW FAMILY. HERE OUR LIVES BEGIN TO INTERTWINE.
SAY WHAT?
WHO HAS NOT HEARD THE LEGEND OF THE JUGGERNAUT, THE LIVING WILL OF CYTTORAK ON EARTH!
YOU AND I HAVE MUCH IN COMMON, CAIN MARKO. I AM ALSO A CONDUIT OF AN ANCIENT POWER.
YEAH...
...THAT'S ME...
DOES NOT...AG-AGA-GGU... COMPUTE.
AND THE ONE WHO WOULD EMULATE THE SPIRITS BEYOND, GHOST.
AHHH... PASSING THROUGH YOUR FORM FEELS LIKE THE CARESSES OF ALL MY DEAD LOVERS AT ONCE.
AND YOUR ARTFUL BODY PULSES WITH THE POWER OF THE MOONSTONE!
I WOULD LOVE TO POSSESS YOU FOR JUST A MINUTE TO FEEL IT COURSE THROUGH MY BOSOM.
I...I DID NOT...

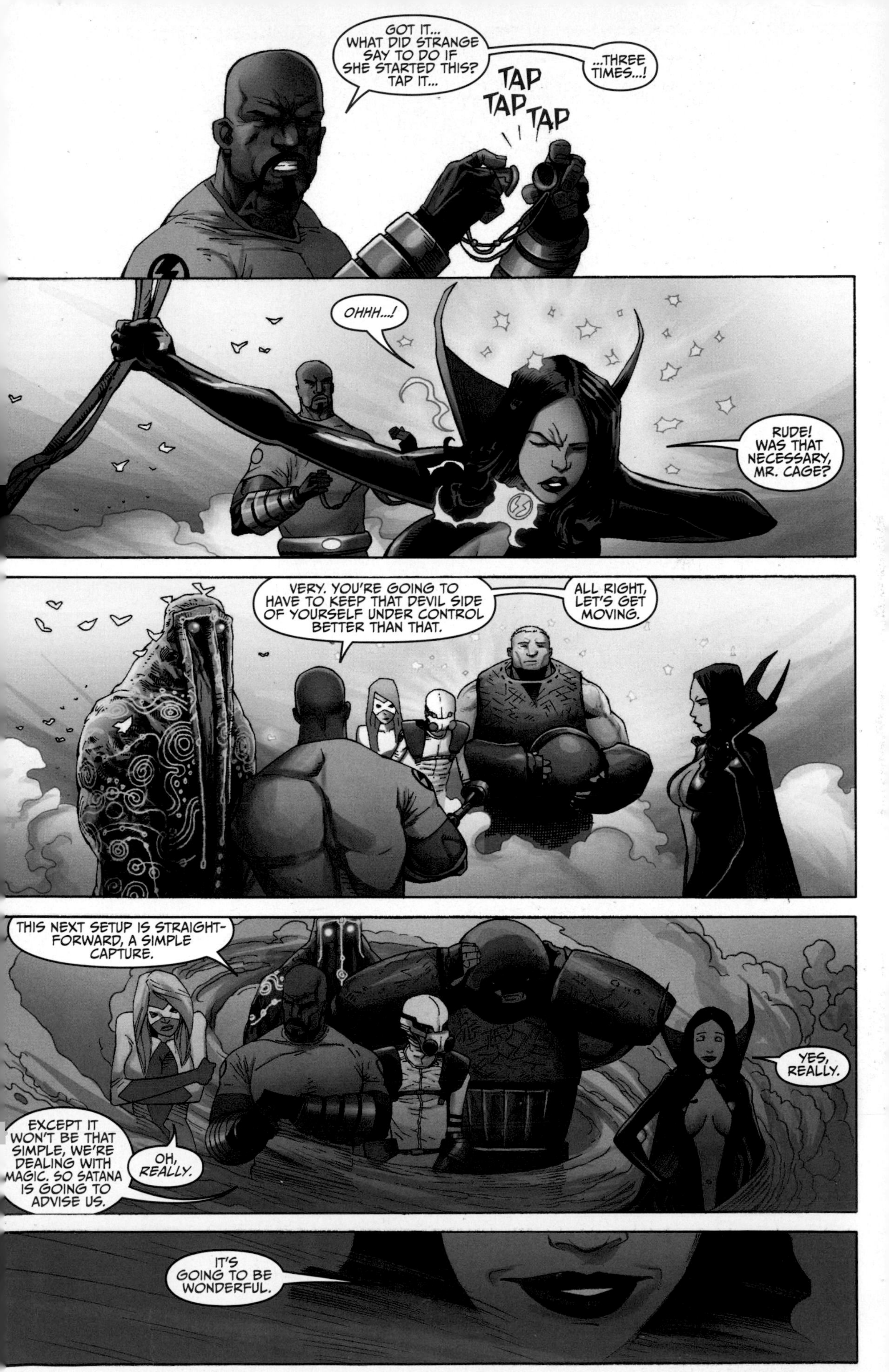
GOT IT... WHAT DID STRANGE SAY TO DO IF SHE STARTED THIS? TAP IT...
...THREE TIMES...!
TAP TAP TAP
OHHH...!
RUDE! WAS THAT NECESSARY, MR. CAGE?
VERY. YOU'RE GOING TO HAVE TO KEEP THAT DEVIL SIDE OF YOURSELF UNDER CONTROL BETTER THAN THAT.
ALL RIGHT, LET'S GET MOVING.
THIS NEXT SETUP IS STRAIGHT-FORWARD, A SIMPLE CAPTURE.
EXCEPT IT WON'T BE THAT SIMPLE, WE'RE DEALING WITH MAGIC. SO SATANA IS GOING TO ADVISE US.
OH, *REALLY*.
YES, REALLY.
IT'S GOING TO BE WONDERFUL.

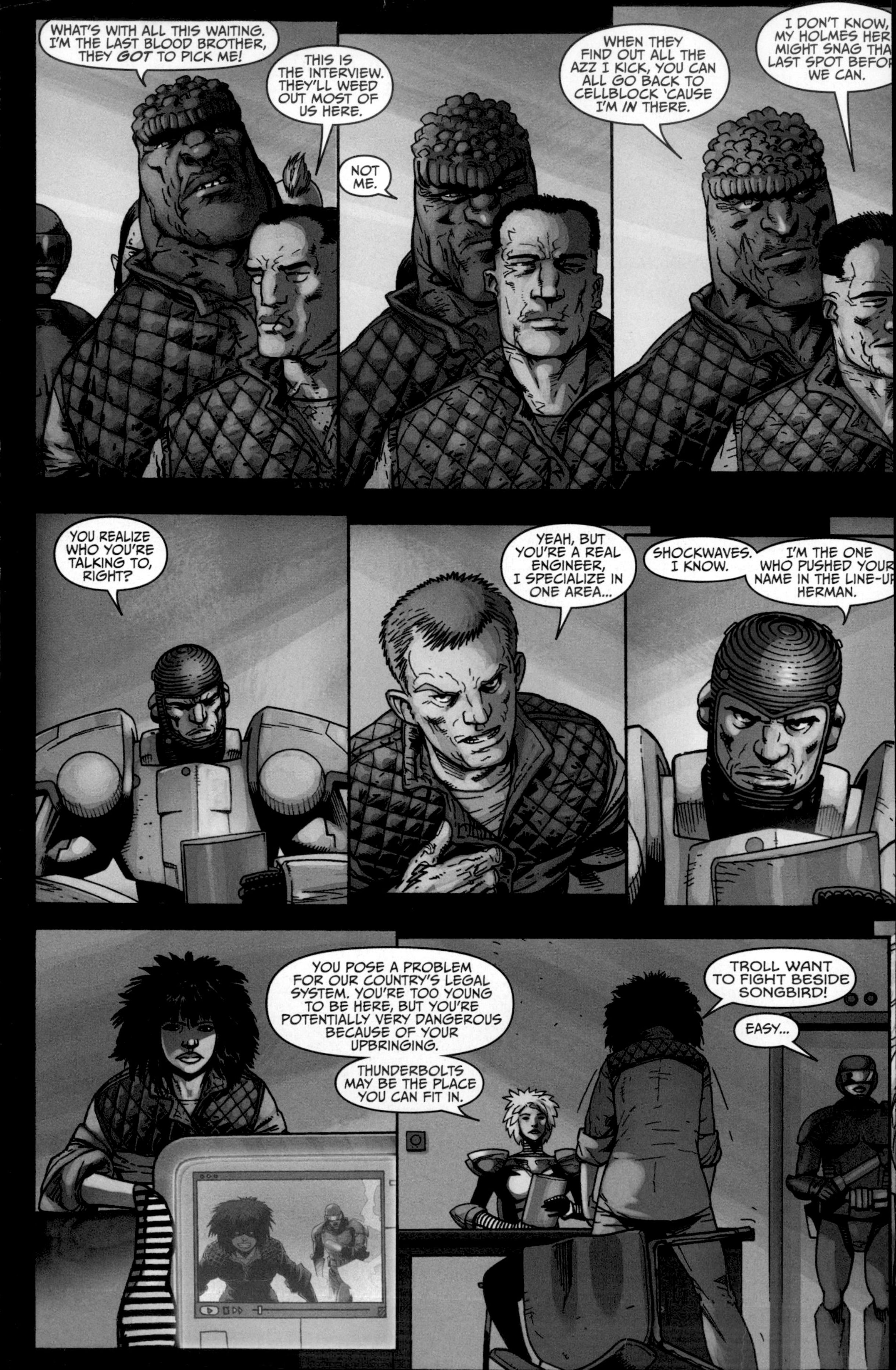
WHAT'S WITH ALL THIS WAITING. I'M THE LAST BLOOD BROTHER, THEY GOT TO PICK ME!
THIS IS THE INTERVIEW. THEY'LL WEED OUT MOST OF US HERE.
NOT ME.
WHEN THEY FIND OUT ALL THE AZZ I KICK, YOU CAN ALL GO BACK TO CELLBLOCK 'CAUSE I'M IN THERE.
I DON'T KNOW, MY HOLMES HER MIGHT SNAG THA LAST SPOT BEFOR WE CAN.
YOU REALIZE WHO YOU'RE TALKING TO, RIGHT?
YEAH, BUT YOU'RE A REAL ENGINEER, I SPECIALIZE IN ONE AREA...
SHOCKWAVES. I KNOW.
I'M THE ONE WHO PUSHED YOUR NAME IN THE LINE-UP HERMAN.
YOU POSE A PROBLEM FOR OUR COUNTRY'S LEGAL SYSTEM. YOU'RE TOO YOUNG TO BE HERE, BUT YOU'RE POTENTIALLY VERY DANGEROUS BECAUSE OF YOUR UPBRINGING.
THUNDERBOLTS MAY BE THE PLACE YOU CAN FIT IN.
TROLL WANT TO FIGHT BESIDE SONGBIRD!
EASY...

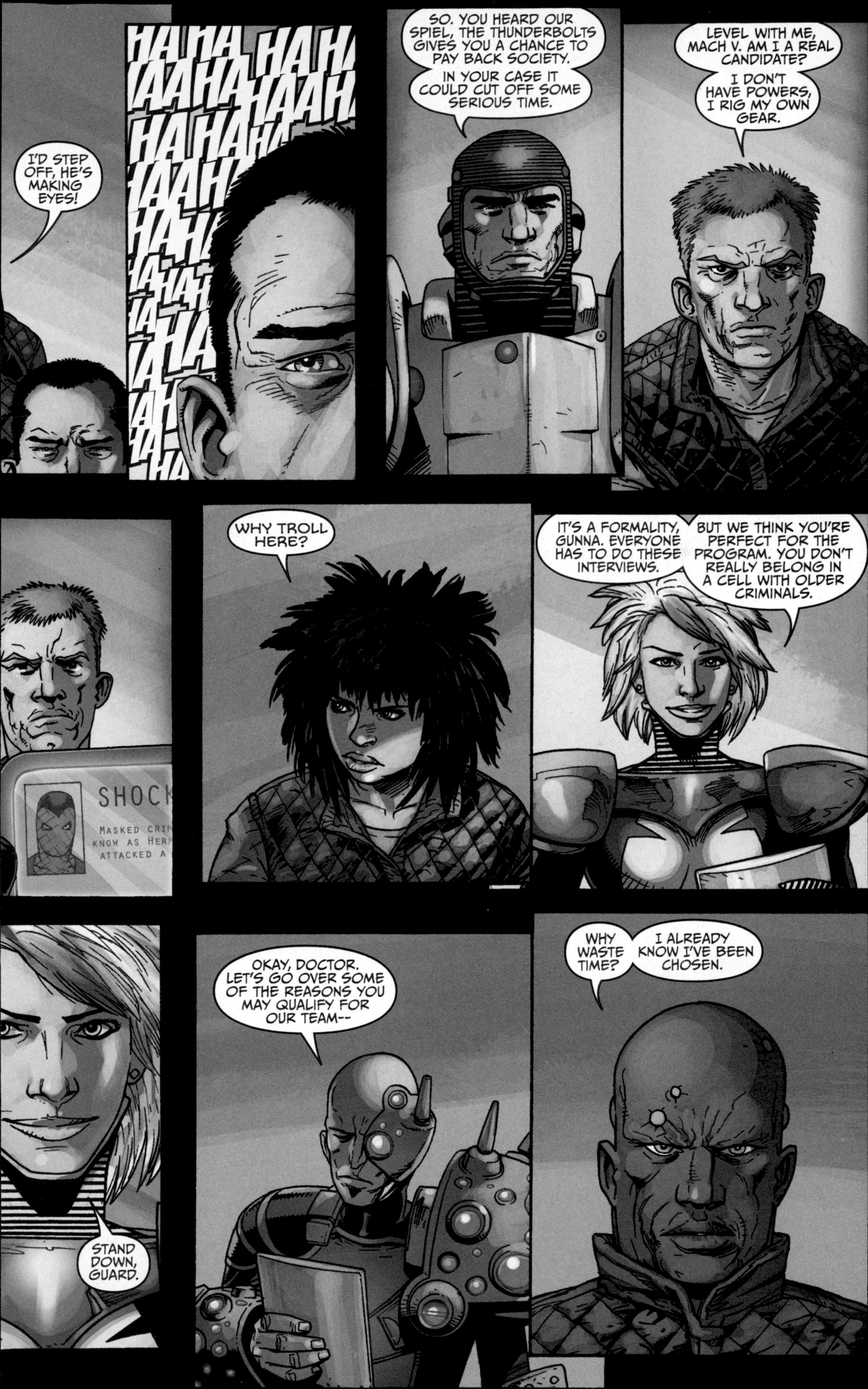
I'D STEP OFF, HE'S MAKING EYES!
HA HA HA HA HA HA HAAHA HA HA HA HA HAH HA HA HA HA HA HA
SO. YOU HEARD OUR SPIEL, THE THUNDERBOLTS GIVES YOU A CHANCE TO PAY BACK SOCIETY.
IN YOUR CASE IT COULD CUT OFF SOME SERIOUS TIME.
LEVEL WITH ME, MACH V. AM I A REAL CANDIDATE?
I DON'T HAVE POWERS, I RIG MY OWN GEAR.
SHOCK
MASKED CRIM
KNOW AS HERM
ATTACKED A
WHY TROLL HERE?
IT'S A FORMALITY, GUNNA. EVERYONE HAS TO DO THESE INTERVIEWS.
BUT WE THINK YOU'RE PERFECT FOR THE PROGRAM. YOU DON'T REALLY BELONG IN A CELL WITH OLDER CRIMINALS.
STAND DOWN, GUARD.
OKAY, DOCTOR. LET'S GO OVER SOME OF THE REASONS YOU MAY QUALIFY FOR OUR TEAM--
WHY WASTE TIME?
I ALREADY KNOW I'VE BEEN CHOSEN.

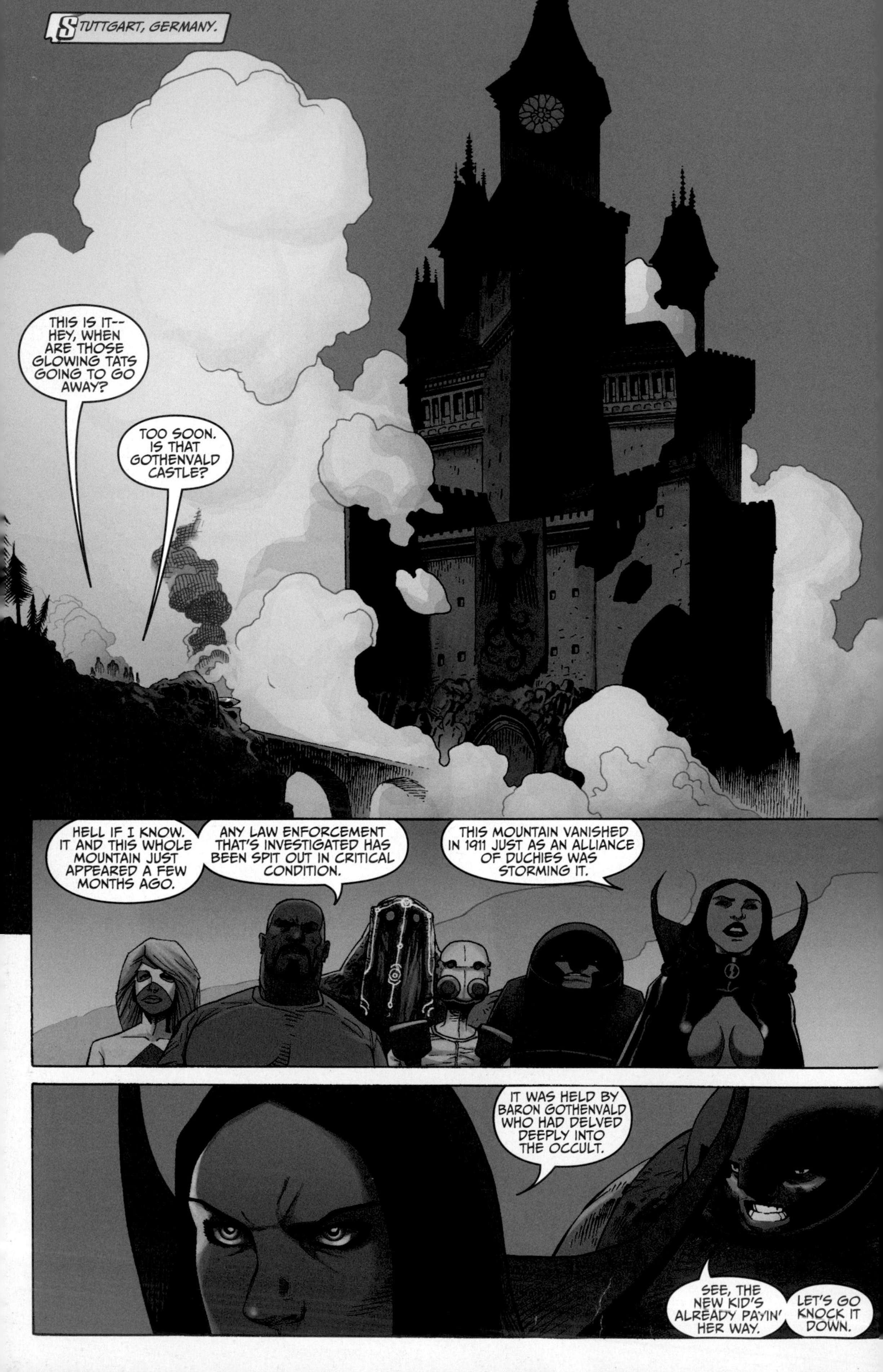
STUTTGART, GERMANY.
THIS IS IT-- HEY, WHEN ARE THOSE GLOWING TATS GOING TO GO AWAY?
TOO SOON. IS THAT GOTHENVALD CASTLE?
HELL IF I KNOW. IT AND THIS WHOLE MOUNTAIN JUST APPEARED A FEW MONTHS AGO.
ANY LAW ENFORCEMENT THAT'S INVESTIGATED HAS BEEN SPIT OUT IN CRITICAL CONDITION.
THIS MOUNTAIN VANISHED IN 1911 JUST AS AN ALLIANCE OF DUCHIES WAS STORMING IT.
IT WAS HELD BY BARON GOTHENVALD WHO HAD DELVED DEEPLY INTO THE OCCULT.
SEE, THE NEW KID'S ALREADY PAYIN' HER WAY.
LET'S GO KNOCK IT DOWN.

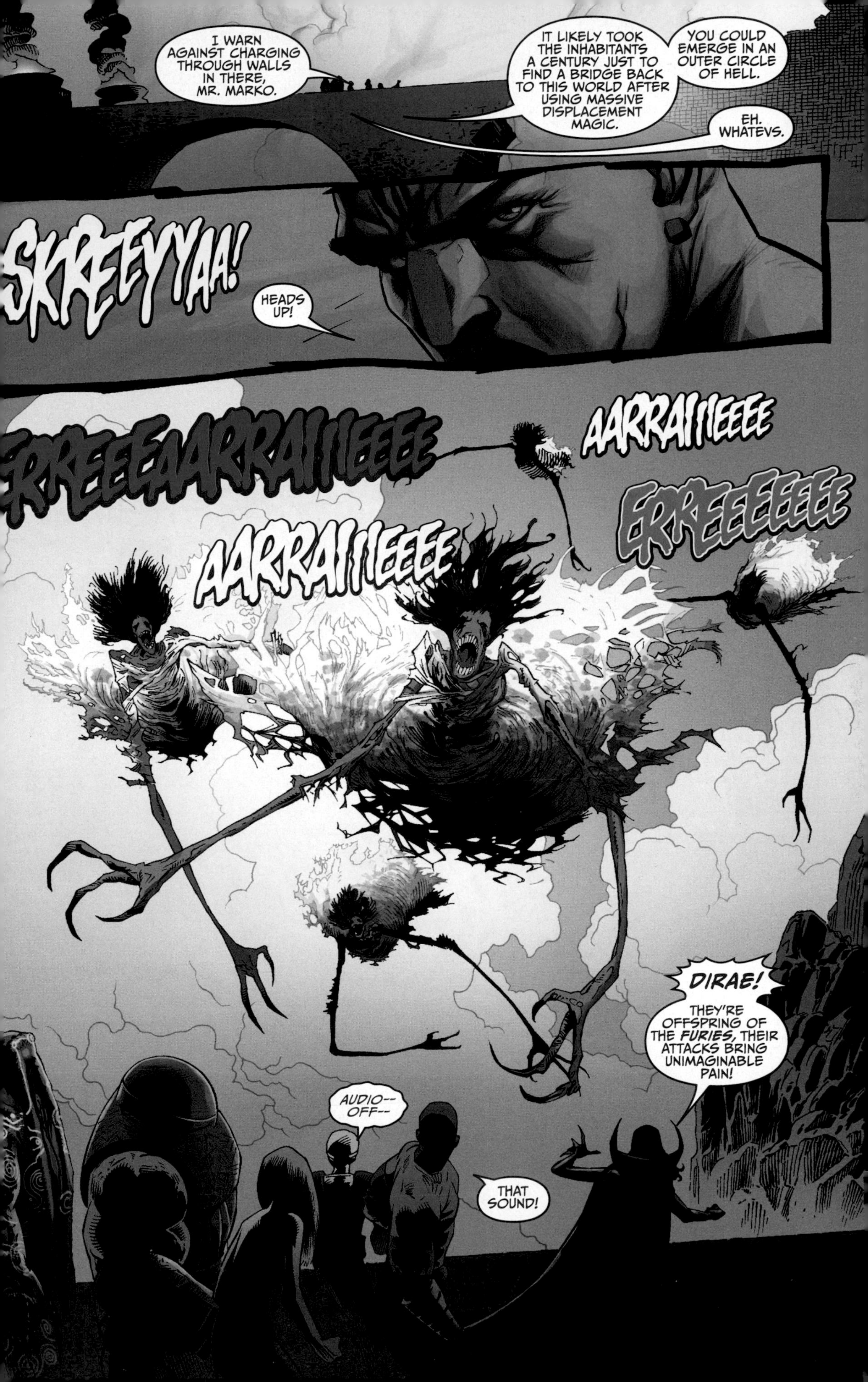
I WARN AGAINST CHARGING THROUGH WALLS IN THERE, MR. MARKO.
IT LIKELY TOOK THE INHABITANTS A CENTURY JUST TO FIND A BRIDGE BACK TO THIS WORLD AFTER USING MASSIVE DISPLACEMENT MAGIC.
YOU COULD EMERGE IN AN OUTER CIRCLE OF HELL.
EH. WHATEVS.
SKREEYYAA!
HEADS UP!
ERREEEAARRAIIIEEEE
AARRAIIIEEEE
ERREEEEEEEE
AARRAIIIEEEE
DIRAE!
THEY'RE OFFSPRING OF THE *FURIES*, THEIR ATTACKS BRING UNIMAGINABLE PAIN!
AUDIO-- OFF--
THAT SOUND!

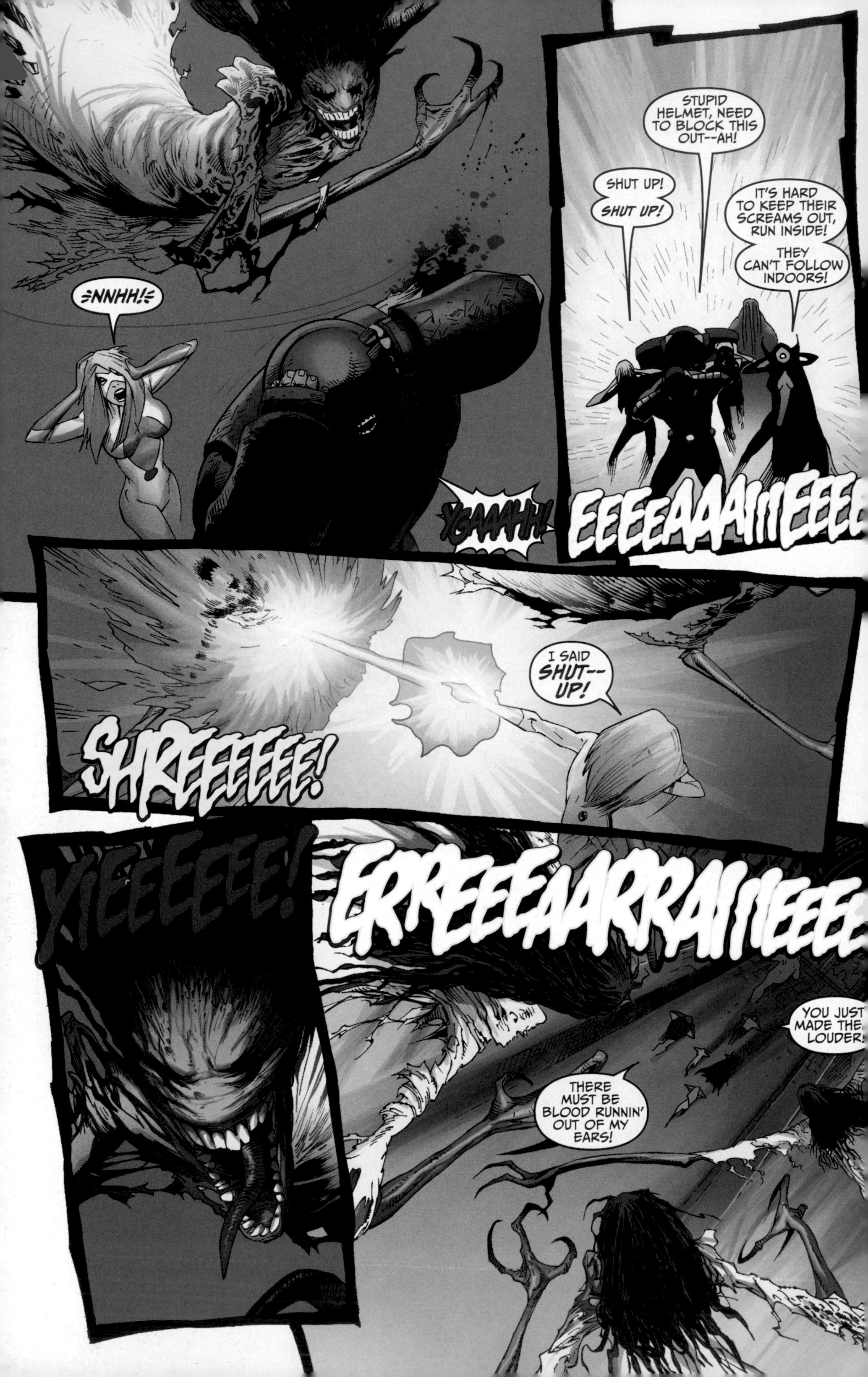

NNHH!
YGAAAHH!
STUPID HELMET, NEED TO BLOCK THIS OUT--AH!
SHUT UP!
SHUT UP!
IT'S HARD TO KEEP THEIR SCREAMS OUT, RUN INSIDE!
THEY CAN'T FOLLOW INDOORS!
EEEEAAAIIIEEEE
I SAID SHUT-- UP!
SHREEEEEEE!
YIEEEEEE!
ERREEEAARRAIIIEEEE
YOU JUST MADE THE LOUDER!
THERE MUST BE BLOOD RUNNIN' OUT OF MY EARS!

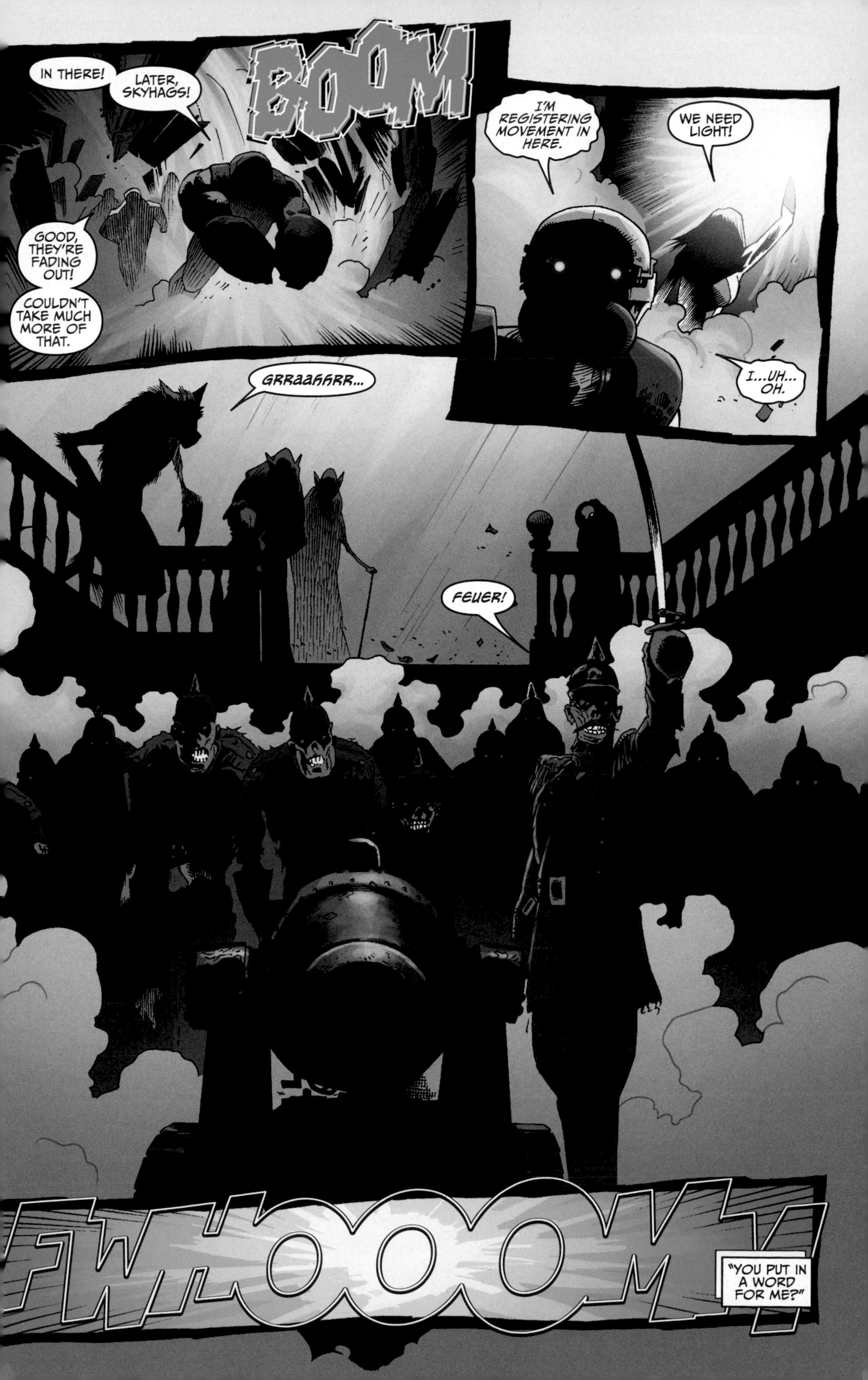
IN THERE!
LATER, SKYHAGS!
BOOM
GOOD, THEY'RE FADING OUT!
COULDN'T TAKE MUCH MORE OF THAT.
I'M REGISTERING MOVEMENT IN HERE.
WE NEED LIGHT!
I...UH... OH.
GRRAAHHRR...
FEUER!
FWHOOOOM
"YOU PUT IN A WORD FOR ME?"

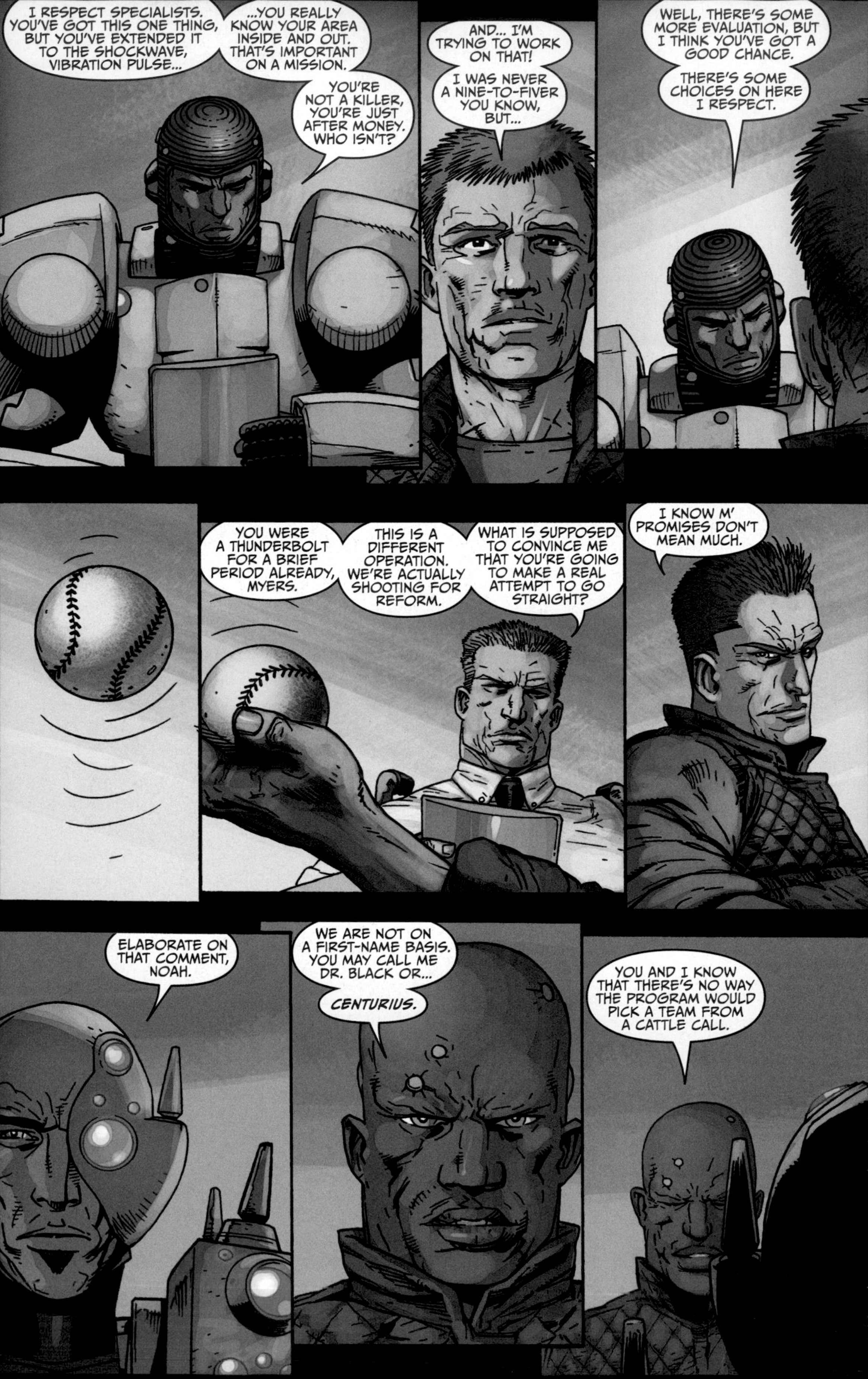
I RESPECT SPECIALISTS. YOU'VE GOT THIS ONE THING, BUT YOU'VE EXTENDED IT TO THE SHOCKWAVE, VIBRATION PULSE...
...YOU REALLY KNOW YOUR AREA INSIDE AND OUT. THAT'S IMPORTANT ON A MISSION.
YOU'RE NOT A KILLER, YOU'RE JUST AFTER MONEY. WHO ISN'T?
AND... I'M TRYING TO WORK ON THAT!
I WAS NEVER A NINE-TO-FIVER YOU KNOW, BUT...
WELL, THERE'S SOME MORE EVALUATION, BUT I THINK YOU'VE GOT A GOOD CHANCE.
THERE'S SOME CHOICES ON HERE I RESPECT.
YOU WERE A THUNDERBOLT FOR A BRIEF PERIOD ALREADY, MYERS.
THIS IS A DIFFERENT OPERATION. WE'RE ACTUALLY SHOOTING FOR REFORM.
WHAT IS SUPPOSED TO CONVINCE ME THAT YOU'RE GOING TO MAKE A REAL ATTEMPT TO GO STRAIGHT?
I KNOW M' PROMISES DON'T MEAN MUCH.
ELABORATE ON THAT COMMENT, NOAH.
WE ARE NOT ON A FIRST-NAME BASIS. YOU MAY CALL ME DR. BLACK OR...
CENTURIUS.
YOU AND I KNOW THAT THERE'S NO WAY THE PROGRAM WOULD PICK A TEAM FROM A CATTLE CALL.

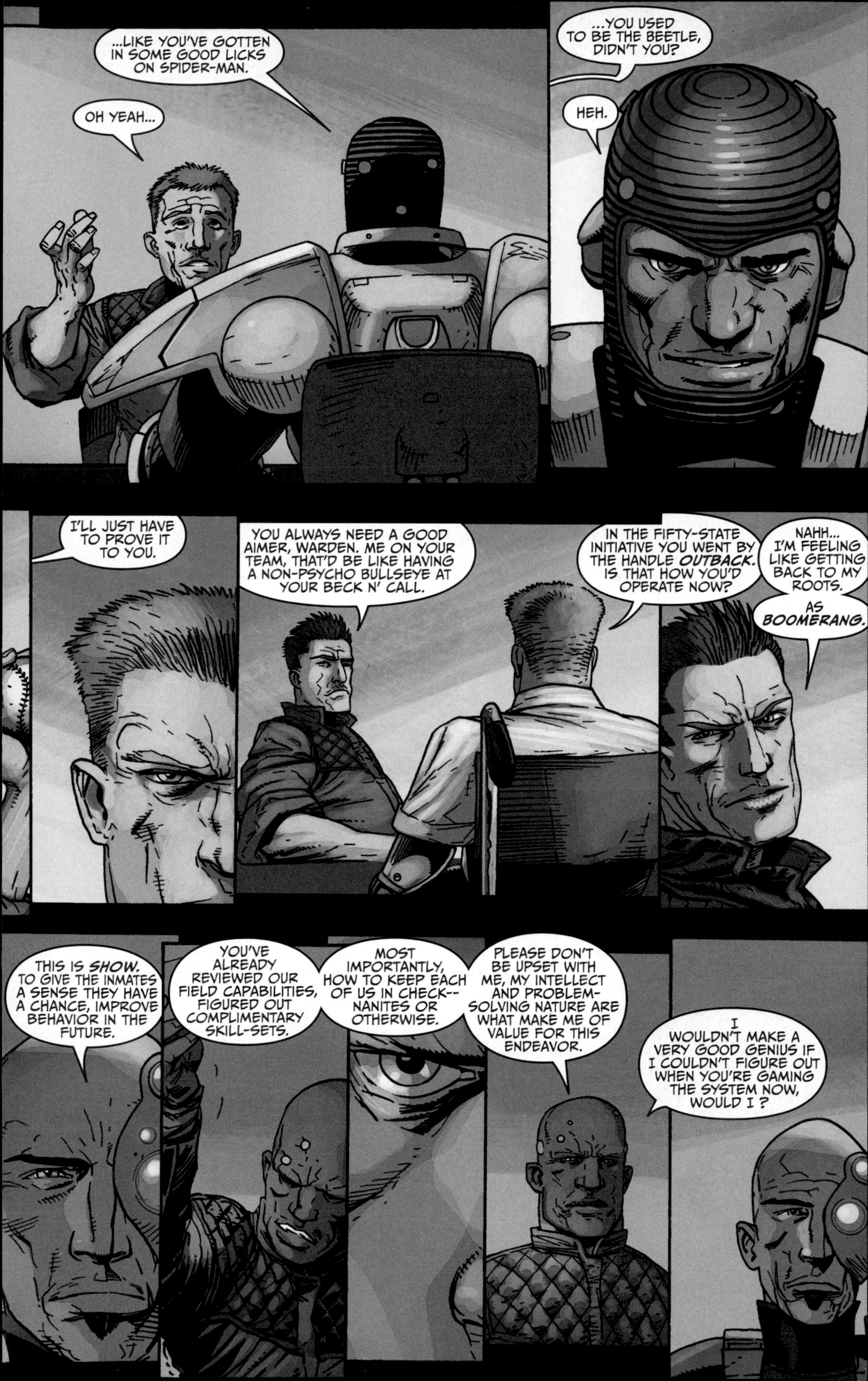
...LIKE YOU'VE GOTTEN IN SOME GOOD LICKS ON SPIDER-MAN.
OH YEAH...
...YOU USED TO BE THE BEETLE, DIDN'T YOU?
HEH.
I'LL JUST HAVE TO PROVE IT TO YOU.
YOU ALWAYS NEED A GOOD AIMER, WARDEN. ME ON YOUR TEAM, THAT'D BE LIKE HAVING A NON-PSYCHO BULLSEYE AT YOUR BECK N' CALL.
IN THE FIFTY-STATE INITIATIVE YOU WENT BY THE HANDLE OUTBACK. IS THAT HOW YOU'D OPERATE NOW?
NAHH... I'M FEELING LIKE GETTING BACK TO MY ROOTS.
AS BOOMERANG.
THIS IS SHOW. TO GIVE THE INMATES A SENSE THEY HAVE A CHANCE, IMPROVE BEHAVIOR IN THE FUTURE.
YOU'VE ALREADY REVIEWED OUR FIELD CAPABILITIES, FIGURED OUT COMPLIMENTARY SKILL-SETS.
MOST IMPORTANTLY, HOW TO KEEP EACH OF US IN CHECK-- NANITES OR OTHERWISE.
PLEASE DON'T BE UPSET WITH ME, MY INTELLECT AND PROBLEM-SOLVING NATURE ARE WHAT MAKE ME OF VALUE FOR THIS ENDEAVOR.
I WOULDN'T MAKE A VERY GOOD GENIUS IF I COULDN'T FIGURE OUT WHEN YOU'RE GAMING THE SYSTEM NOW, WOULD I ?

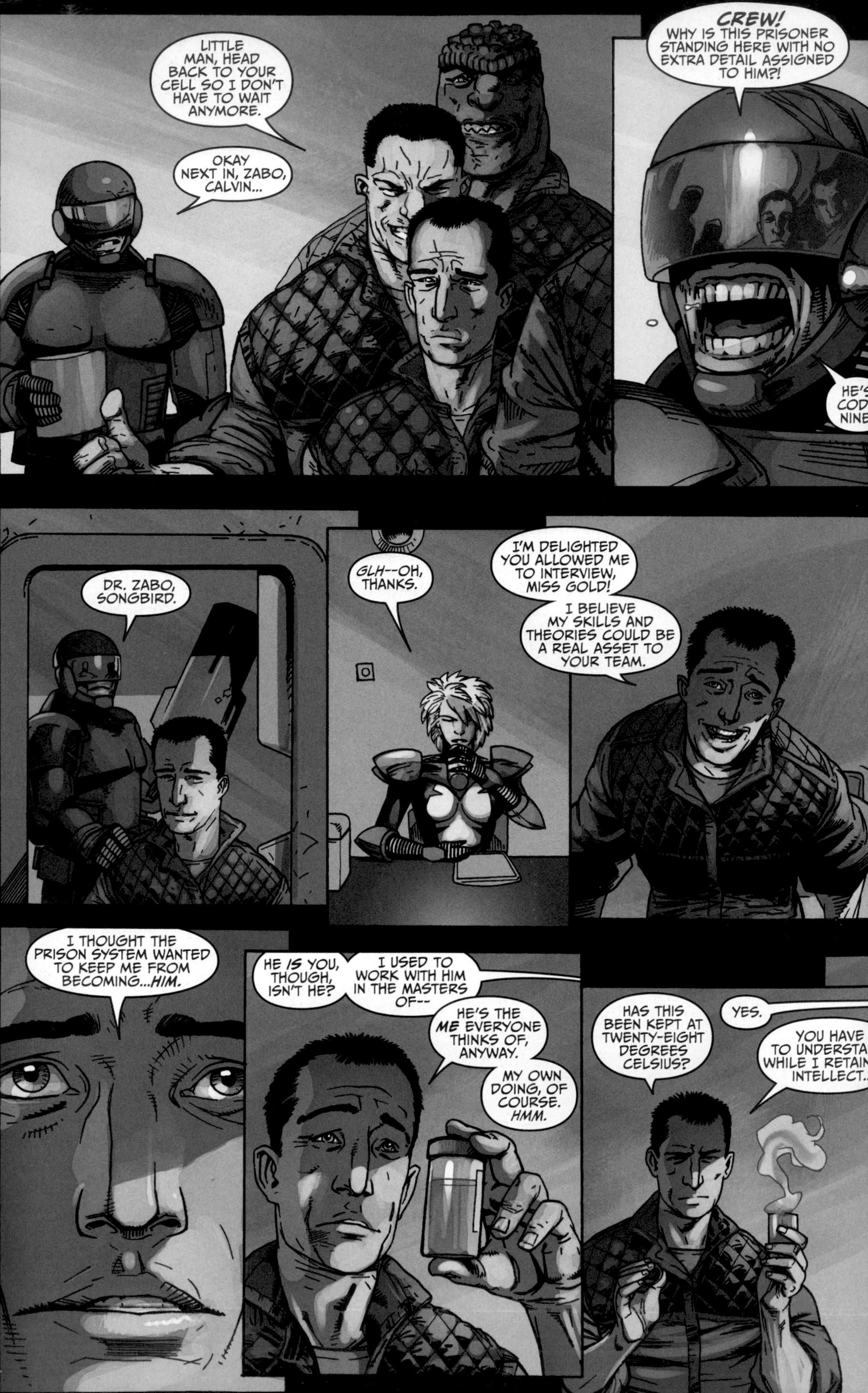

LITTLE MAN, HEAD BACK TO YOUR CELL SO I DON'T HAVE TO WAIT ANYMORE.
OKAY NEXT IN, ZABO, CALVIN...
CREW! WHY IS THIS PRISONER STANDING HERE WITH NO EXTRA DETAIL ASSIGNED TO HIM?!
DR. ZABO, SONGBIRD.
GLH--OH, THANKS.
I'M DELIGHTED YOU ALLOWED ME TO INTERVIEW, MISS GOLD!
I BELIEVE MY SKILLS AND THEORIES COULD BE A REAL ASSET TO YOUR TEAM.
I THOUGHT THE PRISON SYSTEM WANTED TO KEEP ME FROM BECOMING...HIM.
HE IS YOU, THOUGH, ISN'T HE?
I USED TO WORK WITH HIM IN THE MASTERS OF--
HE'S THE ME EVERYONE THINKS OF, ANYWAY.
MY OWN DOING, OF COURSE. HMM.
HAS THIS BEEN KEPT AT TWENTY-EIGHT DEGREES CELSIUS?
YES.

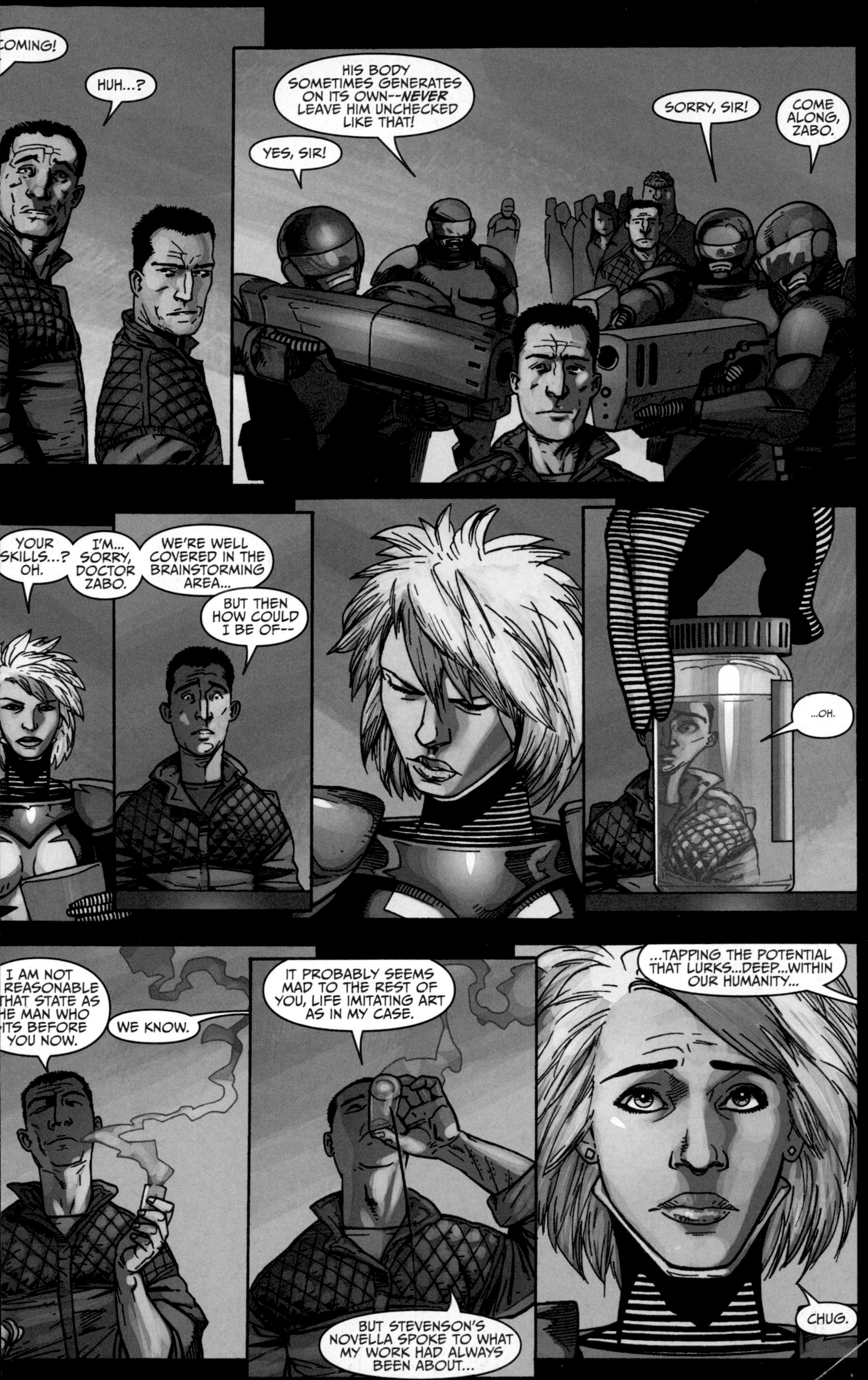

COMING!
HUH...?
HIS BODY SOMETIMES GENERATES ON ITS OWN--NEVER LEAVE HIM UNCHECKED LIKE THAT!
YES, SIR!
SORRY, SIR!
COME ALONG, ZABO.
YOUR SKILLS...? OH.
I'M... SORRY, DOCTOR ZABO.
WE'RE WELL COVERED IN THE BRAINSTORMING AREA...
BUT THEN HOW COULD I BE OF--
...OH.
I AM NOT REASONABLE THAT STATE AS HE MAN WHO ITS BEFORE YOU NOW.
WE KNOW.
IT PROBABLY SEEMS MAD TO THE REST OF YOU, LIFE IMITATING ART AS IN MY CASE.
BUT STEVENSON'S NOVELLA SPOKE TO WHAT MY WORK HAD ALWAYS BEEN ABOUT...
...TAPPING THE POTENTIAL THAT LURKS...DEEP...WITHIN OUR HUMANITY...
CHUG.

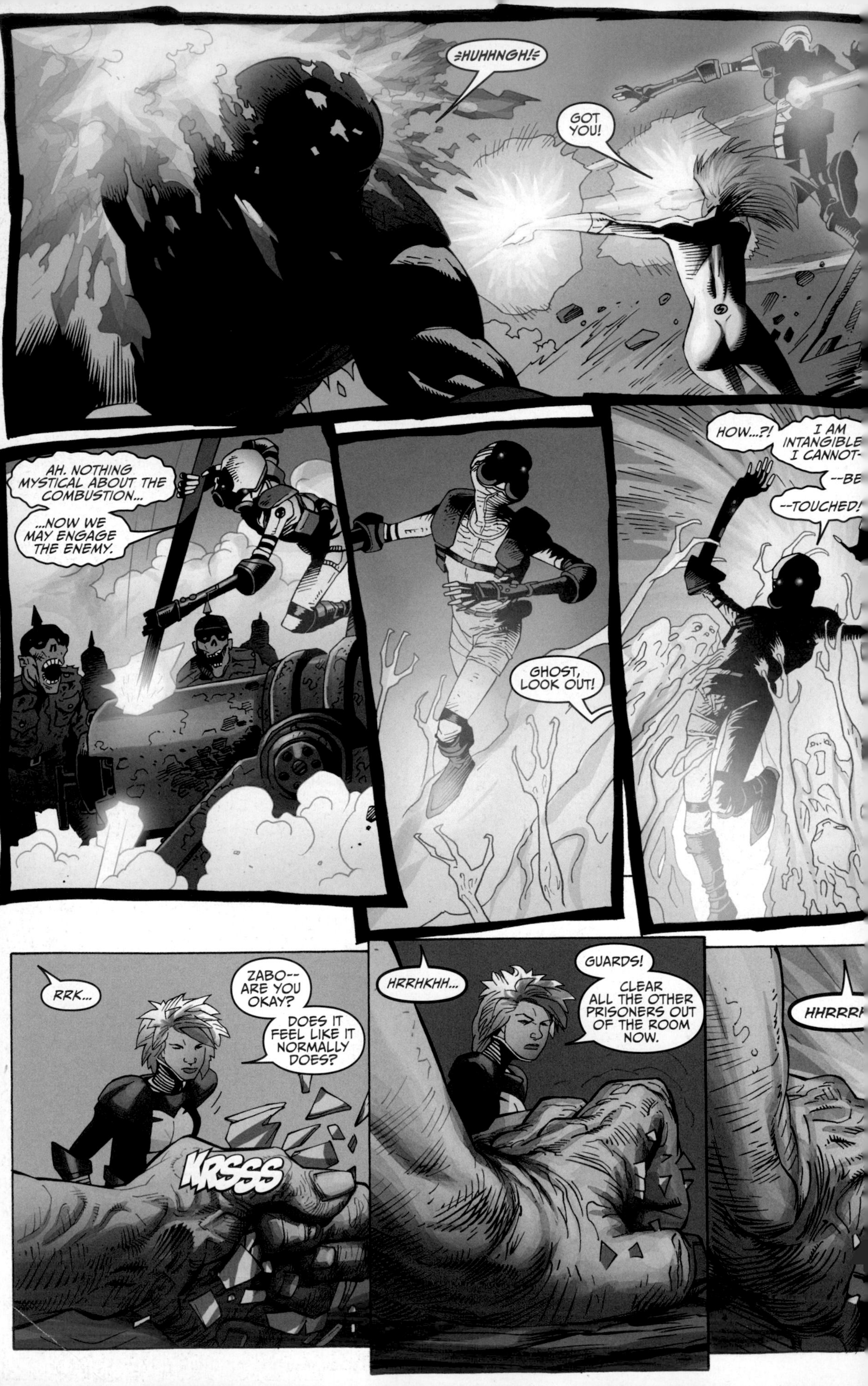
HUHHNGH!
GOT YOU!
AH. NOTHING MYSTICAL ABOUT THE COMBUSTION...
...NOW WE MAY ENGAGE THE ENEMY.
GHOST, LOOK OUT!
HOW...?!
I AM INTANGIBLE I CANNOT-
--BE
--TOUCHED!
RRK...
ZABO-- ARE YOU OKAY?
DOES IT FEEL LIKE IT NORMALLY DOES?
KRSSS
HRRHKHH...
GUARDS!
CLEAR ALL THE OTHER PRISONERS OUT OF THE ROOM NOW.

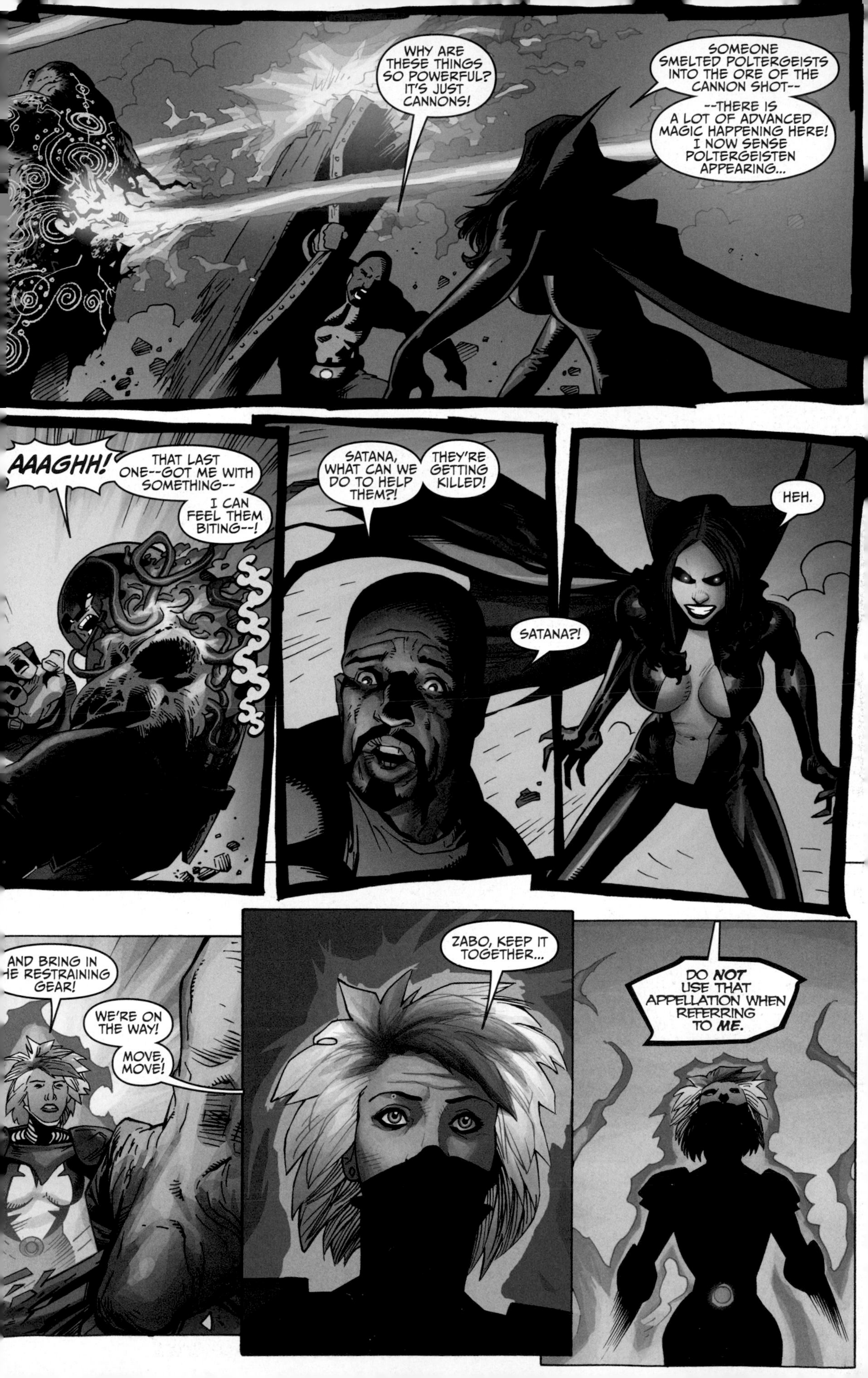
WHY ARE THESE THINGS SO POWERFUL? IT'S JUST CANNONS!
SOMEONE SMELTED POLTERGEISTS INTO THE ORE OF THE CANNON SHOT--
--THERE IS A LOT OF ADVANCED MAGIC HAPPENING HERE! I NOW SENSE POLTERGEISTEN APPEARING...
AAAGHH!
THAT LAST ONE--GOT ME WITH SOMETHING--
I CAN FEEL THEM BITING--!
SSSSSSS
SATANA, WHAT CAN WE DO TO HELP THEM?!
THEY'RE GETTING KILLED!
HEH.
SATANA?!
AND BRING IN HE RESTRAINING GEAR!
WE'RE ON THE WAY!
MOVE, MOVE!
ZABO, KEEP IT TOGETHER...
DO NOT USE THAT APPELLATION WHEN REFERRING TO ME.

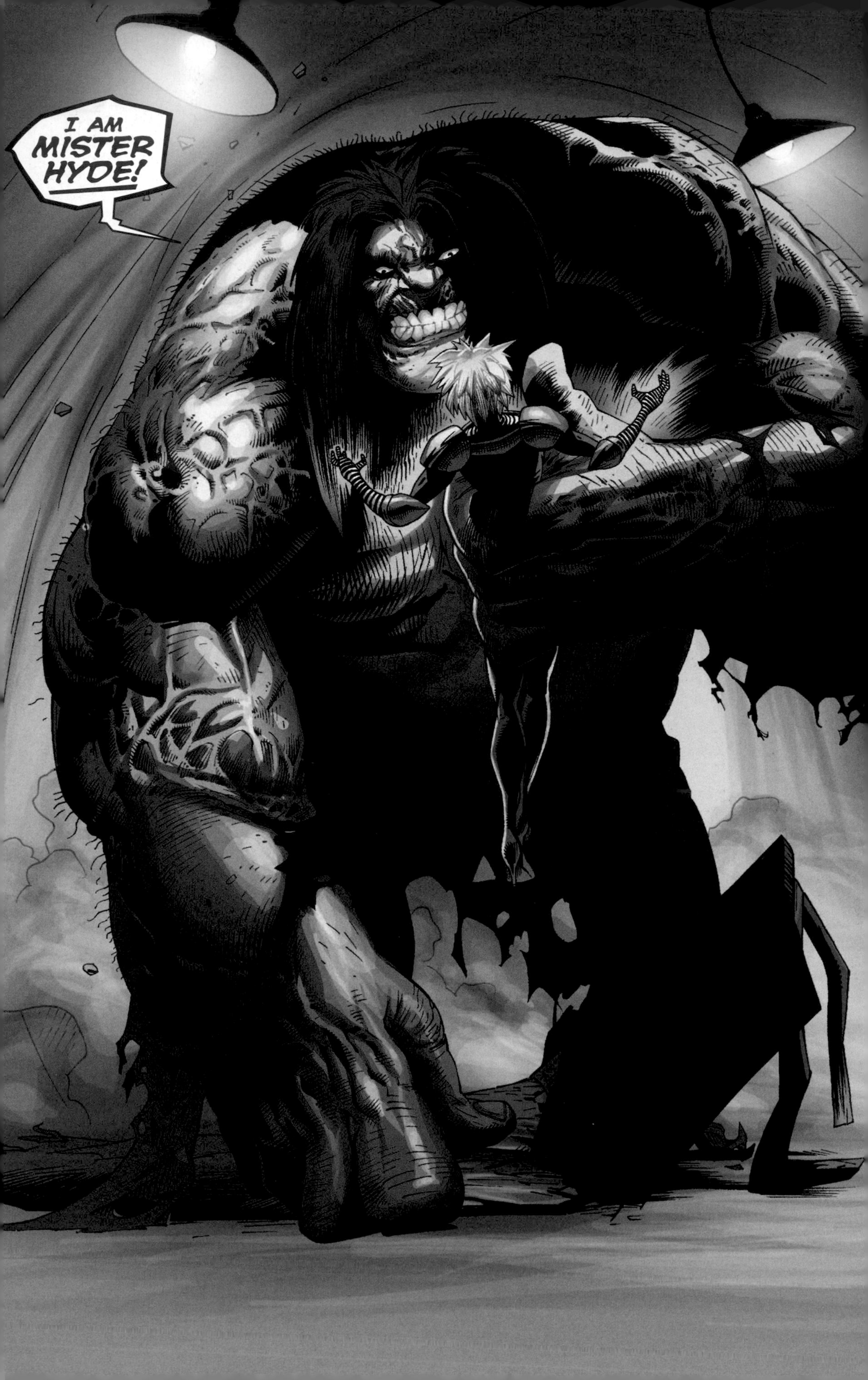
I AM MISTER HYDE!

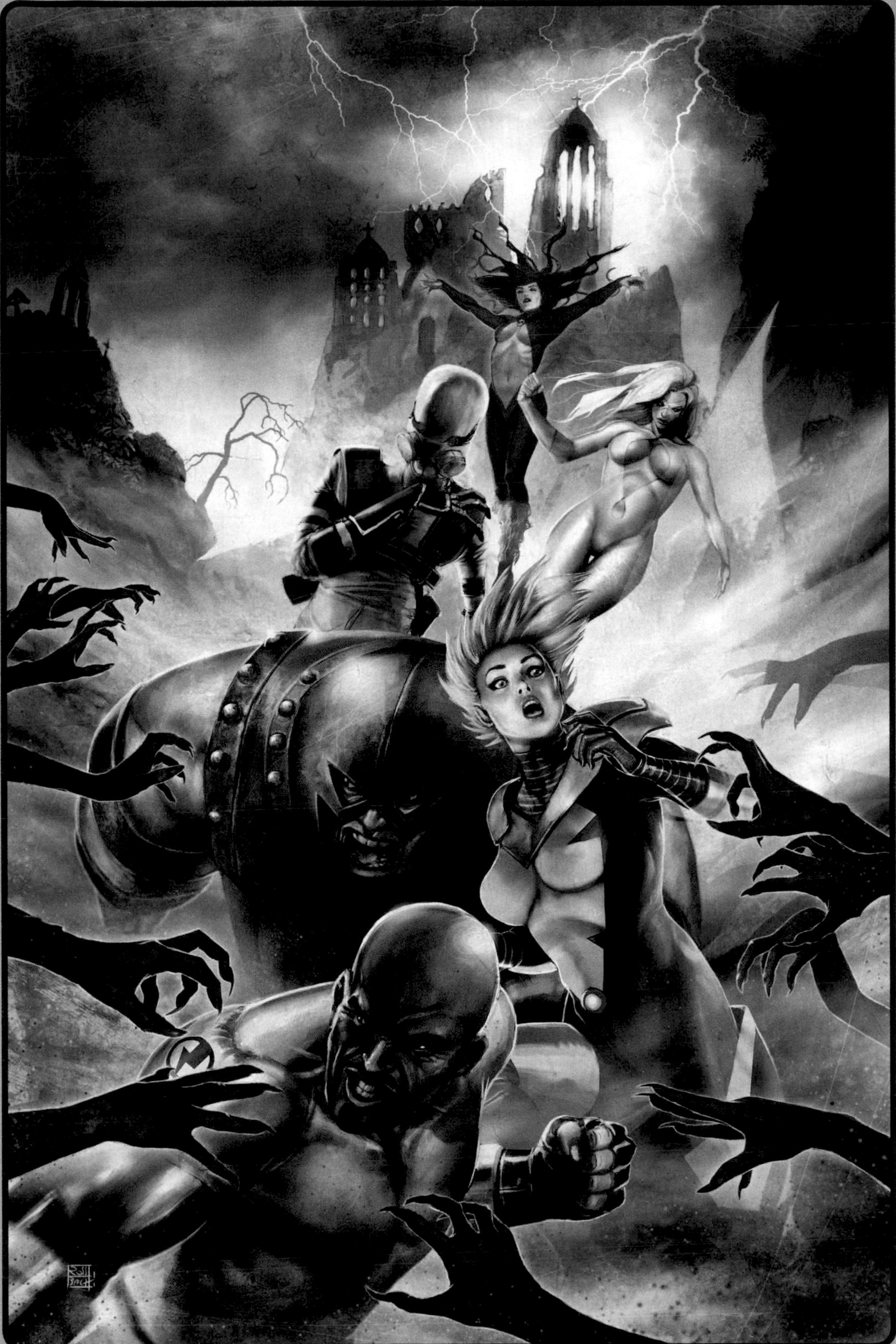

#157

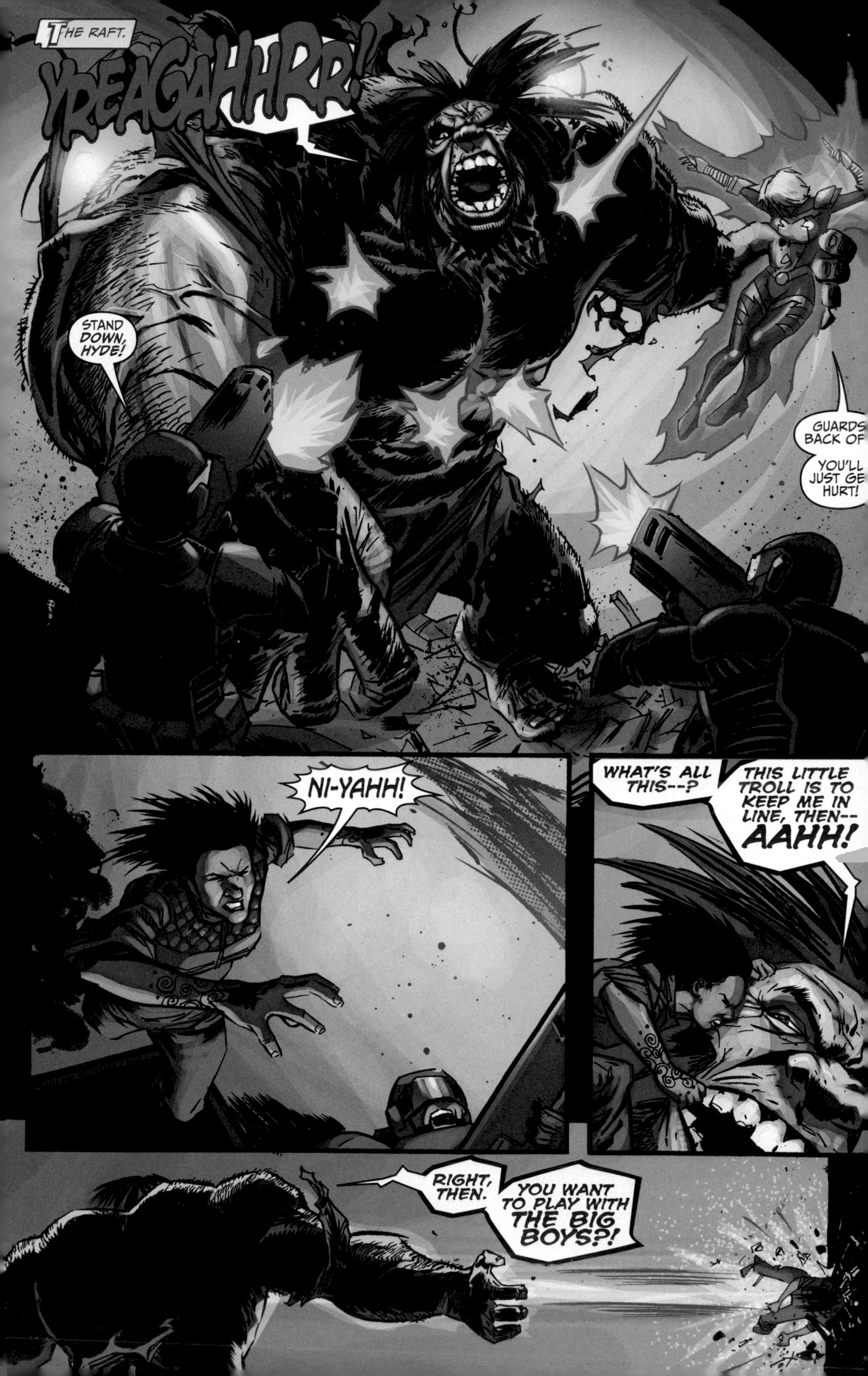
THE RAFT.
YREAGAHHRR!
STAND DOWN, HYDE!
GUARDS BACK OF
YOU'LL JUST GE HURT!
NI-YAHH!
WHAT'S ALL THIS--?
THIS LITTLE TROLL IS TO KEEP ME IN LINE, THEN-- AAHH!
RIGHT, THEN.
YOU WANT TO PLAY WITH THE BIG BOYS?!

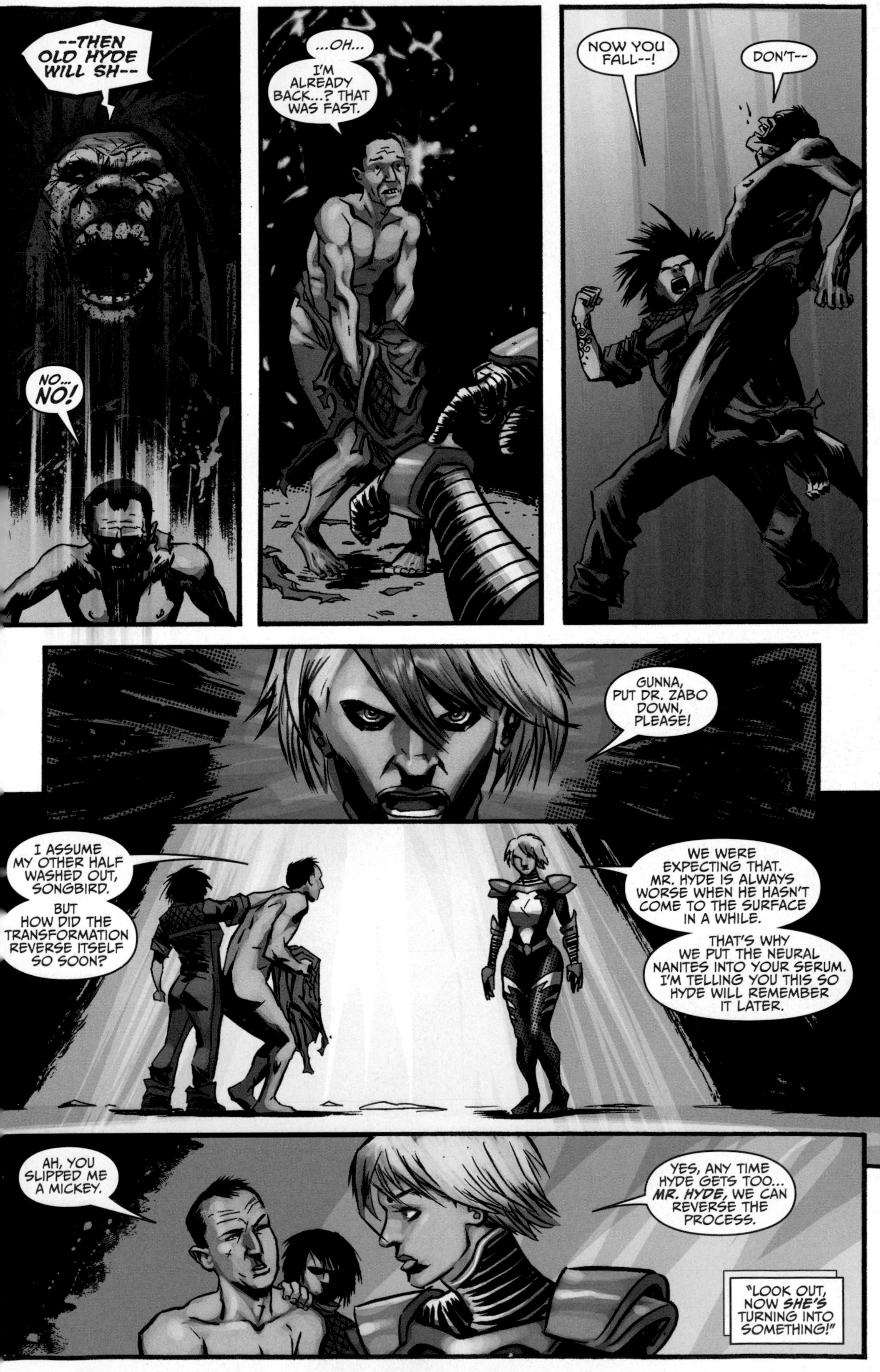
--THEN OLD HYDE WILL SH--
NO... NO!
...OH...
I'M ALREADY BACK...? THAT WAS FAST.
NOW YOU FALL--!
DON'T--
GUNNA, PUT DR. ZABO DOWN, PLEASE!
I ASSUME MY OTHER HALF WASHED OUT, SONGBIRD.
BUT HOW DID THE TRANSFORMATION REVERSE ITSELF SO SOON?
WE WERE EXPECTING THAT. MR. HYDE IS ALWAYS WORSE WHEN HE HASN'T COME TO THE SURFACE IN A WHILE.
THAT'S WHY WE PUT THE NEURAL NANITES INTO YOUR SERUM. I'M TELLING YOU THIS SO HYDE WILL REMEMBER IT LATER.
AH, YOU SLIPPED ME A MICKEY.
YES, ANY TIME HYDE GETS TOO... MR. HYDE, WE CAN REVERSE THE PROCESS.
"LOOK OUT, NOW SHE'S TURNING INTO SOMETHING!"

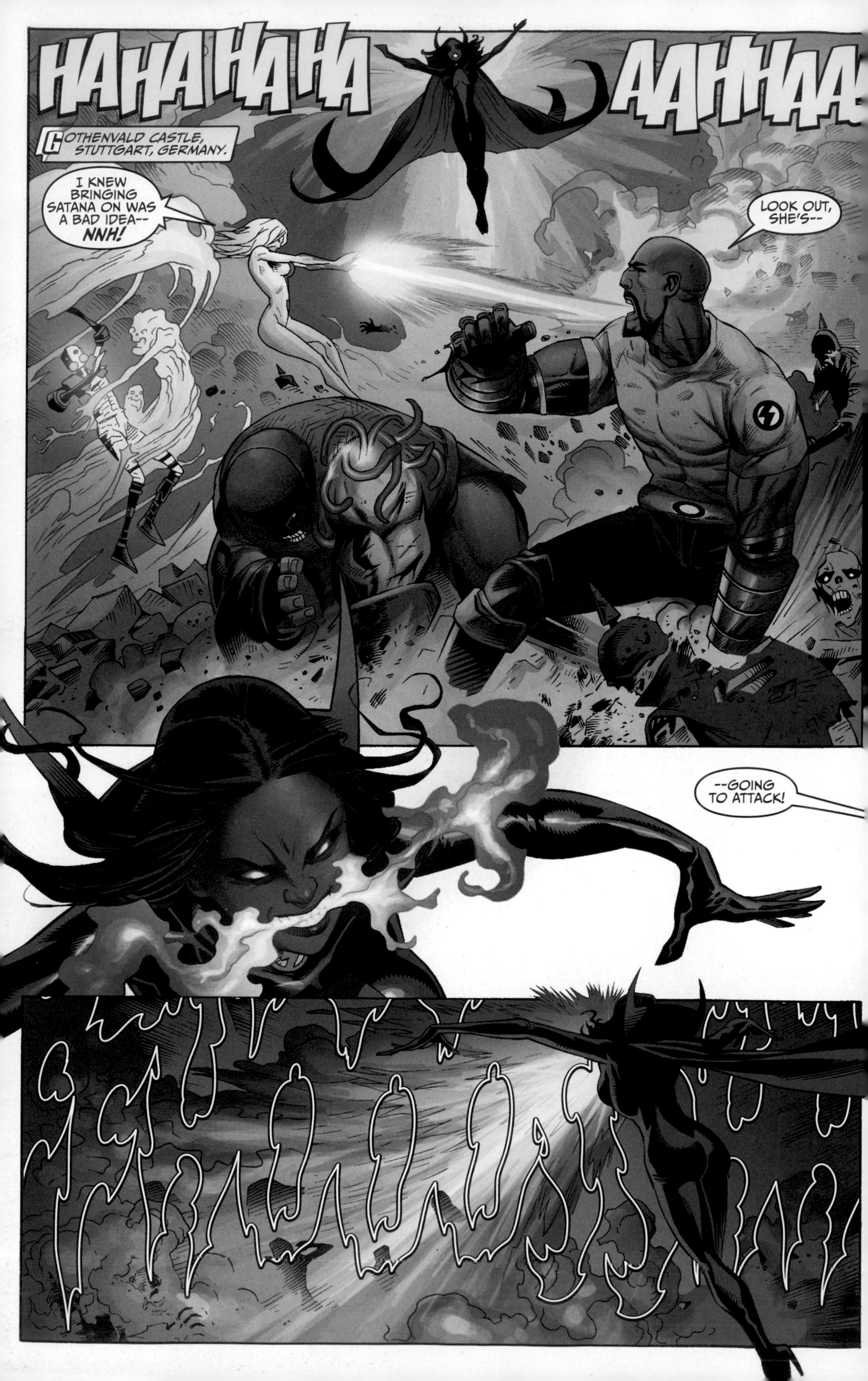
HAHAHAHA
AAHHAA
GOTHENVALD CASTLE, STUTTGART, GERMANY.
I KNEW BRINGING SATANA ON WAS A BAD IDEA-- NNH!
LOOK OUT, SHE'S--
--GOING TO ATTACK!

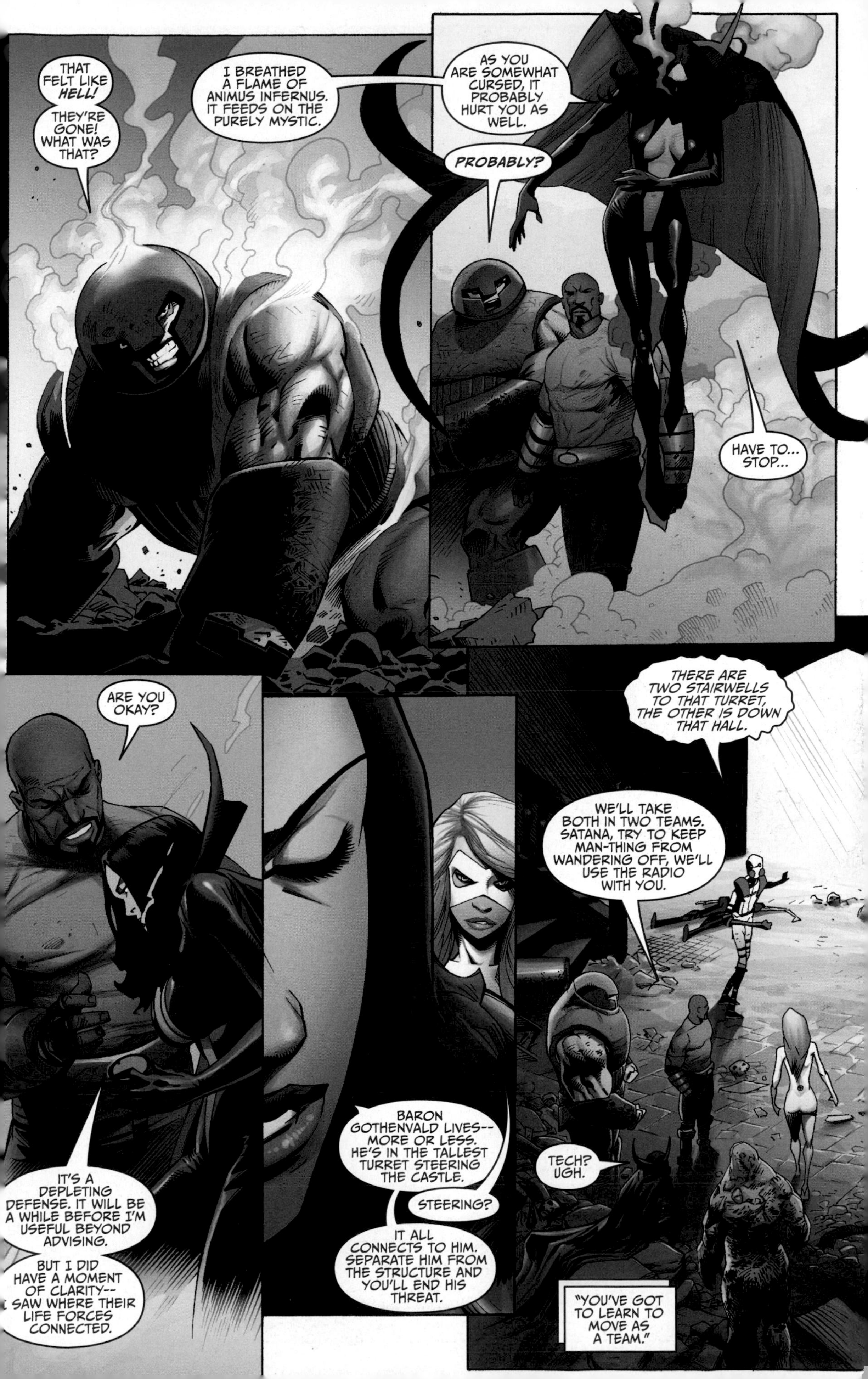
THAT FELT LIKE *HELL!*
THEY'RE GONE! WHAT WAS THAT?
I BREATHED A FLAME OF ANIMUS INFERNUS. IT FEEDS ON THE PURELY MYSTIC.
AS YOU ARE SOMEWHAT CURSED, IT PROBABLY HURT YOU AS WELL.
PROBABLY?
HAVE TO... STOP...
ARE YOU OKAY?
IT'S A DEPLETING DEFENSE. IT WILL BE A WHILE BEFORE I'M USEFUL BEYOND ADVISING.
BUT I DID HAVE A MOMENT OF CLARITY-- I SAW WHERE THEIR LIFE FORCES CONNECTED.
BARON GOTHENVALD LIVES-- MORE OR LESS. HE'S IN THE TALLEST TURRET STEERING THE CASTLE.
STEERING?
IT ALL CONNECTS TO HIM. SEPARATE HIM FROM THE STRUCTURE AND YOU'LL END HIS THREAT.
THERE ARE TWO STAIRWELLS TO THAT TURRET, THE OTHER IS DOWN THAT HALL.
WE'LL TAKE BOTH IN TWO TEAMS. SATANA, TRY TO KEEP MAN-THING FROM WANDERING OFF, WE'LL USE THE RADIO WITH YOU.
TECH? UGH.
"YOU'VE GOT TO LEARN TO MOVE AS A TEAM."

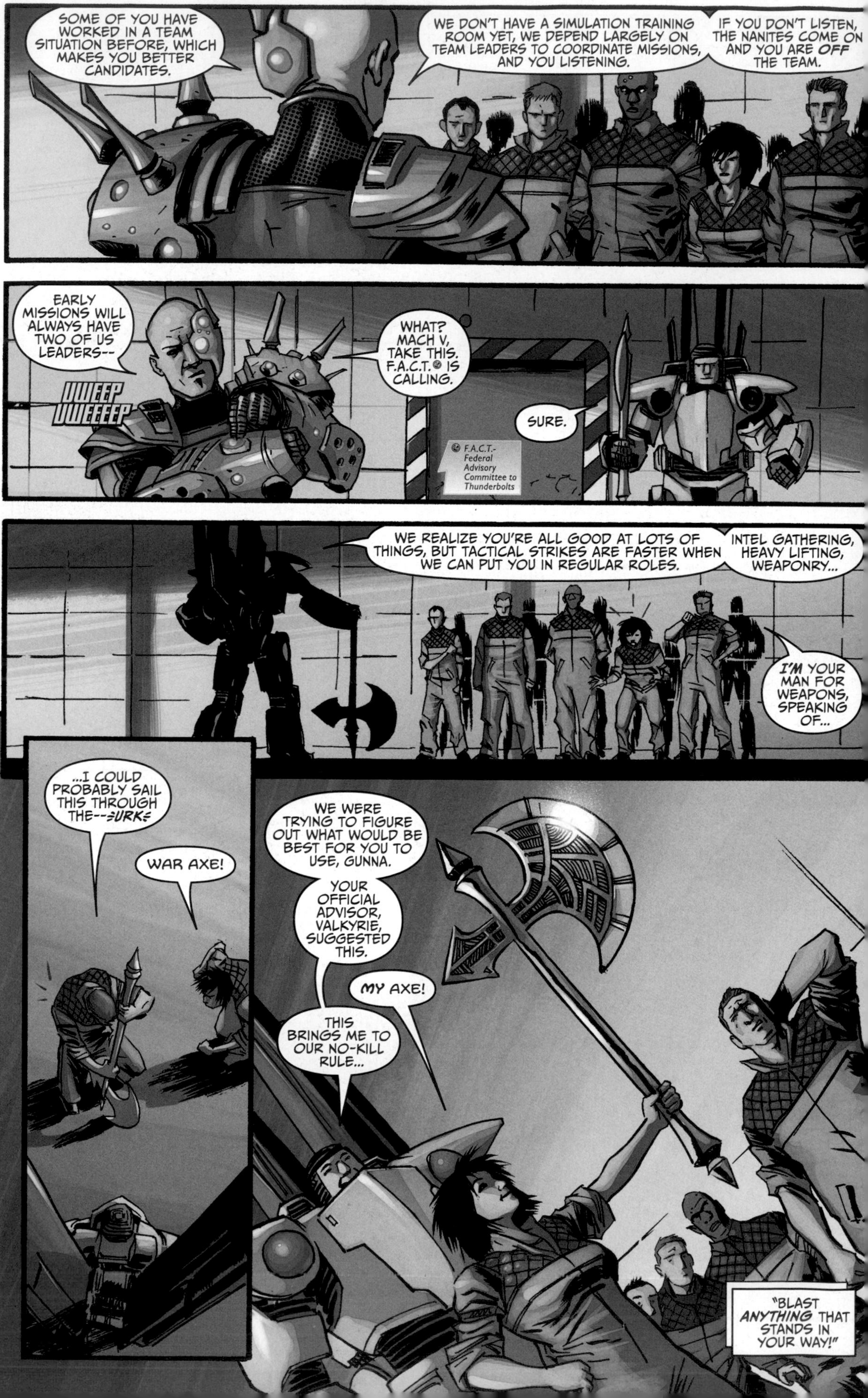
SOME OF YOU HAVE WORKED IN A TEAM SITUATION BEFORE, WHICH MAKES YOU BETTER CANDIDATES.
WE DON'T HAVE A SIMULATION TRAINING ROOM YET, WE DEPEND LARGELY ON TEAM LEADERS TO COORDINATE MISSIONS, AND YOU LISTENING.
IF YOU DON'T LISTEN, THE NANITES COME ON AND YOU ARE *OFF* THE TEAM.
EARLY MISSIONS WILL ALWAYS HAVE TWO OF US LEADERS--
UWEEP UWEEEEP
WHAT? MACH V, TAKE THIS. F.A.C.T.® IS CALLING.
SURE.
® F.A.C.T.- Federal Advisory Committee to Thunderbolts
WE REALIZE YOU'RE ALL GOOD AT LOTS OF THINGS, BUT TACTICAL STRIKES ARE FASTER WHEN WE CAN PUT YOU IN REGULAR ROLES.
INTEL GATHERING, HEAVY LIFTING, WEAPONRY...
I'M YOUR MAN FOR WEAPONS, SPEAKING OF...
...I COULD PROBABLY SAIL THIS THROUGH THE--*URK*
WAR AXE!
WE WERE TRYING TO FIGURE OUT WHAT WOULD BE BEST FOR YOU TO USE, GUNNA.
YOUR OFFICIAL ADVISOR, VALKYRIE, SUGGESTED THIS.
MY AXE!
THIS BRINGS ME TO OUR NO-KILL RULE...
"BLAST *ANYTHING* THAT STANDS IN YOUR WAY!"

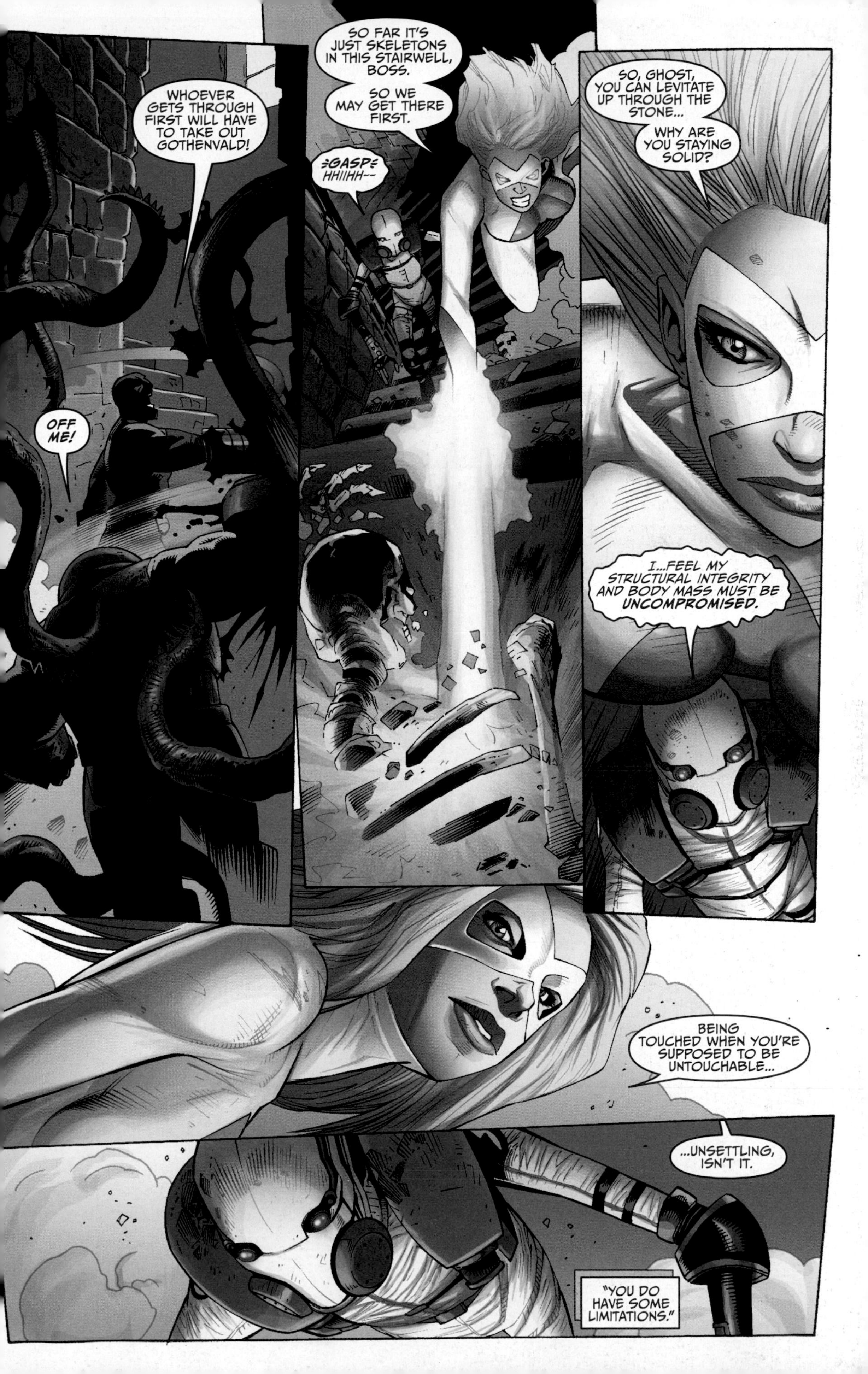
WHOEVER GETS THROUGH FIRST WILL HAVE TO TAKE OUT GOTHENVALD!
OFF ME!
SO FAR IT'S JUST SKELETONS IN THIS STAIRWELL, BOSS.
SO WE MAY GET THERE FIRST.
GASP HHHHH--
SO, GHOST, YOU CAN LEVITATE UP THROUGH THE STONE...
WHY ARE YOU STAYING SOLID?
I...FEEL MY STRUCTURAL INTEGRITY AND BODY MASS MUST BE UNCOMPROMISED.
BEING TOUCHED WHEN YOU'RE SUPPOSED TO BE UNTOUCHABLE...
...UNSETTLING, ISN'T IT.
"YOU DO HAVE SOME LIMITATIONS."

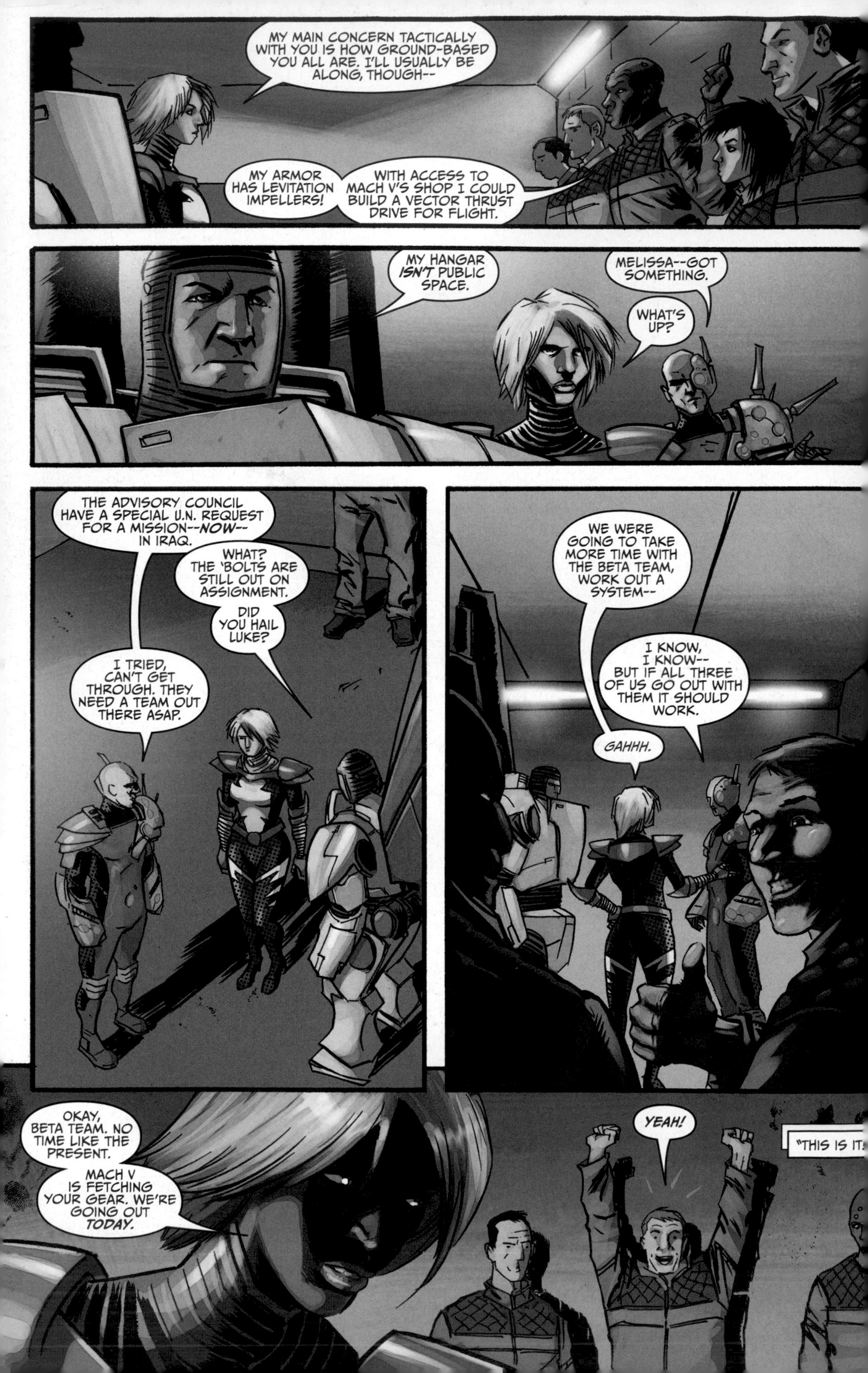
MY MAIN CONCERN TACTICALLY WITH YOU IS HOW GROUND-BASED YOU ALL ARE. I'LL USUALLY BE ALONG, THOUGH--
MY ARMOR HAS LEVITATION IMPELLERS!
WITH ACCESS TO MACH V'S SHOP I COULD BUILD A VECTOR THRUST DRIVE FOR FLIGHT.
MY HANGAR ISN'T PUBLIC SPACE.
MELISSA--GOT SOMETHING.
WHAT'S UP?
THE ADVISORY COUNCIL HAVE A SPECIAL U.N. REQUEST FOR A MISSION--NOW--IN IRAQ.
WHAT? THE 'BOLTS ARE STILL OUT ON ASSIGNMENT.
DID YOU HAIL LUKE?
I TRIED, CAN'T GET THROUGH. THEY NEED A TEAM OUT THERE ASAP.
WE WERE GOING TO TAKE MORE TIME WITH THE BETA TEAM, WORK OUT A SYSTEM--
I KNOW, I KNOW-- BUT IF ALL THREE OF US GO OUT WITH THEM IT SHOULD WORK.
GAHHH.
OKAY, BETA TEAM. NO TIME LIKE THE PRESENT.
MACH V IS FETCHING YOUR GEAR. WE'RE GOING OUT TODAY.
YEAH!
"THIS IS IT

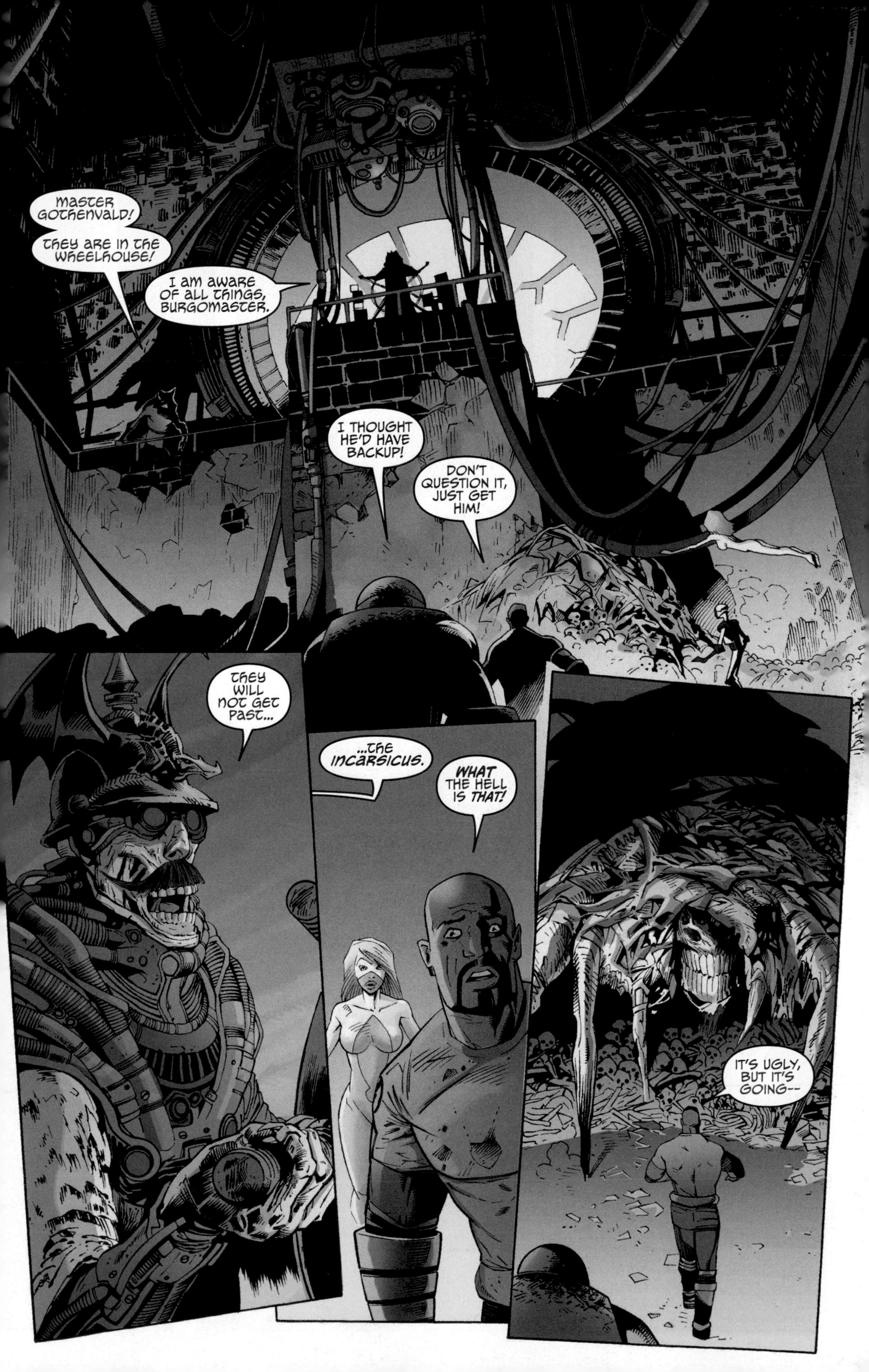
MASTER GOTHENVALD!
THEY ARE IN THE WHEELHOUSE!
I AM AWARE OF ALL THINGS, BURGOMASTER.
I THOUGHT HE'D HAVE BACKUP!
DON'T QUESTION IT, JUST GET HIM!
THEY WILL NOT GET PAST...
...THE INCARSICUS.
WHAT THE HELL IS THAT!
IT'S UGLY, BUT IT'S GOING--

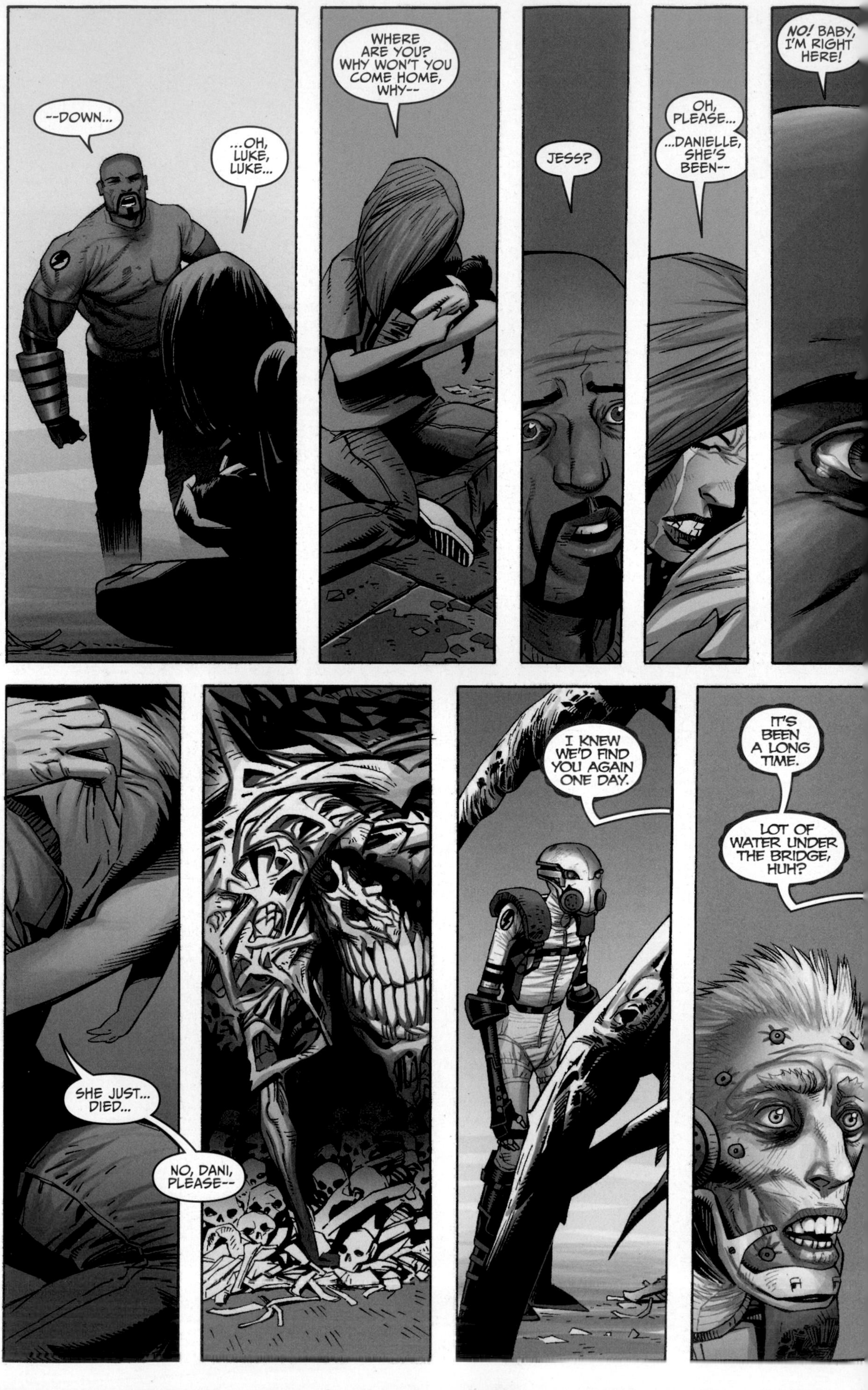
--DOWN...
...OH, LUKE, LUKE...
WHERE ARE YOU? WHY WON'T YOU COME HOME, WHY--
JESS?
OH, PLEASE...
...DANIELLE, SHE'S BEEN--
NO! BABY, I'M RIGHT HERE!
SHE JUST... DIED...
NO, DANI, PLEASE--
I KNEW WE'D FIND YOU AGAIN ONE DAY.
IT'S BEEN A LONG TIME.
LOT OF WATER UNDER THE BRIDGE, HUH?

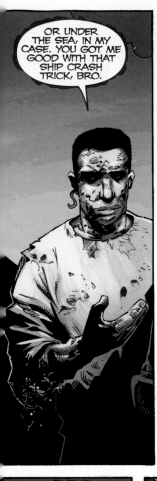

OR UNDER THE SEA, IN MY CASE. YOU GOT ME GOOD WITH THAT SHIP CRASH TRICK, BRO.

STILL, LET BYGONES BE BYGONES, I SAY. WE'VE GOT A NEW VENTURE, AND WANT TO PUT THE TEAM BACK TOGETHER.

IT'S NOT OMNISAPIENT WITHOUT OUR CHIEF DESIGNER.

AND GUESS WHO ELSE WE'VE GOT ON BOARD?

I KNOW YOU REMEMBER SHANA.

HEY, LOVER.

REMEMBER WHAT IT WAS LIKE TO BE ALIVE?

WITH ME?

AAH... SHANA...

WHERE DID HE GO?

THERE WAS NO GOTHENVALD, SILLY GIRL.

THIS IS MY CASTLE, AND I WANTED TO GO HOME. SO I GAVE US THIS MISSION.

I KNEW IT! I KNEW YOU COULDN'T BE TRUSTED!

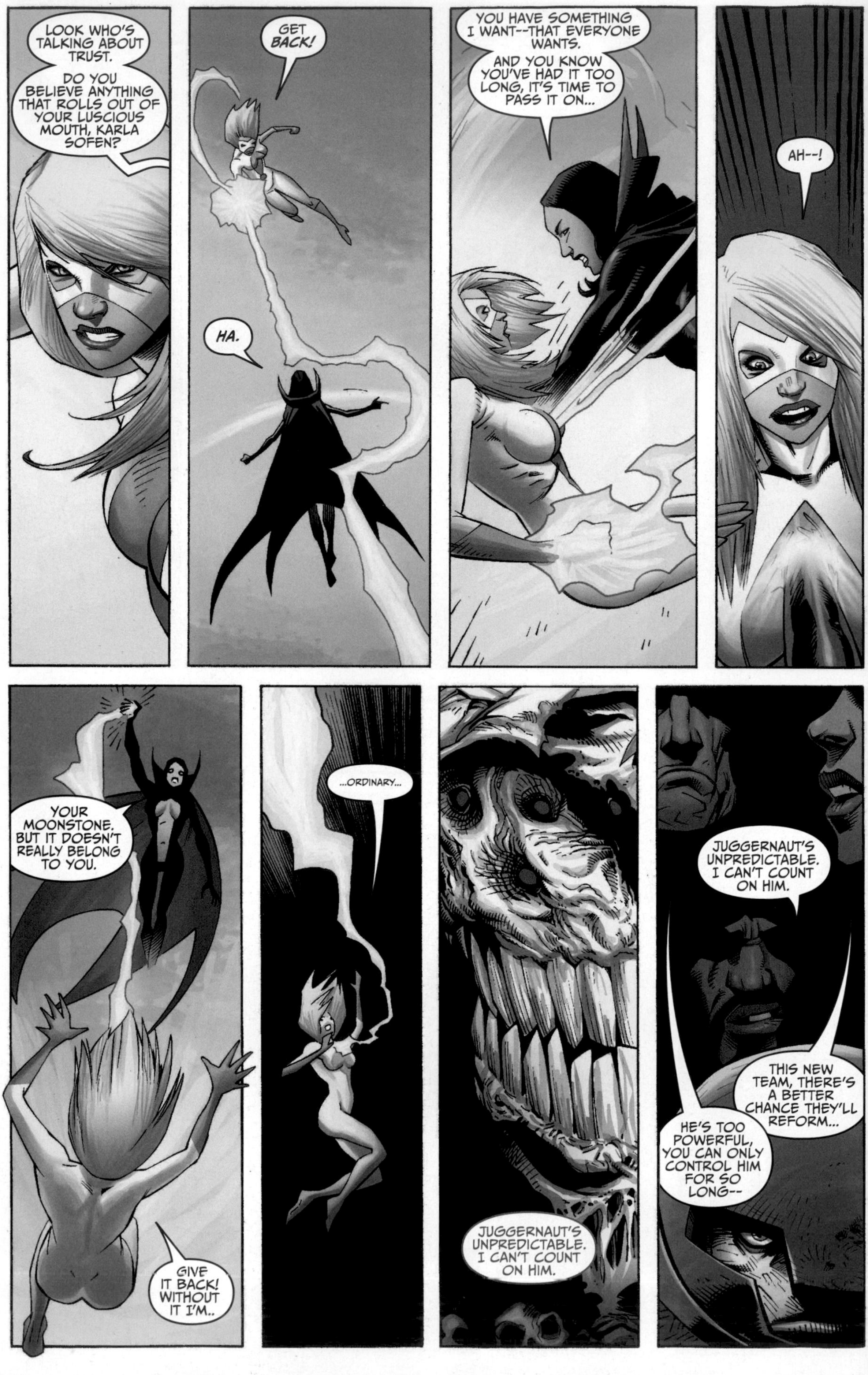
LOOK WHO'S TALKING ABOUT TRUST.
DO YOU BELIEVE ANYTHING THAT ROLLS OUT OF YOUR LUSCIOUS MOUTH, KARLA SOFEN?
GET BACK!
HA.
YOU HAVE SOMETHING I WANT--THAT EVERYONE WANTS.
AND YOU KNOW YOU'VE HAD IT TOO LONG, IT'S TIME TO PASS IT ON...
AH--!
YOUR MOONSTONE. BUT IT DOESN'T REALLY BELONG TO YOU.
GIVE IT BACK! WITHOUT IT I'M..
...ORDINARY...
JUGGERNAUT'S UNPREDICTABLE. I CAN'T COUNT ON HIM.
JUGGERNAUT'S UNPREDICTABLE. I CAN'T COUNT ON HIM.
THIS NEW TEAM, THERE'S A BETTER CHANCE THEY'LL REFORM...
HE'S TOO POWERFUL, YOU CAN ONLY CONTROL HIM FOR SO LONG--

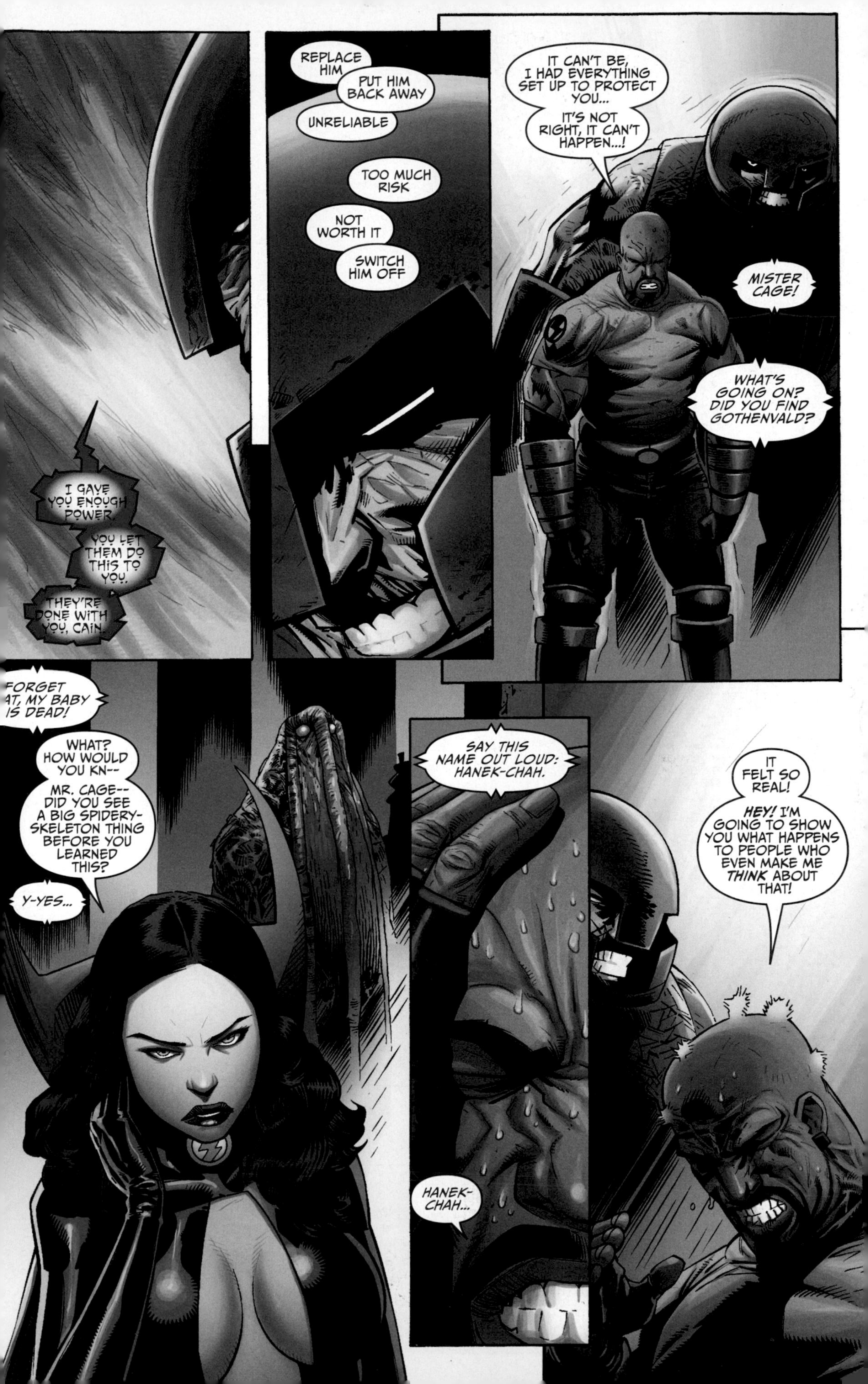
I GAVE YOU ENOUGH POWER.
YOU LET THEM DO THIS TO YOU.
THEY'RE DONE WITH YOU, CAIN.
REPLACE HIM
PUT HIM BACK AWAY
UNRELIABLE
TOO MUCH RISK
NOT WORTH IT
SWITCH HIM OFF
IT CAN'T BE, I HAD EVERYTHING SET UP TO PROTECT YOU...
IT'S NOT RIGHT, IT CAN'T HAPPEN...!
MISTER CAGE!
WHAT'S GOING ON? DID YOU FIND GOTHENVALD?
FORGET AT, MY BABY IS DEAD!
WHAT? HOW WOULD YOU KN--
MR. CAGE-- DID YOU SEE A BIG SPIDERY-SKELETON THING BEFORE YOU LEARNED THIS?
Y-YES...
SAY THIS NAME OUT LOUD: HANEK-CHAH.
HANEK-CHAH...
IT FELT SO REAL!
HEY! I'M GOING TO SHOW YOU WHAT HAPPENS TO PEOPLE WHO EVEN MAKE ME THINK ABOUT THAT!

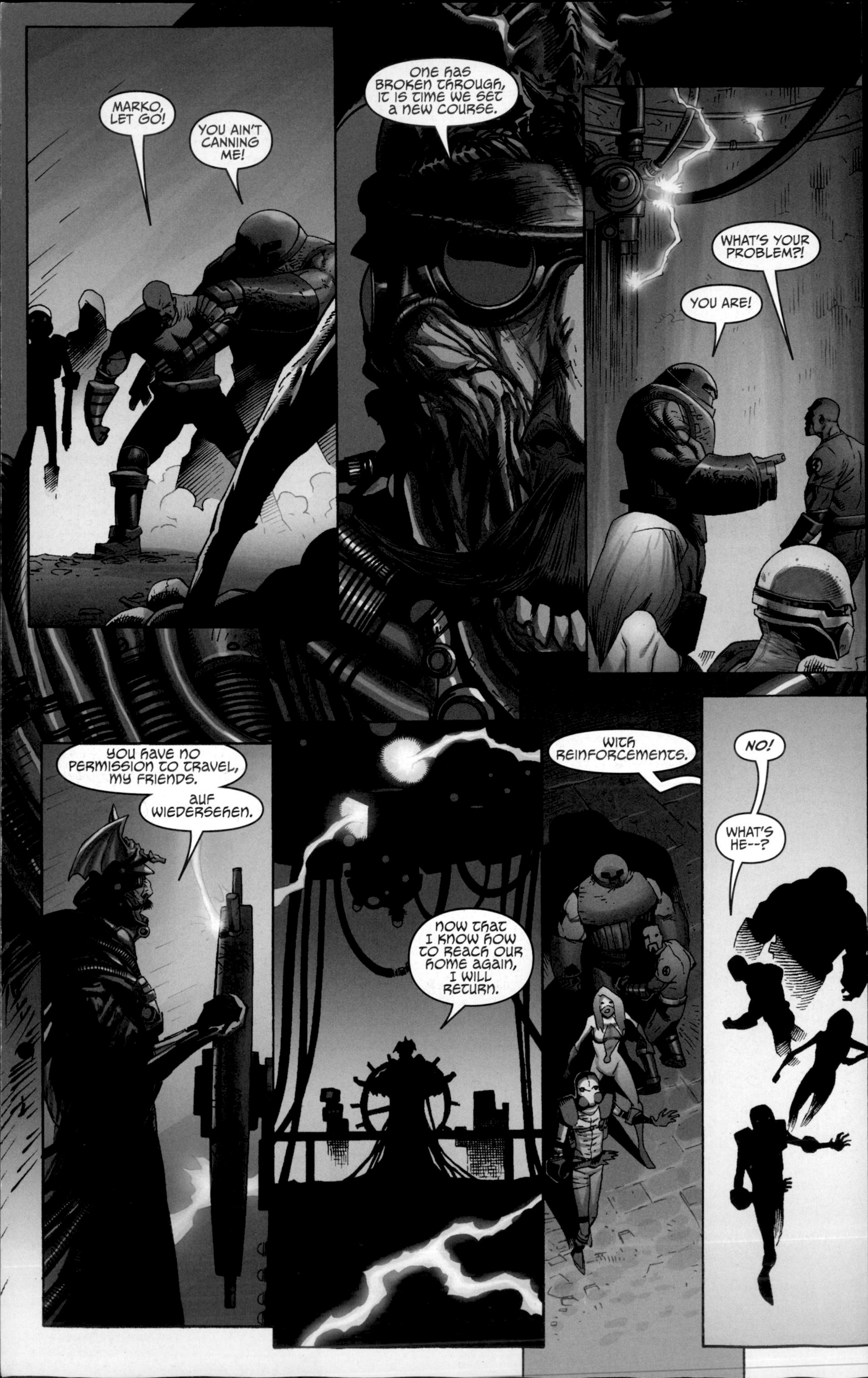

MARKO, LET GO!
YOU AIN'T CANNING ME!
ONE HAS BROKEN THROUGH, IT IS TIME WE SET A NEW COURSE.
WHAT'S YOUR PROBLEM?!
YOU ARE!
YOU HAVE NO PERMISSION TO TRAVEL, MY FRIENDS.
AUF WIEDERSEHEN.
NOW THAT I KNOW HOW TO REACH OUR HOME AGAIN, I WILL RETURN.
WITH REINFORCEMENTS.
NO!
WHAT'S HE--?

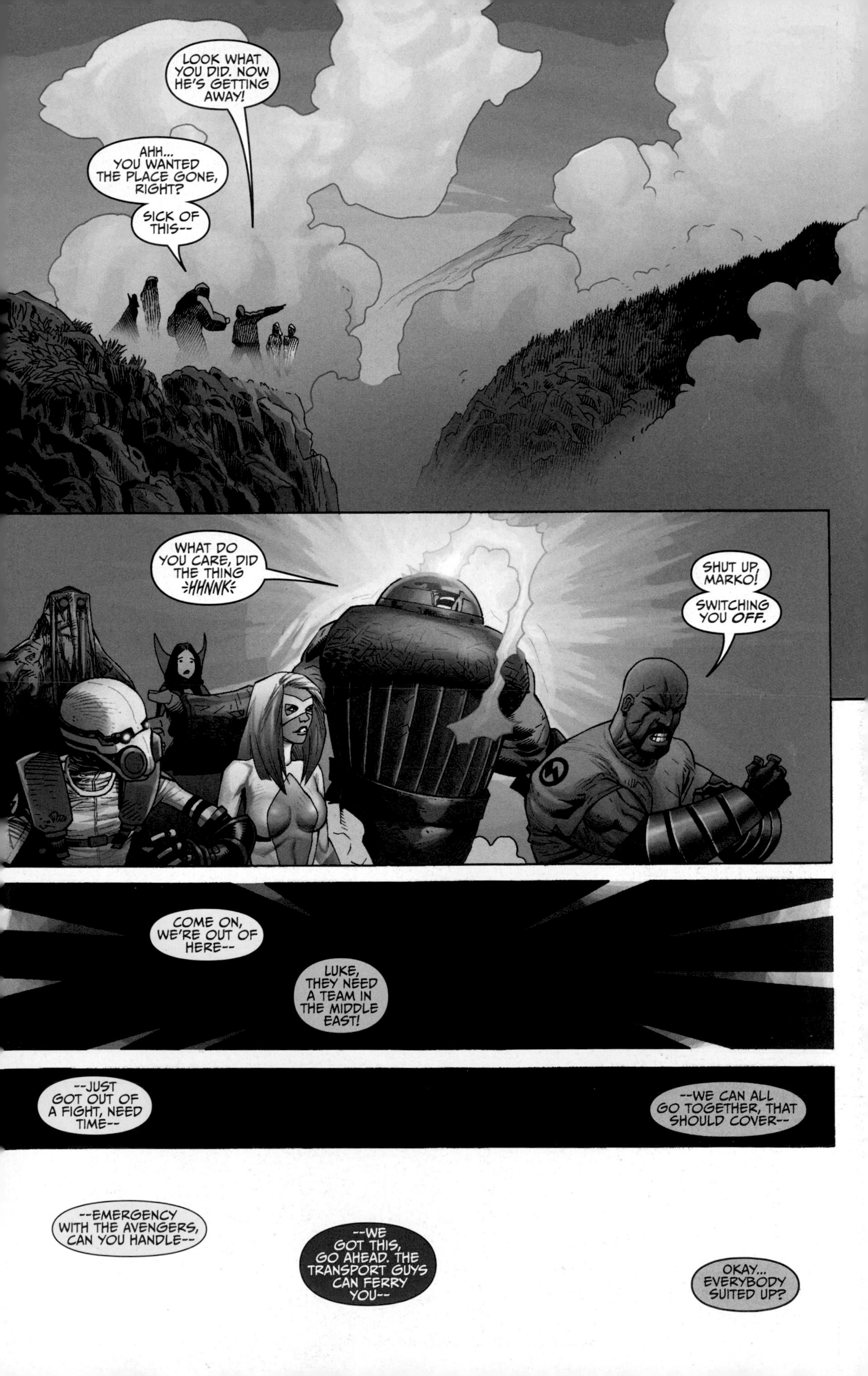
LOOK WHAT YOU DID. NOW HE'S GETTING AWAY!
AHH... YOU WANTED THE PLACE GONE, RIGHT?
SICK OF THIS--
WHAT DO YOU CARE, DID THE THING -HHNNK-
SHUT UP, MARKO!
SWITCHING YOU OFF.
COME ON, WE'RE OUT OF HERE--
LUKE, THEY NEED A TEAM IN THE MIDDLE EAST!
--JUST GOT OUT OF A FIGHT, NEED TIME--
--WE CAN ALL GO TOGETHER, THAT SHOULD COVER--
--EMERGENCY WITH THE AVENGERS, CAN YOU HANDLE--
--WE GOT THIS, GO AHEAD. THE TRANSPORT GUYS CAN FERRY YOU--
OKAY... EVERYBODY SUITED UP?

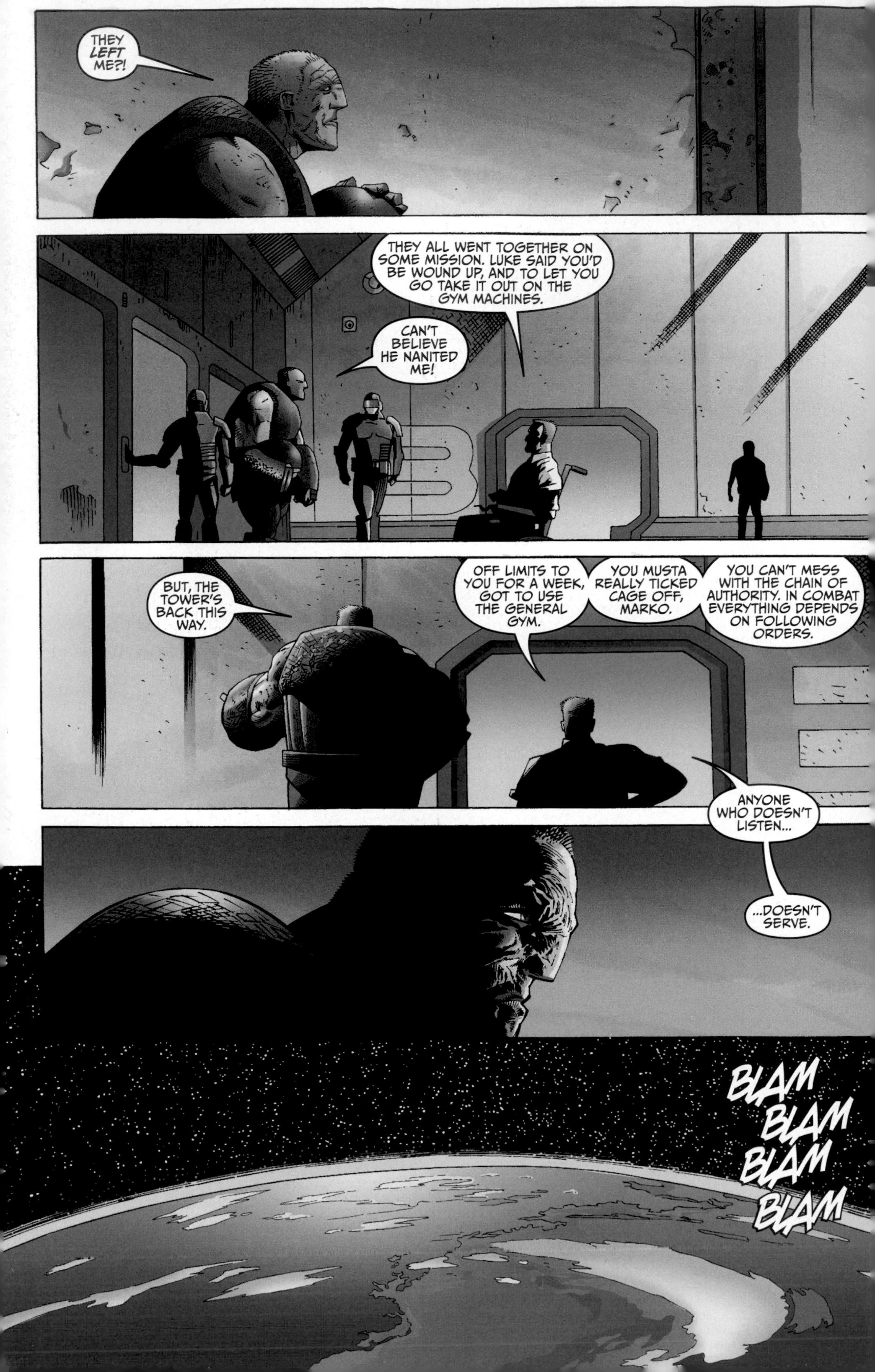
THEY *LEFT* ME?!
THEY ALL WENT TOGETHER ON SOME MISSION. LUKE SAID YOU'D BE WOUND UP, AND TO LET YOU GO TAKE IT OUT ON THE GYM MACHINES.
CAN'T BELIEVE HE NANITED ME!
BUT, THE TOWER'S BACK THIS WAY.
OFF LIMITS TO YOU FOR A WEEK, GOT TO USE THE GENERAL GYM.
YOU MUSTA REALLY TICKED CAGE OFF, MARKO.
YOU CAN'T MESS WITH THE CHAIN OF AUTHORITY. IN COMBAT EVERYTHING DEPENDS ON FOLLOWING ORDERS.
ANYONE WHO DOESN'T LISTEN...
...DOESN'T SERVE.
BLAM BLAM BLAM BLAM

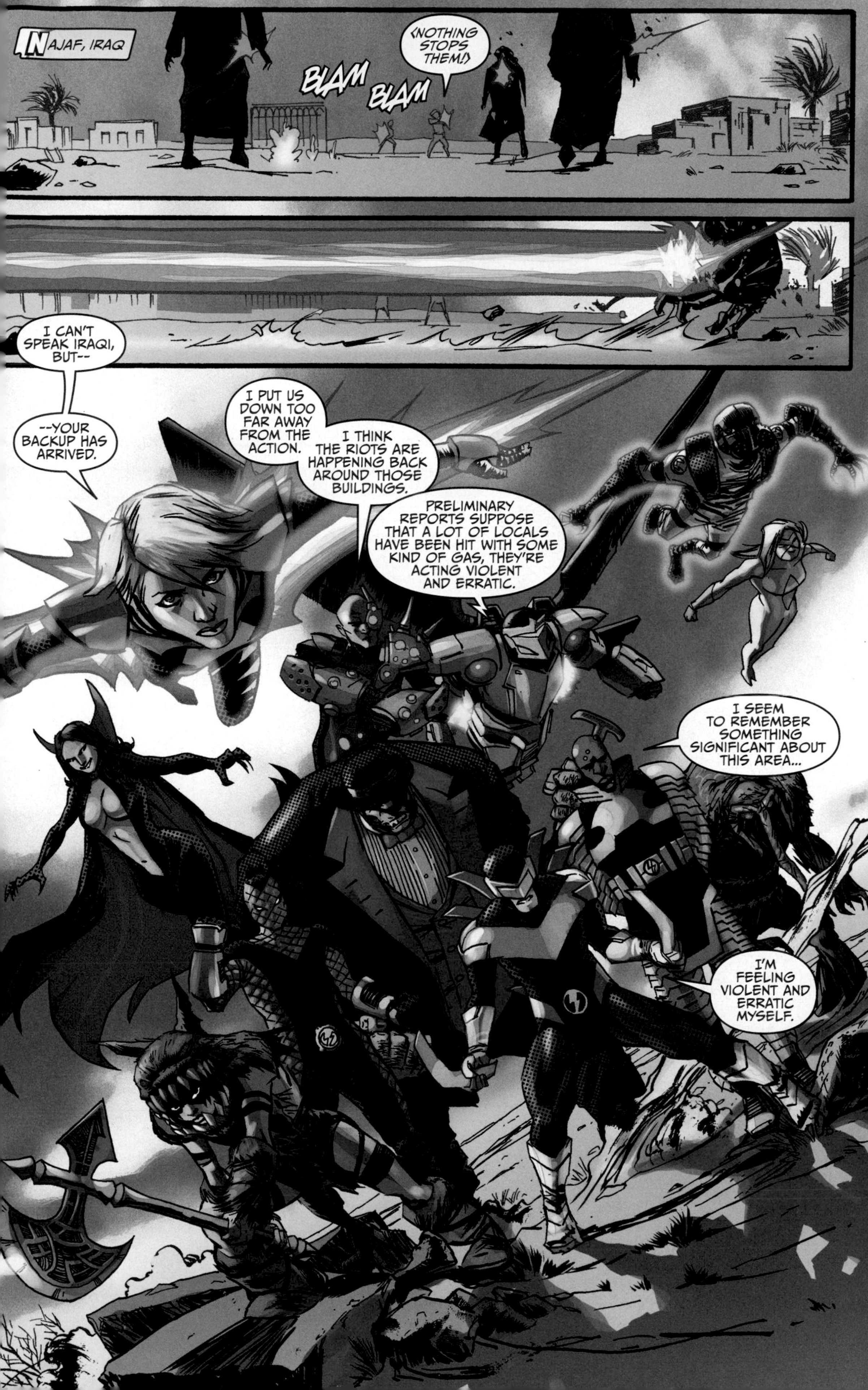
NAJAF, IRAQ
BLAM
BLAM
<NOTHING STOPS THEM!>
I CAN'T SPEAK IRAQI, BUT--
--YOUR BACKUP HAS ARRIVED.
I PUT US DOWN TOO FAR AWAY FROM THE ACTION.
I THINK THE RIOTS ARE HAPPENING BACK AROUND THOSE BUILDINGS.
PRELIMINARY REPORTS SUPPOSE THAT A LOT OF LOCALS HAVE BEEN HIT WITH SOME KIND OF GAS, THEY'RE ACTING VIOLENT AND ERRATIC.
I SEEM TO REMEMBER SOMETHING SIGNIFICANT ABOUT THIS AREA...
I'M FEELING VIOLENT AND ERRATIC MYSELF.

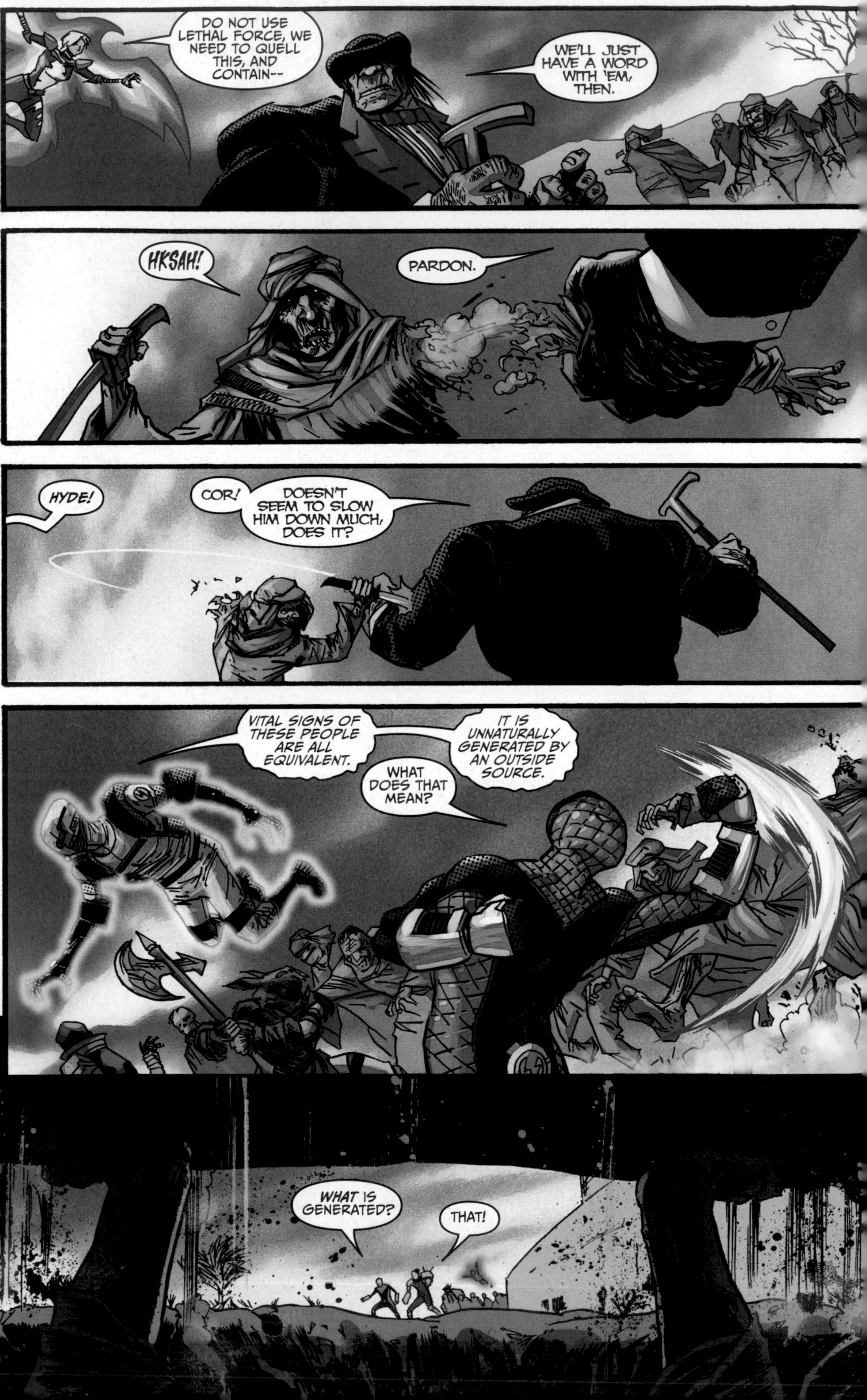
DO NOT USE LETHAL FORCE, WE NEED TO QUELL THIS, AND CONTAIN--
WE'LL JUST HAVE A WORD WITH 'EM, THEN.
HKSAH!
PARDON.
HYDE!
COR!
DOESN'T SEEM TO SLOW HIM DOWN MUCH, DOES IT?
VITAL SIGNS OF THESE PEOPLE ARE ALL EQUIVALENT.
IT IS UNNATURALLY GENERATED BY AN OUTSIDE SOURCE.
WHAT DOES THAT MEAN?
WHAT IS GENERATED?
THAT!

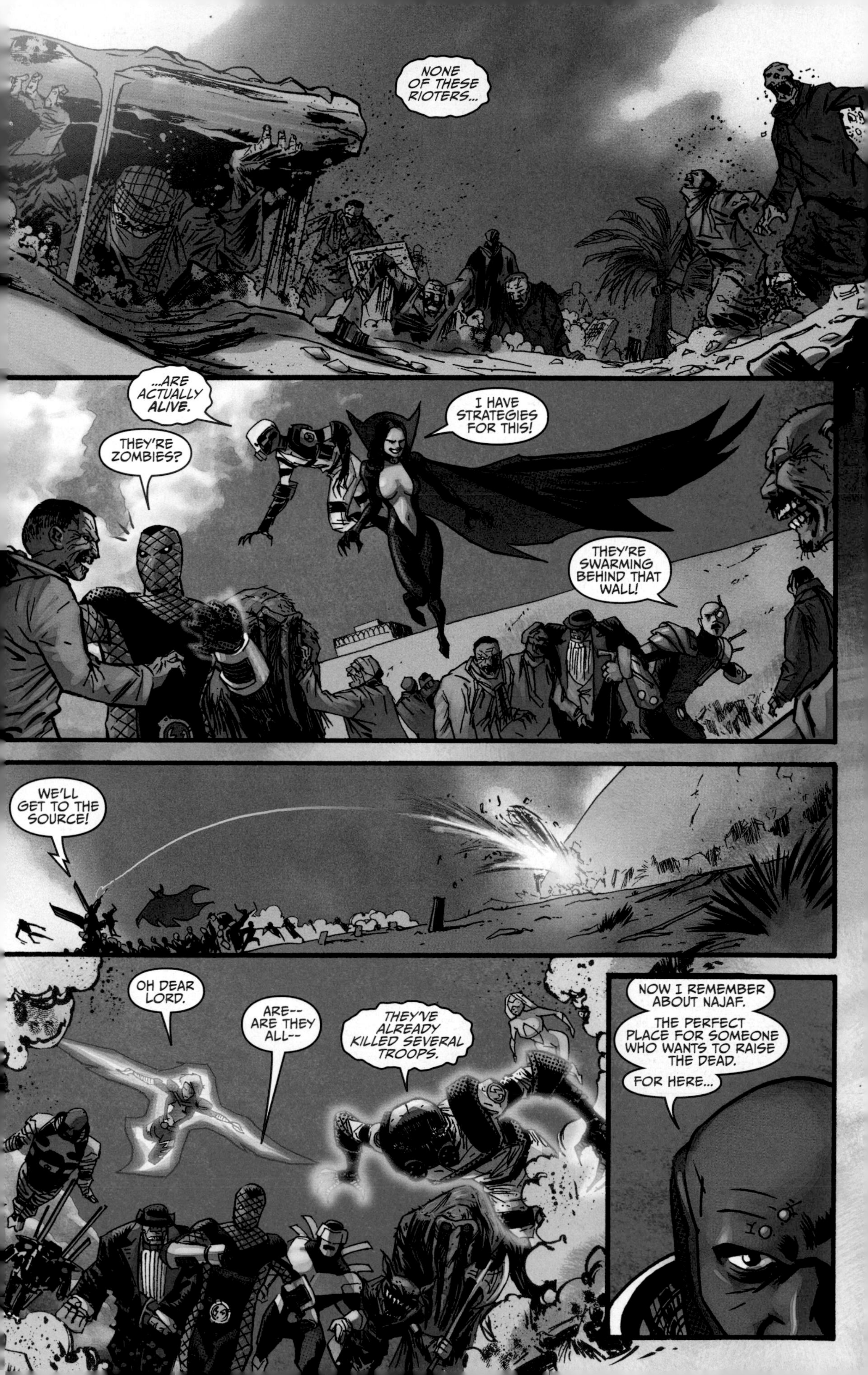
NONE OF THESE RIOTERS...
...ARE ACTUALLY ALIVE.
THEY'RE ZOMBIES?
I HAVE STRATEGIES FOR THIS!
THEY'RE SWARMING BEHIND THAT WALL!
WE'LL GET TO THE SOURCE!
OH DEAR LORD.
ARE-- ARE THEY ALL--
THEY'VE ALREADY KILLED SEVERAL TROOPS.
NOW I REMEMBER ABOUT NAJAF.
THE PERFECT PLACE FOR SOMEONE WHO WANTS TO RAISE THE DEAD.
FOR HERE...

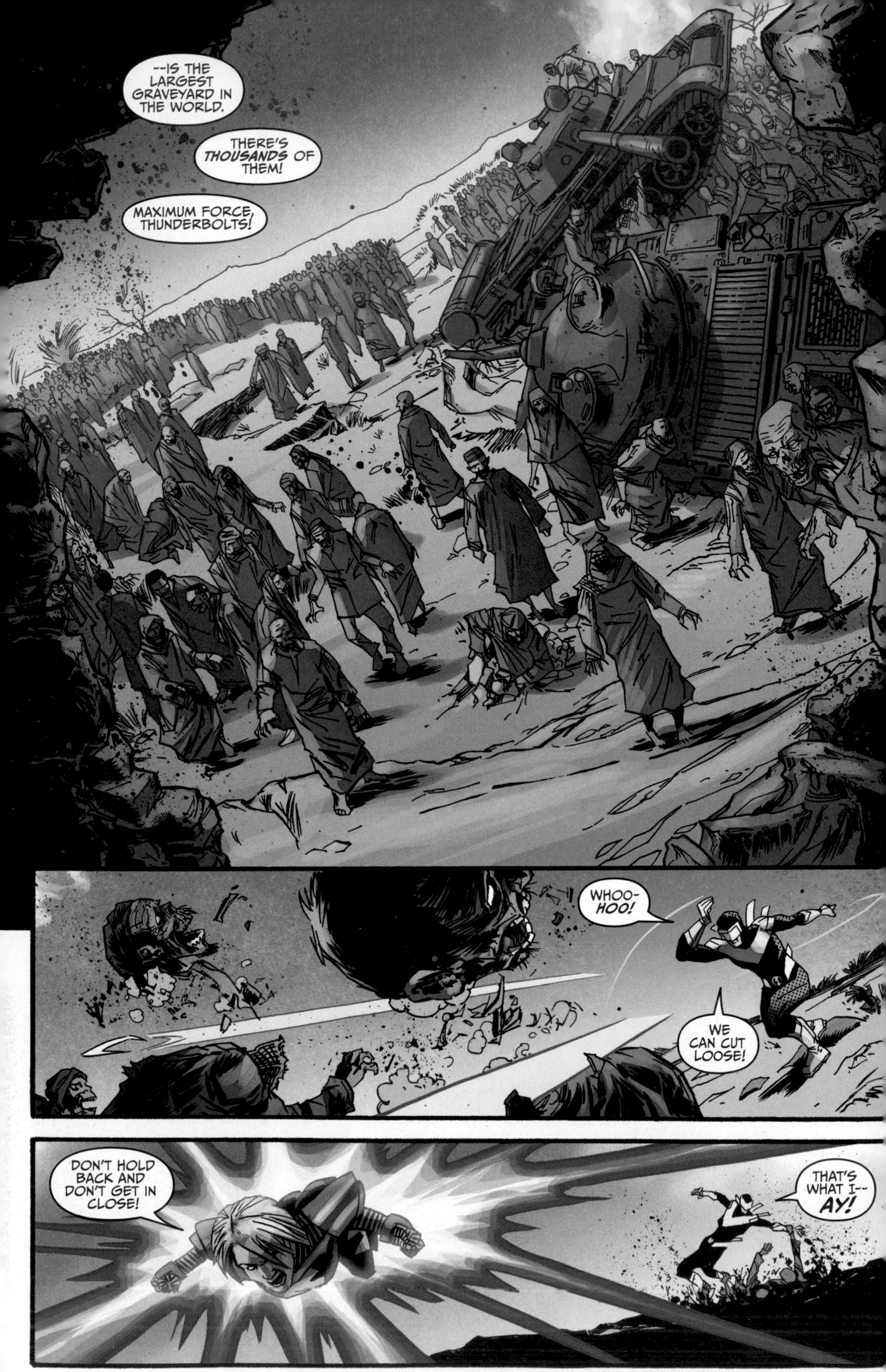
--IS THE LARGEST GRAVEYARD IN THE WORLD.
THERE'S THOUSANDS OF THEM!
MAXIMUM FORCE, THUNDERBOLTS!
WHOO-HOO!
WE CAN CUT LOOSE!
DON'T HOLD BACK AND DON'T GET IN CLOSE!
THAT'S WHAT I-- AY!

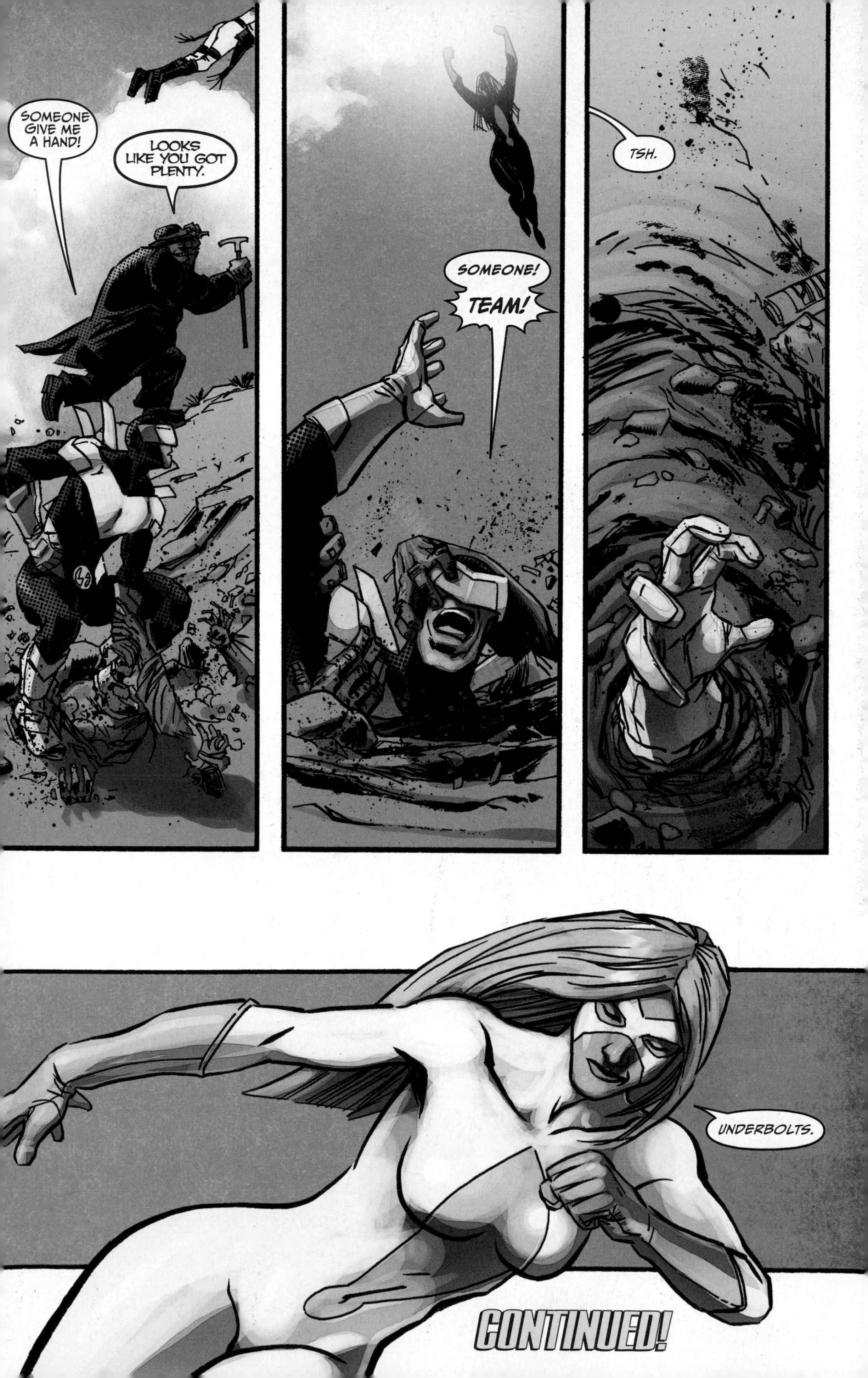
SOMEONE GIVE ME A HAND!
LOOKS LIKE YOU GOT PLENTY.
SOMEONE!
TEAM!
TSH.
UNDERBOLTS.
CONTINUED!

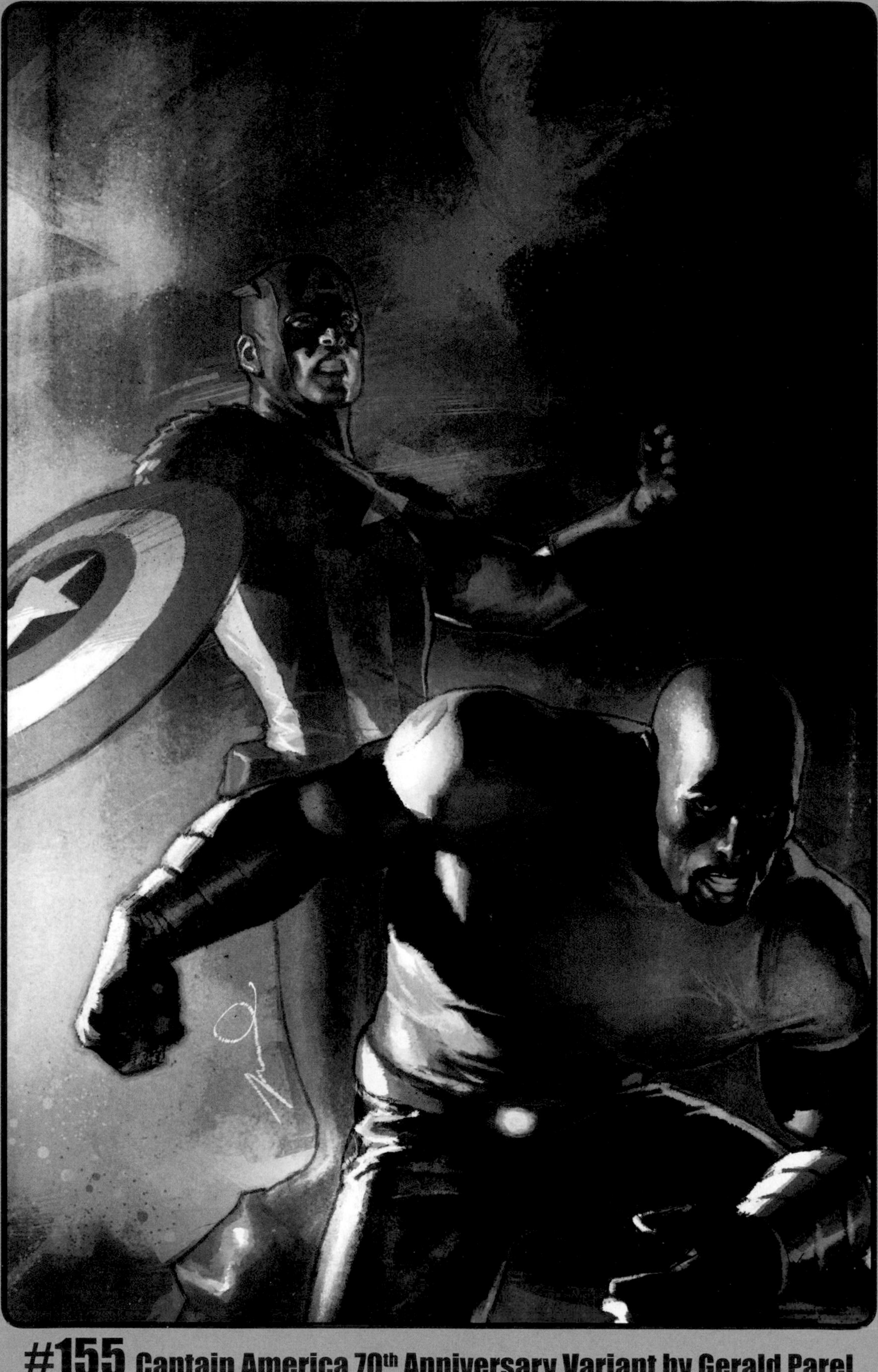

#155 Captain America 70th Anniversary Variant by Gerald Parel

HYPERION (EARTH-4023)

HISTORY: On Earth-4023, Hyperion strove to become his planet's ruler and destroyed all of his reality's heroes. The population resorted to nuclear warfare to stop him; ultimately, he was his world's only survivor. Recruited by an unidentified species of insectoid alien explorers (aka Timebreakers) to join the dimension-fixing Weapon X team, he immediately rebelled and decided to become king of the world to which they sent him (Earth-94831), killing those who opposed him. Magneto refused to submit and dropped an asteroid on the planet. Hyperion was unable to stop it, and the planet's entire population was killed. With nothing left to rule, Weapon X completed their mission by killing the world's remaining mutants on Asteroid M, including Hyperion's own teammate Colossus (Earth-1917). Hyperion rebelled again on Earth-4400, slaughtering its super heroes and seizing control of that world. The insectoids decided to cut their losses and via their Time Broker interface hologram ordered Weapon X and their similar Exiles team to battle each other until only six remained. Hyperion was defeated when Blink (Earth-295) used a warp portal to redirect Hyperion's eye-blasts into his own back, crippling him; Gambit then thrust an energy-charged sword into his back, apparently killing both men.

The insectoids placed Hyperion's remains in a stasis wall, where he regenerated and escaped. Hyperion took over the Panoptichron (aka the Crystal Palace) and, posing as the Time Broker, sent the Exiles on suicide missions while adding disruptive members to their ranks. The Exiles used the reality-bending M'kraan Crystal (the Nexus of All Realities) to travel to the Panoptichron and discovered Hyperion's involvement. Hyperion killed two Exiles, Holocaust (Earth-295) and Namora (Earth-2189), and injured Mimic (Earth-12) and Morph (Earth-1081). The remaining Exiles found themselves on the run. The insectoids retrieved former Exile Beak (Earth-616, later Blackwing), who recruited two heroic Hyperions from Earth-712 and Earth-5764. The three Hyperions battled to a standstill until the renegade Hyperion was finally trapped, in a prison where he could neither escape nor do further harm: his own lifeless world, Earth-4023.

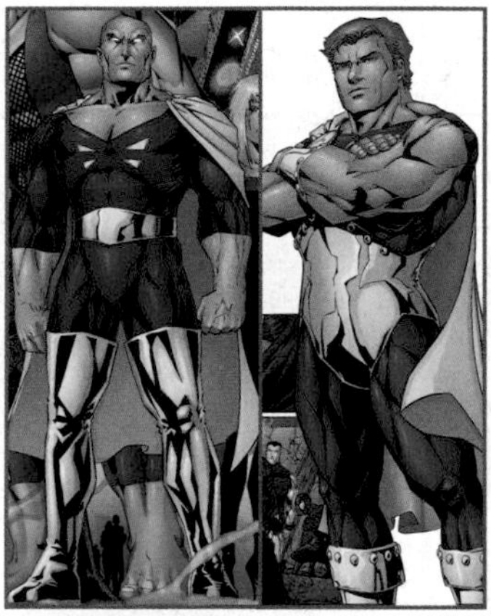

Art by Jim Calafiore

REAL NAME: Unrevealed
ALIASES: King Hyperion
IDENTITY: Secret
OCCUPATION: Would-be world conqueror
CITIZENSHIP: USA
PLACE OF BIRTH: Unrevealed
KNOWN RELATIVES: Unrevealed
GROUP AFFILIATION: None; formerly Weapon X
EDUCATION: Unrevealed
FIRST APPEARANCE: Exiles #38 (2004)

HEIGHT: 6'4"
WEIGHT: 470 lbs.
EYES: Red
HAIR: Red (shaved bald)

ABILITIES/ACCESSORIES: Hyperion possesses Class 100 strength, endurance, durability and speed. His life force is augmented by radiant energy stored in specialized enclaves of his body's cells. Combined with his highly efficient physiology, this renders him virtually immortal, immune to all terrestrial diseases, ageless, and invulnerable to conventional forms of injury. Hyperion is highly durable and resistant to pain and his skin can resist extreme temperature variations (from -455 °F to 11,000 °F), extreme pressure and great impacts. Hyperion can survive without nourishment and in the vacuum of space for months by storing energy within his cells. While he can be injured, Hyperion also has vastly superhuman healing, enabling him to regenerate body tissue (including internal organs) within seconds to minutes; it once took him minutes to recover from a broken neck. It is not known what type of injury could kill him; he once survived a biokinetic energized Soul Sword that blew his body into pieces, proving able to reintegrate his form over a period of several months drawing energy from constant contact with sunlight. Hyperion is virtually tireless due to his metabolism continuously counteracting fatigue poisons by converting them into cellular energy. This process also allows him to store energy, causing a corresponding escalation of strength and vibration at hyper speeds allowing objects to pass through him. Hyperion can fly at speeds of approximately 17,000 mph (orbital velocity) by manipulating gravitons around himself. He can project "flash vision" through his eyes, generating heat up to 12,000 °F. It takes about one minute to attain this temperature and has a maximum range of approximately 200 feet. Hyperion's flash vision can see into all forms of the electromagnetic (EM) spectrum, allowing him to see through any substance except lead. Hyperion also has enhanced smell (can smell others within 40 feet of himself), and hearing (can hear sounds far beyond the range of human hearing).

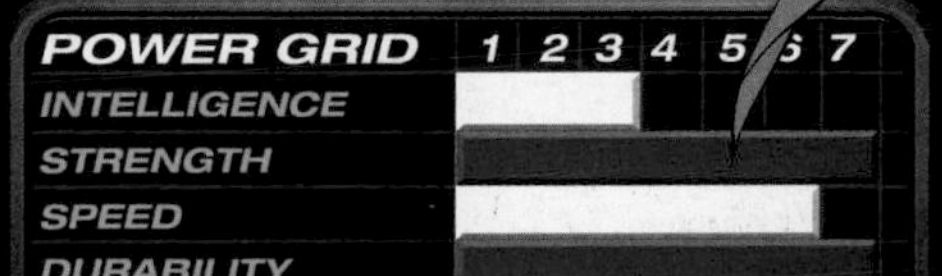
POWER GRID
1 2 3 4 5 6 7
INTELLIGENCE
STRENGTH
SPEED
DURABILITY
ENERGY PROJECTION
FIGHTING SKILLS

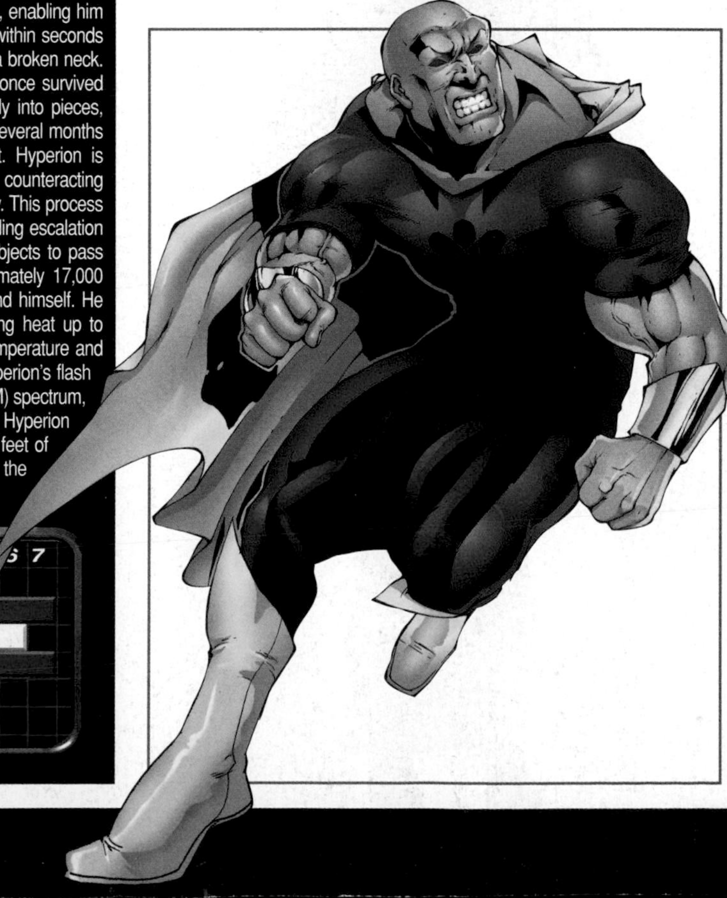

Art by Mizuki Sakakibara,
text by Mark O'English & David Wiltfong

SATANA

REAL NAME: Satana Hellstrom
ALIASES: The Devil's Daughter, Julia Lensky, Satana the Damned, Satana the Succubus, Mistress of the Basilisk, "Queen of Hell," Judith Camber
IDENTITY: No dual identity, though most do not believe her to be Satan's daughter
OCCUPATION: Adventurer, succubus, mystic advisor
CITIZENSHIP: USA; Hell
PLACE OF BIRTH: Fire Lake, Greentown, Massachusetts
KNOWN RELATIVES: Marduk Kurios ("Satan," father), Victoria Wingate Hellstrom (mother, deceased), Daimon Hellstrom (Hellstorm/Son of Satan, brother), Patsy Walker (Hellcat, ex-sister-in-law), Jaine Cutter (Daimon's consort); Asmodeus, Beelzeboul, Lucifer, Mephisto, Satannish, Thog and other Hell-lords (apparent quasi-fathers); Blackheart, Mikal Drakonmegas (Hellfire), Mephista (apparent quasi-half siblings); Gene & Paul Camber (false husband & son)
GROUP AFFILIATION: Formerly SHIELD's Howling Commandos, the Witches
EDUCATION: Tutored by demons
FIRST APPEARANCE: Vampire Tales #2 (1973)

HISTORY: Satana is the daughter of the archdemon Satan. Over 30 years ago, a coalition of demons ruling various Hells — including Marduk Kurios, Asmodeus, Beelzeboul, Lucifer, Mephisto, Satannish, Thog and possibly others — desired a son via a human woman to serve as a living battery drawing in mankind's black energy (sin), storing it as a charge of pure evil. This would empower the Hell-lords to pierce reality's walls in force and overwhelm humanity. In an early attempt, the Hell-lords bonded their collective essence within Beelzeboul who seduced and impregnated Cassandra Dragonmekas, but upon learning his true nature she magically banished him back to Hell. Kurios (usually known as Satan) subsequently took human form for their next attempt. Apparently unknown to the Hell-lords, the Chapel of Dresden cult sought to create a half-human, half-demon messiah from the pit through which they could rule mankind. Purchasing Victoria Wingate Hellstrom from her Satanist parents, they tattooed her womb with Satanic symbols, enabling her to bear such a child. In human form, Kurios was drawn to and seemed to seduce Victoria. Marrying quickly, they moved to Fire Lake's mansion, where Daimon was born a year later. More attached to his mother, Daimon remained unaware of his father's true nature; but his sister, Satana, born when he was three, was always daddy's little girl. Like her brother, she was weaned on human blood and tended by her father's servants. Even as a toddler, Satana pleased her father by killing birds or other such behavior. Both Satana and Daimon were home schooled, as their father did not want them to be defiled by the townfolk. When Satana was six, Victoria walked in on an animal sacrifice Satana was performing for her father; Victoria was driven mad and institutionalized upon seeing her husband's true face. Driving out the memory of willingly mothering the Antichrist, Victoria described herself as an innocent victim of Satan in her diary. Kurios, Victoria and their children remained utterly unaware that Devil-Breaker Stephen Loss, an agent of Heaven's assassins, the Asura, had since exterminated the Chapel of Dresden.

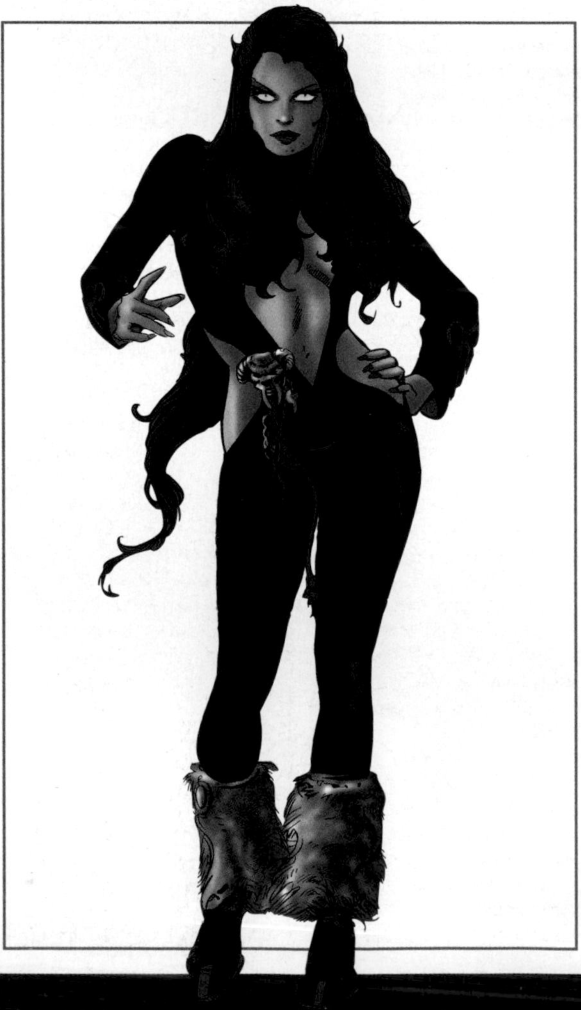

Satana and Daimon were split up to be placed in homes, but the car carrying Satana disappeared en route along with the driver and the young nurse escorting her. Satana was taken to her father's Hell realm. She was schooled in the use of her demonic powers, some of which she inherited, while others Satan granted to her. Satan also bonded Satana's soul to the immensely powerful Basilisk demon. At ten years old, Satana was given her costume by Dame Aramanthe of Eleom, and soon after, Satan gave her a feline familiar, Exiter, and she was tutored in warfare by the ancient demon Dansker. The demon Zannarth was forced to become Satana's companion and slave, and he began to resent her after she once jokingly stole his soul. As part of a graduation test of sorts, Satana battled Dansker, landing a few good strikes before he easily humbled her, showing her he was her master and could have slain her.

As a young woman, Satana was banished to Earth and Zannarth to a netherworld, all seemingly the work of a cabal known as the Four, though Satan was secretly behind it. Arriving in Manhattan, Satana attracted a would-be human predator, but smoothly led him into an alley and consumed his soul's power. Tracking the Four, Satana relocated to Los Angeles, where she saved the Church of the Dark Father's members by dispersing a frenzied mob rallied by politician Harry Gotham. She befriended the Church's Ruth Cummins (who apparently carried Satan's mark), but when Gotham sent assassin Darkos Edge after Satana, he unwittingly slew Cummins instead; Satana subsequently consumed Edge's and Gotham's souls. After moving in with Church member Gloria Hefford, Satana was reunited with Exiter. Continuing to feed on men she encountered, such as Hank Johnson, Satana identified Miles Gorney as the Four's leader, then seduced and sent former soldier Rich Corbett to assassinate Gorney. Too late, she learned Gorney's sacrifice at her hands was the Four's real goal and would power the Four's spell to close a portal to Hell she might have used to return home; frustrated at her own stupidity, she drained Corbett's soul. Using the hidden Cave of the Seven Winds to reach a

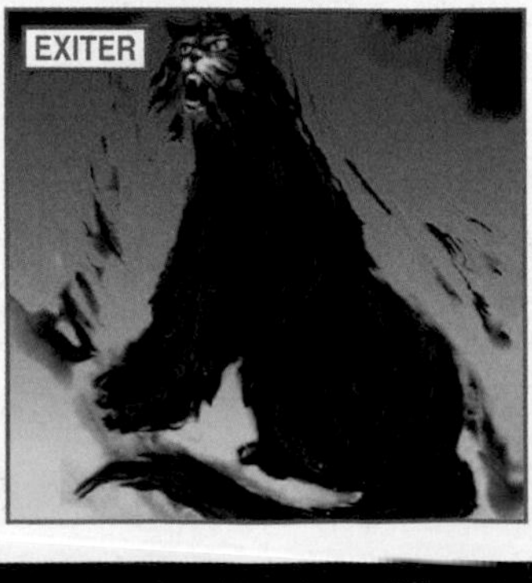

EXITER

Art by Pablo Marcos

Art by Esteban Maroto

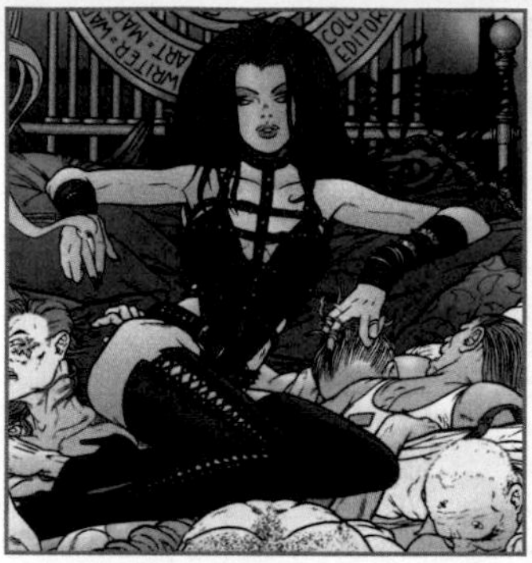

Art by Martin Chaplin

netherworld from which she hoped to access Hell, she found Zannarth and coerced him into assisting her. After battling the Four's demons, they found the corpse of the bull-headed Trachos, the Four's apparent true leader. They were then attacked by the rest of the Four: Lion-headed Karath, hawk-headed Raga, and snake-headed Ellin, the latter of whom slew Zannarth. Satana sought to distract her assailants by forcing them to see their inner selves, but this caused the Four great agony and reverted them to human forms, which Satana fed upon in rapid succession. Arising, Trachos revealed himself to be a still-living Miles Gorney and vanished, laughing. Satana felt the Four's barrier fade, but returned to Earth to gain answers and perhaps vengeance.

Monsignor Jimmy Cruz, a secret member of the Camarilla of the N'Garai (a demon race who long ago battled Lucifer, whom they identified as her father), sent an army of soldiers who savagely beat Satana; she called to her father but found the portal to Hell closed again. Exiter saved Satana by leading surgeon and former priest Michael Heron into the alley to help her. Exiter then slaughtered a man who returned to confirm her death and brought Satana a man on whom to feed, regain her strength, and heal her wounds. Upon awakening, Satana tried to feed on Heron as well, but he resisted her call — the first ever to do so. Cruz led a squad to kill Satana, but she escaped, and they abducted Heron instead. Exiter reached Cruz first, but he summoned the N'Garai who slaughtered the cat. Forewarned of this, Satana later ambushed and fed on Cruz before he could summon his masters. Parting ways with Heron, Satana gave him the Azshiran, a ring that could protect him from any demon born of Satan. Still seeking Gorney, Satana slew Walter Dean, a Hollywood producer/director who had aspired to Camarilla of the N'Garai membership. The demon Agathon then subdued Satana and brought her before Gorney, who had captured Heron and cut off his ringed hand. Slaying Agathon and the other demons upon awakening, Satana recognized Gorney as her father, as no one else could have injured a man wearing the Azshiran. Satan revealed that everything involving the Four had been a test to prove her power and loyalty, but she turned her back on him by allowing Heron to die and pass on to a higher plane without her consuming his soul. Furious, Satan banished her to Earth until the time of her death.

Gloria Hefford later unwittingly summoned and was possessed by the demon-mother Kthara, attracting the attention of both Satana and Daimon Hellstrom (who had since accepted his identity as the Son of Satan, though he still opposed his father). As Gloria, Kthara duped Daimon into believing that Satana was the threat, mystically goading him into combat with his sister and enhancing his power. Daimon's hellfire consumed Satana, but the Basilisk restored her just as Kthara was about to slay Daimon in a ritual sacrifice that would free her ravagers to claim the Earth. Unable to oppose Kthara's power, Satana summoned the Basilisk to slaughter Kthara. Satana refused Daimon's apology, threatening to take his soul when next they met. Magical energies subsequently drew Satana north to Chandler, California, where men were about to burn the witch Deborah Hirsch, who was secretly possessed by Satana's former tutor Dansker. The assaults on Hirsch enabled Dansker to take control, and he slew his attackers and stunned Satana, then prepared a spell that would physically transport him to Earth. Satana defeated Dansker (whose power was limited in this form) and summoned the Basilisk to slay him.

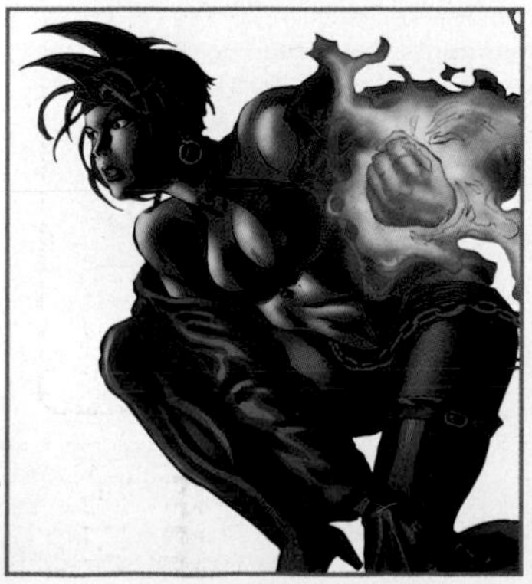

Art by Will Conrad

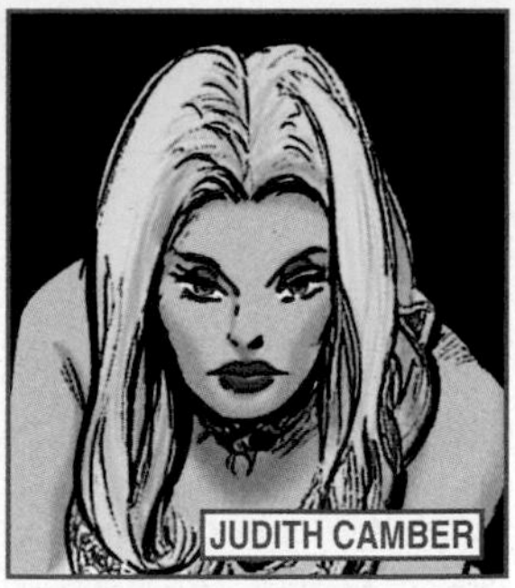
JUDITH CAMBER

Art by Vicente Alcazar

Realizing that slaying Satana outright would release the Basilisk, which might destroy the entire world, the Camarilla of the N'Garai mystically transformed Satana into the mortal Judith Camber, complete with false memories of her past life with her family. However, within an hour of the transformation, the Basilisk rebelled against these constraints and slew Judith's family. Their deaths devastated "Judith," which briefly allowed Satana's personality and form to become dominant. While Camber was confused by her dual memories and personalities, the Camarilla extracted Satana's spirit from Camber, planning to sacrifice it to the N'Garai; however, realizing that would end her own false existence, Camber tracked the Camarilla to the Church of Dis and unleashed the Basilisk. The archdemon destroyed the entire church and slew the Camarilla. Regaining her true form and memory, Satana destroyed the soul of the Camarilla's leader, Brian Abelard, before it could pass on to any final resting place.

Having grown in power and will due to its frequent use, the Basilisk sent a wolf-demon to possess Sorcerer Supreme Dr. Stephen Strange. Sensing this, Satana allied with Spider-Man (Peter Parker) to cure Strange. She mystically transported the trio to an astral plane, where they fought the Basilisk's demon legions as they neared Strange's soul. Satana summoned her full power to destroy the demons and shatter the casing containing Strange's soul; but the effort exhausted her, and the Basilisk broke free from her and struck her down from behind with its sword. As Satana died, however, so did the Basilisk, which had become intrinsically attached to her soul. In death, Satana returned to her father's realm of Hell.

Years later, the Rev. Joshua Crow began having dreams in which the Lord seemed to speak to him; in reality, it was Satan who had contacted him. Crow had visions of innocent souls trapped in Hell, and the voice charged him with rescuing them from the eternal fires. Goingto New York, Crow used his new power to summon these souls from Hell and placed them in the bodies of people in a seemingly hopeless comatose state. Crow performed six such "resurrections" over the following three weeks, unaware that Satan intended to use the souls Crow had reincarnated as "lightning rods for evil" — focal points Hell would use as anchors to their reality as it tried to take them back. Through them, Hell would begin to manifest itself on Earth, escalating as it gained strength. Daimon (now Hellstorm) dealt with five of these "Souls of the Damned," but was unable to locate the sixth, secretly Satana, who had taken the form of Julia Lenksy. Realizing what he had done, Crow was praying for forgiveness when Julia thanked him with a kiss, draining his soul and sending it down into the abyss.

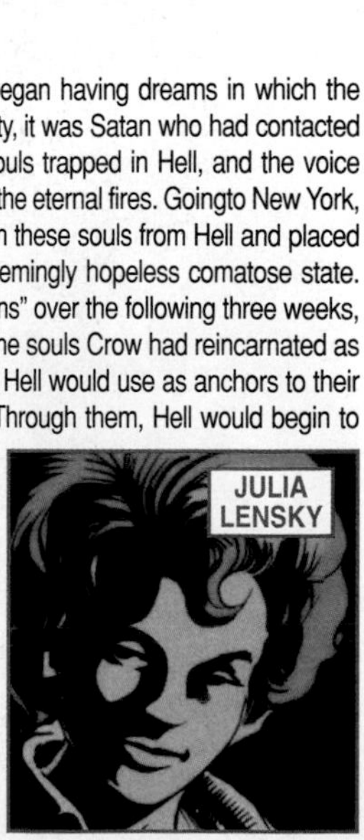
JULIA
LENSKY

Art by Peter Gross

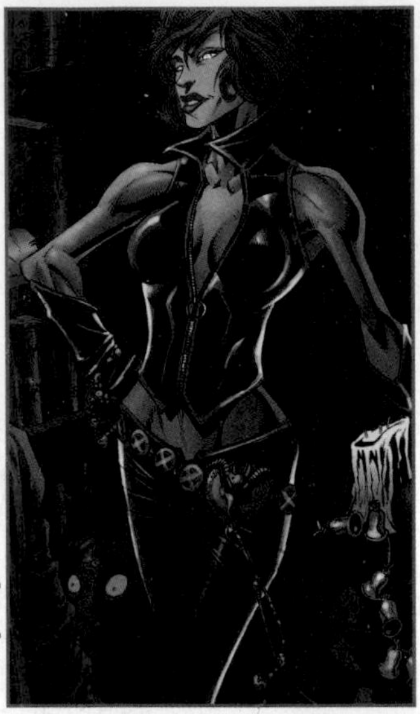

Art by Kyle Hotz

Learning she could increase her own might by consuming more souls than she needed to survive, Satana plotted to amass great power and conquer Hell. She created the Body Orchard, a deconsecrated church in which she kept multiple victims chained to the walls and ceiling, wrapped in a spell that continually regenerated their life forces, which Satana constantly fed on. Detective Gunyon, who had lost his job (and much of his sanity) through an encounter with Hellstorm, sought to kill Satana to punish Daimon, but Satana instead enslaved Gunyon. She branded him with a magic symbol, such that all his actions would be attributable to her. She also gave him a box of bullets, each impregnated with her body fluids and inscribed with her mark, instructing him to use them to commit mass murder. Those shot by Gunyon with these bullets would have their souls consigned to Satana, and she intended to grow powerful enough to challenge the supremacy of Heaven and Hell. She rewarded Gunyon with sex, though she consumed progressively more of his soul. Her activities attracted the perverse lust of Stephen Loss, who wrote about her in his Fur Journal, allegedly bound in the skin of the first man, Adam. The outcome of Satana's efforts is unrevealed, but she apparently perished and/or was sent to Hell again.

Satana was later returned to Earth by Dr. Strange to serve as the underworld representative to assist sorceresses Jennifer Kale and Topaz against the immensely powerful magic-user-slaying Hellphyr, which Satan had secretly manipulated Jennifer's brother, Andrew, into releasing from the mystic Tome of Zhered-Na; Satan sought to eliminate all potential challengers to his regaining control of his Hell, which Daimon had usurped. Satana initially clashed with Kale and Topaz, but after Satan revealed his involvement and offered Satana a chance to rule at his side, she rejected him again and helped Kale and Topaz destroy the Hellphyr. The three women banded together as the Witches, but split up not long after. Satana was subsequently recruited into SHIELD's Howling Commandos monster unit, and she opposed the world-conquering plot of a corrupt Merlin.

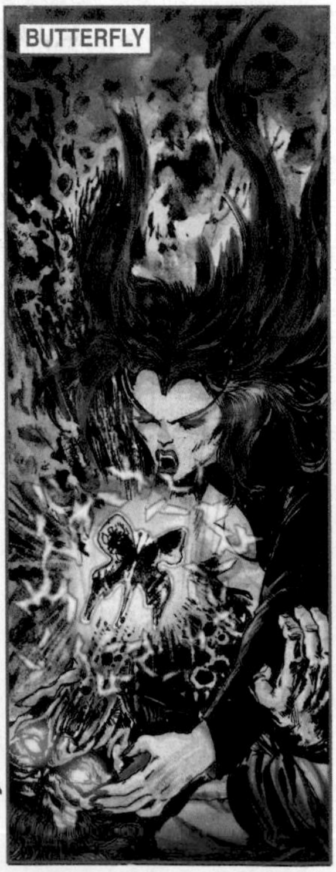
BUTTERFLY

Art by Pablo Marcos

After Satan apparently regained control of Hell, Satana began delivering a monthly soul tithe to him; one such soul was Jason Silence. Returning to the Body Orchard, Satana was eventually ambushed by Jason's sister, Jennifer, who had obtained the Fur Journal, enabling her to use the mystic Electric Pentagram to trap Satana. Jennifer had Satana write a contract in blood to bring Jason back to Earth alive and unharmed, and not to harm any of the Silences or their friends, family, or associates. Upon writing the contract, Satana was released from the Electric Pentagram, but she bound Jennifer to a man near death in her Orchard and claimed the Fur Journal herself. Satana then magically enhanced an electromagnetic sensing device to track Jason Silence's soul, and traveled to Hell to recover Jason. En route she was attacked by the Scorpion Queen, who had possibly taken Jason's soul for herself, and slew the Scorpion Queen and her offspring. Satana returned Jason to Earth, fulfilling the contract, but then killed him again and added Jennifer Silence to her Body Orchard. Briefly considered as a potential successor to Dr. Strange as Sorcerer Supreme, Satana was later sought out by the Hood (Parker Robbins) for aid in managing his bond with Dormammu, ruler of the Dark Dimension, and she became his occult advisor.

HEIGHT: 5'7" **EYES:** Red
WEIGHT: 120 lbs. **HAIR:** Black with red highlights

ABILITIES/ACCESSORIES: Satana is a succubus, draining souls to survive, though how long she can go without taking a soul is unrevealed. She prefers to feed on men, kissing each victim as she draws forth his soul, causing his body to shrivel. The soul then takes the form (visible at least to Satana) of a butterfly-like being, which she would crush in her fingers, seemingly disintegrating it, but actually absorbing its psionic energy. After she feeds on the soul's power, the spirit is cast down into her father's Hell realm. Following time in Hell after her death, Satana learned she can increase her power by consuming more souls than she needs, and by partially feeding on a man, she can enslave him. She also learned that by impregnating weapons with her body fluids, she can gain the soul power of victims slain with those weapons. It is unclear whether this is only true when said weapons are used by her servants.

Satana can fire soulfire, which causes intense psychic or spiritual pain, but can also be perceived by its target as heat or physical force if its wielder so wills it. She can also form shields, levitate (though she apparently cannot fly), cast illusions, mesmerize others and strip away others' false images, laying bare their souls and forcing them to see themselves as they truly are. She has superhuman strength (Class 10), durability, longevity and other physical abilities. She is resistant to conventional disease and does not require food, air, or most other human needs. Even if she dies, her spirit is sent to her father's Hell, and she can be reincarnated on Earth under various circumstances. She has extensive knowledge of black magical lore, and she has added magic to technological devices, for instance utilizing a tracker of electromagnetic energy to locate a specific soul in Hell. She occasionally casts spells, but her magical abilities are undefined.

She was formerly assisted by her familiar, the demon cat, Exiter. She was also previously bound to the Basilisk, an immensely powerful archdemon capable of slaughtering virtually any who encountered it. It was contained within Satana (or a pocket realm accessed by her), and released only at her discretion. It grew stronger, more powerful, and more willful with each use, and its life force was tied to hers.

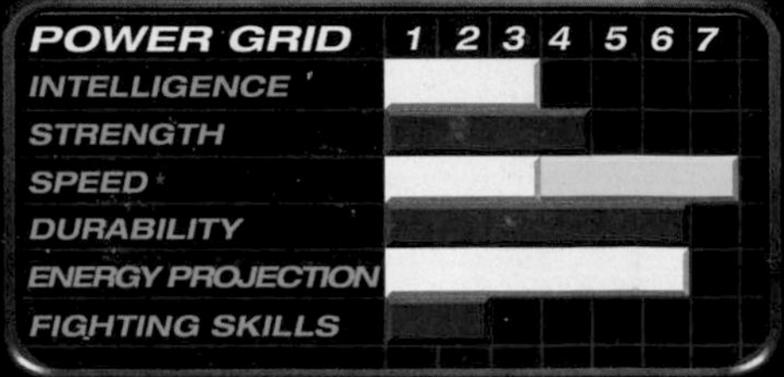
POWER GRID
1 2 3 4 5 6 7
INTELLIGENCE
STRENGTH
SPEED*
DURABILITY
ENERGY PROJECTION
FIGHTING SKILLS

*SATANA IS A TELEPORTER

Text by Jeff Christiansen